Protesting with Rosa Parks

Protesting with Rosa Parks

FROM STAGECOACHES TO DRIVING WHILE BLACK

John K. Bollard

NewSouth Books
an imprint of
The University of Georgia Press
Athens

NSB

Published by NewSouth Books,
an imprint of the University of Georgia Press
Athens, Georgia 30602
https://ugapress.org/imprints/newsouth-books/

Set in 10.25/13.5 Minion Pro by Classic City Composition LLC

Printed and bound by Sheridan Books, Inc.
The paper in this book meets the guidelines for
permanence and durability of the Committee on
Production Guidelines for Book Longevity of the
Council on Library Resources.

Most NewSouth/University of Georgia Press titles are
available from popular e-book vendors.

Printed in the United States of America
25 26 27 28 29 P 5 4 3 2 1

EU Authorized Representative
Easy Access System Europe—Mustamäe tee 50, 10621 Tallinn, Estonia,
gpsr.requests@easproject.com

Library of Congress Cataloging-in-Publication Data
Names: Bollard, John K. author
Title: Protesting with Rosa Parks : from stagecoaches to driving while Black / John K. Bollard.
Description: Athens : NewSouth Books, an imprint of the University of Georgia Press, [2025] |
Includes bibliographical references and index.
Identifiers: LCCN 2024053268 | ISBN 9781588385529 paperback alk. paper |
ISBN 9781588385536 epub | ISBN 9781588385543 pdf
Subjects: LCSH: Segregation in transportation—United State—History—20th century |
Civil rights movements—United States—History—20th century | African Americans—
Segregation | African Americans—Legal status, laws, etc. | African Americans—Biography
Classification: LCC E185.61 .B678 2025 | DDC 323.1196/0730904—dc23/eng/20250305
LC record available at https://lccn.loc.gov/2024053268

Action is everything. With it we are successful.
Without it all our enthusiasm is worse than nothing.
—DAVID RUGGLES, 1841

If you're looking for me, here I am. But you needn't think that your big brass buttons and your shiny bullets are going to scare me, because I have rights, they're substantial, and I'm sitting on them.
—ADELENE MCBEAN, 1940

Many people don't know the whole truth. . . . I was just one of many who fought for freedom.
—ROSA PARKS, 1988

To Margaret, Brynley, Catrin, Jesse, Owen, and Emrys,
and in honor of those who continue the struggle for equality, tolerance,
and human rights everywhere

CONTENTS

PREFACE

Public transportation, race, segregation, the law, and, in the early period, the abolition of slavery have been intricately woven together throughout U.S. history. Racism in transportation was and still is widespread, persistent, and frequently contested, not just in the South but in all parts of the country. The need to travel on public conveyances, by its very nature, put Black and white people together in confined and often crowded spaces. Such close proximity enabled racist violence toward Black passengers in a very public venue. Because of its intrinsically public nature, travel was not only physically dangerous for African Americans, it was demeaning, as was noted some years ago by Catherine Barnes: "For Southern blacks, segregated transportation was long one of the most despised forms of discrimination."[1] Furthermore, the violence and the degradation of Black travelers was not merely condoned, it was enforced and frequently perpetrated by conductors, police, and others in authority. This kept transportation racism painfully visible daily. Nor is it surprising that the white owners and shareholders of railroads and bus lines would want to protect their profits and keep their white customers happy by forcing Black travelers onto the roofs of stagecoaches and the outside platforms of streetcars, into separate railway cars, or into the backseats of buses.

Much of this history is in danger of being forgotten. During the years I was researching and writing this book, it became increasingly clear that very few people today know or can readily recall without prompting the name of anyone other than Mrs. Parks who protested the same way she did. Of the many people I asked as I traveled around the country, only once did someone give me a name. A ten-year-old girl came up to me after I had given a public talk and asked enthusiastically, "Will Claudette Colvin be in your book?" She made my day!

I am greatly indebted to many works by excellent scholars of the history of protest against racism. Most such studies have focused on a particular set of events or specific period of time, though some have taken a somewhat broader view.[2] *Protesting with Rosa Parks* brings a new perspective to this field, especially by examining the span of time from the earliest-known incidents protested publicly by Emiliano Mundrucu and David Ruggles in the 1830s to the social upheaval and unrest of the mid-to-late twentieth century, with a brief foray into the twenty-first. Rather than relating this history through historical analysis, I chose to present it through the lives and experiences of the people themselves who have been part of the long struggle against oppression. Some engaged in that struggle knowingly and willingly; many were thrust into it by the cruelty of others. Setting out their experiences over time reveals a sweeping narrative of the foundations of protest and activism as a persistent component of American history writ large.

For five decades now, the civil rights movement has been widely remembered as a series of events, protests, and legal developments over the short span of eleven years, beginning with the Supreme Court's 1954 decision in *Brown v. Board of Education*, which declared segregation unconstitutional, continuing through the arrest of Rosa Parks, the Montgomery Bus Boycott, and the Freedom Rides, and culminating in the Civil Rights Act of 1964 and the Voting Rights Act of 1965. In 2005 Jacquelyn Dowd Hall proposed the "long civil rights movement," arguing that the movement began as early as the 1930s and continued beyond 1965 up to the present.[3] She also extended the conceptual parameters of the movement beyond the borders of the South and recognized the intertwined arenas of civil rights, workers' rights, and women's rights, as well as the migration of many African Americans out of the rural South into southern, northern, and western cities, which often precipitated social and political backlash. Hall's analysis began an important debate about the extent and the nature of the civil rights movement, with some arguing for the traditional limits.[4] Others suggested extending the movement back to the early twentieth century or even to the Emancipation Proclamation (1863).[5] *Protesting with Rosa Parks* provides evidence of the history of familiar modes of protest against racial oppression since the early 1830s. However we define the civil rights movement, the legal and nonviolent strategies introduced by Emiliano Mundrucu and David Ruggles have remained a major tool of social protest, both on and off the roads, for almost two hundred years.

A Note on the Structure of This Book

Chapter headings give a general idea of the tenor of the times and prominent themes during a particular period, but, given the book's chronological structure, no chapter is strictly limited to a single theme. For example, in Chapter 5, "World War II and the Black Soldier," though Irene Morgan, Langston Hughes, and Sarah Ray were not soldiers, their accounts reflect the uneasy transition to a "peacetime" in which civil rights took on increasing importance, as is illustrated horrifically in the case of Sgt. Isaac Woodard. With a few exceptions, each individual account has as a focal point an incident in which someone protested the denial of a seat. These provide the threads that weave together a chronological narrative of the long struggle for equal rights. While an attempt has been made to include incidents that led to the most significant court cases, boycotts, protests, and other developments, the primary principle of inclusion is the personal experience underlying each incident, though there is no intent to produce a full biography of any particular person. In the case of a leader with a long career (e.g., David Ruggles, Frederick Douglass, or Bayard Rustin), multiple incidents may be separated in the book's chronological sequence. This helps us to see the continuing commitment and the role each played in influencing the progress of the struggle in concert with the work of others.

INTRODUCTION

In the early evening of Thursday, December 1, 1955, Rosa Parks was riding home from work on a crowded city bus in Montgomery, Alabama. According to Montgomery city law, the ten front seats of the bus were reserved for the use of white passengers only. When an eleventh white rider boarded the bus, the driver told Mrs. Parks and three other African Americans in the same row to get up and move back so that a white man could sit down, even though they were already sitting in the section designated for Black passengers. There were no empty seats further back, but, even if there had been, Rosa Parks might have done precisely what she so famously did—she refused to give up her seat.

What happened during the next hours, days, and months brought to a head a long, long campaign against inequities in U.S., state, and local laws and customs pertaining to race—a campaign that in many ways shaped the course of our national history. The arrest of Rosa Parks has often been written about, and millions of people watched as subsequent events unfolded on television. But what was it that led her to that moment? To fully appreciate the background to Mrs. Parks's refusal to move, we must go back to a time before buses were invented, before the first segregation laws were written, before slavery was abolished, to a time when people traveled by stagecoach and the very first railroads were just being built.

Of course, racial prejudice in the Western Hemisphere was far older than the formation of the United States. Both free and enslaved Africans had come or been brought to North America in companies of European explorers and conquistadors as early as 1513, perhaps even in the 1490s. St. Augustine, Florida, was a center of the Spanish slave trade in the sixteenth century, and in 1619 enslaved Africans were brought to be sold to the Virginia Colony.[1] The enslavement of Indigenous Americans was also a persistent feature of the Spanish and English conquest of the continent. In the late eighteenth and early nineteenth centuries, slavery was gradually eliminated from the northern states of the newly independent and expanding United States. However, racial antipathy toward persons of color remained among white citizens, and as the antislavery movement grew in the North it began to expose the ways that prejudice continued to manifest itself and even to increase.

On Thanksgiving Day, 1828, Hosea Easton, a black minister living in Bridgewater, Massachusetts, preached to "the Coloured Population of Providence, Rhode Island." In his speech Easton encouraged the free Black people of New England to raise themselves up to claim the equal place in society that was being denied them, and in the course of doing so he enumerated many of the stark realities of racial discrimination. In a passage touching on the matter of transportation, Easton asked his listeners to consider the situation of a traveling Black minister: "How does he fare on his journey from place to place? I am bold to say that he cannot purchase a seat on the public stage, only by sufferance. I have known men of that profession to be detained in towns and cities, not far distant from this place, ten days, before they could prosecute their journey, and then be under the necessity of getting some white man as an intercessor to the driver or owners for a passage on the outside of the carriage, by paying full price for fare."[2]

Similarly, in its third week of publication, on January 15, 1831, William Lloyd Garrison's abolitionist newspaper the *Liberator* noted that a clergyman on his way to New Bedford had been expelled from a stage when a white passenger objected to his presence. The following December, Garrison included a brief account of a Black clergyman with his wife and two other women being driven from the cabin of a sloop sailing from Nantucket to New Bedford and required to sit in the rain on the deck. Garrison appended a note to this article clarifying that it was not an unusual incident: "The above is but a single specimen of the ill-treatment under which our free colored citizens groan. They cannot obtain seats in any of our stages; they are ousted from the cabin of the most insignificant packet; even in houses dedicated to the worship of the great Creator, they are driven to the wall. . . . On whatever side they turn, contempt and prejudice meet them. . . . Shame on our hypocrisy!"[3]

While segregation in transportation gradually lost any legal status it might have had in some parts of the country after the 1840s, in other parts it burgeoned. In January 1950 there were fourteen states that did not simply tolerate but had laws on the books *requiring* racial segregation in railroad facilities. Eleven states enforced segregation on buses and streetcars, and four enforced segregation on steamboats and ferries. Nine states required separate waiting rooms.[4] The long-standing fact of segregation in public transportation in general is well known, as are some of the specific incidents involving notable figures (e.g., Frederick Douglass, Homer Plessy, and Rosa Parks). Less well known is the fact that the refusal to relinquish both one's seat and one's dignity, even at great personal risk, remained one of the most persistent and powerful modes of resistance to racism in an unbroken line from the early nineteenth century through the middle of the twentieth. The incremental progress accomplished by generations of protesters, the various legal setbacks they endured, and most tragically the pain, humiliation, and even death that so many suffered made possible the successes of those who followed them.

However, a survey of this specific practice through time teaches us about more than the continuity of just one aspect of U.S. legal, social, and racial history. On a more personal level, it helps us to get a feel for the weight of that history as it has been and continues to be borne by African Americans. Each instance of segregation, each attempt to deny someone a seat, was perpetrated against an individual —who may, in response, have felt frightened, ashamed, humiliated, helpless, angry, indignant, outraged, or all of these at once—as well as against an entire race. And each act of defiance against this particular mode of discrimination contributed its portion to the fierce determination of the human spirit to oppose an injustice so deeply embedded in the worldview of many who did not suffer under it. Such discrimination seemed, as one judge expressed it in 1841, "in the very nature of things and supported by common sense."[5]

One might wonder if collecting so many examples of being denied a seat might simply result in predictable repetition. To this I have three responses. Firstly, we need to recognize and understand the nature and cumulative effects of actual, continual, predictable, culturally sustained oppression. Daily, mundane, malevolent acts lie at the heart of oppression and of what Hannah Arendt taught us to recognize as the banality of evil. Experiencing something of that quotidian malice, even from a distance through the pages of a book, can bring us to a deeper understanding. Secondly, both for those of us who inherited the weight of this history by virtue of being African American and for those of us (like myself) who do not live directly under that persistent oppression, knowledge of the underlying details of history allows us to see that history not as something that happened to "important" people whom we learn about in school but rather as the combined experience of all of us.

Thirdly, there is a fluctuating but gradually progressive narrative movement to this long series of incidents. On the legal front, we see the slow but very real effects of putting pressure on the courts, from the offhand dismissal of cases beginning in the early nineteenth century to the more rigorous defining of "separate but equal" in increasingly narrow terms later in that century and well into the next. While the focus had long been on greater equality in the material accommodations and accoutrements of segregated travel, toward the mid-twentieth century much of the emphasis shifted to the intangible personal and psychological effects on the people being segregated. On the social front, we can discern over time how the continued persistence of protest kept the matter of racial inequality in the public eye. At times and in various regions, in both North and South, such resistance may have seemed counterproductive, hardening the resolve of segregationists. But in the long run, we can see, public opinion at large shifted sufficiently to have an effect on the legal decisions, especially Supreme Court cases, that exposed and finally dismantled Jim Crow.

Some of the people whose stories are retold in this book already were or subsequently became important people, people who very directly helped shape our nation, our communities, and our culture. Some of them, Ida B. Wells and Pauli Murray, for example, became well known and influential activists precisely *because* they had been forced out of their seats and awakened to the imminent need for action. Some, like David Ruggles, Frederick Douglass, Bayard Rustin, and John Lewis, would intentionally sit in a seat to provoke action against themselves in order to challenge the status quo and the laws that propped it up. Most, however, were just ordinary people trying to get from one place to another for their own personal reasons, and tragically some of them never made it to their destination. These, and the many others whose stories are not included here, are the true heroes of this book.

In 1833 Lydia Maria Child published *An Appeal in Favor of That Class of Americans Called Africans*, the first book-length treatise in the country calling for the immediate end of slavery without compensation for the slave owners. In this book, Child addresses briefly the mistreatment of African Americans in public transportation and gives several anecdotal instances. Following her summary of the expulsion of Harriet and Emiliano Mundrucu from the steamboat *Telegraph* in 1832, Child raises a question that continued to be asked for more than 130 years, though the modes of transportation may have changed: "Will any candid person tell me why respectable colored people should not be allowed to make use of public conveyances, open to all who are able and willing to pay for the privilege?"[6] This book will follow that question down the years through the stories of those who persisted in asking it and insisted on an answer that never came.

Protesting with Rosa Parks

CHAPTER 1

The Rise of Jim Crow

When the American Revolution came to an end, slavery was legal in the entire country. In 1780 Pennsylvania adopted a system of gradual emancipation (not completed for more than sixty years). Massachusetts became the first state to abolish slavery altogether in 1783. Other northern states adopted various systems of gradual emancipation throughout the first half of the nineteenth century. As the population of free Blacks gradually increased, so did their need and desire to travel, both locally and over longer distances. The simultaneous development of the steam engine and the expansion of the antislavery movement led to increasing tensions as some white travelers and the employees of railroad and steamship companies took offense at the presence of Black passengers.

Emiliano Mundrucu and David Ruggles may not have been the first travelers to protest being denied equal treatment, but they are the first whose experiences we learn of from published accounts and court records. Ruggles was an important figure in abolitionist circles in New York and New England, and his example undoubtedly encouraged other Black travelers to protest, especially those on their way to antislavery meetings in the very busy summer and autumn of 1841. Those protests, in turn, established a model that became familiar across the North.

Emiliano and Harriet Mundrucu, November 1832

Emiliano F. B. Mundrucu was a *pardo* ("mixed-race") Brazilian army officer and revolutionary who fled to the United States in 1824 after being sentenced to death in Brazil for his involvement in a revolt, inspired in part by the Haitian revolution, to establish an independent republic in northeastern Brazil. He settled in Boston, married Harriet Jerdine, an educated African American Bostonian, in 1831, and ran a secondhand clothing business. In her description of the incident recounted below, Lydia Maria Child describes Mundrucu,

Nantucket Harbor, 1852, with the steamer *Telegraph (broadside)*. Pencil sketch by George G. Fish (1822–1906). Nantucket Historical Association Collection, gift of George G. Fish, 1895.143.1.

anonymously, as "shrewd, enterprising, noble-spirited, and highly respectable in character and manners."[1]

In November 1832, on the advice of her doctor, Harriet and her husband were planning to sail to Nantucket on the newly built steamboat *Telegraph*, with their infant daughter, Emiliana, and their horse and cabriolet. They paid "the highest or cabin fare"—four dollars for Emiliano and Harriet, three dollars for the horse and carriage. The boat's captain, Edward H. Barker, denied Harriet entry into the after or ladies' cabin, which included private berths. They were instructed instead to go to the forward cabin, which was open to the use of the crew and to seawater from the deck and which lacked any privacy. As Emiliano quarreled with Barker, Harriet continued toward the ladies' cabin but was blocked by the captain. Weather conditions then forced the *Telegraph* back into port, and everyone disembarked. The following morning Harriet was once more prevented from entering the ladies' cabin, as her husband again argued heatedly with Barker that since he had paid the highest fare they should be treated accordingly. The captain ordered them off the boat, and Mundrucu parted with a promise to "go and get a writ out immediately."[2]

Mundrucu sued Captain Barker for breach of contract, and the case was heard October 14, 1833, in the Massachusetts Court of Common Pleas. Mundrucu was represented by two prominent abolitionists, the renowned orator Daniel Webster and David L. Child, the husband of Lydia Maria Child. After four hours of deliberation and several instructions from the judge on what payments were allowed, the jury awarded Mundrucu $125.[3] Barker immediately appealed, and in January the decision was overturned in the Massachusetts Supreme Judicial Court on the basis that the court could see no explicit guarantee of access to the ladies' cabin.

Whether or not the Mundrucus had considered beforehand that their protest might serve as a civil rights test case is unanswerable, but certainly before April 1833 Mundrucu had become a member of the New England Anti-Slavery Society.[4] The importance and perhaps novelty of the case is reflected in the fact that the story was picked up by newspapers in Boston, New York, Philadelphia, Baltimore, and even Virginia and London, England. Mundrucu intended to appeal his case to the U.S. Supreme Court, but in 1834, when the Brazilian government granted him a pardon, he returned to Brazil and resumed his military career.

When Emiliano failed to gain a desired command post, the Mundrucus returned to Boston in 1841, where they continued to campaign for abolition and equal civil rights. The growing network of antislavery societies and newspapers, and frequent travel to antislavery meetings by members both white and Black, provided a visible public platform for addressing the related matter of racial intolerance in the North. In 1863 Mundrucu was a vice president of the Union Progressive Association, a literary and improvement society of Black activists and intellectuals in Boston, which held a daylong New Year's Day celebration of the Emancipation Proclamation, featuring speeches by William Wells Brown, Frederick Douglass, William Cooper Nell, and other notable abolitionists.[5] He died later that year on September 16.[6]

David Ruggles, January 14, 1834, and Autumn 1833

On January 14, 1834, David Ruggles set out to travel by stagecoach from New York City, across the Hudson River by ferry, and on to Newark, New Jersey. It was common practice to require Black passengers to ride on the top of coaches, reserving the sheltered and more comfortable inside for white passengers. But Ruggles was not about to acquiesce willingly to such demeaning treatment. After Ruggles entered the coach, the coachman told him repeatedly that he would have to give up his seat inside and ride on the outside, so that white passengers boarding in New Jersey could ride inside. Ruggles cleverly avoided doing so—until the exasperated driver finally resorted to violence. That coach driver (the prototype of many drivers and train conductors we will meet in the following pages) probably had no idea that Ruggles was a sales agent for the *Emancipator and Journal of Public Morals*, the weekly newspaper of the American Anti-Slavery Society, much less that he would publish a lively and intentionally dramatic account of that very journey in the *Emancipator*, with a headline and subhead that reveal the dry, sardonic wit that runs through much of his writing.

> Men and Manners,
> Or, a memorandum of the way in which Americans, in the nineteenth century, are in the habit of treating their neighbors and fellow citizens, when their complexions do not happen to resemble their own.

After detailing his preliminary negotiations and arrangements with the coachman, Ruggles embarks on his tale:

> A few minutes before 3 o'clock, he mounted his stage and drove off, and returned about half past 3, with a lady and her little son.
>
> He cries out, "Stage ready!"
>
> I immediately left the office, and proceeded toward the ferry; he hailed me to get in.
>
> Said I, "I will cross the ferry first."
>
> "No, no; I am going to the other ferry."
>
> I stepped to the stage, and getting in, said he, "You had better ride up here with me, until you cross the river."
>
> "No, I thank you, I'll get in now and make one job of it."
>
> [I accordingly took my seat, and soon found myself in Cortlandt Street.] He stopped, opened the door, and said, "You can go to the ferry." We were directly over a little pond of water. The lady says, "Dear me! we cannot get out in this water!—Do you wish us to get out here, driver?"
>
> "No, madam." He shut the door, and moved on to the ferry boat; and before we reached the Jersey shore, he opened the door, and invited me out of the stage.
>
> I thanked him, and told him that I did not wish to get out.
>
> "But you must get out, because I have other passengers."
>
> "Isn't there room for them, sir?"
>
> "They wish to ride inside."
>
> "Why! I have paid my fare to Newark, and I wish to keep my seat."
>
> "But you are a COLORED man, and you must get out and ride out side, if you go to 'Newark' with me."
>
> "Why sir? I should have no objections to riding out side, but I think that your reasons for demanding me to give up my seat are unjust; for your FIRST reason would leave me behind, if other passengers enough wished to ride with you; and your SECOND reason is most unpardonably unrighteous; because it is not my

person, it is the complexion that the Creator has bestowed upon me, that is the reason why you treat me in this ill manner."

"Yes, you are unfortunate to be colored, it's true; and it is not customary, and it is against my rules to allow colored men to ride inside."

"Must I not have what I PAID FOR, because I am a colored man? An honest principle, truly!"

Ruggles then delivers to the driver a detailed, logical, metaphorical argument (omitted here) to illustrate that principle, undoubtedly intending to confuse the driver. The exasperated coachman declares, "It is useless to talk about it." He moves on to pick up three more passengers and then drives to the stage office, where he renews his demand:

"I tell you that you must get out, and if you want to ride, get upon the outside!!"

"I don't think your invitation an honest one, and therefore I don't feel disposed to accept of it, sir."

"Gentlemen, get out, and I'll fetch him out. I am the proprietor of this stage, and when I tell any body to get out of it, he shall come, or I will break his neck!!" This threat he had previously made.

[Two of the gentlemen alighted, and the lady and her little son being alarmed, as I should suppose, at the idea of a human being's having his "neck broke," for the crime only of wearing the skin that the God of nature had bestowed upon him, begged to be removed from the stage.]

The animal in human shape entered the stage with the ferocity of a tiger, and with his hands like claws tore both clothes, buttons and skin; and nature was at that moment prepared to give up even my heart's blood, had he chosen to take it, for he had taken my LABOR, trampled upon my FEELINGS, and he was robbing me of my RIGHTS, my LIBERTY, my ALL! And by the assistance of another white gentleman, (!) he now forced me out into the street. I felt no wound on the body, at the time, but am now quite lame. I proceeded to Newark on foot, where I arrived about 7 o'clock.

Such, Mr. Editor, is the treatment I received from Mr. _____, a Christian! an American! in the broad glare of day light, in a Christian community, in this our "boasted land of liberty," this "asylum for the oppressed," this "land of the free!"

My soul is sick, my heart is faint. Oh! when will men learn that they are all children of one great and benevolent Father!

Your despised brother,
David Ruggles
New York, Jan. 17, 1834[7]

Whether or not Ruggles's initial statement that he "did not wish to get out" was meant to be intentionally provocative, this is the earliest detailed first-hand record we have of an African American protesting with his own body the custom—for segregation was not yet embedded in law—of discrimination in public transportation. But this was not Ruggles's first such encounter with racial antipathy on his travels. Later in 1834 he printed and published an antislavery pamphlet that includes a long footnote recounting a stagecoach trip he had taken through Pennsylvania the previous autumn. This journey began, significantly, in the dark, around 12:00 or 1:00 a.m., along with two ladies, two gentlemen, and another man identified only as a "two-leged animal" [*sic*]. Ruggles relates that the conversation in the coach turned to the question of slavery. All the passengers were opposed to it, but they could not agree on a plan to end it. Some were in favor of colonization, that is, freeing the slaves and relocating them to Africa along with other free Black people. The man Ruggles identifies as "the animal" was "a vociferous colonizationist" whose chief fear was "amalgamation" of the races—that is, miscegenation or even marriage between Black and white women and men. Ruggles replied that amalgamation had nothing to do with the question of slavery: "If I could gain the hand and heart of a colored lady, I would consider myself honored to accompany her to the Hymeneal altar." The man was shocked to hear such a thing: "Heavens! *marry a black! marry a negress!*" After further discussion, the passengers all dozed off. As dawn approached, Ruggles awoke. "As soon as I thought my complexion would appear to an advantage, I raised the curtain. The animal screamed out, 'Good heavens! a negro! why you are a black man!!' [Every other passenger was ready to burst with laughter.]"

When the coach stopped at an inn, the same man objected to Ruggles sitting at the breakfast table with the white passengers. The others, however, all agreed that Ruggles should sit with them, and his adversary simply left the room. Biographer Graham Hodges points out, "Ruggles's description of the 'animal' indicates that he despised the racist for his beliefs and offensive statements and considered him to be less than human. Rather than be defined by racial accusation, Ruggles in fact turned it around, indicating through his description that he was superior to the racist."[8]

Who was this man who so ardently defied long-standing custom and defended his right to travel as an equal? David Ruggles was born in Lyme, Connecticut, in 1810, the son of David and Nancy Ruggles, who were both free. Soon after his birth, the family moved to the Bean Hill neighborhood just north of Norwich. The Ruggles family, which grew to include eight children, was poor, but both David's father, a blacksmith, and his mother, a cook and caterer, worked at occupations that afforded them a degree of recognition and respectability in the mostly white, in places even elite, neighborhood. The family attended the Norwich Methodist Episcopal Church, for which there is no evidence that people of color were restricted to a segregated gallery or discriminatory "Negro pew." Nor does Ruggles recount, in his later writings, any incident that woke him suddenly as a child to the harsh realities of racial prejudice. Indeed, in his 1834 pamphlet he paints an idealized picture of his childhood that shows no evidence of early rancor: "Do not colored and white children play together promiscuously until the white child is taught to despise the colored? . . . Then *nature*, never, *never*, taught us such sinful 'repugnance!' She was *strong* to the contrary."[9]

The confidence that young Ruggles gained moving among the mixed social strata of Norwich stood him in good stead during his subsequent career, as did the sound classical and religious education he received at the Sabbath School for the Poor. But life for African Americans in early nineteenth-century New England was by no means the idyll that Ruggles makes it out to be to score a few rhetorical points. The question of slavery was rapidly becoming the most fraught issue facing the young nation during the early nineteenth century, and the abolitionist movement was growing apace in New England. The Norwich Methodist Episcopal Church played a part in helping fugitive slaves to safety, and we cannot doubt that he was aware of the difficulties pertaining to race from an early age.

Slavery was still legal in Connecticut: the state had legislated a form of gradual emancipation in 1784 and 1797. The complete abolition of slavery in Connecticut was not accomplished until 1848. In 1810, the year Ruggles was born, there were twelve slaves in Norwich alone. More importantly, a significant portion of the New England economy, especially shipbuilding, commerce, and related professions, benefited either directly or indirectly from the slave trade. Nor were free Blacks in Connecticut or elsewhere in the North accorded a full measure of equality or dignity. The steady increase in the free Black population led to a concomitant rise in racial animosity at all levels of white society. Among the working class, this often expressed itself as a fear that Black workers would take their jobs, and the flames of this fear were often fanned by those better off, with their dire predictions of racial "amalgamation."[10]

When he was fifteen, Ruggles left home to become a coastal mariner, and by 1827 he had taken lodgings in New York City. As many as three quarters of the free Black men in the city worked as seamen, and from them Ruggles learned of the complexities of urban life for Black residents. On July 4, 1827, slavery officially ended in New York State, and some two thousand African Americans in the city celebrated with a grand parade followed by orations and revelry. Whether or not Ruggles was in town at the time, he would certainly have been aware of the event and the encouragement and hopes it gave the city's Black population of about fourteen thousand. Nevertheless, slavery and racial prejudice remained problematic issues throughout the city and the state.

In 1828, at the age of eighteen, Ruggles opened a grocery shop at 1 Cortlandt Street, near Broadway, in lower Manhattan. His advertisements in Samuel Eli Cornish's abolitionist newspaper *Freedom's Journal* indicate that Ruggles, better educated than many, kept himself informed of relevant issues and events both in the city and elsewhere. His earlier ads announced: "A quantity of superior Canton and Porto Rico Sugars. ALSO—Coffee, Teas, Flour, Goshen Butter, Cheese, &c. Rum, Gin, Brandy, Wine, Cordials, Porter and Cider, &c which will be sold cheap for cash." By December that year Ruggles had appended: "The sugars above mentioned are free sugars—they are manufactured by free people, not by slaves."[11]

His engagement with slavery as an issue both ethical and practical had begun. By the fall of 1829, perhaps under the influence of Cornish, he no longer sold alcoholic beverages. He moved his store to new premises on Cortlandt Street, but in early December someone broke in, stole $280 and other items, and started a fire, completely destroying his stock. Ruggles reopened the grocery in 1831, and by 1833 he was combining his business with antislavery activities. The career of one of the great early African American civil rights leaders was under way in earnest.[12]

In 1833 Ruggles quit the grocery business and became one of the few Black agents for the *Emancipator and Journal of Public Morals*. His travels for the *Emancipator* were tiring and dangerous, but they allowed him to develop connections with abolitionists and sympathizers throughout the Northeast. Ruggles devoted much of his time, energy, and money to helping fugitive slaves get through New York City to Canada or to safer places in upstate New York and New England, while simultaneously working both on the streets and in the courts to protect or rescue Black adults and children from kidnapping by slave traders who would take them south or even out of the country to be sold into slavery.

The following spring Ruggles opened the Anti-Slavery Bookstore on Lispenard Street, about a mile uptown from Cortlandt. The first Black-owned bookstore in the country, it also served as a lending library. He began to speak publicly and to write pamphlets supporting the cause of immediate abolition. In 1835, Ruggles and other "Friends of Human Rights" both Black and white formed the New York Committee of Vigilance, which became renowned and provided a model for other cities and towns to provide support for former slaves and to protect their free Black citizens from illegal capture. Three years later he published the first of five issues of *The Mirror of Liberty*, the first

David Ruggles (*center*) with white abolitionists Isaac T. Hopper (*left*) and Barney Corse. Detail from "The Disappointed Abolitionists" political cartoon, 1838, by Edward Williams Clay and lithographer Henry R. Robinson. Library Company of Philadelphia.

African American magazine. *The Mirror* reported on the activities of the Committee of Vigilance, on other related news, and on the activities of various African American organizations. Ruggles estimated that over his years in New York from the early 1830s until 1842 he helped over six hundred people to freedom. His own home was not only the meeting place for the Committee of Vigilance. It also became one of the most important and frequent stops in that interlocking network of covert communications and activity that became known as the Underground Railroad.

As Ruggles's name and reputation spread, many fugitive slaves, on reaching free territory (and perhaps even before that), were directed to his house. One of these was Basil Dorsey, who emancipated himself from Maryland in 1836 and after a year in Pennsylvania found his way to Lispenard Street. Ruggles then sent him on to Northampton, Massachusetts, where they would later meet again. The most notable former slave to pass through the gateway to freedom guarded by Ruggles was a frightened young fugitive also fleeing from Maryland—Frederick Augustus Bailey. Ruggles took him in, sheltered him, and began to educate him in the necessities for negotiating life as a free man. While at Ruggles's home, Bailey changed his surname to Johnson and married Anna Murray, a free woman who had come north from Maryland to join him. Ruggles made arrangements for them to go to New Bedford, where Johnson took the name Frederick Douglass and set out on the road to becoming the most prominent African American of the nineteenth century.

Steam Power and the Segregation of Passengers

The steam engine had been developed during the late eighteenth and early nineteenth centuries. In 1807 Robert Fulton's *Clermont* became the first commercially viable steamboat, plying the Hudson River between New York City and Albany. Within a few years steamboats were carrying passengers along rivers and coastal waters throughout the country. Another new mode of transportation was also growing out of industrial tramroads using horse-drawn cars on wooden rails to haul heavy loads during the late eighteenth and early nineteenth centuries. Horse-drawn streetcars on rails were first established by the Harlem Railway Company in New York City in 1832, and similar lines soon became a familiar feature of many cities. In 1826 the New Jersey lawyer and inventor John Stevens had demonstrated the viability of using steam-powered engines on steel rails, and the development of steam-driven railroads was rapid and widespread. By the latter half of the 1830s there were rail lines in Maryland, South Carolina, Pennsylvania, New Jersey, New York, and Massachusetts, making it easier, quicker, and less expensive to travel what had until then seemed like long distances.

Discrimination in public transportation, as in other aspects of public life, had been the norm in the early years of the republic. As they campaigned specifically for an outright end to slavery, northern abolitionists also began to address the more general manifestation of racial intolerance on public carriers and in taverns and churches. On June 14, 1834, the *Liberator*, William Lloyd Garrison's abolitionist newspaper, published an article under the headline "Cost of Prejudice," stating the problem forthrightly:

> The manner in which our colored citizens are generally treated by the proprietors of stages and steam-boats, whenever they attempt to go from one town or State to another, is vulgar and shameful in the extreme. If they travel as servants

William Lloyd Garrison. Carte de visite. Boston Public Library.

or slaves, in company with their masters or mistresses, no offence is given, and none taken; but as intelligent, virtuous, and independent passengers, they are not permitted to enjoy what is granted to the most rude, profligate, and vulgar whites. We have some facts on this subject to communicate to the public, which ought to make every true American blush for his country. It is a humiliating truth, that prejudice against persons of a colored complexion is more exclusive and venomous in New-England, than in any other portion of this republic. We are consoled, however, in believing—nay, in *knowing*, that it is rapidly declining—precisely in proportion to the growth of the anti-slavery cause.

Garrison then included a resolution adopted by the New England Anti-Slavery Convention just two weeks earlier:

Resolved, That it is the duty of all the friends and well wishers of the anti-slavery cause, to inquire out, and encourage with their custom and their influence, those taverns, stages, and steamboats, which receive and accommodate our colored fellow citizens, without making an illiberal and disgraceful distinction either of charges or of treatment on account of color.

This resolution makes no mention of railroads, for none existed in New England at the time. Passenger service on trains was only just beginning and had not yet become a daily commodity. To show that abolitionists intended to practice what they preached, Garrison included in this article a letter, signed by himself and seven others, offering public thanks to a certain Captain Lewis Davis of the steamboat *Philadelphia* for treating his passengers equitably, without regard to color. On a trip to New York in early May 1834, these men and "an esteemed female member of the Society of Friends" had chosen to sail on the *Philadelphia* rather than to travel by train on the Camden and Amboy Railroad, one of the first rail lines in the country, founded in 1830 by John Stevens himself. The boat was slower than the train and required that they take a more circuitous route. The implication, therefore, is that discrimination was standard practice on the railroads from the very beginning. Though the word "boycott" would not enter the English language for more than forty years, even at that early date Garrison points hopefully toward a similar strategy to end such unfair treatment by affecting the pocketbooks of the railroad owners, concluding, "Let this example be extensively imitated by anti-slavery men, and every barrier of caste will soon be overthrown."[13]

Several railroads began passenger service in southern New England in the later 1830s, and protests against the segregation and harsh treatment of colored passengers became increasingly common as the popularity and accessibility of both steamboat and rail travel grew. The Taunton Branch Railroad in Massachusetts was chartered in 1835 and began carrying freight and passengers over the eleven and a half miles from Taunton to Mansfield in 1836. In 1840 the line was extended south to New Bedford. The New York, Providence and Boston Railroad began operation in November 1837, whereby travelers could take a steamboat from New York City to Stonington, Connecticut, and thence travel by rail to Providence and Boston. This route considerably shortened travel time between these cities, and it eliminated many of the discomforts and inconveniences of the earlier stagecoach on the overland leg of the journey. The first stretch of the Eastern Railroad from East Boston to Salem, Massachusetts, was completed in 1838, and by 1840 it extended to Newburyport and the New Hampshire state line.

These three railroads in particular soon became infamous among abolitionists for their discriminatory, often violent, treatment of passengers of color. The annual report of the Massachusetts Anti-Slavery Society in January 1837 included a much stronger and more explicit statement than the resolution of 1834, noting in exclamatory parentheses the curious state of affairs that allowed slaves but not free Black persons to ride in the first-class cars: "Our colored brethren . . . are still deprived of their rights in the tavern, in the stage coach, in the rail-car, and the steam-boat, (except such as are *slaves*, who travel with their lordly masters!)—so that in travelling, they are exposed to every indignity, great mental and physical suffering, and frequently subjected to great expense. Their treatment, in this particular, would be quite insupportable to any other people."[14]

In July 1840 at a meeting in Salem, Massachusetts, the Essex County Anti-Slavery Society resolved: "The unchristian arrangement upon the Eastern Rail Road, of excluding people from equal privileges, on account of color, and barbarously dragging them from a seat to which they have an indisputable right, ought to receive the united condemnation of every friend to impartial liberty."[15]

The railroads soon began to dominate overland transportation. In January 1837 there were about 145 miles of railroad operating in eastern Massachusetts, including the line to Providence, Rhode Island. By the end of 1840 this had grown to 285 miles.[16] By late 1841 there were 3,300 miles of railroad in use throughout the country, with 2,000 more under construction.[17] A number of railroad companies in the North, often after some initial protest, were willing to accept both white and colored passengers equally in their cars; others were notorious for their refusal to do so. Enforced segregation on some New England railroads seems to have been de facto policy from the outset. As steel rails were laid across the country and throughout many cities for horse-drawn and later electric streetcars, the stage was set for public conveyances to become one of the most common sites where white and Black people came into close personal contact in a narrow, confined space daily. Conflict was likely, if not inevitable, and it is not surprising that public transportation should become the most frequent arena in which tensions mounted, discrimination became codified, and eventually segregation became law.

In 1842 Charles Dickens toured the United States and Canada, and in the description of his train journey from Boston to Lowell, Massachusetts, he noted that railroad companies ran three categories of passenger car:

> There are no first and second class carriages as with us; but there is a gentleman's car and a ladies' car: the main distinction between which is that in the first, everybody smokes; and in the second, nobody does. As a black man never travels with a white one, there is also a negro car; which is a great, blundering, clumsy chest, such as Gulliver put to sea in, from the kingdom of Brobdingnag. There is a great deal of jolting, a great deal of noise, a great deal of wall, not much window, a locomotive engine, a shriek, and a bell.[18]

The "negro car," as we shall see, came to be known by a variety of other names as well. Lest we think Dickens's characterization is Swiftian hyperbole, we might compare it to a passage from the *Voice of Freedom* reprinted in the *Liberator* in July 1840. G. W. Clark wrote of his journey by steamboat, then by rail from New York to Philadelphia. On the boat he met a Presbyterian pastor from Philadelphia leading a group of ten or twelve men and women. Together they enjoyed the scenery along the river and then took a train across New Jersey. On noticing that they had been given tickets of a different color than his, Clark "thought that all was not as it should be," and he described the significance of that difference in some detail:

> I found that the tickets given to this proscribed company of Christians, entitled them to a seat, not in a comfortable, easy and splendidly finished car, such as was fitted up for the *white gentry*; no, not even in a *decent* car; but they were driven into a rough, close, dismal, dirty car, called the *dog* car, a vehicle which resembles more a cage for wild beasts, than any thing else to which I can liken it. It was about seven feet wide, ten feet in length, and so low that no person of ordinary height could stand erect. There was not, if my recollection serves me, a single slide or window [in] it; and I should judge it had never been painted or cleaned. It was literally a *dark, filthy cage*. . . . It was a most shameful outrage upon human rights, and cruel in the extreme, and should cover with infamy those who were concerned in it. Inhuman and disgraceful as these things are, they are acted over and over, every day in our boasted land of "*equal rights*"!![19]

A "Colored Man and His Wife" and Elizabeth Chace, May 30, 1838

Especially on their way to or from antislavery society meetings or conventions, sympathetic white passengers might find themselves traveling with Black friends or acquaintances on the same journey. Elizabeth Chace, who published her *Anti-Slavery Reminiscences* at the age of eighty-five in 1891, provides an early but typical example. A member of a white family of abolitionist Quakers from Rhode Island, Chace articulates clearly the practical differences between the belief that slavery was wrong and the racial prejudice embedded in many people's personal feelings: "I remember making an appeal to a Quaker brother-in-law of mine, by asking him if he did not think the slaves should be freed, and his only reply was, 'I shouldn't want to see a Black man sitting on the sofa beside my daughter.'" She notes too that even as a devoted Quaker among Quakers, "to be an Abolitionist, put me down among the ostracized." She and her sister organized the Female Anti-Slavery Society in Fall River, Massachusetts, in 1835. On one occasion some members objected when she invited "a few very respectable young colored women, who came to our meetings[,]" to join the society. "[Some of the leading members] said they had no objection to these women attending the meetings, and they were willing to help and encourage them in every way, but they did not think it was at all proper to invite them to join the Society, thus putting them on an equality with ourselves. We maintained our ground, however, and the colored women were admitted."[20]

Here Chace quietly reveals her disapproval of such distinctions as can often be made between a theoretical equality and the emotional, personal, and social responses that can affect even those we might expect to be the most sympathetic to that theory. The Black abolitionist and newspaperman Samuel Ringgold Ward was more direct in his assessment of this Quaker ambivalence: "They will give us good advice. They will aid in giving us a partial education—but never in a Quaker school, beside their own children. Whatever they do for us savors of pity, and is done at arm's length."[21]

Chace begins her account of the following incident with the words "At that time," but she does not give a precise date. Nevertheless, the likely time can be deduced from internal evidence.[22]

> At that time, the prejudice against color, throughout New England, was even stronger than the pro-slavery spirit. On one occasion, my husband and myself went to Boston, to attend the annual meeting of the New England Anti-Slavery Society. Accompanied by a gentleman friend, we drove to Taunton from Fall River, there to take the railroad, which I think, at that time, furnished only one car for the journey. As we entered the car, Samuel Rodman, an Anti-Slavery man from New Bedford, and a highly respectable, well-dressed colored man and his wife, from the same town, took seats therein also. The conductor came and ordered the colored people to leave the car. We all remonstrated, of course, but without avail. He called the superintendent, who peremptorily repeated the order. They got out quietly, and we did the same, (but not so quietly,) and retired to the waiting-room, leaving the car empty. The officials held a conference outside, and the conductor soon informed us that an extra car had been put on for the negroes, and invited us to take the seats we had left. We held a little conference among ourselves, and then every one of us entered the car with the colored people. The superintendent was very angry, but he did not quite dare to order us out, so he assured us that our conduct would avail nothing, for negroes would never be permitted to be mixed up with white people on that road. They were mixed up with us, however, on that day, and we found them intelligent, agreeable companions.[23]

This is the earliest-known account of a segregated car actually being added to a train—one of the first "Jim Crow cars," as David Ruggles designated them later that summer.

The Chaces not only sat with that unnamed Black couple on the Taunton line, they became friends in their joint opposition to slavery. Chace includes a later anecdote about integrated seating in which the same couple were involved:

> At one time, when we had an Anti-Slavery Convention at Fall River, a large number of visitors dined at our house. Among them were the two New Bedford people, who had so shocked the sensibilities of the railroad officials at Taunton, and, I think, Charles Lenox Remond, a young colored Anti-Slavery orator. We had then in our house, in some useful capacity, a devoted Baptist woman, who usually sat at the family table. When the dinner was ready, I asked her to come. She replied, "No; I don't eat with niggers." When the dinner was over and the guests had retired to the parlor, I called her again. And again she answered, "No; I don't eat *with* niggers nor *after* 'em." Whether she went hungry that day, I never inquired.[24]

David Ruggles, August 7, 1838

The stagecoach incident in New Jersey in 1834 was by no means the last time that David Ruggles insisted on his right to travel without discrimination or harassment. Indeed, Ruggles rarely missed a chance to draw attention to discrimination of any sort when he saw it or suffered it. In August 1838 he made a hurried trip on the steamboat *Rhode Island* to Stonington, Connecticut, and then by rail to Providence, Rhode Island. He was in hot pursuit of Thomas Lewis, a ship's officer who had sold three young free Black sailors from New York into slavery in New Orleans. Lewis had been in custody in the Florida Territory for "taking off a man's head there with a Bowie knife," but he had escaped. When Ruggles got word that Lewis was aboard a revenue cutter in the Providence area, he rushed to Philadelphia to obtain the proper papers and followed Lewis posthaste to Providence and Newport, and then to New Bedford, Massachusetts, arriving just hours before Lewis was planning to leave. Ruggles presented the summons to the sheriff, who arrested Lewis. Ruggles then wrote to the territorial governor of Florida that they had Lewis in custody. The governor replied and requested that Lewis be held until a bill of indictment could be obtained. On August 30, 1838, the *Emancipator* printed a first-page article under the headline "David Ruggles and the Daily Papers," demonstrating how the commercial dailies vilified Ruggles outrageously for his pursuit of this case and for his abolitionist activities in general.[25]

It is indicative of Ruggles's energies and his dedication to equal rights that even while on such a pressing journey he nevertheless took the time to inform the papers of the prejudicial behavior of boat and rail officials on his way. Ruggles sent a letter of complaint to the Providence, Rhode Island, *Courier*. Disappointed in that paper's editorial cutting of the letter, he expanded on it in his inimitable style and sent it to be reprinted in the *Emancipator*, along with some "additional remarks." There the letter was given an attention-grabbing headline: A Trip to the East—Defrauded on the Steamboat Rhode Island—and Lynched on the Stonington Rail Road.[26]

> *Mr. Editor.*—Permit me to say to your readers, that my trip to the East, after the notorious Thomas Lewis, who participated in kidnapping and selling three of our fellow-citizens into slavery at the South, was attended with outrage and violence from New York to Providence, which I did not expect to meet on the route through "the land of steady habits," as explained in the following article which appeared in the Providence Courier of the 9th instant.
>
> "CAUTION TO TRAVELLERS.
>
> "I left New York, on Tuesday evening, for this city, in the steamboat Rhode Island, on the route through Stonington, on which I was most egregiously defrauded and lynched.
>
> "The clerk of the boat having received full fare [viz four dollars,] agreed to send me through in the enjoyment of the same privileges that all passengers [who had paid full fare] enjoyed. But from the treatment I received from the rail road conductor, I consider myself defrauded and lynched, from the consideration that I paid full fare to the clerk of the boat who furnished me with a deck ticket. After arriving at Stonington, and the conductor of the car failing to extort fifty cents more from me, insisted that I should not have that car, saying you are a d——d Abolitionist. He and three others forcibly ejected me from the car, and forced me into what they call the pauper [or Jim Crow] car.
>
> "David Ruggles
>
> "*Providence, R.I.* August 8, 1838"
>
> The following additional remarks were excluded by the editor of that paper, viz
>
> "Abolitionists are cautioned against taking the route over the Stonington Rail Road."
>
> I wish to state here, that highway robbery is a crime that used to be punishable by death in New England, but now "*forties*" are employed in steamboats and on rail roads, that will commit larceny upon men's pockets and rights, and lynch them with impunity. Travellers assent to the outrages committed on the defenceless and unprotected, by their neutrality in such cases of plunder.

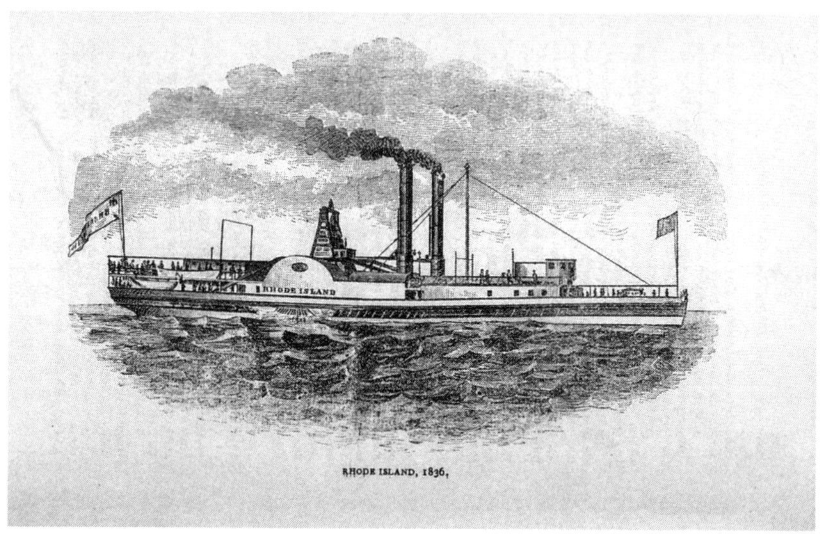

The *Rhode Island*, built in 1836. William A. Fairburn, "The Great Steamers of Long Island Sound," *Engineering Magazine*, April–September 1895.

> I send it to your paper, that your readers may understand that travellers are liable to be defrauded and lynched on the route to Boston over the Stonington Rail Road.
>
> Yours, respectfully,
> David Ruggles
> New York, August 11, 1838[27]

Why Was It Called the "Jim Crow Car"?

The precise origins of the term "Jim Crow" are somewhat obscure, but its adoption and spread can be confidently attributed to an early nineteenth-century white actor and early (though not the first) blackface minstrel performer named Thomas D. Rice, who billed himself as "Daddy Rice."[28] His most popular bit was a song and dance routine called "Jump Jim Crow," which he began performing in the late 1820s. The words and lyrics were published around 1832, printed in an orthography derogatorily imitative of Black speech:

> Come, listen, all you gals and boys,
> I'm just from Tuckyhoe; (Tuckahoe)
> I'm gwine to sing a little song, (going)
> My name's Jim Crow.

Chorus:
Weel about, an' turn about, (Wheel)
An' do jis so; (just so)
Eb'ry time I weel about, (Every)
I jump Jim Crow.

Rice and the song, which he accompanied by dancing a wild, rhythmic jig and flailing about with his arms and legs, became immensely popular in both the South and the North. Rice claimed, rather dubiously, that he learned the song and the dance from an African American, perhaps a stableman or a slave, named Jim Crow, who had a crooked leg and a deformed shoulder. Alternatively, it may have been adapted from some earlier version of an African American song featuring a bragging trickster-type narrator named Jim Crow. Rice often added new verses in his performances, as did other later performers. As a parody of Black dialect, dance, and behavior, the song "Jump Jim Crow" soon led to the use of "Jim Crow" as a generalized, mocking term for a Black person.

The earliest-known reference to a separate railway car designated for passengers of color as a "Jim Crow car" is found in David Ruggles's letter to the Providence *Morning Courier* on August 8, 1838, and in the *Emancipator* on August 23: "He . . . forced me into what they call the pauper [or Jim Crow] car." The brackets suggest that Ruggles assumed the bracketed term would be understood by his readers. Strikingly, the next known printed reference to a "Jim Crow car," just two months later, is in the account of a drunken white sailor. Upon causing a disturbance on the Eastern Railroad, he was compelled by the train crew "to take his seat in the 'refuse' or 'Jim Crow' car, at the end of the train."[29] It seems that the *Gazette* editor did not think any explanation of the term was necessary, either.[30]

Railroad companies began designating separate seating for Black passengers in the late 1830s. However, in lieu of a separate car, the Jim Crow was often merely a sectioned-off part of the uncomfortable, unheated, and unventilated baggage car. Just after the likely date of the incident in which Elizabeth Chace describes a car being added to a train, and a month before Ruggles wrote his letter in August 1838, the *Liberator* reprinted a short article from the New York *Colored American* suggesting that it had already become common to force Black passengers to ride on the platforms outside the cars, as had been the long-standing practice on stagecoaches. In addressing the hypocrisy of the "colonizationists, knaves, and fools" who decried "amalgamation" of the races without objecting to the frequent rape of female slaves in the South, the writer continued: "But let a colored Christian be seated in the house of God, let him be given a berth and a comfortable place in a Steam Boat cabin, or an inside passage in a Rail Road car or a stage coach; and the cry Amalgamation ! ! Amalgamation ! ! ! is at once raised by ten thousand polluted tongues."[31]

Numerous other words for the "proscribed car" came into use: Negro car, Colored car, pauper car, dog car, dirt car, dirty car, refuse car, forward car, front car, combination car, cage. As the nineteenth century progressed, "Jim Crow car" became the common term in everyday use, especially among African Americans. At least officially and in court, the railroad companies and conductors avoided terms that implied discrimination by color, preferring euphemisms such as "forward car," "smoking car," and "combination car." The term "Jim Crow" soon spread beyond the rails to refer to the many laws and customs enforcing segregation and to the systematic practice of segregation as a whole, though it never completely lost its connection to public transportation.

Thomas Van Renselaer, October 25, 1838

Thomas Van Renselaer, a Black New York abolitionist, traveled to Boston to attend the New England Colored Temperance Convention in October 1838. On his return trip by steamboat he suffered the same treatment as had David Ruggles the preceding August, though on a different boat. The very next day, Van Renselaer related the event in a letter to the New York abolitionist Joshua Leavitt, editor of the *Emancipator*. Garrison reprinted it in the *Liberator,* adding in a headnote, "His case is not a rare, but a very common one. . . . Had he been a servant or a slave, in company with his master, he might have remained in the cabin with impunity—no one would have thought of quarreling with his presence; but being an independent traveller, it was an outrage for him to think that he was entitled to the treatment of a man!" By "opposition boat" in the following account, Van Renselaer means a boat opposed to slavery and the segregation of Black passengers. It is noteworthy that he graciously acknowledges the kinder treatment he received from some of the employees working on the boat, in contrast to the captain and the man who initially accosted him.

> Boston, October 26, 1838
> Dear Brother,—I stepped on board the Steamboat J. W. Richmond in your city, yesterday afternoon, for Providence. I had previously understood that *this* being an opposition boat, people were treated irrespective of complexion; so, full of hope of a pleasant entertainment, I went to the office and paid $3.50 (fifty cents

more than regular fare,) for my passage and a berth, No. 15, which was assigned me in the after cabin, and obtained my ticket. I walked about until dark, when, feeling chilly, I repaired to the cabin in which my berth was. I had not been there long before a man came up to me in a very abrupt manner, and said, "Whose servant are you?" I at first gave no answer; he repeated, and I replied, I am my own, Sir. "Well," said he, "you must go on deck." I asked, why so? "Because you ought to know your place." I said, this is my place. Said he, "Go on deck, I tell you." Said I, I cannot go on deck. Said he with an oath, and running upon deck, "I'll make you." He returned in a moment with the captain, who came trembling, and said, "I want you to go on deck immediately." I asked the reason. "Not a word from you, sir." I asked, what offence have I committed? "Not a word, sir," said he, and laid hold of me with violence, and ordered two men to remove me. But when I saw him in such a rage, and fearing that he might do *himself* harm, I retired, and walked the deck till late at night, when I had another talk with the captain. I then told him he had not treated me well, and that an explanation was due from him; but he refused to allow me to go below, or to give me a berth. I then told him I should publish the treatment I had received. He again flew in a passion, and I said no more to him. Between 11 and 12 o'clock, one of the waiters invited me to occupy a bed which he had prepared. I accepted it and was rendered comfortable; and feel very grateful to three of the waiters for their sympathy in these trying moments, as well as to some of the passengers. One gentleman in particular, the Rev. Mr. Scudder, (Methodist) gave me great consolation by identifying himself with me at the time.

Now, dear brother, I have made this communication of facts for the information of the friends of human rights, who, I believe, have patronized *this boat* from principle, that they may act accordingly hereafter.

Yours in affliction,
Thos. Van Renselaer[32]

Nathaniel A. Borden, December 1840

One of the few recorded early instances of successful protest against railroad segregation policies took place on the notorious Taunton line to New Bedford. In a letter of January 1, 1841, to Debora Weston, William C. Coffin, a Nantucket banker and abolitionist, writes of an incident on the train to New Bedford, probably returning from the annual Christmas fair of the Boston Female Anti-Slavery Society held to raise funds for the cause. Coffin was a principal organizer of the first Nantucket Anti-Slavery Convention held the following summer that would bring Frederick Douglass to prominence. Debora Weston and three of her five sisters were founding members of the

Boston Female Anti-Slavery Society in 1834. The man Coffin calls "our friend Borden" was Nathaniel A. Borden, a well-respected Nantucket whaleman who became secretary of both the Nantucket Anti-Slavery Society and the Nantucket Colored Temperance Society. Coffin writes,

> We had taken our seats in the cars when on looking round our friend Borden was missing. Suspecting the cause and not being willing to lose so good a companion I immediately went in search of him, and found him colonized without his consent in the "Jim Crow." I persuaded him to leave it and take a seat with us. He had hardly got himself comfortable [*sic*] seated, before the Conductor appeared, full of wrath, and ordered him out. This of course we could not consent to without first telling the *gentleman* what we thought of such an unrighteous proceeding, and immediately opened our fire upon him. Arnold, Ann, Mary and myself,—all joined, the girls (forgetting they were out of their "appropriate sphere," in their eagerness to protect an insulted brother) did their part and our poor conductor not expecting such opposition, retreated, leaving us in possession of the field.[33]

In his account of the trial of the men who threw him off a train the following July, David Ruggles notes that on that same New Year's Day, William A. Crocker, one of the railroad line's directors, instituted the "rule" about passengers taking "such seats as may be assigned them by the conductor." It is not unlikely that this rule was codified in response to the incident involving Borden and Coffin in order to give employees of the railroad written documentation to support their actions in removing colored passengers from the first-class cars. This may indeed be the earliest written regulation used as a foundational excuse for segregating the railroads.

Thomas Downing, December 30, 1840

In the early 1830s, David Ruggles was working to assist fugitive slaves through New York City and was publishing tales of the harsh treatment he met with on stagecoaches. At the same time the world's first streetcar line, the Harlem Railroad, was built to carry passengers in horse-drawn trolleys from Prince Street north to Fifteenth Street. As the line expanded, steam engines were introduced in 1837, but only north of Twenty-Third Street. By 1839 the rails had reached south to City Hall and north to Harlem.

On December 30, 1840, Thomas Downing entered a Harlem line car at Fifteenth Street, heading downtown. A brief account of what happened was recorded in the New York *Journal of Commerce* and reprinted in the *Liberator*:

> Reported for the Journal of Commerce.
>
> POLICE OFFICE—Yesterday.
>
> *Outrage.* Thomas Downing, a colored man, who keeps a well known oyster cellar in Broad street, yesterday forenoon got into one of the railroad cars at Fifteenth street, with the intention of returning down town. But he had scarcely taken his seat, when the agent of the car peremptorily ordered him out, saying, that "no nigger shall be in the car." Downing, however, refused to leave the car, and the agent and driver immediately seized hold of him, dragged him out, and assisted by two other men, gave him a severe beating, and inflicted a wound in his neck. A warrant has been issued for their apprehension.

The *Liberator* then appends the comments of the editors of the *Journal of Commerce*, testifying to Downing's good standing in the community and his heroism during the Great Fire of 1835:

> The abuse of Downing by the Harlem rail-road agents, is an act which we hope will be dealt with according to its merits. Downing is an intelligent, respectable citizen, possessing considerable property, and universally esteemed by those who have been accustomed to visit his refectory. At the time of the great fire in December, 1835, Downing was one of half a dozen persons, who, by indefatigable and somewhat hazardous exertions, saved the buildings in the rear of the South Dutch church from burning, although *we* had neither engine nor water, but (what was better than water in such tremendous cold weather) vinegar, several pipes of which happened to be in the adjoining yard. Nothing but these exertions of Downing and a few others prevented the conflagration from extending through to Broad street. A million dollars at least was thus saved from destruction. But Downing is a *colored man*, and therefore he may be kicked out of a railroad car, and wantonly beaten at pleasure. . . . It is time those outrages were put a stop to.[34]

Six weeks later, the *Liberator* reprinted, again from the *Journal of Commerce*, an account of the trial of "William W. Skirving, agent, and Lucius Deleber, driver, of Rail Road car No. 7," who were charged with assault and battery on Downing. This account describes the injuries Downing suffered: "The agent seizing him by the collar, the driver struck him under the ear, and with two others beat and kicked him, broke his hat, and forced him violently out of the car. The cartilage of one ear was divided for half an inch, and both ears cut, and the skin torn down under one of them. His leg was badly bruised and swollen, until it was 3 1-2 inches larger than the other, as Dr. Bliss deposed." The court determined that there was a regulation "that no colored persons were to ride inside of the car, but on the top, in accordance with the tone of public opinion, though some rode inside almost every day." As with the stagecoaches, "colored persons" were expected to ride with the driver on top of the cars, exposed to the elements. However, it is also significant that the regulation was frequently ignored. Indeed, the *Journal*'s summary stated that on his journey uptown Downing rode inside the car "without opposition." Thus, there was an arbitrariness in Skirving's decision to forcefully oust Downing from the car that day.

The *Journal* also recounted in some detail instructions to the jury members. They were to determine whether the regulation was reasonable, whether "due notice had been given of the regulation, that those interested in it could have known, and might conform to it," and whether Downing might have been thrown off his guard by the fact that he had ridden inside the car on his way uptown, though the agent may not have known that fact. Downing testified "that he was not aware of any rule to exclude colored persons from an inside seat." However, one intriguing sentence implies that Skirving and Deleber or their lawyers went to some lengths to contradict him. Per a judge's instructions, "The jury were at liberty to draw inferences, as to whether their notice was known to the complainant, from the fact that those regulations having been last spring enforced against part of Mr. Downing's family, at which time his son told his mother of the occurrence, but did not tell it to his father." They were also to consider, "Was the blow he received necessary to remove him, or did he receive any blow?" Perhaps he received his injuries "from being pushed against the railing or door post." Had the agent used "a greater violence . . . than was necessary"? The jury members were also to keep in mind the fact that "no violence was offered to the complainant until the order was repeated to him to leave the car."

All of these instructions look very much like ways in which judges and the courts for the next 130 years were able to coach juries to arrive at verdicts that would preserve the status quo. The final sentence of the report gives us an intimation of the atmosphere in the courtroom that day: "Verdict, not guilty;—which caused loud applause from the audience, but which was immediately suppressed by order of the Court."[35]

Thomas Downing was born in 1791, the son of freed slaves in Chincoteague, Virginia. He came north and joined the army during the War of 1812. After some years as a domestic servant in Philadelphia, he moved to New York around 1820. Downing's oyster cellar, established in 1825 at the intersection of Broad Street and Wall Street, was for many years a popular meeting place for bankers, financiers, and politicians. Over time, through his friendly personality and excellent provisions, Downing gained a considerable reputation and eventually became quite wealthy.[36] But, as we shall see, this was not the last time that he would be threatened on a New York streetcar.

The First Freedom Riders, 1841

In spite of protests and the occasional success, such as that of Nathaniel Borden at the end of 1840, the racial animosity exhibited by the railroads did not diminish. Throughout the summer and fall of 1841 there was a spate of incidents in which African Americans who took their seats in the first-class cars on the railroads of New England were forced into a Jim Crow car or off the train altogether. This was the result of a number of converging forces. Rail travel was becoming more common in general, and the growing antislavery movement gave rise to the establishment of local and statewide antislavery organizations, meetings, and conventions. This, of course, led to an increase in the number of people, both Black and white, traveling to attend those meetings, at times in the company of one another. It is unclear how planned, organized, or coordinated the resultant campaign of protest against such incidents throughout the year might have been, but Black abolitionists and their white allies regularly began to challenge the abrogation of passengers' rights on public conveyances that summer, and there was a growing concern for the rights of free Black people in regions of the North where slavery had recently been, or was soon to be, eliminated. Confrontations multiplied as railroad officials and employees became increasingly bullheaded and heavy-handed in their efforts to keep passengers of color separated in inferior accommodations, making the abolitionists, in turn, even more determined. As the railroad companies and their owners began to receive more and more criticism in the press and in the courts, the railroad cars were bound to become an important venue for public protest and action. The intentionality of these protesters justifies applying to some of them, at least, the title of "Freedom Riders," albeit 120 years before that term came into public use.

Thomas Jinnings, May 28, 1841

The earliest of numerous incidents on Massachusetts railroads during the summer of 1841 is recorded in a letter written on May 31 by Thomas Jinnings Jr., describing how three days earlier he had been threatened with violence by a conductor on the Eastern Railroad at Salem, Massachusetts. Having bought a first-class ticket and seated himself in the first-class car, Jinnings was told by the conductor to "accompany him to another car" in accord with the rules of the company. Jinnings appealed to the other passengers in the car. "Several

An Eastern Railroad train, possibly at South Boston station, 1840–41. Courtesy of Historic Beverly.

said I had a perfect right to the seat I had occupied, and that it was the conductor's duty to wait until he had received complaints from the passengers before he ordered my removal. Others called for 'the rules.' . . . In rushed baggage masters and brakemen!" The conductor, along with these railroad employees and one of the passengers, then seized Jinnings "like giants, and cried—*Clear the road!*" Several men intervened and prevented violence, and Jinnings gave in: "For peace sake, I retired to another car."[37]

Thomas Jinnings Jr. was the son of Thomas L. Jennings, a successful New York tailor and businessman and the first African American to be awarded a U.S. patent. Thomas Jr. and his brother William moved to Boston. (They appear in Boston city directories for 1839 and 1840 under the spelling "Jinnings."[38] Thomas Sr. and the family in New York appear most frequently in the record as Jennings, but sometimes as Jinnings.) Like their father, both brothers were active in the antislavery movement. William, however, died of consumption (tuberculosis) at the age of thirty in September 1840.[39] Thomas Jinnings Jr. first appears in the *Liberator* on July 31, 1840, in an announcement that he was to address the Plymouth County Anti-Slavery Society the following day. That August he began advertising his dental services at Dr. Daniel Mann's office on Summer Street. Mann, who was white, was a dentist and a prominent Boston abolitionist. Though his race is not indicated, Jinnings is listed in the Harvard catalog for the academic year 1841–42 as a medical school student, under the instruction of "D. Mann, M.D." Thomas Jinnings Jr., therefore, is the earliest-known African American to attend Harvard.[40]

Because of Jinnings's standing in the community as both a well-educated professional man and an abolitionist, his expulsion from a first-class Eastern Railroad car captured the attention of abolitionists across the state and elsewhere, and notices appeared in various papers. An unsigned letter to the editor of the *Bay State Democrat* in Boston, on the general subject of the principles of democracy in relation to questions of race and slavery, concludes with a description of the forced removal of Jinnings and a question posed to the *Democrat* editor, "Is this one of the forms of tyranny to which you declare uncompromising hostility?" Though Jinnings is not named in this piece, it is clearly a reference to that event.[41] On June 4, 1841, just a week after the railroad incident, Jinnings participated in a meeting in Boston honoring David Ruggles, supporting the activist minister and editor Henry Highland Garnet, and discussing the formation of a Boston Vigilance Committee on the model of the New York Committee of Vigilance founded in 1835 by Ruggles. Both Jinnings and Mann were elected as members of the executive committee.

A short but impassioned item describing the threat against Jinnings appeared in the *Colored American* under the heading "Rail Road Abuse." The writer's concluding statement makes it clear that there had been similar incidents in Massachusetts in the past: "Wonder how much longer such a game is to be played upon the rail roads of Massachusetts, which is classed among the purest states in the Union? We now hear of more such outrages upon colored men in that State, than in all the rest of the States in the Union, free or slave States. She has, in this respect, her character to redeem. Will her free and enlightened citizens tolerate much longer such outrages upon colored men? It remains for the people, who incorporate such companies, to say."[42]

Another response to the harassment of Jinnings, extracted from the *Lynn (Mass.) Record*, was published in the *Liberator* in early July. The publisher and editor of the *Record*, Alonzo Lewis, was a staunch abolitionist, and he articulated explicitly the relevance and importance of a distinction between people and corporations—an issue that would again come into prominence in the political arena of the twenty-first century. Though Lewis erred in believing that such mistreatment occurred only on the Eastern Railroad, he forcefully laid out the principles in question:

> Case of Mr. Jinnings
>
> The editor of that well-conducted journal, the Lynn Record, (who seldom omits to improve every suitable opportunity to vindicate the cause of our colored population, both bond and free,) notices the recent outrage committed

upon the person of our respected fellow-citizen Thomas Jinnings, in his exclusion from the cars on the Eastern rail-road, on account of his complexion, in the following manner:

> The above is undoubtedly a gross and palpable outrage on equal rights, and individual rights. "Corporations have no souls," and the agents and individuals who act under them sometimes act as if they had worse than none. Railroad companies are incorporated for the public good. They have special powers, privileges and favors conferred on them for the purpose of being serviceable to the public, like turnpike companies and others, and they have no right to make arbitrary distinctions between individuals, and deny to any one or more persons, rights which belong to all equally. They have no more right in selling their tickets and furnishing cars to regard the color of the skin than they have the color of the clothes of individuals. The law does not allow it, and public sentiment does not allow it. In no other place than *Essex county and on the Eastern Railroad* is such tyranny practised. Even in the slave states, colored people ride in the same cars with white people, and no one thinks of making any objection. So through all the states and counties south of us, no distinction is made. But on the Eastern Railroad, if a colored man, however well educated and well behaved, after paying for his ticket, takes his seat like other people, where he chooses, he is dragged from his seat by violence and force, thrust out of the cars, and perhaps kicked after he is out. No law and no justice will tolerate such conduct. The subject is important, and may receive further attention hereafter.[43]

As we shall see, Jinnings was again assaulted, along with two white friends, on the New Bedford and Taunton line a few months later, on October 21, 1841. Thirteen years later, his sister, Elizabeth Jennings, about sixteen years younger than he, was expelled from a New York streetcar in 1854, in a case that became key to the eventual elimination of segregation on the streetcars of that city.

"Treatment of Colored Citizens," June 17, 1841

Many of the published instances in which Black passengers were denied seating on trains and steamboats during this early period involve active abolitionists with access to one or another of the antislavery newspapers. However, the following report from the Cambridgeport Anti-Slavery Society demonstrates that such discrimination was not limited to just one or two train or boat lines, or to cases in which the principal figure, perhaps on the way to or from an abolitionist meeting, might be expected to resist mistreatment. By way of contrast, here we have an unnamed man and his wife simply in need of local transportation from Cambridgeport to Boston, a distance of less than four miles. A stagecoach line between Cambridge and Boston had been established in the 1820s, and during the 1830s it was expanded by the addition of smaller omnibuses, drawn by two horses rather than four, running hourly into the city from both Harvard Square and Cambridgeport.[44]

Treatment of Colored Citizens

At a meeting of the Cambridgeport Anti-Slavery Society, held Thursday evening, June 17, the following preamble and resolution were adopted:

Whereas, it having been stated to this Society, that a gross outrage has lately been committed upon the personal feelings, and the inalienable and constitutional rights of a highly respectable colored lady and gentleman of Boston, by the driver of a Cambridge omnibus, who rudely refused to allow them to ride as passengers from Cambridgeport to Boston, the lady being in a feeble state of health;

And whereas, it is among the objects of this Society to vindicate and secure the rights of our colored fellow citizens, and to bear a faithful testimony against that unnatural and unholy prejudice, which so extensively prevails against them; therefore,

Resolved, That a committee of three be appointed, respectfully to make known the facts, in regard to the outrage aforesaid, to the proprietors of the Cambridge line of omnibusses—to remonstrate against the repetition of such an act—and to ascertain whether the driver aforesaid acted on his own responsibility, or in accordance with any rules or regulations laid down for his guidance by the proprietors; the committee to make their report to this Society at their earliest convenience, that such further action may be taken in the [pr]emises as may be deemed expedient.[45]

David Ruggles, June 19 and July 6, 1841

Having been defrauded in 1838 on the steamboat *Rhode Island*, David Ruggles was perhaps even more outraged when it happened to him again during the active summer of 1841. Writing with his usual fervor, Ruggles set out the details of another encounter during a trip from New Bedford to Nantucket Island on June 19:

NEW BEDFORD, June 23d, 1841.

To the Editor of the New Bedford Daily Register:—

SIR,—Permit me to inquire of your readers, what is Highway Robbery? and if the following outrage is not Robbery, and Assault and Battery. I left New Bedford on Saturday last, the 19th inst., on board the Steamboat Telegraph, for Nantucket.[46]

> On the passage thither, when called upon to pay the fare, I stepped forward to the Captain's office, and inquired the price of the passage. I learned that there were two prices; one $2, the other $1.50. The passenger who pays the first price is entitled to all the privileges of the Boat. The one who pays the second price purchases a forward deck privilege. I concluded to pay $2, which the Capt. repeatedly refused to take, and insisted on my purchasing the forward deck privilege, which I did not choose to take, on the grounds, first, no man or body corporate has a right to decide for another person what he or she shall purchase; second, no man can justly compel another to pay for what he does not want. The Capt. became furious at my position, commenced an assault and battery upon my person, took from me by force my private papers. Finding myself "a stranger in a strange place," shorn of hat and important papers, I was compelled to leave the Island without accomplishing the object of my visit; on my return passage, Capt. Lot Phinney received $2 fare. I state these facts to *caution* the public, who may travel in the Steamboat between New Bedford and Nantucket.
>
> Yours for Equal Rights,
> David Ruggles[47]

The *New-Bedford Register* for July 7 includes the notice of a "Meeting of Colored Citizens," chaired by Frederick Douglass, some months before he began to attract the attention of white abolitionists. During this meeting the following resolution was passed unanimously:

> *Resolved*, That we consider the unjust assault inflicted on the person of our devoted friend, David Ruggles of New York, Editor and proprietor of the Mirror of Liberty, by Capt. Lot Phinney of steamboat Telegraph, while on his passage from this place to Nantucket, an open violation of the laws of this commonwealth and unworthy the head or heart of any man who claims an inheritance to the Bay State, and we call on the friends of Liberty to discountenance so insufferable an outrage on equal rights. Frederick Douglass, Chairman. Edward B. Lawton, Secretary.[48]

The day before the above notice appeared in the *New-Bedford Register*, however, David Ruggles was back in the news after being forcibly removed from a first-class railroad car at New Bedford. In response, he brought a charge of assault and battery against the conductor and others involved. A trial was held two weeks later, a summary of which appeared in the *New-Bedford Mercury* on July 23, under the heading "Rights of Rail Road Corporations." According to the *Mercury*, Justice Henry Crapo decided the case on two points: "1st. Whether said Corporation have a legal right to adopt and enforce regulations of such character as those that had been presented, and whether any such regulations had been adopted" (i.e., regulations denying colored passengers seats in the first-class cars), and "2d. Whether any more force and violence was used . . . than was necessary in effecting the removal of Mr. Ruggles from the car . . . and also, whether due notice was given him of such regulation." Justice Crapo decided on the first point that "they have such right—the right being implied in the very nature of things and supported by common sense." On the second point, he determined that due notice had been given to Ruggles, adding, "It further did not appear that any more force was used in removing Mr. Ruggles from the car to the platform, than was necessary to effect that object,—except from the testimony of Mr. Ruggles himself, and even this witness had been unable to say by whom the blows had been inflicted." Accordingly, the defendants were found not guilty.

In response to the bias evident in the *Mercury* article, Ruggles sent his own account of the incident to the *Liberator*, under the title "Justice Henry A. Crapo and Lynch Law."[49] In his report Ruggles prints the "regulation" in question, as it was testified to at the trial. This rule seems to have been established by William A. Crocker, an agent of the railroad company, on January 1, 1841: "Passengers who go in the cars of the Taunton and New Bedford branch railroad, will take such seats as may be assigned them by the conductor." Coincidentally or not, this instruction was instituted on the same day that William Coffin wrote to Debora Weston describing the failed attempt to ouster Nathaniel Borden, in which the train conductor had backed down, perhaps for the lack of just such a written rule. Similar rules and laws, often just as vaguely worded, were subsequently adopted on other rail and bus lines well into the twentieth century.

The brief headnote "Case of David Ruggles" that preceded Ruggles's report would have been written by his friend, the *Liberator*'s renowned editor, William Lloyd Garrison. In addition to characterizing the assault and battery upon Ruggles as "dastardly," Garrison refers to the court proceedings as a "mock trial," and he calls Justice Crapo's conduct "unspeakably atrocious," thus setting a tone quite different from that of the *Mercury* article. Not surprisingly, Ruggles's version of the trial is even more acerbic, and he offers his opinions as to Justice Crapo's conduct and abilities in caustic terms, equating the trial from the outset with lynch law.[50] Ruggles recognized that a conviction for assault and battery against those who threw him off the train was "without even a hope." Rather, he took a longer view of the problem, and he explains:

> [My] action was brought for the purpose of compelling the New-Bedford and Taunton Branch Rail Road Company to explain, under oath, the object of their

> pretended rule and their fraudulent practices upon the public, that I might be better prepared to proceed against them in a civil court of law. . . . It was hardly to be supposed that his honor could give an equitable decision in this case—himself being a stockholder in said company, and therefore lawfully rendered incapable of occupying the bench of justice under such circumstances.

The explanation that Ruggles was seeking came in no uncertain terms directly from Joseph Grinnell, the president of the railroad company, who testified, "This regulation was made to render the passage pleasant and convenient to passengers and the public. It has operated very beneficially. The rule or regulation separates the drunken, dirty, ragged and colored people from others." Under cross-examination, Grinnell testified: "I myself think color alone offensive—that a colored man should be put in the cars with the dirty and intoxicated; and if I was going to Boston with my family, I would not go in the same car with a colored person. I once knew a colored woman to be annoyed by drunken sailors, and the conductors put her in a car with me."

In his report Ruggles cannot here refrain from noting sardonically in brackets, "[Query—Must not the woman have been highly honored, to sit in the presence of such 'small potatoes!']" He then offers his own unvarnished opinion of Grinnell's employees:

> But, seriously, according to Mr. Grinnell's testimony, the servants of his rail-road company are a gang of pickpockets or highwaymen. One of these marauders is authorized to receive two dollars fare from all persons who apply at the ticket office for a passage to Boston. After receiving the money, and persons are seated, search is made to find an object of prey. If a person is found guilty of wearing a colored skin, he becomes a victim of plunder, and must crawl into the 'Jim Crow' or dirty car, so called, or become a subject of lynch law! Defenceless persons are in great danger, when travelling on the New Bedford rail-road to Boston, or from Boston to New Bedford, of being robbed, assaulted and lynched, at the bidding of his hired pimps.

Ruggles follows this with a brief reference to another incident that helps us to envision the conditions in the Jim Crow or "dirty car," which was often divided into separate sections for colored passengers and white second-class ticket holders: "It is not long since a respectable female, going from Boston to New-Bedford, was most grossly insulted and assaulted by a ruffian in the dirty car, where she was compelled to sit. He crawled through a window from another part of the same car, and the conductor permitted him to remain, without affording the defenceless woman the least protection!"

He also makes note that of sixty or seventy passengers in the car from which he himself was ejected, there were only two "who were sufficiently tainted with ruffianism" to urge on his assailants.[51]

On Monday, July 12, a public meeting, which Ruggles attended, was convened at the old Congregational meetinghouse in New Bedford. A resolution was passed remonstrating "in the most solemn manner against such *inhuman* proceedings as took place at the rail-road Depot in this town on the 6th of the present month, in expelling David Ruggles of New-York, from the car, for the unworthy cause of his having a color which the God of nature was pleased to give him."[52]

Suffering from ill health and from near blindness perhaps caused by cataracts, Ruggles left New York City in 1842. At the recommendation of the prominent white abolitionist Lydia Maria Child, he joined the Northampton Association of Education and Industry, a recently founded utopian, abolitionist society in Broughton's Meadow (later called Bensonville, now Florence), Massachusetts. The association was guided by the principle that "the rights of all are equal without distinction of sex, color or condition, sect or religion." When the association was dissolved in 1846, Ruggles remained in Florence. He continued his communications with white and Black abolitionists, and a community of former slaves and other people of color grew up in the neighborhood around him, attracted in part, no doubt, by his personality and his reputation.[53]

Having experienced some improvements to his health through "water cure" treatments he received from Dr. Robert Wesselhoeft of Cambridge, Massachusetts, Ruggles began to use a similar regimen to treat himself and other members of the association and the local community, including Sojourner Truth, who had joined the community in 1844, as well as such notables as Frederick Douglass and William Lloyd Garrison. Though he was almost completely blind, during the later 1840s Ruggles established a hospital, the first of its kind in this country, for patients to come for his water cure, and his reputation extended even as far south as Georgia.[54] Ruggles's final patient was himself. Suffering from a variety of ills that had plagued him periodically for years, he died on December 16, 1849, at the age of thirty-nine. As short as his life and his career were, David Ruggles was by any standard a remarkable man whose energy and accomplishments made him one of the most active, effective, and outspoken proponents of the abolition of slavery and of equal rights.

"Corporations Have No Souls," August 1841

In his editorial responding to the mistreatment of Thomas Jinnings in May 1841, Alonzo Lewis, the editor of the *Lynn Record*, had commented that "corporations have no souls." In August he expanded on that theme as he again addressed the racism evidenced—and indeed encouraged—on railroad trains. The absurdity that, even in a free state, slaves could accompany their masters in first-class cars where free Black passengers were not allowed, no matter how respectable or well-behaved, was frequently pointed out. Here Lewis coupled that logical inconsistency with the objection that impersonal corporations should have the power to limit the rights of people, as he called out Stephen A. Chase, a Quaker and the first superintendent of the Eastern Railroad, to answer for the hypocrisy of his policies:

> Eastern Rail-Road Company.
>
> The TYRANNY OF CORPORATIONS has perhaps a more deadly influence in destroying the liberties of our country than any thing else, and should be watched with vigilance by the whole community. They have no souls, no bodies, no consciences, no personal responsibility, but selfishness in abundance. They are sure to take all the power they can get, without regard to the welfare of the people or the rights of individuals.
>
> The arbitrary distinctions of rank, and color, and caste, which one or two Rail-road Companies are attempting to make, against our Bill of Rights, our constitution and laws, against the liberties of the people, and the equal rights of citizens, call loudly for animadversion and redress; and should excite general alarm. If we *must* be enslaved, give us a tyrant in his *private capacity*, and not in the shape of a servant to a corporation, which has no regard for the rights of individuals. We refer to the *negro car*, more abominable, illegal, and inexcusable, than slavery itself. Indeed, it appears evident from some late movement to have been done for the accommodation of *slaveholders*, and not freemen.
>
> *The Eastern Rail-road* takes in black *slaves* or *servants* among the white people, without objection, but drags out by brute force, intelligent, well educated *freemen* of color, or we have been wrongly informed. How is this, superintendent, friend Chase? One of thy own Friends, of thy own society, neighborhood and name, so informed us, and we have no reason to doubt his word. The circumstances as related to us are these.
>
> A colored person was seen on board one of the cars, among the white people. The observer, not supposing it possible that such an occurrence had escaped the vigilant eye of friend superintendent, congratulated and complimented him, at the first landing, on his liberality in having abolished the old, barbarous, tyrannical, and shameful custom, of obliging colored people to withdraw from the cars of the whites.
>
> "What do you mean?" said the superintendent or conductor. "We have made no alteration."

"Well, I saw a colored person in the car I have just left, and concluded without doubt, he was there by your permission."

"O—ah—hem—true—to be sure—*there is a black* in that car *but*—that is a *servant* (or *slave*) to a white person there."

So here we have the whole story. It is not the *color*, but the *freedom* of the color, that is so much hated and persecuted by our broad brim nobility. And what says the slaveholder? Hear ye—"*We treat our slaves better than you do your colored freemen.*" And this is strictly true. *The slaveholders don't object* to riding in the same car with their slaves. *They will not ride without them.* They love to have their slaves about them, near them, to feed and fan them, and take care of them and their children. There is no "offensive odor" to a servant or slave, but the colored freeman emits an intolerable stench. Ah, Friend Chase, this is sheer pretence, too glaringly so to be denied or doubted. Thou knowest it; and the sooner such hypocrisy is cast away, the sooner thou wilt clear the skirts of thy garments. Do it quickly, or the whole land will cry *out upon thee* for very shame.[55]

A "Respectable Colored Woman" and Isaac Bassett, September 1, 1841

The first page of the *Liberator* for October 1, 1841, devotes a full column to the Eastern Railroad and "the arbitrary and tyrannical rule they have adopted, of compelling people of color to take a car by themselves." A letter from Isaac Bassett again addresses the inconsistent application of Jim Crow practices on the Eastern line. Bassett describes what happened on the train from Lynn to Boston as he was traveling with his daughter and her two children, ages three and one, "together with a respectable *colored woman*, who had been residing with my family, and who accompanied us for the purpose of assisting with the children . . . on our way to Philadelphia."[56]

Soon after leaving the Lynn station, the conductor came to Bassett and whispered in his ear, "*You must not think to take a colored person in with you again—this is the second time—and if you ever do it again, she shall be taken out.*" Bassett replied that "under such circumstances it would be next to impossible to get along without her assistance—if she is removed, we must go with her." To this the conductor answered, "*No, you shall not!*" Bassett's arguments had no effect, and the conductor insisted that "the like *offence* should not be repeated." By way of contrast, Bassett notes, "On the train from Boston to Stonington, we had no trouble in not being all of one *shade of complexion*. My daughter, her children and servant, took the saloon car, and on the steamboat they all took lodgings in the cabin. Comment on such outrageous proceedings is unnecessary. Will the public tolerate them longer on the Eastern Rail-Road?"

To this letter, Garrison, editor of the *Liberator*, appends some remarks and a notice:

> Remarks: A slave or servant of color has heretofore been considered an exception on the Eastern Rail-Road, and allowed to take a seat among the whites. Why *this* colored female was not allowed the same privilege, is known best to the conductor. A Justice of the Peace in New-Bedford, it is said, decided that the conductors of the cars *had a right to seat the passengers*. That does not decide that they have a right to be arbitrary, or to make color a reason for dragging out a person from one car and thrusting him into another; if it does, we should appeal to a higher Court. . . . Let the question be decided, whether there is any such thing as equal rights, and whether we are slaves or freemen.
>
> Since the above occurrence, the following notice has been published by the superintendent:
>
> NOTICE: The Directors of the Eastern Rail-Road Company have ordered the following rule of the road to be published, viz.:
>
> All passengers upon the road are required to take such seats in the cars, and in such cars as shall be designated by the respective conductors; and all tickets are sold subject to this rule.
>
> STEPHEN A. CHASE, *Sup't.*
> September 2d, 1841

Isaac Bassett's letter reveals that from the beginning the exception allowing slaves or servants in the cars was applied as arbitrarily as an individual conductor or driver, or his employer, wished. The justice of the peace Garrison refers to was Henry H. Crapo, who justified with heavily biased logic the Jim Crow rule in the case of David Ruggles about six weeks earlier, saying that the right for companies to make such a rule was "implied in the very nature of things and supported by common sense."[57] It may have been mere coincidence, but just one day after Isaac Bassett objected to the conductor's implied threat, Superintendent Chase published the company's version of the Jim Crow rule (sanctioned by the courts, though not yet law). Within a week placards stating that rule had been posted in the railroad cars themselves, as we learn from J. A. Collins's account of the experience of Frederick Douglass on September 8.

Frederick Douglass, September 8 and 28, 1841

Frederick Douglass was born into slavery as Frederick Augustus Washington Bailey in February 1818, in Talbot County, Maryland. As was often the case with infants born into bondage, within a year Frederick was separated from

Frederick Douglass, circa 1850. Courtesy of the Onondaga Historical Association.

his mother. He spent his early years in a cabin with his grandmother, Betsy, who died when he was six or seven. At the age of eight he was sent from the plantation to be the boyhood "companion" of the son of his master's brother, Hugh Auld, in Baltimore. It is fortunate that Sophia Auld, Hugh's wife, looked on Frederick with such favor that she taught him his ABC's and the rudiments of reading. But when Frederick reached eleven years old, Hugh forbade his wife to teach him any further. It was, after all, unlawful. Douglass quotes Hugh as saying (among harsher and cruder words), "It would forever unfit him to be a slave. He would at once become unmanageable and of no value to his master."[58] Hugh proved to be more right than he could have imagined.

Having been introduced to reading, Frederick proceeded to teach himself secretly. He acquired and carried with him a copy of the "Blue-Back Speller," as Noah Webster's widely used spelling book was popularly known. He took spelling lessons from young white playmates near his master's shipyard: "For a single biscuit, any of my hungry little comrades would give me a lesson more valuable than bread."[59] Earning some money by shining gentlemen's boots, he bought a copy of Caleb Bingham's *The Columbian Orator*, with its numerous examples of famous speeches and knowledge of the world beyond Frederick's experience, including a dialogue between a slave and his master in which the slave's replies lead to his emancipation.[60] Some of his learning Frederick literally took from the streets: "I have gathered scattered pages of the Bible from the filthy street-gutters, and washed and dried them, that in moments of leisure I might get a word or two of wisdom from them."[61]

However, in 1832 Frederick became a pawn in a feud between Hugh and Thomas Auld. Thomas, his master, demanded that the boy be returned to him in the small town of St. Michaels on Maryland's Eastern Shore. There, bored, angry, deprived of the friends he had made in Baltimore, and working under a stingy master and his cruel wife, Frederick was even reduced to stealing food to sustain himself. He became troublesome, and Auld began whipping him and taking out his rage mercilessly on Frederick's disabled cousin Henny.

In response to Frederick's recalcitrance, Auld rented him out for all of 1833 as a field hand to a small-time farmer named Edward Covey, a well-known slave breaker. For six months Covey whipped the sixteen-year-old about once a week, until one day the boy fought back fiercely and prevailed against Covey in a battle lasting nearly two hours:

> This battle with Mr. Covey was the turning-point in my career as a slave. . . . It recalled the departed self-confidence, and inspired me again with a determination to be free. . . . I now resolved that however long I remained a slave in form, the day had passed forever when I could be a slave in fact. I did not hesitate to let it be known of me, that the white man who expected to succeed in whipping, must also succeed in killing me.[62]

Douglass's only explanation for why Covey never turned him over to the constable and the inevitable whipping post for striking a white man was that doing so would have ruined Covey's reputation as "a first-rate overseer and negro-breaker."[63]

The following year Frederick was leased out to William Freeman, a farmer with both a better disposition and a better-run farm than Covey. During that year Frederick was able to teach other slaves how to write, and he soon became the leader of an ad hoc Sunday school with up to forty students of all ages. Freeman renewed his hire for 1835, and it was during this time that Frederick and four others developed a plan to escape. The plan failed, and they were all imprisoned briefly. Auld returned Frederick to Baltimore to live again with Hugh. There he was hired out to a ship builder, and he learned to be a caulker, sealing the seams between the planks of wooden ships. By 1838 he had determined to escape.

On Monday, September 3, Douglass says, "I bade farewell to the city of Baltimore, and to that slavery which had been my abhorrence from childhood."[64] He borrowed a free sailor's identification papers from a friend and then engaged a friendly hack driver to put his bag on a train bound for Wilmington, Delaware, which was still slave territory. Rather than attempt to buy a ticket at the depot, Frederick waited until the train began moving, and then he jumped aboard and purchased a ticket from the conductor without raising his suspicion. A steamboat ride up the Delaware from Wilmington to Philadelphia was then followed by another train ride to New York.

Within twenty-four hours Frederick found himself a free man in the dazzling and bewildering city. But the "unspeakable joy" he felt was soon dampened when by chance he met another fugitive, who schooled him about the dangers of being recaptured.[65] He spent "at least one night among the barrels on one of the wharves."[66] Then he was lucky to encounter a sailor named Stuart, who sheltered him for the night and took him the next day to meet David Ruggles.

Frederick remained hidden at Ruggles's home on Lispenard Street, and he wrote to summon his beloved, Anna Murray, a free woman he knew in Baltimore. They were married in Ruggles's apartment by the Presbyterian minister James W. C. Pennington. That same day they set out for New Bedford, Massachusetts, where Ruggles suggested Frederick might find both greater safety and familiar work among the shipyards. On the steamer to Newport they had to spend the night on the open foredeck but on this occasion did so willingly: "Unjust as this regulation was, it did not trouble us much. We had fared much harder before."[67]

In New York, Frederick had assumed the surname Johnson, a common one among African Americans at the time. Upon reaching New Bedford, the couple received the protection and hospitality of Nathan Johnson. Following Johnson's recommendation, Frederick, determined to keep his first name, adopted the surname Douglass, based on the character of "Douglas of the stalwart hand/ . . . exiled from his native land" in Sir Walter Scott's popular poem "The Lady of the Lake."[68] As busy as the New Bedford shipyards were, the caulker's trade was restricted to white workers. Douglass, therefore, turned to other less-skilled and less-remunerative work as a common laborer.

A few months after arriving in New Bedford, Douglass became a subscriber to the *Liberator*: "I was brought into contact with the mind of Mr. Garrison, and his paper took a place in my heart second only to the Bible.

It detested slavery and made no truce with the traffickers in the bodies and souls of men. It preached human brotherhood; it exposed hypocrisy and wickedness in high places; it denounced oppression and with all the solemnity of 'Thus saith the Lord,' demanded the complete emancipation of my race. I loved this paper and its editor."[69]

He also began to attend church, but finding the segregation of the Elm Street Methodist Church unacceptable, he made his way to the AME Zion Church, led at first by William Serrington and later by Thomas James.[70] Here Douglass soon began teaching Sunday classes and even preaching on occasion.[71] In his 1886 autobiography James would note that Douglass had spoken before Black audiences, and he took credit for first introducing Douglass to a white audience.[72] Douglass began to attend antislavery meetings in New Bedford, and by 1840 he was attracting the attention of white abolitionists.[73]

Douglass spoke at several meetings of the Bristol County Anti-Slavery Society in New Bedford during 1841, and on one such occasion he was invited by William C. Coffin to attend an antislavery convention on Nantucket, beginning on August 10. It is likely that Douglass spoke at a meeting in New Bedford on August 9, in which several "col'd individuals" spoke to the matter of segregation in public transportation and churches. This meeting was also attended by William Lloyd Garrison, John A. Collins, and other prominent Massachusetts abolitionists. The following day about forty Black and white abolitionists, including Douglass, boarded the steamer *Telegraph* for the trip to Nantucket—the same boat on which Emiliano Mundrucu, David Ruggles, and Thomas James had been denied cabin access. True to form, the captain of the *Telegraph* required the African Americans on board to stay on the open foredeck. In response, the white abolitionists accompanied them, and during the passage they held a meeting during which they passed a resolution condemning the steamship company's practice.[74]

Douglass had not been scheduled to speak at what he described as the "grand anti-slavery convention" on the island, but at the invitation of William Coffin he did speak before the large, mostly white crowd. Douglass gave his own estimate of its size: "That night there were at least one thousand Garrisonians in Nantucket!"[75] The summary sent to the *Liberator* by the convention president, David Joy, noted that Douglass spoke a few words on the second evening of the meeting, in support of a resolution against northern prejudice, gave way for an adjournment, and then resumed his remarks in the morning.[76]

He was so nervous that he did not later remember what he had said.[77] Still, that speech introduced Douglass to the larger abolitionist community, and it moved John A. Collins, general agent of the Massachusetts Anti-Slavery

Society, to offer him a position promoting the antislavery cause and soliciting subscribers to the *Liberator*. In spite of his initial reluctance—fearing exposure to recapture as a slave and uncertain as to his ability—Douglass agreed to a three-month engagement that ended up lasting six years. Such a position inevitably required almost constant travel, and in this capacity Douglass suffered from both the conditions of travel and the racism perpetrated by the railroads. He became staunchly determined and adept at resisting mistreatment when it came to him.

On September 8, a mere four weeks after the Nantucket convention, Douglass and Collins boarded a train at Newburyport en route to a meeting in Dover, New Hampshire. They took seats in one of the "long cars," as the cars in which white passengers rode were called (distinguishing them from the Jim Crow car). Collins sent a detailed description of the ensuing incident to the *Liberator*: "No sooner were we seated, than the conductor made his appearance, and peremptorily ordered Douglas to leave, and to take his seat in the forward car; meaning the '*Jim Crow*,' though he felt ashamed to call it by that name." When Collins demanded the authority by which the conductor could remove Douglass, the conductor pulled down a placard from near the door, stating the company rule that gave the conductor the right "to seat passengers where it might please him." Collins responded that that did not give him the right to order Douglass out of the car, upon which "the conductor's ire was fiercely kindled, and his little fist flourished above my head quite gracefully."[78]

Collins refused to move to allow the conductor to drag Douglass out of his seat. The conductor replied by citing the authority of the recent decision against David Ruggles by Justice Crapo. Collins's letter to Garrison and the *Liberator* describes what came next:

> The conductor left the cars, and returned in a few moments, followed by four or five of the Company's minions, with a fiendish smile and a careless indifference expressed in their countenances, appearing like so many bloodhounds, waiting for the orders of their master to seize him, which were no sooner given than they all laid hold of him, like so many hyenas, and snaked him out over me in a tangent, and thrust him into the "negro car," with a "Go there, that's good enough for you, d——n you!"

George Foster, another abolitionist who was with them, went to join Douglass in the Jim Crow car, but he, in turn, was forced out because he "was not black enough to ride there."[79]

Collins notes that he himself was injured in the struggle and that Douglass's clothes were damaged. To add further insult to the affair, after the train got under way, one of the other conductors went into the Jim Crow car to "console" Douglass and remarked that "this rule of the Directors can't be so bad, for the *churches*, you know, have their 'negro pews.'" As printed in the *Liberator*, this conductor's comment is highlighted with sardonic pointing index fingers at both ends. Collins concludes: "What a commentary upon our christianity!"[80]

Three weeks later, on September 28, a similar but even more violent encounter took place at the Lynn station. In both the second and third versions of his autobiography, Douglass takes some delight in recounting what happened, but Collins, in the same *Liberator* article, gives an even more dramatic and detailed version.[81] Collins traveled up from Boston to be joined by Douglass and others at Lynn, and they all planned to continue on to a meeting in Newburyport. When the train stopped at Lynn, Collins disembarked to help an unnamed woman in their party to board, and she was followed aboard by Douglass and J. N. Buffum. Collins sat next to Douglass, with the woman in front of them and Buffum directly behind. The conductor soon appeared, apparently the same one as earlier.

The conductor took Douglass by the collar and ordered him to go into the forward (i.e., Jim Crow) car. Buffum asked, "Can't I ride with him if he goes into the forward car?" and the conductor replied, "No, I'd as soon haul you out of his car, as I'd haul him from this." Douglass then persisted in asking the question that the conductor finds difficult to answer out loud: "There are but very few in this car . . . and why, since no objection has been made, do you order me out?" Buffum's call for a vote among the passengers in the car was ignored by the conductor, and Collins's description of the impact Douglass's question has on him aptly conveys the tense atmosphere of such a confrontation:

> "If you will give me any good reason why I should leave this car, I'll go willingly; but, without such reason, I do not feel at liberty to leave," said Douglas; "though," he continued, "you can do with me as you please, I shall not resist." "You have asked that question before," quoth the trembling conductor. "I mean to continue asking the question over and over again," said my colored friend, "as long as you continue to assault me in this manner." "Give him the reason," cried one voice after another, in tones too positive to be misunderstood. The conductor found himself in quite an embarrassed situation. He felt it would not do to force him out without a reason, and yet *the* reason amounted to no reason at all. He finally made up his mind to say, in a half-suppressed, half-audible voice, "Because you are black." The giving utterance to this thought oppressed him. It stuck in his throat, like Macbeth's *Amen*. He could not speak out boldly, "Because you are black."[82]

The conductor called some eight or ten of the company's minions to his aid. "'Snake out the d——d nigger,' cries one. 'Out with him,' responded another. . . . The word was given—'Take him out!' Five or six, like so many tigers, laid hold of Douglas [*sic*], but he happened to be exceedingly heavy, as the laws of gravity were in full force." Douglass held on to his seat firmly, as did Collins, who refused to move from the seat next to him, and they were seized fiercely. "In consequence . . . our seat gave way, and we, with five or six of these villains hold of our head, arms and legs, were dragged out head foremost, and deposited upon the ground in no very gentle manner." They were both kicked and beaten, and Douglass's baggage was thrown out after him. Collins, but not Douglass, was suffered to reboard, but when the train reached Salem, he was kicked off by none other than the president of Eastern Railroad.

Only in his shorter account of this incident in *Life and Times*, his 1881 autobiography, after twenty-five years of retrospection, does Douglass admit that some African Americans had disagreed with his persistent challenges to the Jim Crow rule: "The colored people generally accepted the situation and complained of me as making matters worse rather than better by refusing to submit to this proscription."[83] To have acknowledged this opposition during his antislavery travels in the 1840s and 1850s would surely have diminished the effect of his narrative, when the opponents of abolition would have gleefully seized on any hint of dissension, disagreement, or weakness in the abolition movement.

On the whole, Lynn, Massachusetts, was an amenable, antislavery town. Thus, in spite of the treatment he had received at the Lynn train depot, Douglass moved his family from New Bedford to Lynn at the end of 1841, even though he would often be required to travel on the Eastern Railroad to get to Boston and north to more distant towns.

Mary Newhall Green, September 30, 1841

On various occasions, Mary Newhall Green, secretary of the Lynn Anti-Slavery Society, had ridden in the first-class car, perhaps unnoticed because of her light complexion. She had also traveled in the Jim Crow car, where she had been severely frightened previously at least once. In the long letter that John Collins sent to the *Liberator* describing the two occasions when Frederick Douglass was thrown off the Eastern Railroad on September 8 and September 28, he also includes his firsthand account of an incident involving Mary Green just two days later.

Collins had attended a meeting in Lynn on the evening of September 29 to discuss the railroad's mistreatment of people of color. The following morning he went to take the train back to Boston to deliver a report on the meeting to the *Liberator.* While he was at the Lynn depot talking with a friend, there was a disturbance. He boarded the train and saw three men carrying a woman off, hitting her, and laying her on the ground "in no very gentle manner."

Discussing with Mary Green what had happened, Collins learned enough to give this detailed description of the event:

> This morning, she got into the cars, as usual, with her infant, only five months old. The conductor ordered her out, but she refused, not feeling at liberty to debase herself by voluntarily entering the proscribed negro car, and particularly after having paid a full price for her ticket. Five ruffians, with abundance of oaths and horrid imprecations, were ordered to carry her out. Mrs. Greene [*sic*] informed me that an attempt was made by one of these blood-hounds to wrench her infant from her arms, but she held on to it, and the consequence was, the side of the babe was hurt by the grip of the conductor. Mrs. Greene's husband, learning that his wife and child were being roughly handled, and being moved with the feelings of a parent and husband, rushed to their rescue, but was repulsed from the car, and sent back with a bloody face! By this time, the mother of Mrs. Greene, learning what was going on, ran up to the aid of her daughter, and, though unable to write, left her *mark* upon the face of one of the mobocrats, which will not disappear by a month's washing.[84]

Mary Green herself wrote a letter to the stockholders and directors of the Eastern Railroad, from which a selection was printed in the November 5 edition of the *Liberator* under the headline "Eastern Rail-Road Outrage." In an introductory note to this letter, the editor adds details: "Mrs. Green says that her knee and shoulder were badly hurt, and her finger severely cut. After having been thrown from the car, she went to the ticket office to sit down, but was ordered out in a very insulting manner!" In her letter, Green describes an experience she had had earlier when riding in the Jim Crow car:

> I will tell you the reason why I do not wish to ride in what is called the Jim Crow car. In the first place I have been grossly insulted in said car by one of the hirelings of the rail-road; and had it not been that the life of my babe would have been endangered, I would have jumped from the car, though the train was going at a rapid rate. In the second place, I do not think it is proper for a woman to go in that car, by herself, liable to be insulted by the servants in attendance. In the third place, I do not think that I have any more right in that car than any other person. It is a proscribed car, in which, for that reason alone, I do not wish to ride. I think I have a right, in common with others, to go in any car I choose. When I behave disorderly, it will be time to order me out.[85]

She then addresses rumors that grew up about the episode on September 30: "It has been said that the abolitionists prompted me to go into the car, from which I was ejected. It is not true. I am not aware that any of them knew I was going to Boston. I need no prompting. I hope I have intelligence and courage enough to assert my rights when I see them invaded." The editor then summarizes other aspects of her letter:

> Mrs. Green adds, that, so ashamed are the miscreants who committed the outrage upon her person, they have circulated the story that she was a man dressed in woman's clothing, and that her infant was a rag baby! This proves that they are ashamed of themselves, and that the moral outburst of manly indignation which has followed their barbarous conduct is producing a salutary effect. The most guilty persons, however, are not those who, at the bidding of their employers, did the deed, but those who have established a rule which violates the most sacred rights, and tramples under foot the claims of humanity:—we mean, *the Directors of the Road*.[86]

A "Colored Man" and Dr. Mann, September 30, 1841

On the same day that Mary Green was dragged off the Eastern Railroad, a second incident occurred on the same line, involving the same conductor, resulting this time in a claim of assault and battery against him. Coming so close on the heels of the two expulsions of Frederick Douglass on September 8 and September 28, the ensuing trial attracted considerable attention, and the *Boston Daily Mail* published a detailed account.[87] This account shares a number of similarities with descriptions of the earlier treatment of Douglass, but it further illustrates dramatically the extent to which prominent white abolitionists were willing to engage in the defense of wronged Black passengers. As for the railroad company itself, this case was seen as sufficiently important that the president of the company and the superintendent, Stephen A. Chase, whom we have several times met above, as well as other "persons of distinction," attended the trial.

One of the striking aspects of the trial is that "a colored man" thrown off the train was neither the plaintiff nor a participant in the trial of the conductor, George Harrington. Rather, Harrington was charged with assaulting a white dentist, Dr. Daniel Mann. In planning their suit, the abolitionists may have believed that identifying the Black man thrown out of the car that day could well have exposed him to physical danger, or even, if he were a fugitive slave, to recapture and return to slavery. In response to a rumor that soon arose, one of the witnesses testified explicitly, "The colored man was not Frederick Douglas [*sic*], as has been supposed."

Daniel Mann, a prominent Boston abolitionist, shared his dental office with Thomas Jinnings, whose expulsion from an Eastern Railroad train five months earlier ignited the ensuing campaign through the summer and autumn. Among their other antislavery activities, Jinnings and Mann were both on the executive board of the Boston Vigilance Committee that had been formed that June.

As a follow-up to a meeting in the town of Lynn on September 29, "to consider the cases in which colored people had been excluded from the cars on this road," a second meeting was scheduled for the evening of September 30. On the ferry on his way to catch the train that afternoon, Mann had entered into a conversation with a stranger "about the propriety of permitting colored men to ride in the public cars." He himself was in favor, and the stranger was opposed. Mann had also heard that "there had been some trouble that morning about a negro that had been pulled out of the cars." That was Mary Newhall Green, though her name is not mentioned in the report of Mann's trial. Clearly, the Jim Crow car was very much a matter of public interest and heated debate that Thursday around Boston.

When he boarded the train at East Boston, Mann "took his seat in the cars . . . near a colored man, who was a stranger to him." His seat was facing that of the Black man, and he "saw the conductor come in, storming with passion, followed by two or three others. He cried, 'There's the man I want taken out.' The men seized the colored person, and thrust him out." In addition to Mann, there were several other abolitionists in the car on their way to that meeting in Lynn, one of whom, Joel P. Bishop, testified, "I did intend, so far as my influence would go, to prevent the exclusion of colored people from the cars, by all lawful and proper means. . . . I took my seat near the colored man, by design. Thought it probable an attempt would be made to remove him." They all remonstrated with Harrington, the conductor, and tried to prevent the man's expulsion.

Harrington's lawyer asked Mann, "Did you intend to assist the colored man in resisting the authority of the conductor?" to which he replied,

> I determined that I would not use violence, but that I would interpose my body, and remonstrate against any attempt to exclude him from the car.
>
> I did interpose my body, when the attempt was made to take him out, and endeavored to shield him. I caught hold of the seat, and when they were pulling the man out, took hold of his arm, and attempted to hold him back. I had a strong wish for him to remain in the cars; I caught hold of him instinctively.

Mann went on to describe what happened after that man was dragged out of the car: "There was at this time a good deal of noise outside of the car.

The conductor then came back in a passion, and cried out, 'Drag out every d——d one of them!' 'Drag out every d——d nigger and abolitionist!'" A fracas broke out, and Mann, Bishop, and one other person were thrown from the car. Charles P. Bosson testified that Mann was "thrust out of the car with great violence," that "Mr. Bishop [was] thrust out, more violently than Dr. Mann," and that both were "prostrated upon the earth."

Mann and other witnesses on his behalf agreed that Harrington had not first asked the Black man to move to the Jim Crow car, he simply came in and told the others to take him out. That Harrington expected a confrontation is clear, for he had earlier told Robert Blake, the ticket master, that "he anticipated some difficulty about a colored man in the cars." Blake came along to help him, and at the trial added further details, perhaps with some narrative fervor to make the case stronger in favor of Harrington:

> With considerable difficulty he was taken out. The resistance was made by the persons on the seat with him, and those near him. They held onto him until he was drawn up, over the back of the seat. The passage way was full of people. Dr. Mann said to the conductor, "You have stolen my hat." The conductor said he had not seen it. Dr. Mann repeated the charge several times; the conductor denied it. The conductor said, "all I ask is, that you behave quietly and peaceably, or I shall be under the necessity of having you taken out of the cars." One said, "I should like to see you do it." Don't know who it was. Another said, "I should like to have you put me out! I defy you and your whole hosts! bring on your forces!" At least five persons were concerned in resisting the conductor. Mr. Harrington then ordered his men to put the disorderly persons out. They took Dr. Mann first, because he charged the conductor with stealing his hat. No more force was used than was necessary; no blows were used. He held on to the seats, but was dragged out. One other person was also put out.

There is much talk about hats in the testimony on both sides, and it is not clear that Mann was the one who accused Harrington of stealing his hat. As Joel Bishop explained,

> There were two inquiries about a hat—one for Dr. Mann's cap, and one for my hat, which was lost in dragging me out. I should also like my gloves, if the gentlemen of the Rail-Road have got them.... I don't think I accused the conductor with stealing my hat; can't say I did not.

As well as being a costly item, a man's hat can be an important marker of his public identity. The accounts of the expulsions of Thomas Downing, David Ruggles, Thomas James, and J. W. C. Pennington all mention the taking or damaging of a hat as part of the insult inflicted, and Basil Dorsey, in recounting how he made his challengers back down, notes that he first removed his hat and coat.[88]

> Lord, the company's lawyer, argued for the defendant that the colored man came into the public car . . . in violation of a known rule of the Company; that the [plaintiff], and others, were there aiding and assisting him in this violation of the rules; . . . that the [plaintiff] and his associates acted in an improper and disorderly manner, and the conductor . . . put them out, using no more force than was necessary; and that no offence against the laws was committed in this act.[89]

After hearing five witnesses for the prosecution and eleven for the defense, Judge Simmons "decided that . . . the conductor was justified by the disorderly and unlawful conduct of Dr. Mann and his friends, in ejecting them from the cars—and ordered that the defendant be *discharged*." Once again the court upheld the legitimacy of private companies, even in the service of public transportation and funded in no small part from the state coffers, to enforce a prejudicial Jim Crow rule, though no law to that effect had been passed.

Thomas Jinnings, October 21, 1841

On Saturday, October 21, 1841, the Boston abolitionist Hiram Cummings and J. W. Alden, professor of Latin and political economy at Williams College, were returning on the New Bedford and Taunton Railroad from Fall River, Massachusetts, to Boston. During the stop at Taunton, they met "Dr. Jennings, a highly respected, well-educated colored gentleman of Boston, returning from New Bedford."[90] Though Cummings uses the spelling "Jennings," this is undoubtedly Thomas Jinnings, the Boston dentist who shared an office with Daniel Mann and who had been forced into an Eastern Railroad Jim Crow car the preceding May, initiating the long summer and autumn of protests. Cummings's narrative of this later incident, reprinted in the *Liberator* from the *New-England Christian Advocate*, reveals once again the arbitrariness, single-mindedness, and violence with which the offending railroads attempted to retain their right to discriminate among their passengers.

For a while the three friends stood talking on the platform between cars, Cummings says.

> We rode some little distance and then we invited Dr. Jennings to take a seat with us in the car where there were but few passengers. He did so, and we seated ourselves in one end of the car, some ten or twelve feet from any of the passengers. Soon the conductor came in and took our tickets, but made no objection to the Dr.'s riding in the car, and no passenger objected. But when we arrived at

> Norton, the first stopping place, the conductor came in and ordered Dr. Jennings into the "jim crow" car, at the same time seized him by the collar, and violently began to drag him out. We informed the conductor who the Dr. was, and that, being a friend of ours, we had invited him to take a seat with us. The conductor replied, "I don't care who he is, *damn him*, he has abused me enough at New-Bedford, and he *must* and *shall go out*."
>
> He continued pulling the Dr., who refused to go, with all his might. I appealed to the passengers to protect the Dr. from such a violent outrage, and took hold of the Dr. to prevent them from injuring him, still remonstrating. Upon that I was seized by two of the brakemen, who attempted to drag me out also, but not succeeding, I still holding to Dr. Jennings to protect him instead of myself, they jammed me back against the window and smashed it. By that time, another great "two-fisted fellow" arrived and made an effort to seize me, but was diverted from his purpose by Br[other] Alden. Well, sir, we kept our places against the whole force of this band of highwaymen, until our clothes were badly torn, and the Dr. said he would go out. When he said that, I let go of him, but the conductor and another man still handled him very roughly, throwing him upon the platform outside, and striking him, and otherwise bruising him.

After describing this melee, Cummings astutely draws attention to that particular conductor's immediate underlying motive:

> Mark the *cause* assigned for the outrage: "*Damn him, he has abused me enough at New-Bedford*." He did not state what that abuse was, but pounced upon him like a tiger upon a lamb. He did not turn him out because of the illegal, lynch law rule of the corporation; but to gratify *private revenge*. This augments the heinousness of the offence.

This is an explicit reminder that, while racial prejudice is a socially, culturally, and at times even legally, sanctioned stance, in practice it is exercised by individual people, often for personal reasons. Cummings then returns to his general excoriation of the corporations and their employees, recommending the ballot box as a solution and reminding readers forthrightly, "Colored men's rights are not only annihilated in the South, they are violently wrested from them in the North."

In 1843 Jinnings returned to New York. He married and lived with his wife, A. Augusta Jinnings, a dressmaker, just up the block from his father and younger siblings on Church Street.[91] By 1855 they had moved to New Orleans, where he established the New Orleans Dental Depot, a supplier of dental equipment. According to the 1860 New Orleans census, Jinnings's personal estate was valued at $5,000.[92]

In January 1861 Louisiana seceded from the Union, and in February it joined the Confederacy. What was life like in New Orleans for a northern abolitionist in such times? We can glean much from an incident reported in the New Orleans newspapers in late May of that year. Jinnings and his wife had attended a charity bazaar sponsored by several churches to raise funds for an orphan's home, and he was arrested, according to the *Daily Picayune*, for "intr[u]ding himself among the white congregation . . . and conducting hisself [*sic*] in a manner unbecoming the free colored population of this city."[93] Before launching into grossly racist descriptions of Jinnings and his wife, an article in the *New Orleans Daily Crescent* rather snidely describes Jinnings as "a genius who has several times been in the hands of the police for his sharp practices." This hints intriguingly at the possibility that Jinnings's egalitarian beliefs might have caused some trouble on earlier occasions. The article comments that "many ladies were greatly astonished and offended at the presumption of the negroes" for simply being there, and for "taking refreshments, and otherwise putting themselves on a par with the white people at the fair." At the subsequent hearing before the mayor, people were even more surprised when a white witness spoke on his behalf. A "lady of respectability, a member of Christ Church, a teacher in the Sunday School," this witness acknowledged that she had given the Jinningses tickets to the fair and had "treated them to ice-cream and cake." "[She] seemed to think it perfectly right that they should visit the fair."[94]

Further consternation was caused when it came out that Jinnings and his wife taught both free and enslaved children in Sunday school, though Jinnings's lawyer then stressed that the instruction was entirely oral; in other words, they were not illegally teaching slaves to read. When it came out that Jinnings was from Boston, the mayor withheld judgment until it could be determined whether Jinnings should be charged with "being in the State in contravention to law."[95] Whatever the outcome of that case, Thomas Jinnings Jr. died in New Orleans on January 30, 1862.[96]

Frederick Douglass in a Jim Crow Car, December 18, 1841

In December 1841, Frederick Douglass and George Foster, a white abolitionist from Andover, Massachusetts, traveled by rail on their way to South Kingston, Rhode Island, to attend an antislavery convention. Foster sent an account of this trip to the *National Anti-Slavery Standard*, and it was reprinted in the *Liberator* on January 14, 1842. Even allowing for a certain amount of dry sarcasm, Foster gives us a vivid picture of the Jim Crow car itself and of its effects on the strong, healthy, six-foot-one, twenty-three-year-old Douglass. This Jim Crow car, as Foster vividly evokes it, was very much like the "*dog car*" described by

G. W. Clark in New Jersey in 1840. Indeed, both of them use the word "cage" as a more precise descriptor than "car." An important distinction in this later journey, however, is that it was made even more unbearable by the winter weather.

> South Kingston, R.I., Dec. 20, 1841.
>
> On Saturday afternoon last, amidst a most furious snow storm, Frederick Douglas [*sic*] and myself, took passage in the cars of the Stonington and Providence Rail-road Company, for Westerly, twenty-four miles distant. Several *spare* cars were on the train, which would have accommodated more than a *hundred* passengers; but not more than ten or twelve were on board.
>
> I entered a long car, and Frederick followed immediately after; but before he had entered the door, the conductor seized hold of his coat, and ordered him into the "*Jim Crow car*." I, of course, followed, and took a place with Frederick, in the "*cage*;" in which we found several shovels, and other implements used in *breaking paths*; the seats were covered with snow, one door was fastened open to *let out* the cold, and produce a free circulation of air. All the light admitted through glass, was one pane 7 by 9. To render our situation more agreeable, after a few miles, four smokers came in; three had their mouths stopped with cigars, the other had a pipe or rather an apology for one, which, to say the least, ought to be "burnt out." We felt inclined to open the shutters and suffer from the cold and snow, rather than endure the stifling smoke. If this does not already appear a serious matter, the sequel will prove it to be so. Frederick did not sit down, but stood, stamping his feet. He contracted a severe cold, in consequence of which, he has been scarcely able to leave the house for two or three days, and from which he may never fully recover.[97]

Learning of these circumstances, the members of the South Kingston convention expressed their sympathy toward Douglass, who was unable to attend, and they adopted the following resolution: "Resolved, That prejudice against our colored population, as developed in proscription on our railways, in churches, and almost all departments of society, is vulgar, cruel and murderous."[98] Fortunately, Douglass did recover from his illness and continued on his way toward becoming the most powerful spokesman for racial equality throughout the nineteenth century—and well into the twentieth.

Thomas James, 1841 or 1842

No specific date or even year is given for the train and steamboat incidents that Thomas James recounts in his 1886 memoir, but the chronology and the events he relates are similar to other events in the same locations during the summer and autumn of 1841 and are most likely from that same period.

Tom (the only name he had as a boy) was born in Canajoharie, a small town in upstate New York, in 1804, enslaved by a farmer named Asa Kimball. When Tom was eight years old, Kimball sold his mother, his brother, and his elder sister to purchasers elsewhere in the state. He never saw his mother or sister again, though he was reunited with his brother many years later. He further states, "Of my father I never had any personal knowledge, and, indeed, never heard anything."[99]

When Tom was seventeen, Kimball was killed in an accident, and Tom was sold along with the rest of the farm to a neighboring farmer who soon traded him to yet another farmer for "a yoke of steers, a colt and some additional property, the nature and amount of which I have now forgotten." His new owner treated Tom harshly. After Tom was whipped he fled west along the route of the Erie Canal, which was still under construction. When he reached Lockport, he was told how to get to Canada and freedom. He worked in Canada as a laborer for about three months and then crossed back into the United States. After a stint as a woodchopper near Youngstown, Ohio, he made his way to the recently settled Rochesterville, which rapidly grew into the city of Rochester, New York. There he found work doing chores in two homes. When the Erie Canal opened in Rochester, he took a job in a warehouse and lived with the manager, for whom he also did chores. He began to learn to read at a Sunday school class, and he studied on his own during the winter months when the canal was closed. Soon he was placed in charge of the freight business at the warehouse. He joined the African Methodist Episcopal Society and was ordained a minister in May 1833 under the name Thomas James. As he explains, "I had been called Tom as a slave and they called me Jim at the warehouse. I put both together when I reached manhood, and was ordained as Rev. Thomas James."[100] He then built a church on a lot he had purchased in 1830.

James had been given some antislavery literature, he writes in his memoir. "It was these documents that turned my thoughts into a channel which they never quitted until the colored man became the equal of the white in the eye of the law, if not in the sight of his neighbor of another race."[101] When an antislavery group in the region bought a press and started a fortnightly paper called the *Rights of Man*, James became its traveling agent, for which he suffered repeated attacks.

In 1835 James founded a church in Syracuse and then moved to Ithaca, to Sag Harbor on Long Island, and finally to New Bedford, Massachusetts, where he became deeply involved in the abolitionist movement. There he met Frederick Douglass, who "had already begun to talk in public, though not before white people," and who briefly became a member of James's church.

Though he does not specify the time or place, James takes credit for introducing Douglass to a white antislavery audience: "On one occasion, after I had addressed a white audience on the slavery question, I called upon Fred. Douglass, whom I saw among the auditors, to relate his story. He did so, and in a year from that time he was in the lecture field with Parker Pillsbury and other leading abolitionist orators."[102] James may have invited Douglass to speak at a New Bedford antislavery meeting in the summer of 1841, prior to the Nantucket convention at which Douglass famously spoke that August.

James participated in several high-profile court cases, including freeing an enslaved woman named Lucy, who had been brought north by her owner from Virginia in the summer of 1841.[103] He took an active role in gaining the release of fifty-three Mende captives from Sierra Leone who had seized control of the schooner *Amistad*, on which they were being transported to be sold into slavery in Cuba. When the *Amistad* was discovered and taken by an American ship off Long Island Sound, the Mende were held in prison in New Haven, Connecticut, until the U.S. Supreme Court determined in 1841 that they had been illegally enslaved and ordered them to be set free. James records, "On their release we tried hard, but vainly, to persuade them to stay in this country. I escorted them on shipboard when they were about to sail from New York to their native land."[104]

It was probably in that year or the next that James purposely tested the custom of segregating passengers on trains and steamboats of New England. He notes in his account of the case of Lucy that he had met her while riding in the Jim Crow car. However, on a later journey, having been denied first-class tickets, he decided to make his opposition to Jim Crow more public. James had a white friend buy two tickets for him. "[Then] a colored friend and myself quietly took seats in the corner of the regular passenger coach." On being discovered by the brakemen, they refused to leave when ordered to do so by the ticket agent. "They sent in trainmen, baggagemen, and hackmen; we resisted passively, and three seats to which we clung as they were dragging us along were torn up before they got us out." James had them arrested under a warrant he obtained from the same Judge Crapo before whom David Ruggles had fruitlessly brought similar charges. A hearing was held that same day, and on the morrow Judge Crapo "ruled that custom was law, and that by custom colored people were not allowed to ride in cars in company of white people." James appealed the case to the Massachusetts Supreme Court, which reversed Judge Crapo's decision.

> The court decided that the word "color," as applied to persons, was unknown to the laws of the commonwealth of Massachusetts, and that the youngest colored

> child had the same rights as the richest white citizen. No company chartered as a common carrier had a right to enact regulations above the laws of the state. The decision of Judge Crapo was reversed, and I was given $300 damages besides. That broke up the practice of consigning colored railway passengers to "Jim Crow" cars.[105]

However optimistic Thomas James had been when the higher court reversed Judge Crapo's decision regarding the railroads, the future proved less tractable. As the active season of protest continued into 1842, James and others continued the struggle in the cars, on the boats, and in the courts.

James recounts an incident on the steamboat from New Bedford to Nantucket, when he was refused a first-class ticket allowing him access to the cabin. The captain—whom he names as "Captain Nottfinney"—was undoubtedly the same Lott Phinney with whom Ruggles contended on the *Telegraph* in June 1841. Upon James refusing to pay for a second-class foredeck ticket, Phinney seized James's hat, presumably as collateral for payment. On landing in Nantucket, the captain sent a servant to return his hat to James, but James refused it and went ashore with a handkerchief tied about his head. During his lecture that evening he recounted the shipboard events, after which three ladies presented him with a new hat. On the return journey, James was again refused a first-class ticket, so he boarded without a ticket, as he had earlier. "But no one asked for my ticket, and no one said a word to me, although I went where I pleased on the boat."[106]

In 1849 James took an active interest in the case of William and Ellen Craft, who had escaped from Georgia to freedom in Philadelphia and thence to Boston. Ellen Craft was very light-skinned, and she disguised herself as an ailing southern gentleman, with her chin swathed in bandages to conceal her lack of a beard and her arm in a sling so that she would not have to write. Her dark-skinned husband then traveled as her servant, and together they boldly entered separate compartments on the Macon-to-Savannah railroad that Ellen's former owner had built. They arrived in Philadelphia on Christmas and traveled on to Boston in January. In 1850 the Fugitive Slave Act was passed, requiring the return of runaway slaves who had made it to the North. The Crafts, who had become prominent in abolitionist circles, then had to live underground, often separately, until they sailed to England where they could live in freedom more safely.[107]

James was also involved in the attempts of the Boston Vigilance Committee to prevent the return of Anthony Burns, who had escaped to Boston from captivity in Virginia. Burns's case became a cause célèbre that increased abolitionist sympathies in the North. Though Burns himself was returned to slavery in Virginia, the Boston abolitionist community was later able to buy his freedom for $1,300.

James returned to Rochester in 1856, but during the Civil War he was sent to Louisville, Kentucky, where he worked to help many slaves, who were being secretly held, move to government camps outside the city where they became free. Colored men who came to the camps were immediately enlisted as soldiers; thus the camps came to hold mostly women and children. Because Kentucky had not rebelled, Kentucky slaves were not included under the Emancipation Proclamation. In order to subvert the Fugitive Slave Act, James writes, "I was ordered by General [William Jackson] Palmer to marry every Black woman that came into camp to a [Black soldier] unless she objected." This gave them and their children the same freedom granted to Black soldiers.

Shadrach Howard, February 1, 1842

A number of abolitionists from New Bedford had come to Taunton, Massachusetts, to attend the quarterly meeting of the Bristol County Anti-Slavery Society, and on February 1, 1842, they were returning by the evening train. Shadrach Howard, a New Bedford sailmaker, market victualler, and member of the Massachusetts Anti-Slavery Society, had traveled down from Boston that morning and boarded the same evening train on his way home to New Bedford.

A brief article in the white-owned *New-Bedford Mercury* two days later records rather benignly a "disturbance" in which "[a] negro . . . intruded himself upon the passengers of the 'Long Car,' contrary to a standing rule of the Directors." The report continues, "The negro . . . resolutely persisted in maintaining his position, so that gentle force became necessary to effect his removal." The article concludes, "Mr. Bird, the conductor, was the greatest sufferer in the fray, having received some severe bruises, and a wound in the face, from his assailants, while at his part, no improper violence was used."[108]

A more detailed report based on eyewitness accounts, printed in the *New Bedford Register* and in the *Liberator*, gives a quite different view of the event.[109] That same evening, a "large public meeting" was convened in Taunton to inquire "into the barbarous and inhuman assault committed by the servants of the Taunton and New-Bedford Rail Corporation, upon the person of Shadrach Howard." At this meeting a committee of five prominent abolitionists, including William C. Coffin, Nathan Johnson, and J. B. Sanderson (who was himself involved in the incident), was designated to examine the case and present its findings to the press. These findings were "made up entirely from the statements . . . made to the committee."

According to the testimony compiled by the investigating committee, the train from Boston had two passenger cars, and on reaching Taunton the conductor suggested that most of the passengers in the rear car move to the forward "long car," presumably to make the rear car available for a large group of African American and white abolitionists. The abolitionists then filled the rear car. As the train was about to start, Shadrach Howard and a Black friend, most likely Jeremiah Sanderson, boarded and went into the long car, the only one with empty seats. "A solitary individual remarked, that there were two persons in the car who had no business there." A few minutes later the conductor, George W. Bird, entered and said, "Get out here," to which Howard replied, "There are no seats in the other car," and Bird rejoined, "Get out, I'll find you a seat." Howard's friend then got up to leave the car, and Howard followed him. "The conductor, impatient of their speed, gave Howard a shove to hasten them along. Howard said, 'take off your hands.' To this, Bird replied, 'I'll do no such thing,' and forced him along. Howard said, 'What do you want to push me along for? I am going out.' No sooner had they reached the car step, than Bird clenched Howard by the collar, and with a very enraged look and angry tone of voice, said, 'Now I'll let you know why I put my hands upon you,' and shoved him off the car."

Howard was then set upon by several of the company's strongmen. "[They] seized hold of Howard, pulled his hair, struck him in his face, kicked his person, forced him back fully fifty or sixty feet from the car from which he was rejected, and thrust him down two or three feet upon the track of the rail road. Howard with his face scratched and bloody, threw off his coat, drew out his knife (unopened, and not a 'spanish knife' as falsely reported, but a common three-bladed one,) and made an attempt to regain the platform, but was repulsed by a kick."

Another car was added to the train, which Howard and four other Black passengers entered. When the train had gone about six miles down the line, the conductor came to collect tickets. Howard and the friend he had traveled with from Boston had not yet purchased their tickets. His friend paid with a bank note. "Howard said, 'you are the man that abused me,—why did you push me out of the car?' and said, 'I've got no ticket,' and thrusting his hand into his pocket, said, 'how much is it?' The conductor replied, '*I want your ticket*.' 'I told you,' said Howard: 'I had no ticket, how much is to pay?' and added, 'you are the man that insulted me.'—'You must get out of this car: you can't ride any further,' said Bird[.]"

As the train came to the next stop, other passengers asked Bird to tell Howard what the fare was, and one even offered to pay it. The conductor opened the car door, called for assistance, and attempted to haul Howard out of the car. Howard threw off his coat and said, "You take no one out of this car." Again "four or five bullying fellows" forced their way in while others stood around outside ready to help. During the struggle, Howard again drew out his knife, but one of his friends took it out of his hand. "Many who stood round were fearful that the conductors and others, might, under the influence of passion, kill Howard. . . . The excitement was tremendous." In a brief lull in the fight, Howard broke loose and ran to the far end of the next car, which was filled with both Black and white passengers, many of whom blocked the aisle to prevent Bird from getting to him. At several points, but especially here, the account in the *Liberator* reveals how the other passengers aided Howard. A number of them challenged Bird as to why he was so intent on getting Howard off the train, and his response reveals the level of his personal animosity, as well as the power he relished exercising as conductor. "'That fellow can't ride, I've said it, and that's enough; my commands must be obeyed,' sung out Bird. 'He must,' he continued, 'get out of this car, or, I'll detach and leave you.'—'That you can do if you please. The man can go out or stay, if he likes. We shall neither detain him, [n]or force him out,' added nearly all in the car.—'He must get out, or I'll run the cars back to Taunton,' said Bird. 'Run them back if you like; run them any way you please,' cried out the multitude."

Bird indeed ran the train back to Taunton, where a crowd largely hostile to Howard gathered. Howard, fearing for his life, left the train with a friend (possibly Sanderson) and thought to find a magistrate to issue a warrant to arrest Bird and his henchmen. They were so closely hounded by the mob, however, that they abandoned that plan and disappeared. The train then went on to New Bedford.

In David Ruggles's earlier account of the suit he brought against the New Bedford and Taunton Railroad for the mistreatment he received on July 6, 1841, Ruggles notes that an action had been brought against the same railroad "for a similar outrage inflicted upon the person of Shadrach Howard, of New-Bedford."[110] Such a previous encounter might account for the intense level of animosity shown by Bird toward Howard.

Although Howard did not register a complaint, Bird did. The case was brought before the Taunton Court of Common Pleas, and on March 16 a grand jury returned fifteen bills of indictment to the court. As the *New Bedford Register* put it, "The only case of any great interest is that of Shadrach Howard." The paper noted that the charge was for "assault and battery against Geo W. Bird, Conductor of the New Bedford and Taunton Railroad."[111] The trial began on Monday, March 28, and on Wednesday Howard was convicted and sentenced to a fine plus court costs—a ten-dollar fine according to the

Register, twenty according to the *New Bedford Mercury*.[112] A long article in the *Liberator* on April 22 expresses outrage at the verdict. One correspondent cited was "compelled to declare, in view of the testimony that was given on the occasion, that, in his opinion, a more unjust or unexpected verdict was never rendered in a court of justice in this Commonwealth: there was not a particle of evidence to warrant it." The article also points out that the court costs would be "not less than two hundred and fifty dollars!" and concludes with a call for people to send financial aid to Howard.[113]

Probably in the 1850s, Howard went to California, as did Sanderson. In late 1863, after the Emancipation Proclamation had been issued but before emancipation was universal throughout the country, Howard gave a long speech, published as a supplement to the *Pacific Appeal* on December 19, 1863, "to give proof positive, not mere assertions, that immediate and unconditional Emancipation [was] the only true and dignified platform to stand upon."[114]

Charles Lenox Remond, February 10, 1842

Charles Lenox Remond was born in 1810 in Salem, Massachusetts, the eldest child of John Remond, who had emigrated from Curaçao as a boy, and Nancy Lenox, the daughter of Cornelius Lenox, a Revolutionary War veteran. Working together, John and Nancy became successful caterers in Salem. Their eldest child, Charles, was educated for a while at the Salem African Free School, and then he and his siblings received private lessons at home.[115]

Around 1830 Remond became acquainted with the writings of William Lloyd Garrison, and he heard Garrison speak in Salem in 1831, the year Garrison began publishing the *Liberator*. Remond soon became a subscription agent for the paper, and his mother helped to found the Salem Female Anti-Slavery Society. Remond traveled through much of New England soliciting subscribers to the *Liberator* and encouraging the formation of local antislavery societies. Through this work he became a polished and effective speaker, and in 1838 he was hired as the first Black lecturer for the American Anti-Slavery Society. Following the principles espoused by Garrison, Remond was a firm believer in immediate emancipation, relying solely on moral suasion—that is, persuasion by invoking moral arguments to convince others to reject slavery, rather than on political action, violence, or military force.

The American Anti-Slavery Society also advocated in favor of women's rights and accepted women as equal members. Some men's opposition to admitting women led to a split, and in 1840 Arthur and Lewis Tappan and others left to form the American and Foreign Anti-Slavery Society, which barred women from its ranks. Garrison then hired as a field agent the outspoken

Charles Lenox Remond, circa 1851–56. Boston Public Library.

Abby Kelley, who scandalized many by speaking openly before audiences of both men and women.

Remond was chosen as a delegate to the World Anti-Slavery Convention in London during the summer of 1840, and his trip was financed largely by female antislavery societies. Even though Lucretia Mott and five other American women had been selected as delegates to the convention, men had voted to exclude women from the floor, and the six were consigned to seating in the gallery. Garrison, Remond, and several other prominent male delegates from America protested and caused a public stir by segregating themselves with the women. Elizabeth Cady Stanton and her husband, both staunch abolitionists, were attending the convention while on their honeymoon, and this event played a significant role in drawing her into the cause of women's rights.

Following the London convention, Remond toured England, Scotland, and Ireland for nineteen months, lecturing on slavery and racial prejudice. The welcome reception he received in Britain went far toward increasing his reputation as an African American orator, equaled only in the years to follow by Frederick Douglass. In a report in the *Liberator* on a meeting in Boston's Faneuil Hall shortly after his return, during which a number of fiery speakers addressed the problems of slavery, northern prejudice, and segregation on the trains, Remond's oratory was described. "Charles Lenox Remond . . . well maintained his laurels, won as an elegant, correct and forcible speaker, on the other side of the water. The meeting paid him the most respectful and profound attention, and had Quaker Stephen Chase, the railroad overseer, been there, he would sooner have thought of taking passage himself in the boiler of the engine, than of asking the colored orator to the Jim Crow car."[116]

Remond had returned to the United States in late December 1841, after a long summer and autumn that had seen numerous belligerent clashes over segregation on trains in New England. Although he had been out of the country for nineteen months, he was asked to speak on the issue on behalf of petitioners to a joint special committee of the Massachusetts legislature on February 10, 1842, making him the first African American to address that body. He was preceded by Wendell Phillips, who laid out the arguments against separation in the cars, including a reading of the entire committee report on the assault against Shadrach Howard in Taunton just nine days earlier.[117]

Remond's address, which came to be known by the title "The Rights of Colored Persons in Travelling," began with a clever rhetorical flourish, addressing head-on the fact of his color in such a way as to preempt any prejudices harbored by the members of the committee as to how a Black man might speak.[118]

> Mr. Chairman and Gentlemen of the Committee:
>
> In rising at this time, and on this occasion, being the first person of color who has ever addressed either of the bodies assembling in this building, I should perhaps, in the first place, observe that, in consequence of the many misconstructions of the principles and measures of which I am the humble advocate, I may in like manner be subject to similar misconceptions from the moment I open my lips in behalf of the prayer of the petitioners for whom I appear, and therefore feel I have the right at least to ask, at the hands of this intelligent Committee, an impartial hearing, and that whatever prejudices they may have imbibed, be eradicated from their minds, if such exist. I have, however, too much confidence in their intelligence, and too much faith in their determination to do their duty as the representatives of this Commonwealth, to presume they can be actuated by partial motives.

After some general remarks on discrimination, he specifically highlighted the persistent ubiquity of daily acts of racism and prejudice: "The grievances of which we complain, be assured, sir, are not imaginary, but real—not local, but universal—not occasional, but continual, every day matter of fact things—and have become, to the disgrace of our common country, matter of history."

Rather than recapitulate the arguments that Phillips had presented, Remond devoted much of his speech to a comparison between his experience in the United States and his reception abroad: "Mr. Chairman, the treatment to which colored Americans are exposed in their own country, finds a counterpart in no other; and I am free to declare, that, in the course of nineteen months' travelling in England, Ireland and Scotland, I was received, treated and recognised, in public and private society, without any regard to my complexion."

He contrasted his experience as a steerage passenger on the American packet ship to Liverpool—"it was unfit for a brute"—to that on the British steamer *Columbia* on his return. For financial reasons, Remond had booked steerage for his journey back as well. Though the accommodations in steerage, below decks in the rear of a ship, were far less amenable and comfortable than a cabin, they were considerably less expensive for such a long trip. The steamers were much faster than sailing ships had been, but Remond's return took seventeen days. As it turned out, his expectations of an unpleasant voyage were overturned by unexpected kindness:

> On the first day out, the second officer came to inquire after my health; and finding me the only passenger in that part of the ship, ordered the steward to give me a berth in the second cabin; and from that hour until my stepping on shore at Boston, every politeness was shown me by the officers, and every kindness and attention by the stewards. . . .
>
> In no instance was I insulted or treated in any way distinct or dissimilar from other passengers or travellers, either in coaches, rail-roads, steampackets, or hotels; and if the feeling was entertained, in no case did I discover its existence.

Immediately upon arriving in Boston, however, Remond was back in the land of the Jim Crow car, although in his speech he chose not to give it that colloquial name. And while on that occasion he acceded "peaceably" to the railroad's regulation, he made his opposition to the practice quite clear:

> On my arrival home from England, I went to the railway station, to go to Salem, being anxious to see my parents and sisters as soon as possible—asked for a ticket—paid 50 cents for it, and was pointed to the American designation car. Having previously received information of the regulations, I took my seat peaceably, believing it better to suffer wrong than to do wrong. I felt then, as I felt on many occasions prior to leaving home, unwilling to descend so low

as to bandy words with the superintendents, or contest my rights with conductors, or any others in the capacity of servants of any stage or steamboat company, or rail-road corporation.

Remond then related an encounter he had shortly after his return with none other than Stephen Chase, who also lived in Salem and who must have known Remond at least by sight and reputation:

> On returning to Salem some few evenings afterwards, Mr. Chase, the superintendent on this road, made himself known to me, by recalling by-gone days and scenes, and then enquired if I was not glad to get home, after so long an absence in Europe. I told him I was glad to see my parents and family again, and this was the only object I could have, unless he thought I should be glad to take a hermit's life in the great pasture; inasmuch as I never felt to loathe my American name so much as since my arrival.

Remond closed with a plea that the legislature act favorably on the wishes of the petitioners:

> Finally, Mr. Chairman, there is in this and other States a large and growing colored population, whose residence in your midst has not been from choice, (let this be understood and reflected upon,) but by the force of circumstances, over which they never had control. Upon the heads of their oppressors and calumniators be the censure and responsibility. If to ask at your hands redress for injuries, and protection in our rights and immunities, as citizens, is reasonable, and dictated alike by justice, humanity and religion, you will not reject, I trust, the prayer of your petitioners.

Twelve days later, the Massachusetts House of Representatives did indeed pass an "An Act Relating to the Rights of Rail-Road Passengers," though it was subsequently defeated in the Senate, and then the following year it passed in the senate and failed in the lower house (see below).

Remond's return to the United States, along with the arrival of Frederick Douglass onto the New England abolition circuit, considerably increased the rhetorical power of the movement and public interest in it. The two traveled and lectured together often, especially on the "One Hundred Convention" campaign, which ranged across Vermont, New York, Ohio, Indiana, and Pennsylvania during the last half of 1843.[119] That they had become close friends is evidenced by the fact that when Douglass's third son was born in October 1844, he was named Charles Remond Douglass.

Whatever disappointment or resentment Remond might have felt as Douglass's star began to outshine his own, it was exacerbated during the 1850s as

Douglass broke from Garrison's insistence on moral suasion alone to consider direct political action and even violence as necessary tactics to bring an end to slavery. The Garrisonian abolitionists believed that the U.S. government was in essence pro-slavery and based on a pro-slavery document, the U.S. Constitution. Thus they came to believe that the union should be dissolved; hence the motto of the American Anti-Slavery Society: "No Union with Slaveholders." Remond and the Garrisonians criticized Douglass for abandoning this uncompromising, idealistic stance, and Douglass, in turn, felt betrayed by the Garrisonians. In 1852 Remond announced publicly that he had canceled his subscription to *Frederick Douglass' Paper*.[120] The following year Douglass said that he considered Remond, Robert Purvis, and William Cooper Nell "my *bitterest enemies,* and the *practical* enemies of the colored people."[121]

As the 1850s progressed, the issue of slavery grew ever more intense. Preservation of the union became increasingly tenuous as the southern states moved toward secession in order to preserve slavery, while Garrisonian abolitionists (admittedly a small minority of the general population) advocated dissolving the union precisely *because* it was founded on slavery. Following the notorious *Dred Scott* decision by the Supreme Court in March 1857, the abolitionist cause was severely damaged. Just nine days later Douglass and Remond met in New York City in a fierce debate on the question "Is the American plan under the Constitution, anti-slavery or not?" Douglass argued for the affirmative and Remond for the negative.

Unfortunately, the main message of abolitionists was often drowned out in the arguments over ideology that beset the movement. As war approached, however, political action and the use of violence came to dominate that debate. Remond, too, gradually moved away from strict Garrisonianism. During the war, when Massachusetts opened enlistment to Black soldiers in 1863, he, Douglass, and other Black leaders worked throughout the North to recruit members for the famed Fifty-Fourth Massachusetts Infantry Regiment.

After the war Remond continued to travel and lecture on behalf of civil and political rights for African Americans through 1867, when his health began to deteriorate after contracting tuberculosis. Beginning in 1865 he worked as a streetlight inspector and then as a stamp clerk in the Boston Custom House. One of the most renowned Black abolitionists, he died in 1873.

An Act Relating to the Rights of Rail-Road Passengers, February 22, 1842

While Shadrach Howard was awaiting trial, a petition to address the wrongs of segregation on the railroads was submitted to a joint special committee of the Massachusetts Senate. As related above, on February 10 Charles Lenox Remond and Wendell Phillips, both renowned as orators, addressed the state legislature in Representatives' Hall on the evils and effects of segregation on the railroads. The committee's report focused in particular on the violation of passengers' rights as citizens of a state whose constitution recognized that "all men are born free and equal, and have certain natural, essential, and unalienable rights," including "that of acquiring, possessing, and protecting property" and "that of seeking and obtaining their safety and happiness." The committee's principal concern was whether the legislature had the authority to restrict the practices of the railroads.[122] The committee determined that indeed it did, and on February 22 its members unanimously voted to report the following bill for the consideration of the full Senate:

> **AN ACT**
> *Relating to the Rights of Rail-Road Passengers.*
>
> Be it enacted by the Senate and House of Representatives, in General Court assembled, and by the authority of the same, as follows:
>
> Sec. 1. No rail-road corporation shall, by themselves, their directors, or others, make or establish any by-law or regulation, which shall make any distinction, or give a preference in accommodation to any one or more persons over others, on account of descent, sect, or color.
>
> Sec. 2. Any officer or servant of any rail-road corporation, who shall assault any person for the purpose of depriving him of his right or privilege, in any car or other rail-road accommodation, on account of descent, sect, or color, or shall aid or abet any other person, in committing such assault, shall be punished by imprisonment in the county jail not less than six days, or by fine not less than ten dollars; and shall also be answerable to the person assaulted, to the full amount of his damage in an action of trespass.[123]

It began to seem that the power of the state might at last kick Jim Crow off the railroads. The Massachusetts House of Representatives voted in favor of the bill, but then the state senate defeated it.

Travellers' Directory, April 8, 1842

In April 1842, William Lloyd Garrison began to devote a full column of the *Liberator* to the train schedules he received from the agents of the various railway lines operating in Boston. In the first issue to do so he printed the following notice: "To serve the convenience of our readers, in this locomotive age, we devote a column of our paper to railroad notices, though we receive no corporation pay for it; on the contrary, insult and abuse still mark the course of some of them towards abolitionists. We have designated the character of each in this respect."

By printing these schedules with an explicit comment on a railroad's acceptance or rejection of Black passengers in their first-class cars, Garrison made it easier for people of color to plan their travel and to avoid—or to challenge—the racism that some companies practiced. But this was also a not-so-subtle way to put pressure on the offenders and to keep the issue visible every week, whether or not there were any new incidents to report.

Each heading naming a railroad in the Travellers' Directory is preceded with an indexed note—and a dose of sarcasm as Garrison felt appropriate. (The actual timetables are omitted here.)

> **TRAVELLERS' DIRECTORY.**
> ☞ *Humanity respected.*
> BOSTON AND LOWELL RAILROAD. . . .
>
> ☞ *No exclusiveness.*
> BOSTON AND WORCESTER RAILROAD. . . .
>
> ☞ *A vile and complexional distinction, enforced by brutal assaults. "Hail Columbia, happy land"! The noble Eagle has become a* BIRD *of prey, fattening on "the blood of all the* HOWARDS."
> BOSTON AND PROVIDENCE, TAUNTON AND NEW BEDFORD RAILROAD. . . .
>
> ☞ *Human rights not invaded.*
> BOSTON AND MAINE RAILROAD. . . .
>
> ☞ *An odious distinction on account of color, and a bullying propensity to carry it out, even to a Quaker* CHASE *and overthrow of equity.*
> EASTERN RAILROAD. . . .
>
> ☞ *Equality of privileges.*
> WESTERN RAILROAD. . . .
>
> ☞ *Equally free to all.*
> NASHUA AND LOWELL RAILROAD. . . .
>
> ☞ *No unwarrantable distinctions.*
> NORWICH AND WORCESTER RAILROAD.[124]

The quoted phrase "the blood of all the Howards" is taken from a passage on the true nature of greatness in *An Essay on Man*, Epistle IV, by the English poet Alexander Pope.[125] The full couplet reads, "What can ennoble sots, or slaves, or cowards? / Alas! not all the blood of all the Howards." The Howards were an important and ancient noble family in England, and Pope's point is that true greatness stems from one's character, not from one's bloodline. Garrison's point in quoting this line was to suggest that "the noble Eagle" (i.e., America) was growing fat and rich on the profits of those corporations and people who had made themselves wealthy at the expense of others. Garrison's literary allusion would have undoubtedly been obscure to many readers, and it was omitted in later editions of the Travellers' Directory.

The reference to "a Quaker CHASE" is to Stephen A. Chase, the superintendent of the Eastern Railroad. The abolitionists were fond of criticizing him for allowing the violence perpetrated on his railroad, though he was a prominent Quaker. Whether to save space or for some other reason, the personal reference to Chase was not included in the following weeks.

Jabez P. Campbell, March 29, 1843

A brief summary of the incident in which the Rev. Jabez P. Campbell, an African Methodist pastor in Providence, Rhode Island, and Boston, was beaten on a New Jersey train appeared in the *Liberator* on April 21, 1843. The following week Campbell himself sent in a more detailed description. On March 27, Campbell took a steamboat from Providence to New York on his way to Philadelphia. Two days later he went to the New York office of the Jersey City Railroad and bought a ticket there after being assured that he would be "accommodated with a comfortable seat in the cars." Seating himself in a secluded part of the car, the first part of the journey went without incident, until there was a change of conductors. Here we pick up Campbell's account:

> Sometime after we left Trenton, we came to another stopping-place, and when the cars were about to move again, the conductor came to me and said, "*Here, old fellow! you must come out of that.*" I asked him why. He said, "*That is none of your business.*" I answered him, "I cannot move until you assign me your reason for it." He rejoined, "*I shall not reason with you about it. All you have to do is to come out, and if you don't I'll pitch you out.*" I answered, "Well, Sir, you will have it to do; for I cannot move myself until you give me a reason for it." I said no more, and this I said as calm and easy as possible to be heard in the noise and bustle that were going on at the time. For some minutes, he stood and said much not worth mentioning. I said nothing. At last, he became much agitated, seized me by the throat, threw me down, and being unable to pitch me out himself, left me on the floor. In a few minutes, before I could regain my seat, he returned with four others—there may have been more, I am sure not less. With violence they fell upon and beat me. From the beginning, I had said not a word, only what I have already named, except to cry for help, after so many had fallen upon

> and beat me, until I had altogether despaired of life. I was gagged—had handkerchiefs crammed into my mouth—was beaten with their fists, and caned—was stamped in the stomach, and beat until almost unable to speak—and was finally thrown into the car where men go to smoke, &c. &c. nearly helpless, and without a friend I knew, except the Rev. N. Colver, of Boston, and one other gentleman, whose name I do not know. To them I wish to return thanks in this letter, for their kindness to me. Some time after, we arrived in Philadelphia, and I was placed under the care of a physician. Since then, I returned to this city, and am now laboring under the influence of the ill treatment I received upon that occasion. I made no attempt to defend myself, by entering into violent combat, because I believe it to be wrong. "The servant of the Lord must not strive." I did not enter suit against the conductor or company for the injuries I sustained, for this plain reason and many others:—I believe there is a just God, who is and will be the avenger of all those that do wrong. "Vengeance is mine; I will repay, saith the Lord." I believe he "hath appointed a day, in which he will judge the world in righteousness by the man Christ Jesus." That day I believe not far distant, and then I expect to meet them at the tribunal of God. God himself will award them according to their works. "Will not the Judge of all the earth do right?" I am sure that he will, and with this assurance I have committed myself into his hands, trusting that the day will come when every man shall be rewarded according to his works.
>
> I am yours, for the cause of truth,
> JABEZ P. CAMPBELL[126]

Campbell's letter is memorable for the first-person viewpoint it gives of such a traumatic occurrence, but it is also remarkable in the determination of his strongly held, faith-based reasons for not responding through the courts or other legal avenues. Whatever one might think about his religious beliefs, he exemplifies the same commitment to nonviolence that became familiar again a century later in the teaching and examples of Bayard Rustin, Martin Luther King Jr., John Lewis, and many others. His reply to the offending conductor not only echoes Frederick Douglass in insisting on an answer to the question of why he must move, it also mirrors the outward calm with which Rosa Parks would respond to a Montgomery, Alabama, bus driver 112 years later.

The Jim Crow Car Leaves Massachusetts, April 1843

As a new season of travel to antislavery meetings and conventions built up steam, abolitionist opposition to segregation on the trains persisted. On January 27, 1843, the Massachusetts Anti-Slavery Society passed a resolution to send a "memorial" to both the state senate and the Massachusetts House of Representatives requesting the legislature to "so . . . define the powers of the railroad corporations, erected by the authority of the Commonwealth, and endowed by it with special privileges, as fully to secure colored persons travelling, on said roads, from proscription, insult and personal violence from their officers."[127]

The act relating to the rights of railroad passengers was brought up again in the 1843 legislative session, and this time the senate, yielding to continued public pressure, passed it. However, when it was sent to the lower house, it was again hotly debated. An amendment was accepted to remove the word "railroad" from the text, and another to add "or common carrier." The resulting more general text only served to strengthen opposition to the act, and when the yeas and nays were called for, the lower house refused to vote on it. Instead representatives voted, 171 to 61, to postpone the bill indefinitely.[128]

On March 11, 1843, the Essex County Anti-Slavery Society passed a resolution that was sustained by Charles Lenox Remond, among others: "Resolved, That among the questions that we are called upon to press home on the people the coming year, no one has a stronger claim on the exertions of the friends of humanity than the odious and wicked distinction on the Eastern rail-road; and we hereby pledge ourselves to urge its abolition with increasing vigilance."[129]

The report of the Essex County meeting, including this resolution, was printed in the *Liberator* on March 31, and in the same edition there is also a ten-line statement about the end of the session of the Massachusetts state legislature on Saturday, March 25. The brief paragraph lists three of the legislature's "good deeds" for the session. Then it concludes, "Among its bad ones is the indefinite postponement of the bill in regard to the rights of rail-road passengers. But we are confident that justice, in this particular, will be done at the next session."[130] Clearly, it would be up to the public to continue to bring their opposition directly to the recalcitrant railroad companies, and abolitionists in Massachusetts were prepared to continue challenging both the railroads and the legislature.

The March 24 edition of the *Liberator* printed the Travellers' Directory for the last time, still identifying the Eastern Railroad and the Boston and Providence, Taunton and New Bedford Railroad as not recognizing the equal rights of passengers of color. Then the Eastern Railroad yielded to public pressure and to the growing threat of legislative action. At a meeting of the Norfolk County Anti-Slavery Society held on April 20, the following resolution was adopted:

> Resolved, That we hail, with unfeigned delight, the removal of the Colored Car from the Eastern Railroad, viewing it as the quailing of a cruel prejudice against color before the indignant rebuke of public opinion—that we congratulate our fellow-citizens on the fall of this, almost the last shackle from their limbs within our Commonwealth—that we will spread the knowledge of this fact far and wide, that slaveholders may know how rapidly Massachusetts hastens to redeem her escutcheon from every stain, and that meeting-houses may blush for their preeminence in being the last to give up the negro seat.[131]

The Jim Crow car was disappearing from the Massachusetts rails, and that particular two-year campaign by Black abolitionist passengers and their allies was winding down. But Jim Crow was far from dead, and segregated cars remained on other lines in other states. The very next item in that same April 28 edition of the *Liberator* is the letter that Jabez P. Campbell had written on April 18 to Garrison, recounting the beating he had received in New Jersey on March 29, as described above.

William Saunders, July 1, 1843

William Saunders was born in Barbados, around 1796, and by September 1820 he was living in Hartford, Connecticut, where he advertised his trade as a tailor in the *Connecticut Courant*.[132] Life for Black residents in Hartford in the first half of the nineteenth century was not easy. Edward Abdy, an English traveler in Connecticut in the 1830s, described Hartford thus: "Throughout the Union there is, perhaps, no city . . . where blacks meet with more contumely and unkindness than at this place. Some of them told me it was hardly safe for them to be in the streets alone at night. . . . To pelt them with stones and cry out nigger! nigger! as they [pass] seems to be the pastime of the place."[133] Nevertheless, Saunders became a successful businessman, and, judging by the polish of the letter printed below, he was well educated and aspired to a dignified and respected middle-class life for himself and his family.

Early in his career Saunders was engaged in the antislavery movement. In 1828 a notice of his wedding to Roxana Cuffee of Sag Harbor, New York, appeared in *Freedom's Journal*, the first African American–owned abolitionist newspaper in the country. From July 9, 1831, to July 7, 1832, Saunders was listed as the Hartford agent of the *Liberator*, which rapidly expanded its circulation after it appeared in January 1831.

In July 1843 Saunders and his family were required to leave a first-class car on the Hartford and New Haven Railroad, although twice previously they had ridden without objection. Saunders gave "a plain statement of the facts" in a letter he sent to the *Christian Freeman*, reprinted at his request in the *Hartford Daily Courant*:

> Mr. Editor:—I wish to give to the public, through the columns of your paper, an account of a brutal outrage to which myself and family were recently subjected, by one of the conductors of the Hartford and New Haven Rail Road. We took our passage on board the cars for New York, on the first of this month, and having paid the *usual price*, went into the car where we saw the other passengers go, and took our seat. The conductor saw us go in and made no objection whatever. Soon after we went in, a woman fixed her eyes upon us as if resolved to magnetize us, and directly her husband, or the man in company with her, left the car, probably to complain of our presence. The conductor immediately came in, and in a loud voice said, "You can't sit here—you must go into the forward car—it is the arrangement of the company." We sat perfectly quiet, feeling neither mortified nor alarmed, though the conductor evidently meant that we should be both. He went out, but soon returned again and said, "You can't sit here—there is no mistake about it!"—casting his eye about the car to see how many looked approval upon his noble deed. There seemed to be no course for us to pursue but to leave the car, which we did, and took our seats in the forward car, though we had paid full price, and were entitled to as comfortable accommodations as any other passenger.
>
> If the company are determined to insist upon these odious and insulting distinctions, I should think it was their duty to keep some person standing by the office to point colored persons to the car they design them to ride in. This would, at least, save them from the insults of their menials, in being ordered out of a car after having taken their seats and from the robbery committed in taking their money for seats in the first class cars. Twice before we have been to New Haven and rode in the large car, without a word or objection from anyone.
>
> This is a plain statement of the facts in the case, in view of which the public are left to form their own opinion of the conduct of all concerned. We cannot say that we are surprised at this treatment, for we remember that we are in a wilderness, surrounded by all manner of beasts of prey, who are constantly seeking to devour us; therefore these things do not take us by surprise.
>
> William Saunders
> Hartford, July 13, 1843[134]

Like Hosea Easton, David Ruggles, and Thomas Van Renselaer before him and numerous others afterward, Saunders emphasizes the inequity of paying first-class fares and then being removed to the Jim Crow car. Like Ruggles, Saunders skillfully reverses the status quo as he refers to white railroad employees as "menials," a term more generally applied by whites to people of color, and by accusing the railroad of committing robbery. He also illuminates the conductor's attitude with a nice touch of irony in the observation that he was "casting his eye about the car to see how many looked approval upon his noble deed."

Though Saunders did not resist the conductor's order to move to the "forward car," one wonders whether the presence of his wife and children might have accounted for his outward acquiescence. While Saunders's suggested remedy for avoiding such incidents falls short of demanding the right to sit where one pleases, some of the language he uses is quite strong and reveals the psychological impact of the mistreatment they received. The anger underlying his restrained complaint, however, is most apparent in his opening description of the incident as "a brutal outrage" and his final characterization of racial conditions in the stark terms of his final sentence, evoking the difficulties of life for a Black family in Hartford at that time.

By 1850 Saunders had become one of the wealthiest Black businessmen in Hartford. Before he died in 1852, Saunders passed his business on to his sons. That the family remained actively interested in the issue of racial equality is evidenced by the fact that in 1862, five years after the *Dred Scott* decision denied citizenship to African Americans, the U.S. Congress received the "petition of T.P. and P.B.H. Saunders, of Hartford, Connecticut, (of mixed blood,) asking the right of citizenship, or, in lieu thereof, exemption from taxation under the revenue law; which was referred to the Committee of Ways and Means."[135]

Basil Dorsey, August 1843?

Basil Dorsey was born in 1810 or 1811 in Liberty, Maryland. (The Northampton, Massachusetts, *Daily Hampshire Gazette* remarked in an article about Dorsey in 1867, "God have mercy on the man who gave the place its name!") For a fugitive slave who left no personal narrative of his slavery or his escape, Dorsey's life and career are remarkably well documented. The story of his escape, recorded in the 1880s by Robert Purvis in R. C. Smedley's *History of the Underground Railroad*, is an exciting one that illustrates the complications and terrors that would often arise even after fugitives reached the relative safety of a free state.[136]

As a slave Dorsey had been known as Ephraim Costly. According to the *Hampshire Gazette*, Dorsey held that his grandfather was an Englishman who had married a colored woman in Maryland and that he was therefore free by birth.[137] His master, Tom Sollers (sometimes spelled Saulers), had agreed to sell Ephraim his freedom for $350, but when a bond was secured for that amount, Sollers reneged, saying that he could get $500. Thus, on the night of May 14, 1836, four brothers set out for Pennsylvania under "the assumed names of Basil, Thomas, Charles and William; all retaining the surname of Dorsey."[138]

The Dorseys made their way to Philadelphia where they were aided by Robert Purvis. Thomas Dorsey remained in the city, while Basil worked on Purvis's farm, near Bristol in Bucks County, and the other two brothers on neighboring farms. Basil's wife, who was free, and their two children were brought to Purvis's farm, and the family was reunited. After Thomas was recaptured, $1,000 was raised in Philadelphia to purchase his freedom. Meanwhile, arrest warrants were issued for the three remaining brothers.

While ploughing one day in July 1837, Basil was seized and taken to the Bristol jail. Purvis had Charles and William conveyed to safety and then negotiated with Sollers's agents to meet before Judge Fox in Doylestown for Basil's fate to be decided two weeks later. Purvis alerted people in the region to be ready to rescue Dorsey if he were to be put in remand of his captors, and he engaged David Paul Brown, an experienced lawyer, to argue the case. Sollers had said earlier that he would free Basil for $500, but then he raised the price to $800. And when that sum was agreed upon, he upped it again to $1,000. According to Purvis, Dorsey responded, "No more offers, if the decision goes against me, I will cut my throat in the Court House, I will not go back to slavery."[139]

As a preliminary legal point, Brown demanded that the plaintiffs satisfy the court that Maryland was by law a slave state. When they failed to produce adequate proof, the judge dismissed the case, with the proviso that Dorsey could be rearrested under a magistrate's warrant. Upon leaving the courthouse, Purvis and Dorsey climbed into a horse and buggy just as the slave catcher came rushing up with such a warrant, but Purvis snapped his whip and the buggy dashed ahead as their pursuer reached for the reins.

With the help of the local free Black population, they escaped, and Purvis accompanied Dorsey to New York, where he introduced him to Joshua Leavitt (editor of the *Emancipator*, the *New York Evangelist*, and other antislavery periodicals) and to David Ruggles. Dorsey was then sent on to Massachusetts. For five years Dorsey and his family lived with Joshua Leavitt's brother, Roger Hooker Leavitt, in Charlemont, Massachusetts. Records show that Dorsey became a paying member of the Massachusetts Anti-Slavery Society. A third child was born in August 1838, and Dorsey's wife, Louisa, died two months later.

During his time in Charlemont, Dorsey accompanied Leavitt on a trip to Rochester, New York (perhaps to attend the four-day antislavery meeting led by Frederick Douglass and Charles Lenox Remond in August 1843, or perhaps earlier). While on the train somewhere beyond Albany, some white passengers in the railroad car in which they were seated insisted that Dorsey move to the forward (or Jim Crow) car. He refused, and "high words ensued," according to the *Hampshire Gazette*. Some of the passengers appealed to the conductor to remove him, but the conductor responded that since he was causing no trouble Dorsey "could ride as other passengers rode." When the objecting passengers threatened to eject him from the car violently, Dorsey rose from his seat, "divesting himself of his hat and coat and threatening to pitch through the window any man who should molest him." His would-be attackers backed down. The conductor was so pleased with the way Dorsey handled the situation that he offered him a free return passage.[140]

In 1844 Dorsey moved to Bensonville (now Florence), Massachusetts, where he worked for many years as a teamster for the Bensonville Manufacturing Company, owned by William Lloyd Garrison's brother-in-law, George Benson, a founder of the utopian Northampton Association of Education and Industry. The association and the village had become a haven for former and fugitive slaves, and here Dorsey renewed his acquaintance with David Ruggles and got to know Sojourner Truth, who joined the association that year. In all likelihood, he also would have met with Frederick Douglass, who was a frequent visitor to the village. Dorsey remarried sometime before 1850. He and his second wife, Cynthia, who was of Irish descent, had eleven children, all of whom were living in 1867.

The Fugitive Slave Act of 1850 was passed on September 18, and one month later, on October 15, Dorsey and nine other fugitive slaves bravely published a letter in the *Hampshire Gazette*, stating in part,

> Aided and directed by a kind Providence, we have effected our escape from this deplorable servitude, and fled to Massachusetts for an asylum and refuge, confidently believing they would not betray the wanderer, nor deliver up the oppressed. . . .
>
> The enactment of this cruel and unrighteous law has thrown us into a state of alarm and consternation for fear we may be torn from our beloved families and friends, and again doomed to a tyranny far worse than death.
>
> We therefore respectfully invite the inhabitants of the town of Northampton, irrespective of party or sect, to assemble in public meeting . . . to express their opinions, and adopt such measures, as they may deem proper to prevent Massachusetts from being made slavery hunting ground.[141]

As a teamster traveling alone throughout the region, Dorsey, in particular, would have been at great risk of recapture. The amount of $150 was raised on his behalf, and a bill of sale dated Baltimore, May 14, 1851, records that Thomas E. Sollers received $150 from George Griscom, a Philadelphia lawyer, and did thereby "grant, bargain, and sell, unto the said George Griscom ... one mulatto man, named Ephraim Costly, otherwise and now called Basil Dorsey, ... now a fugitive from service from said state of Maryland."[142] Griscom would have then filed papers granting Dorsey the legal status of a free man, fifteen years after his escape.

Basil Dorsey died in Florence on February 15, 1872, and is buried there near the graves of his brother Charles Robert Dorsey (d. 1852) and his daughter Louisa A. Dorsey (d. 1868).

Frederick Douglass aboard the Steamship *Cambria*, August 1845, April 1847

On May 1, 1845, Frederick Douglass published his *Narrative of the Life of Frederick Douglass, an American Slave*. While he does not, in this slim volume, give the names, locations, or other identifying details about his former masters, one effect of this printed public record of his earlier life was that it put him at greater risk of recapture and a return to slavery. Partly in order to avoid such a fate, but also to raise awareness of and money to support the abolition movement in the United States and to sell copies of his book, Douglass and James N. Buffum planned a yearlong visit to the British Isles.

The British Cunard Line steamship *Cambria* sailed from Boston on August 16. But the arm of Jim Crow was longer than we might expect, and Douglass tells us in the 1855 edition of his autobiography *My Bondage and My Freedom*, "On applying for a passage to England, ... my friend, James N. Buffum, of Lynn, Massachusetts, was informed that I could not be received on board as a cabin passenger. American prejudice against color triumphed over British liberality and civilization.... The insult was keenly felt by my white friends, but to me, it was common, expected, and therefore, a thing of no great consequence, whether I went in the cabin or in the steerage." He further consoled himself with the reasoning that, if he could not visit friends in the first cabin, they could visit him in the second.

Among the ninety-five passengers were the Hutchinson Family Singers, a white family from New Hampshire who were renowned in abolitionist circles for their songs of liberation, which they sang at many antislavery meetings. On the *Cambria*, they often joined Douglass on the forecastle deck to visit and to sing. Other white passengers on board, learning of the presence of such a widely famed fugitive slave and orator, also began to visit him and even invite him to come to the saloon deck. Although he did not reciprocate very often, he comments in his autobiography that "with the majority of the passengers, all color distinctions were flung to the winds, and I found myself treated with every mark of respect from the beginning to the end of the voyage, except in a single instance."[143]

Although Douglass had been barred from the first-class cabins, the captain of the ship invited him to give a lecture on slavery. Some passengers from Connecticut, Louisiana, Georgia, and Cuba were offended by this and, swearing that Douglass should not speak, threatened to throw him overboard. Douglas recalls, "An end was put to the melee, by the captain calling the ship's company to put the salt water mobocrats in irons. At this determined order, the gentlemen of the lash scampered, and for the rest of the journey conducted themselves very decorously." The entire encounter was actually more contentious than Douglass portrays it, with Douglass shouting insults at them as well as they at him. In the end, peace prevailed, but Douglass retired to steerage and never gave his lecture. Upon landing at Liverpool, the offended passengers ridiculed and denounced Douglass to the press. The effect, however, was opposite to what they intended, for it gave Douglass national coverage in the papers, assuring larger audiences for him, as well as turning the blame back on themselves.[144]

Douglass toured and lectured to great acclaim throughout the British Isles until the spring of 1847. Then, he recalls in his autobiography: "A few weeks before departing from England, while in London, I was careful to purchase a ticket, and secure a berth for returning home, in the 'Cambria'—the steamer in which I left the United States—paying therefor the round sum of forty pounds and nineteen shillings sterling. This was first cabin fare. But on going aboard the Cambria, I found that the Liverpool agent had ordered my berth to be given to another, and had forbidden my entering the saloon!"[145]

Before leaving, Douglass alerted the British press to this "contemptible conduct" and "took the occasion to expose the disgusting tyranny, in the columns of the London Times." As a result of this publicity, Samuel Cunard himself published an apology: "Mr. Cunard came out in a letter to the public journals, assuring them of his regret at the outrage, and promising that the like should never occur again on board his steamers; and the like, we believe, has never since occurred on board the steamships of the Cunard line."[146]

Douglass then concludes the chronological narrative of *My Bondage and My Freedom* with a paragraph that lays bare with stark imagery the psychological effects the imposition of segregation has upon a person subjected to it:

> It is not very pleasant to be made the subject of such insults, but if all such necessarily resulted as this one did, I should be very happy to bear, patiently, many

> more than I have borne, of the same sort. Albeit, the lash of proscription, to a man accustomed to equal social position, even for a time, as I was, has a sting for the soul hardly less severe than that which bites the flesh and draws blood from the back of the plantation slave. It was rather hard, after having enjoyed nearly two years of equal social privileges in England, often dining with gentlemen of great literary, social, political, and religious eminence—never, during the whole time, having met with a single word, look, or gesture, which gave me the slightest reason to think my color was an offence to anybody—now to be cooped up in the stern of the "Cambria," and denied the right to enter the saloon, lest my dark presence should be deemed an offense to some of my democratic fellow-passengers. The reader will easily imagine what must have been my feelings.[147]

Sarah Parker Remond, May 4, 1853

When Sarah Parker Remond was six years old in 1832, her mother and a number of other Black women founded the Salem Female Anti-Slavery Society. That same year, her brother, Charles Lenox Remond, became an agent for the *Liberator*. Her father was a lifetime member of the American Anti-Slavery Society.

Remond was educated in the Salem public schools until the school committee in 1835 voted to disallow Black students. In response, the Remonds moved to Newport, Rhode Island, but they returned to Salem in 1841, where Sarah's education, along with that of her siblings, was completed at home. Thus, as the antislavery movement was gaining strength and adherents throughout the 1830s and 1840s, there can be little doubt as to the milieu in which Sarah grew up. In addition to the Salem Female Anti-Slavery Society, she became an active member of the Essex County and Massachusetts Anti-Slavery Societies. When she was only sixteen, Remond joined her brother Charles on the lecture circuit for the American Anti-Slavery Society, along with Wendell Phillips, Abby Kelley Foster, and later, in 1856, with Susan B. Anthony.

On the evening of May 4, 1853, Remond planned to attend a performance of Donizetti's opera *Don Pasquale* in which the part of Norina was being sung by the renowned soprano Madame Henriette Sontag at the Howard Athenaeum. Remond was accompanied by her married sister, Caroline E. Putnam, and William Cooper Nell, a noted Black abolitionist who wrote for the *Liberator* and who for three years had published Frederick Douglass's *North Star*. As reported in the *Liberator*'s account of the ensuing court case, they had purchased tickets beforehand for seats in the less-expensive, upper-level Family Circle. "At the hour of seven they . . . gave their tickets to the door-

Sarah P. Remond. Collection of the Massachusetts Historical Society.

keeper, and leisurely walked up towards the family circle. . . . Here they were met by Mr. Palmer, who, according to the testimony of Nell, asked to look at their checks, and took them, and upon examining them said they could not occupy those seats."[148] Nell asked for the checks to be returned to him, but Palmer, the agent for Madame Sontag's opera troupe, refused. When Nell demanded that they be shown to their seats, they were told that they had to leave the house, "as there were no seats for them." They asked if they could simply stand where they were to listen to the performance, even if they couldn't see it. Palmer again refused and told them that they could join the reporters in the gallery, which they declined. When Palmer offered them their money back, they refused to receive it. At this point, Henry Willard, the theater manager, arrived with a police officer, Charles P. Philbrick. "After a consultation, Philbrick said that if they insisted on remaining, they must be put out. They said they would not yield their rights, when the officer, as Nell says, caught hold of Miss Remond, pushed her about eight feet, and attempted to push her down the stairs, and after some effort succeeded, tearing her dress and injuring her shoulder."

Remond sued Palmer and Philbrick for assault. The case was heard by Judge Thomas Russell, who at age twenty-seven had just that year been appointed to the bench by the governor. In his written opinion, Russell first ruled that Palmer, as the agent for the opera company, was responsible for the assault because "Palmer ordered Philbrick to eject the complainant." The question was then addressed as to whether the company had the right "to exclude any class of persons from any part of the house, on account of color, occupation, or dress." However, it proved unnecessary to resolve the question of right. Rather, assuming that such a right did exist, any limiting condition applying to the contract entered into by the sale of tickets had to "be made known to the purchaser." No such condition appeared on the tickets, nor were notices posted in the theater that persons of color were restricted only to certain seats. In the past, Willard had "always advertised that persons of color were only admitted to the galleries," but that was no longer the case. Drawing a parallel with the railroads, the judge noted,

> When such an advertisement ceases to appear, it is a strong implication that the rule is no longer to be enforced; and this is strengthened by the fact, that the galleries where colored persons have usually sat are now closed.
>
> The case is precisely like the case of a party purchasing a first-class ticket in the cars. He could not be ordered into the second class, unless he had full notice that such persons as he would be confined to those cars.

The defense also argued, "A universal custom prevails, by which persons of color are confined to the galleries, and . . . this custom modifies the contract of the company." However, a number of Black witnesses testified that they had attended events at the Howard Athenaeum and other venues "and had sat where they pleased, in the dress circle, parquette, or family circle." The judge replied to this defense expansively, again using railroad travel as a comparable situation:

> The evidence shows still further that this alleged custom is unreasonable because unnecessary, for as I have said, persons of color sit at concerts and at the Museum among audiences quite as respectable as those at the Athenaeum. . . . I do not believe that the presence of the complainant would have caused any trouble at the opera.
>
> Upon the whole, it is clear that the complainant had a right to the seat which she had purchased, and that she was only insisting upon her right when she was removed. . . . She had the same right that the holder of a railroad ticket has, to purchase his journey.

It has never been held that such a person was bound to leave the cars, because he was ordered to do so, at the caprice of the conductor. And a conductor or a policeman removing such a person by force, would clearly be liable. The cases are parallel. Mr. Palmer, having no right himself to remove the complainant, could not confer such a right upon the officer. The police officer is as much bound to protect each member of the audience as he is to protect the manager of the theatre. He is not to obey the illegal orders of the manager or of his agents.

On the basis of witness testimony and of his own prior knowledge of Officer Philbrick's "usually peaceable disposition," the judge ruled that Philbrick had not used excessive force, and then he delivered his judgement:

> In fixing the penalty, it must be remembered that this is a criminal prosecution. In a civil case, the measure of damages would be the injury to the complainant, including any injury to her feelings. And the defendants' motives would be no defence. In a criminal case, the motive is the chief test of criminality. The defendants acted under a mistake of law; each thought he was doing his duty; and the officer, especially, felt bound to obey the orders of Mr. Palmer, and supposed that he was doing his duty to the city.
>
> This is the first case of the kind in Boston, and these excuses would not avail in another case. The complainant's counsel has very properly stated that he does not claim a large fine, but wishes to vindicate a right. Mr. Palmer is fined $1 and costs,—Mr. Philbrick $1 without costs.

Following this nominal win in criminal court, Remond filed a civil suit against Palmer and Philbrick in the Essex County District Court. She was awarded $500 in damages, which she accepted "on the condition that she and her friends should have tickets to the opera, for seats as good as those originally purchased on the night they were rejected."[149] While this amount did not cover all her expenses, it did further vindicate the right she claimed.

In late 1858 Remond sailed to Britain to lecture on antislavery issues and to further her own education at Bedford College, the first further education college for women in the United Kingdom. Over the course of the next three years, she delivered some forty-five lectures in twenty-five cities and towns in England, Scotland, and Ireland, becoming one of the first women there to speak publicly before mixed audiences of men and women. Her lectures were well received among both the working class and the socially elite.

But, even in Britain, Remond was not beyond the ability of Jim Crow to impede her freedom of travel. In late 1859 she went to the American legation in London to apply for a visé (a signature equivalent to a visa) to be added to her passport so that she could travel to France. Her application was denied, and she wrote on December 12 to the American minister in London to appeal this decision:

> Upon my asking to have my passport vised at the American Embassy, the person in the office refused to affix the vise, on the ground that I am a person of color.
>
> Being a citizen of the United States, I respectfully demand as my right that my passport be vised by the Minister of my country.

She received a rather imperious reply from an assistant secretary at the legation implying—without saying so outright—that her passport had been issued in error:

> I am directed by the Minister . . . to say, in reply, he must, of course, be sorry if any of his country women, irrespective of color or extraction, should think him frivolously disposed to withhold from them facilities in his power to grant for travelling on the continent of Europe; but when the indispensable qualification for an American passport, that of "United States citizenship," does not exist—when, indeed it is manifestly an impossibility by law that it should exist—a just sense of his official obligations, under instructions received from his Government as long ago as the 8th of July, 1856, and since then strictly conformed to, constrains him to say that the demand of Miss Sarah P. Remond cannot be complied with.[150]

Whatever instructions the legation had received in 1856, they had been strengthened and legitimized in March 1857 by the Supreme Court opinion in *Dred Scott v. Sandford* stating, "A free negro of the African race, whose ancestors were brought to this country and sold as slaves, is not a 'citizen' within the meaning of the Constitution of the United States."[151] Remond took her case to the public, and it became a cause célèbre in the British press for the next six weeks or so and may have even drawn attention of Queen Victoria at Buckingham Palace.[152]

Remond returned to the United States in 1865 to work with the American Equal Rights Association, but the following year she went to Florence, Italy, to study medicine. She was granted a diploma in "Professional Medical Practice" in 1871 and practiced medicine in Florence. She married Lazzaro Pintor, a native of Sardinia. She died in London in 1894 and was buried in the Protestant Cemetery in Rome.[153]

James W. C. Pennington, July 28, 1853

James W. C. Pennington had been born into slavery in Maryland in 1809, and as a boy he was trained as a stonemason and a blacksmith. At the age

James W. C. Pennington. Portrait in W. Armistead, *A Tribute for the Negro*, 1848. National Portrait Gallery, Smithsonian Institution.

of eighteen, however, he escaped to Pennsylvania and worked for a while for a sympathetic Quaker family who taught him to read. "Pennington" was a common Quaker name in the area, so he adopted the name James William Charles Pennington to help mask his identity. Not long afterward he went to Newtown, New York, where the influence of a Presbyterian family led him to seek further education as a Christian. Moving to New Haven, Connecticut, he became a teacher in a Black school and an assistant to the minister of the Temple Street Congregational Church. Though he was unable to register as a student, he would sit in the halls of the Yale Divinity School and listen to lectures, thus gaining an education in theology. After returning to Newtown, he was ordained as a Presbyterian minister.

In 1840 Pennington was called to a Black church in Hartford, Connecticut. His reputation was considerably enhanced as he helped to raise funds to defend, support, and repatriate the West African Mende captives who, under the leadership of Joseph Cinqué, had successfully revolted aboard the slave ship *La Amistad*.

In 1841 Pennington founded the Union Missionary Society, which was later folded into the American Missionary Association. In 1843 he represented the Connecticut Anti-Slavery Society at the World Anti-Slavery Convention and the American Peace Society at the World Peace Convention, both in London. In 1847 he was invited to become the pastor of the First Colored Presbyterian Church (Shiloh) in New York City, one of the largest Black congregations in the country. On a second trip to Europe, in 1849, Pennington was awarded an honorary Doctor of Divinity degree by the University of Heidelberg in Germany—an extraordinary achievement for a fugitive slave. After the passage of the Fugitive Slave Act in 1850, Pennington was encouraged to stay abroad until a friend could negotiate his freedom.[154]

On returning to New York, Pennington resumed his pastoral duties as well as becoming something of a one-man campaign against segregation on trains, omnibuses, and boats. In September 1852 he published in the *New York Evangelist* a letter to the editor outlining the difficulties he had as pastor being denied the ability to travel. He cites, by way of illustration, two times (out of many) that he had been unable to reach, first, his church in time for a service, and second, the funeral of an elderly member of his church, and he asks—and answers—the perennial question:

> And why is it that a man in the public service of one of the largest congregations in the city, has to submit to such a system of oppression? It is not because I smoke segars in the 'busses, as I see some white men do. It is not because I chew and spit tobacco in the 'busses, as some white men do. It is not because I carry a great pet dog with me, and say to every one, "If you love me you love my dog"—not excepting finely dressed ladies in the 'busses. But it is simply and only because I am a black man, obediently carrying about on my person the same skin, with the same color, which the Almighty has seen fit to give me.[155]

This letter was reprinted in the *New York Times*, and the *Times* editor appended a long note decrying "a practice which is infinitely disgraceful to the great body of our fellow-citizens in the Northern States."[156]

Two weeks later, Pennington sent another letter to the *Times*, commending the paper for its comments on the earlier article and recounting an incident. "[It is] so fresh and so amusing that I know you will be glad to hear it," he writes. He then tells of a Black Baptist minister who rode the Broadway line from Sixtieth Street to "far down-town" in pleasant conversation with a white passenger. Only when the minister reached his stop and went to pay the driver his sixpence did the driver notice that he was Black:

> *Driver*—"Why! I didn't know that *you* were there!"
>
> *Colored minister*—"Well, you know it now, don't you? Don't keep me waiting; here's your money—take it and let me go: I am in a hurry."
>
> Here was a pause of a minute or two, which was broken by a hearty laugh from ladies, gentlemen, and all in the 'Bus.[157]

On July 29, 1853, the *New York Times* reported an incident that illustrates racial bias in enforcement of the seating rules on at least some of the city's steam ferries. As on larger ships taking longer journeys, the Manhattan ferries instituted and enforced their own various company-determined "regulations" governing seating and behavior. One such rule was that men could not sit in the ladies' cabin unless they were in the company of a woman. For some years Pennington had taken the Fulton Ferry from his home in Brooklyn to his church in Manhattan without problems. But as racial tensions were gradually but palpably increasing in the city, on July 28 Pennington was prevented from simply walking through the ladies' cabin:

> Scandalous Conduct on Board a Fulton Ferry-boat.—Last evening, while the ferry-boat *Fulton* was crossing from Brooklyn to the slip at the foot of Fulton-street, New York, a colored man, respectably dressed, and having the appearance of a minister of a colored congregation, attempted to pass from one end of the boat to the other, through the ladies' cabin. It is customary to allow the lowest loafers to take seats in the ladies' cabin; but this colored man was peremptorily ordered to withdraw by one of the officers of the boat. The poor fellow explained that he did not wish to take a seat, but desired to pass to the other end of the boat. His explanation was disregarded, and he was driven back. He acquiesced submissively. On inquiry, we were told that the rules of the boat justified this petty tyranny. We publish the fact without further comment. The brutality of the action needs no comment.[158]

A similar incident occurred less than a week later. On August 4 the "Additional City News" column began with a list of the evening's entertainments, including two contrasting items: "National Theatre—Uncle Tom's Cabin" and "Wood's Minstrels—444 Broadway.—Ethiopian Minstrelsy—Overtures, Quicksteps, Choruses, &c." The former was a dramatization of Harriett Beecher Stowe's important antislavery novel. The latter was a troupe of white musicians in blackface, in the mode of D. T. Rice's original "Jim Crow." After this, came the column's lead article, as follows:

More Ruffianism on Board a Brooklyn Ferry Boat.—Yesterday, about 11 ½ o'clock, AM, as the *Manhattan* Ferry-boat was leaving her slip at the foot of Fulton-street, Brooklyn, another of those disgraceful scenes, which have of late become so common on these boats, occurred in the presence of many disgusted passengers. A respectably dressed colored man accompanied by two colored women, one of whom was his wife, attempted to pass through the ladies' cabin to the forward end of the boat. The passage-way of the boat was blocked up with vehicles, and the only way for women to pass through was through the ladies' cabin. The colored women were allowed to pass, but immediately the man attempted to follow them, he was—not ordered back—but seized by the collar by the Captain of the boat, and forcibly thrust back. The negro again came forward and asked to be allowed to follow his wife. The captain then clutched him by the throat, and sent him reeling. Two or three rowdies who were present, applauded, but a loud murmur of disapprobation arose among the respectable portion of the passengers. The captain grew excited, and behaved like a ruffian. He again and again sent the colored man reeling, till at last, notwithstanding the tears of his wife, they were driven off the boat. They repaired to the boat in the next slip, where they were allowed to take their seats in the ladies' cabin. We made inquiries of the authorities, and learned that it was optional with the captains of the Fulton Ferry-boats to allow colored men to walk through the cabin or not, as they (the captains) were disposed.

Vermin-dropping beggars,—low rowdies,—the worst characters with a white skin, may sit and elbow a lady in silk or satin, in those cabins—nothing is said to *them*. But if a decent man with a colored skin only wishes to *walk* through the cabin, he is clutched by the throat, and sent reeling. Does the Company know this fact? We have inquired, and are assured that the Company does not know it. Then why do they tolerate ruffians in their service?[159]

Pennington is not named in either article. However, a letter to the editor signed "Equity," printed in the *Times* on August 10, explicitly identifies Pennington as the subject of the incident on August 3, and Pennington himself wrote a letter published on August 11 identifying himself as the subject of the incident on July 29. Pennington only hints at how he may have been treated prior to that incident, but he clarifies that afterward the ferry company explicitly singled him out:

I forbear to mention here the treatment I have received on the Fulton Ferry, on several occasions within the last few months; but I will state that the servants of the Company have informed me, within a few days, that they have positive orders to deny me the right of way through the ladies' cabin; and I have accord-

> ingly been so denied repeatedly, even for the purpose of going ashore after the boat has been made fast to the bridge.
>
> Have the Company a right to do this? That is my question.
>
> J. W. C. Pennington
>
> P. S.—Supposing the Company to be sincere in conceding me not only the right of way, but also a seat, when I have a lady with me, I have adopted the plan, when I cross in the Company's boats, of taking my wife with me across the Ferry.
>
> This I do simply to avoid insult and annoyance; but the matter cannot rest here. I do this for peace's sake, but under protest.

In his postscript, Pennington would seem to be acquiescing to the seating rule. However, he may have intended to test the company's racial policy by eliminating the "unaccompanied male" objection, thus narrowing the issue to the matter of skin color only. And, clearly, being in the company of two women on August 3 did not resolve the issue.

CHAPTER 2

Streetcars and War

After streetcars were introduced in New York in the 1830s, they quickly spread elsewhere. Cities large and small began to expand rapidly, and streetcar lines proliferated. People could now travel to and from work more quickly and cheaply, to the benefit of all. Through the middle of the century, the population of free Blacks grew, especially in northern cities. And, of course, they had the same need to get to work and back and to simply go about their daily business and interests as white citizens, and their work was also crucial to urban economic and social progress. Yet streetcar conductors and company rules continued to force Black citizens out of their seats. Cultural and political tensions increased, and race relations grew more volatile as the national debate over slavery kept race at the center of public attention. As the country moved inexorably toward war, opposition and outrage in response to persistent mistreatment on streetcars became more frequent and organized among Black passengers.

Elizabeth Jennings, July 16, 1854

Elizabeth Jennings was about fourteen years old when her brother, Thomas Jinnings Jr, was ejected from a railroad car in Salem, Massachusetts, in May 1841 and then again in October.[1] How much might his experience have inspired the forcefulness and determination with which Elizabeth herself responded when the same thing happened to her thirteen years later? The daughter of a successful New York businessman, inventor, and abolitionist, Thomas L. Jennings, Elizabeth grew up to become a New York City school teacher and an organist at the First Colored American Congregational Church on Sixth Street, near the Bowery.

On Sunday, July 16, 1854, while on her way to church, she was forcibly removed from a streetcar owned by the Third Avenue Railroad Company. The following day a meeting was called at the church to condemn the incident. At that meeting a written statement by Jennings was read to the audience,

Elizabeth Jennings. Published in *The American Woman's Journal* in July 1895. Kansas State Historical Society.

"she being unable to attend the meeting, owing to the injuries received at the hands of the railroad conductor and his abet[t]ors." Like similar letters by David Ruggles, Thomas Van Renselaer, and others, it provides a detailed, first-person statement of what happened, written immediately after the event:

> Sarah E. Adams and myself walked down to the corner of Pearl and Chatham Sts. to take the Third Av. cars. I held up my hand to the driver and he stopped the cars. We got on the platform, when the conductor told us to wait for the next car. I told him I could not wait, as I was in a hurry to go to church (the other car was about a block off). He then told me that the other car had my people in it, that it was appropriated for that purpose. I then told him I had no people; it was no particular occasion. I wished to go to church, as I had been going for the last six months, and I did not wish to be detained.
>
> He insisted upon my getting off the car. I told him I would wait on the car until the other car came up. He again insisted on my waiting in the street, but I did

not get off the car. By this time the other car came up, and I asked the driver if there was any room in his car. He told me very distinctly, "No," that there was no more room in my car than there was in his. Yet this did not satisfy the conductor. He still kept driving me out or off the car. [He] said he had as much time as I had and could wait just as long. I replied, "Very well, we'll see."

He waited some few minutes, when the drivers becoming impatient, he said to me, "Well, you may go in, but remember, if the passengers raise any objections you shall go out." I answered again and told him I was a respectable person, born and raised in New-York, did not know where he was born, that I had never been insulted before while going to church, and that he was a good for nothing impudent fellow for insulting decent persons while on their way to church. He then said I should come out and he would put me out. I told him not to lay his hands on me. He took hold of me, and I took hold of the window sash and held on. He pulled me until he broke my grasp from that. (But previously he had dragged my companion out, she all the while screaming for him to let go.) He then ordered the driver to fasten his horses, which he did, and come and help him put me out of the car.

They then both seized hold of me by the arms and pulled and dragged me flat down on the bottom of the platform, so that my feet hung one way and my head the other, nearly on the ground. I screamed murder with all my voice, and my companion screamed out, "You'll kill her! don't kill her!" The driver then let go of me and went to his horses. I went again in the car, and the conductor said, "You shall sweat for this," then told the driver to drive as fast as he could and not to take another passenger in the car; to drive until he saw an officer or a Station House.

They got an officer on the corner of Walker and Bowery, whom the conductor told that his orders from the agent were to admit colored persons if the passengers did not object, but if they did, not to let them ride. When the officer took me there were some eight or ten persons in the car, when the officer, without listening to anything I had to say, thrust me out, and then pushed, and tauntingly told me to get redress if I could. This the conductor also told me, and gave me some name and number of his car. He wrote his name, Moss, and the car No. 7, but I looked and saw No. 6 on the back of the car. After dragging me off the car he drove me away like a dog, saying not to be talking there and raising a mob or fight.

I came home down Walker St., and a German gentleman followed, who told me he saw the whole transaction in the street as he was passing. His address is Latour, No. 148 Pearl St., bookseller. When I told the conductor I did not know where he was born, he answered, "I was born in Ireland." I made answer it made

Hailing a car at the corner of Pearl and Chatham Streets, 1861. New York Public Library.

> no difference where a man was born, that he was none the worse or better for that, provided he behaved himself and did not insult genteel persons.
>
> I would have come up myself, but am quite sore and stiff from the treatment I received from those monsters in human form yesterday afternoon. This statement I believe to be correct, and it is respectfully submitted. Elizabeth Jennings.[2]

The meeting at the church that evening unanimously passed three resolutions: (1) to reprehend the behavior of the company and the conductor, (2) to set up a committee to bring the matter of exclusion to the attention of the legal authorities and to demand equal treatment, and (3) to have notices of the meeting published in Horace Greeley's *New York Daily Tribune* and *Frederick Douglass' Paper*.

The committee referred the case to the law firm of Culver, Parker, and Arthur, well-known advocates for the abolition of slavery. Jennings filed a complaint with the New York Supreme Court against the conductor, the driver, and the company. The case was taken on by the firm's youngest partner, Chester A. Arthur. Arthur would go on to become president of the United States, but at the time he was only twenty-four and had been admitted to the bar only six weeks earlier. The headquarters of the Third Avenue Railroad were in Brooklyn, a separate city altogether at the time; thus the trial was held in the Second District Court in Brooklyn on February 22, 1855.[3] The summary published the following day in the *Tribune* leans, none too subtly, more in favor of Jennings than the railroad: "The conductor finally undertook to get her off, first alleging the car was full, and when that was shown to be false, he pretended that the other passengers were displeased at her presence; but as she saw nothing of that, and insisted on her rights, he took hold of her by force to expel her."[4]

The driver and the conductor offered no defense; thus, it was the company that "took issue" with Jennings's complaint. The judge who heard the case was apparently as sympathetic toward Jennings as was the *Tribune*: "Judge Rockwell gave a very clear and able charge, instructing the jury that the Company were liable for the acts of their agents, whether committed carelessly and negligently, or willfully and maliciously. That they were common carriers, and as such bound to carry all respectable persons; *that colored persons, if sober, well behaved, and free from disease*, had the same rights as others; and could neither be excluded by *any rules of the Company, nor by force or violence*; and in case of such expulsion or exclusion, the Company was liable."[5]

Jennings had sued for $500, and a majority of the jurors were in favor of awarding her the full amount, "but," as the *Tribune* reported, "others maintained some peculiar notions as to colored people's rights, and they finally agreed on $225, on which the Court added ten per cent, besides the costs."[6]

Though her case did not establish a law against segregation on the streetcars citywide, Jennings's victory gave further impetus to the campaign for equal treatment. Although the Third Avenue Railroad announced an end to segregation on its cars the very next day, that did not end the practice on other lines. Thomas Jennings Sr., the Rev. James W. C. Pennington, and James McCune Smith, one of the leading Black intellectuals of the day, were on the committee formed at the church meeting, and they established the Legal Rights Association with the express purpose of keeping attention on the issue of discriminatory seating and to help those who had been wronged and injured to bring their cases to court. It would be some years before success could be claimed across the city.

Elizabeth Jennings taught school under the auspices of the New York Society for the Promotion of Education among Colored Children from 1842 until 1854. She then taught for the New York Board of Education until 1864. In 1860 she married Charles Graham, who died in 1876. In 1895, while in her late sixties, Elizabeth Jennings Graham started a kindergarten in her home on Forty-First Street, the first kindergarten in New York for Black children. She died at her home on June 5, 1901.[7]

William Wells Brown. Frontispiece, William Wells Brown, *Three Years in Europe*, 1852. National Portrait Gallery, Smithsonian Institution.

William Wells Brown, September 26, 1854

William Wells Brown was born enslaved in Lexington, Kentucky, in 1815.[8] His mother, Elizabeth, was enslaved, and his white father was the half-brother of William's first master. As a close relative to the slave-owning family, William was trained as a "house slave" and spared many of the privations of the field hands. After the family moved to St. Louis, William was hired out on various jobs, including a stint in the printing office of the *St. Louis Times* and another on a steamship carrying enslaved people to the New Orleans slave markets. In this latter position he was exposed to the full horrors of the slave trade. In 1833 he and his mother escaped but were caught after ten days. His mother was sold down the river to New Orleans, and William was sold to a steamboat owner.

On January 1, 1834, William walked away from the ship to freedom in Cincinnati, and he adopted the names Wells Brown in honor of a man who helped him escape. Working as a steamship steward out of Cleveland, Brown helped many fugitives get to Canada. He married, and in 1836 he and his wife moved to Buffalo, New York, where they had two daughters. In the 1840s Brown moved to Boston and traveled as an antislavery lecturer. He learned to read and write, and his personal narrative, written in 1847, became very well known, second only to that of Frederick Douglass. The following year he published *The Anti-Slavery Harp: A Collection of Songs for Anti-Slavery Meetings.*

Brown's last slave master, Enoch Price, offered Brown his freedom for $325, but Brown made it known that Price would never receive a dollar from him or his friends. As a well-known figure on the lecture circuit, however, Brown's life and freedom were at risk, and it became prudent for him to sail to Europe. He served as a delegate to the International Peace Congress in Paris in 1849 and then as an antislavery lecturer in Great Britain. Brown's wife died in 1851, and his daughters joined him in England. In 1854 friends convinced Brown to let them purchase his freedom, and he returned to the United States.

After a twenty-day passage aboard the steamer *City of Manchester*, Brown reached U.S. soil on the afternoon of September 26, 1854. The following year he concluded his travel narrative, *The American Fugitive in Europe: Sketches of Places and People Abroad*, with a description of his experience of "the influence of slavery" on the streets of Philadelphia on the very day he returned. He contrasts his exclusion from a Philadelphia omnibus with the respect he had been accorded in France, England, and Scotland, characterizing the "Colorphobia" in Philadelphia as even "more rampant than in the pro-slavery, negro-hating city of New York." His peroration includes the names of many renowned people he met with, sat with, and ate with in Europe, and he even gives us such charming details as the names of some of the omnibuses in London. Driving his point home, however, he ends this comparison—and the book—with a condemnation of the forces that generated racial prejudice in the United States:

> While walking through Chestnut-street, in company with two of my fellow-passengers, we hailed an omnibus going in the direction which we wished to go. It immediately stopped, and the white men were furnished with seats, but I was told that "We don't allow niggers to ride in here." It so happened that these two persons had rode in the same car with me from London to Liverpool. We had put up at the same hotel in the latter place, and had crossed the Atlantic in the same steamer. But as soon as we touch the soil of America we can no longer ride in the same conveyance, no longer eat at the same table, or be regarded

with equal justice, by our thin-skinned democracy. During five years' residence in monarchical Europe I had enjoyed the rights allowed to all foreigners in the countries through which I passed; but on returning to my NATIVE LAND the influence of slavery meets me the first day I am in the country. . . . I had partaken of the hospitality of noblemen in England, had sat at the table of the French Minister of Foreign Affairs; I had looked from the strangers' gallery down upon the great legislators of England, as they sat in the House of Commons; I had stood in the House of Lords, when Her Britannic Majesty prorogued her Parliament; I had eaten at the same table with Sir Edward Bulwer Lytton, Charles Dickens, Eliza Cook, Alfred Tennyson, and the son-in-law of Sir Walter Scott; the omnibuses of Paris, Edinburgh, Glasgow and Liverpool, had stopped to take me up; I had often entered the "Caledonia," "Bayswater," "Hammersmith," "Chelsea," "Bluebell," and other omnibuses that rattle over the pavements of Regent-street, Cheapside, and the west end of London,—but what mattered that? My face was not white, my hair was not straight; and therefore I must be excluded from a seat in a third-rate American omnibus. Slavery demanded that it should be so. I charge this prejudice to the pro-slavery pulpits of our land, which first set the example of proscription by erecting the "negro pew." I charge it to that hypocritical profession of democracy which will welcome fugitives from other countries, and drive its own into exile. I charge it to the recreant sons of the men who carried on the American revolutionary war, and who come together every fourth of July to boast of what their fathers did, while they, their sons, have become associated with bloodhounds, to be put at any moment on the track of the fugitive slave.[9]

Brown made further important contributions to American letters. He was the first African American to write a travel narrative (*Three Years in Europe*, 1853) and a novel (*Clotel; or, the President's Daughter*, 1854, a fictionalized tale of the relationship between Thomas Jefferson and Sally Hemings, Jefferson's slave and mistress). He also wrote two plays (*The Escape, or A Leap for Freedom*, 1848, and *The Doughface Baked, or How to Give a Northern Man a Backbone*, 1858).[10] During the 1860s and afterward, he produced a number of historical works: *The Black Man, His Antecedents, His Genius, and His Achievements* (1863), *The Negro in the American Rebellion* (1867), *The Rising Sun* (1873), and an expanded autobiography, *My Southern Home; or, The South and Its People* (1880).

Brown had a long-standing interest in medicine, and in the mid-1860s he began styling himself William Wells Brown, M.D. He maintained a medical practice throughout the 1870s, as he continued his writing. He died in 1884 and was buried in Cambridge, Massachusetts.

James W. C. Pennington, May 24, 1855

After Elizabeth Jennings won her suit against the Third Avenue Railroad in New York, in February 1855, there was a marked increase in the number of protests mounted in the cars. Rev. J. W. C. Pennington referred to her case after his sermon at Shiloh Church on May 4, 1855, at the beginning of "Anniversary Week," a celebration of various religious and social organizations. He recommended to his congregation that they remind friends who might be coming to the city that week that "colored people could no longer be excluded from the City public conveyances as was formerly the usage," the *New York Daily Tribune* reported. "He said that a judicial decision had already placed the matter of public conveyances in the hands of the colored people themselves, and they would be to blame if they longer continued subject to the great disadvantages involved by the proscriptions of conductors and drivers of cars and omnibuses." Pennington stressed the need to continue challenging troublesome conductors, drivers, and their employers, and he recognized that doing so would require courage. "He hoped that just at this time the colored people would show a bold front in this and other kindred matters of equal importance, so that the coming age might know the value of perseverance when brought to bear upon great and important principles in the development of which are involved the hopes and happiness of the whole human species."[11]

That the Jennings court decision had not brought an end to the prejudicial treatment of Black passengers is demonstrated by a brief article appearing on the same page of the *Daily Tribune* as Pennington's remarks. This notice not only suggests the continuation of the exclusion policy, it also provides a specific example of the complaint often made by Black protesters that troublesome or objectionable white passengers were allowed to ride undisturbed:

> Drunken Rowdies in City Railroad Cars.—Complaint is made that the Conductor of car No. 42, on the Eighth-av. Railroad, admitted four drunken men into the car, on the downward trip, at 11 o'clock on Friday evening, and although their conduct was disgraceful and their conversation obscene, he made no remonstrances, but allowed them to remain, very much to the disgust of the ladies in the car. Had they been clean, well-behaved colored men, they would have been hustled out. Their whitewash saved them.[12]

On the day after Pennington made his remarks in church, Sidney McFarland (perhaps inspired by those remarks) decided to test conditions on the Sixth Avenue line. He got off a "Colored People's Car" and stepped onto the platform of the car just behind it, remarking that he "meant to test the question whether persons of his shade could ride on the white folks' car, or not." After being forced off, McFarland sued the conductor for assault and battery. As the *Times* noted, "The affair has created some considerable excitement, and a large concourse of people visited the court-room to learn the result." The judge, however, dismissed the case on the ground that McFarland had "provoked the assault," adding, like many judges before and after him, that "the conductor did *not* use more force or violence than was necessary to eject the obnoxious passenger."[13]

On Thursday, May 24, Pennington himself became the target of both a driver and a judge, as described under the headline "Outrage upon a Doctor of Divinity":

> Doctor Pennington (Doctor of Divinity of the University of Heidelberg) says he entered the Railroad car No. 16, on the Sixth-avenue, on Thursday morning, for the purpose of coming down town. He was immediately ordered out. On [Pennington's] refusing to alight, the driver became ferocious, forcibly laid hold of him and ejected him. He maintained his hold of the vehicle and again entered. No objection was made by the passengers. The driver again forced him out, and in the attempt knocked his hat off. The Doctor stuck by the vehicle until it arrived at Murray-street; there a boy brought him his hat. Conceiving himself assaulted, he said to the driver, "You are my prisoner." A policeman advised him not to attempt to enter. The Doctor wished the policeman to go with him before the Mayor that he might complain of the driver. Arrived near the City Hall, the policeman carried him before Justice Connolly at the Tombs, who according to his account *turned the tables* upon him completely, threatening to [p]unish him severely if ever brought there again.[14]

Pennington, undaunted, brought the matter to the attention of the mayor of New York, Fernando Wood, and the next day the secretary of the Sixth Avenue Railroad, T. Bailey Myers, replied to the mayor's query, referencing both the McFarland case and Pennington's. In addition to making several snide remarks about Pennington, Myers enumerated at some length what he saw as reasons why people of color should not ride in the cars, stating first: "As to their right to ride in our cars other than those specially assigned to them, we cannot admit it, and shall not until a legal decision to that effect virtually instructs *to take off our colored cars*." The Sixth Avenue line at the time ran "specially assigned . . . colored cars" every half hour, which he believed was "more than [was] required for their convenience—far more than their census ratio entitle[d] them to."[15]

Myers insisted, "[Pennington] certainly must know that a great many people do object to riding next to a colored man; and many others to allowing the ladies of their families to mingle with them in public conveyances." He further claimed, rather mendaciously, "Our business is to carry passengers, and . . . we have nothing to do with the color of their skins, only with the color of their money, and the comfort and convenience of all." Pennington points out in response, "[This is] just the principle I contend for. . . . The Sixth-avenue Railroad Company accedes to my construction of our relative position. Why not act accordingly?"[16] Pennington filed charges against the company, and at a meeting of the Legal Rights Association in the late summer he promised that if he did not win his suit "in one court he would carry it to another; and if he was beat in every court he would carry it to the ballot-box."[17]

Pennington had sued for $1,000 in damages, but in his opening statement Pennington's lawyer admitted, "This action is brought, not so much to recover damages,—for Mr. Pennington did not experience any very great bodily injury,—as to test the question whether in this country, a colored man can or cannot ride in these public conveyances." To limit the issue solely and explicitly to that question, he went on to say,

> I do not know that I can better express the object of this suit, than by giving the words of Rev. Dr. Pennington himself, when he came to my office to solicit my professional assistance in bringing this suit. Said he to me: "Mr. Tallmadge, I know the prejudice which the people of this country have against our color. We do not claim, however, to be their equals. We do not expect to be invited to sit at their tables, or share their beds. But I have yet to learn that I cannot pass from one part of the country to another in your rail cars and steamboats. In that I claim no equality, except the right of passage. If I sit by you on the same seat in a car, that does not imply that I am your equal."[18]

While it may seem that Pennington is abdicating any claims to equality, which is hardly likely, this statement can be better understood as Tallmadge's strategy to restrict the arguments and the court's decision only to that of a railroad company's right to determine who should be allowed to ride.

The *Times* reported on Judge John Slosson's instructions to the jury in considerable detail. While he stressed repeatedly that their decision hinged solely on the question as to whether the regulation denying seats to Black passengers was a reasonable one, he simultaneously expanded the implications of the case to broader issues. For example, he stated, "If it be true that this Company is obliged, by force of law, to admit colored people into their cars indiscriminately with the whites, I see no reason why a hotel-keeper is not equally bound to give any unoccupied room in his house to a colored man who may apply for it," and he charged that the jury had to take into consideration "the probable effect upon the business and interests of the Company, from allowing blacks an equality as passengers with whites." The report concludes, "The jury then retired, and after some hours absence brought in a verdict for the defendant. We understand that this verdict was rendered on the ground that the admission of colored persons would tend to diminish the profits of the Company."[19]

Pennington died in October 1870. In 2011 the University of Heidelberg Center for American Studies and the School of Theology established the James W. C. Pennington Award to honor scholars "who have done distinguished work on topics important to Pennington: slavery, emancipation, peace, education, reform, civil rights, religion, and intercultural understanding."[20]

Thomas Downing, September 24, 1855

By the time Thomas Downing was thrown off a Harlem Line car and beaten in 1840, he was already a successful businessman. During the following years he continued to flourish, and his oyster cellar became the most popular one in the city—a city which was quite particular about its oysters. He was a dedicated abolitionist and an active proponent of Black suffrage. His son George worked with him in the restaurant, where, when the need arose, they would shelter fugitive slaves in the basement, as the New York white elite dined above.[21]

Shortly after J. W. C. Pennington vowed in September 1855 to carry his own lawsuit up to the highest courts in the land, if necessary, Downing too was confronted once again, this time by a conductor on the Sixth Avenue Railroad. Downing related his story to the New York *Evening Post*, and he tells it so well, revealing the assistance and moral support he received from white New Yorkers on the occasion, that it is included here in full, as reprinted in *Frederick Douglass' Paper*.

> COLORPHOBIA ON A CITY RAILROAD.
>
> Mr. Thomas Downing, a well-known colored citizen of New York, in a letter to *The Evening Post,* gives an account of a disgraceful, and, we are glad to say, an unsuccessful attempt to expel him from a car of the Sixth Avenue Railroad. The *Post*, introducing the letter to its readers, says:
>
> "To those who do not know Mr. Downing (everyone knows him here,) it may be proper to say that he is one of the most respectable and aged colored men in this city. His private character is without reproach; he has made a large fortune as the keeper of a refectory, which is frequented daily by throngs of the principal bankers and merchants of Wall and Broad streets and their vicinity; he

THOMAS DOWNING

Thomas Downing, one of the pioneers of New York city. He at one time owned the property at No. 3 Broad street, now occupied by the Morgan-Drexler building, a structure valued at $3,000,000. Born in 1791, he knew intimately every New Yorker of prominence up to the days of the Civil war. It was he who saved James Gordon Bennett's New York Herald from going under by advancing a loan of $10,000 to Bennett.

Thomas Downing.
Unidentified newspaper, after 1872.

has brought up several sons to the same business, to whom he has given a good elementary education, good habits and a good name; and during his long and uninterrupted success had never forgotten the humility and modesty which is one of his most noticeable characteristics.

"He lives where he has lived and as he has lived for nearly half a century; he sells his oysters in the very same cellar—furnished in the same plain way that it was furnished when he opened it, and it would be difficult to detect the slightest change wrought in the dress, in the character or deportment of the old man since he became what he has been for many years, a man of fortune, except in the magnitude of his donations for the relief of his oppressed race."

MR. DOWNING'S STATEMENT.

"Last evening (Monday, Sept. 24,) a lady came to my place of business, No. 3 Broad street, with two letters to be delivered at No. 25 Thirty-eighth street, near Sixth Avenue, and wished me to go with her. She was from her employer's at Flushing. I accompanied her up town and took car No. 27 of the Sixth Avenue Railroad at the corner of Park Place and Church street. As we got in the car the conductor made an objection and threatened to put us out. However, he went along till he got to the corner of Chambers street and West Broadway. Here he stopped the car, and attempted to put us out. This was about 8 o'clock. He came to me, as I was sitting in the car, and putting his hands on my shoulder, told us to get out.

"I told him we had an errand with letters to deliver in haste, and we should not get out, so he had better go on. Then two or three gentlemen, who sat opposite us, told us to sit still, as the conductor had no right to put us out, as we had as much right to ride as they had.

"The conductor then ordered the car to go on, and threatened to call an officer to put us out. This, I said, was the very thing I wanted, as the officers were placed for the purpose of keeping the peace, and he was disturbing me. —'Well,' says he, 'my orders are to put you out.' 'My dear Sir,' says I, 'I would not take a business if I had to break the law to carry it out.'

"The car continued on till it reached the corner of Canal and Varick, when it made a full stop. Here he called to his aid several persons. I asked them what they had to do with the matter, as there was but one conductor and one driver to each car. They said, we are conductors of the line, and we will take you out. I said: 'No, you won't—I don't leave this car till I get to the end of my journey.' The men then made a move toward me, but, from the position I occupied they were afraid to clinch me. I held a brass key in my hand, which I suppose they thought was a knife, as they exclaimed 'don't use your knife!'

"At this time I said, 'Gentlemen, if I have violated or committed a breach of the law, here is my card, and you know where to find me.'—The conductor refused the card; but a number of gentlemen in the car, seeing that I had a handful, took them. The car then started again. From that moment, the passengers, when my name became known, began to manifest an interest in me by saying: 'Don't get out.' One gentleman come [*sic*] and took a seat at my side and says, 'I will sit with you. I have known you for the last thirty years in Broad street.'—The gentleman who sat in the after part of the car went forward and talked the matter over.

"As the car started from Canal and Varick, where a great number of people had collected on the sidewalk and around the car, many of them cried: 'Stay in Downing,' another says, 'Put him out.' Then the car started on an up-trip, and there was a shout among the spectators: 'Three cheers for Downing—hurra, hurra, hurra.'

"The car had proceeded but a very few rods when the conductor rang the bell and stopped it again.[22] The mob then surrounded the car, and filled the platforms, and it was with great difficulty that the conductor could get them off.

"The car at length got under way and went on, and I saw from the conductor's communication with the driver that he did not intend to stop for me when

> I should ring the bell to get out. I noticed that whenever the bell rang, the driver would look into the car to see who wished to get out. When I got to the corner of Thirty-eighth street and Sixth Avenue, I said to the gentleman at my side, 'Will you be kind enough to ring the bell for me?' which he did. The driver looked into the door and, seeing the gentleman standing, stopped the car, when the three of us got quietly out, and no one was hurt."[23]

Thomas Downing continued running his restaurant until a year or two before he died on April 10, 1866, at the age of seventy-five. The obituary printed in the *New York Times* comments on his "presence of mind" in helping to fight the Great Fire of 1835, and, though it does not mention his mistreatment on the streetcars, it does note that he "took a prominent part in all measures for the elevation of the colored race, and lived an active and useful life."[24] His reputation was such that on the day he died the New York Chamber of Commerce closed for the day.[25]

William Howard Day, October 1, 1855

In 1836, at the age of eleven, William Howard Day, the son of a sailmaker and a seamstress in New York City, so impressed J. P. Williston, an ink maker and white abolitionist from Northampton, Massachusetts, that Williston convinced Day's mother to allow him to adopt the boy and educate him in Northampton. Day subsequently became apprenticed to a local newspaper, and in 1847 he graduated from Oberlin College, the first college in the nation to admit Black students, both male and female.[26] The following year, as a delegate to the National Negro Convention in Cleveland, Day worked with Frederick Douglass and others to draft an "Address to the Colored People of America."[27] He became a reporter and editor for the *Cleveland True Democrat* and then briefly published a paper of his own, the *Alien American*. Under the combined pressure of racial discrimination and the economic failure of his paper in 1854, Day and his wife moved to Canada.

On October 1, 1855, Day and his wife were planning to take the overnight steamer *Arrow* from Detroit to Toledo, Ohio. On boarding, Day was refused a cabin ticket, although cabins were available, but was offered deck passage at a lower fare. Rather than travel on the open deck exposed to the autumnal weather, the Days made their way overland to Toledo. Three weeks later, putting his principles into action, Day sued the *Arrow*'s owner, John Owen, in a Michigan court for being "put to great expense, trouble, and delay, and obliged to travel in the night a hundred miles out of his way to reach Toledo."[28] When the suit failed, Day filed an appeal.

The Michigan Supreme Court heard Day's appeal in May 1858. Owen's lawyers presented three familiar arguments:

(1) That it was the prevailing custom and usage on the Detroit River and Lake Erie that "colored persons were not allowed the privileges of cabin passengers."
(2) That such "regulation and course of business" was "reasonable."
(3) That admitting the plaintiff into a ship's cabin "would have been offensive to the other cabin passengers."

Judge Randolph Manning, in writing the court's opinion, focused on the question of reasonability: "All rules and regulations must be reasonable; and to be so, they should have for their object the accommodation of the passengers. Under this head we include everything calculated to render the transportation most comfortable and least annoying to passengers generally." Furthermore, he separated the central matter of race from the more abstract question of the reasonableness of the rule itself: "The reasonableness of the rule, if it be reasonable, does not depend upon the color of the plaintiff, [but rather on] the effect the carrying of such persons in the cabin would have . . . on the accommodation of the mass of persons who have a right, and are in the habit of travelling on his boat." In other words, Manning declared it is a reasonable rule if the presence of a Black passenger among them upset the "mass of persons," (which is to say, *white persons*) on the boat. He failed to consider the question of any harm or effect on the excluded person. Ruling in line with the business interests of the boat's owner, he declared, "[The law] does not require a carrier to make any rules whatever, but if he deems it for his interest to do so, . . . to deny him the right would be an interference with a carrier's control over his own property in his own way." Determining that the rule was reasonable, along with the fact that Day was offered passage on the deck, which he declined, and not denied passage altogether, the court affirmed the original verdict denying Day's lawsuit.

After Day filed his suit but before the appeal was heard and decided in 1858, the U.S. Supreme Court chief justice Roger Taney delivered in March 1857 the decision in *Dred Scott v. Sanford*, which declared, among other things, that African Americans were not U.S. citizens and could not sue in the federal courts.[29] This 7–2 decision, widely regarded as the worst decision the Supreme Court has ever made, gives a good indication of the racial atmosphere in much of the country even outside the slaveholding areas in the years before the Civil War. An unfavorable result in Day's case, therefore, comes as no great surprise. Here we see in Michigan an articulation in legal yet very broad terms of the widespread sentiment that separation between the two races was to the benefit or simply the satisfaction of just one of them. Nearly thirty years later, in 1885, Michigan would pass its own civil rights law promising "full and equal accommodations."[30] Even so, it would take another sixty years beyond that before the right of African Americans to ride on a privately owned steamboat on the Detroit River would finally be established in the case of Sarah Elizabeth Ray.

Though Day and his wife lived in Canada, he remained engaged with the struggle for the abolition of slavery and for civil rights in the United States. In 1859 Day printed the "Provisional Constitution" drafted by the militant antislavery activist John Brown, copies of which were discovered after Brown's attack at Harpers Ferry. By the time of that raid, Day had gone to Britain, where he would spend four years raising funds for the settlement of fugitive slaves in Buxton, Ontario. Returning to New York, Day worked with the American Freedmen's Friend Society and in 1867 became superintendent of schools for the Freedmen's Bureau in Maryland and Delaware. During the 1870s he returned for a few years to newspaper publishing and was then elected to the Harrisburg, Pennsylvania, school board, from which he retired in 1899, having also become a presiding elder of the AME Zion Church. Before he died in 1900, the *Harrisburg Telegraph* declared him "one of the grandest and most refined men of this country regardless of race."[31]

Peter S. Porter, December 16, 1856

J. W. C. Pennington's lawsuit against the Sixth Avenue Railroad in New York was scheduled to be heard on December 16, 1856, but the case was carried over to the following day. However, that afternoon Peter S. Porter, the treasurer of the Legal Rights Association, was forced off an Eighth Avenue car and severely beaten while traveling in the company of his wife and four other women. The attack by the conductor, the driver, and three other company employees was described in the *Daily Tribune* the following day:

> This formidable array of City railroad functionaries pounced upon Mr. Porter and beat, kicked and banged him about most ferociously; also tearing his overcoat and shirt, and breaking his watch. Mrs. Porter endeavored to interfere, but one of the ruffians caught her by the throat and shook her. There were other ladies in the car (white) who offered no objection whatever to ride with Mr. Porter and his friends; and a gentleman, who saw the whole affair, was threatened with the same treatment if he dared to interfere. . . .
>
> Both Mr. P. and his wife have frequently ridden up and down in the Eighth Avenue Railroad cars without being molested before, and why should he be as-

> sailed at this time it is easy to conjecture, when it is stated that he is Treasurer of the New-York Legal Rights Association, under whose auspices the case of Dr. Pennington and the Sixth Avenue Railroad Company is now being tried in the Superior Court.[32]

The Porters sued the railroad, and in February 1858 the New York Supreme Court ruled in their favor, acknowledging that African Americans had the right to equal seating on the streetcars. Unfortunately, as was so often the case, this ruling did not eliminate the practice of ejecting Black passengers.[33]

William Still and the Philadelphia Streetcar Campaign, 1859–1867

The first horse-drawn streetcar company in Philadelphia began operation on January 20, 1858. By 1859 no fewer than nineteen different lines were in operation throughout the city, with more to come. Streetcars were faster than the omnibuses, the rails provided a smoother ride than the streets, fewer horses were required, and the streetcar fares were cheaper, though by and large they were still beyond the range of the poor. In much of the city, the proliferation of streetcars was sufficiently extensive to account for the expansion of residential areas into "streetcar suburbs."[34]

As the city's transportation system was being set on rails, one long-standing practice familiar from trains and omnibuses persisted: Black riders were not welcome. Most streetcar lines allowed no Black passengers, though eight companies would permit them to stand on the front platform exposed to the weather, and for a while some ran separate cars for Black riders. It was not long before William Still, working at the hub of that intangible transportation system, the Underground Railroad, sparked a public campaign to protest the banning of Black citizens from the city's actual cold steel rails.[35]

William Still was born in 1821 in Burlington County, New Jersey, the son of Levin Still, a farmer who had bought his own freedom from slavery, and Charity (maiden name unknown), who had escaped from slavery. As the youngest of eighteen children, Still received little formal schooling, but he persisted in educating himself. At the age of twenty he left home and worked as a farmhand and a handyman. In 1844 he went to Philadelphia, and three years later he was hired as a clerk for the Pennsylvania Society for the Abolition of Slavery, the oldest antislavery society in the country. Still took great interest in the fugitives who came to the society, and he kept meticulous, detailed records, documenting not only their names, personal characteristics, and their escape narratives, but also aliases they used, their origins, and names of relatives and former owners—indeed, any information that might

William Still. Engraved by John Sartain, 1872. National Portrait Gallery, Smithsonian Institution.

be useful for helping them, uniting families, and generally keeping track of them. These records became the basis for his eight-hundred-page book, *The Underground Rail Road*, published in 1872. Still helped hundreds of fugitives through Philadelphia. Among others, he worked with Harriet Tubman to bring a number of her relatives and friends to freedom. In his book Still sometimes includes relevant information about a fugitive's subsequent history, such as his account of two instances during which Miles Robinson had been abused on the streetcars.

On August 31, 1859, Still sent a long letter to the editor of the *North American and United States Gazette*, addressing the sore grievance of genteel colored people in being excluded from the city passenger railroad cars, except when they chose to "stand on the front platform with the driver."

> However long the distance they may have to go, or great their hurry—however unwell or aged, genteel or neatly attired—however hot, cold or stormy the

weather—however few in the cars, as the masses of the colored people now understand it, they are unceremoniously excluded.

Of course my own humble opinion will weigh but little with yourself and readers (being as I am of the proscribed class). . . . Nevertheless pardon me for saying that this severe proscription, for some unaccountable reason, is carried to an extent in Philadelphia unparalleled in any of the leading cities of this Union. This is not imagination or an exaggerated assertion.[36]

Still's claim of unparalleled prejudice in Philadelphia echoes (perhaps intentionally) the statement to the same effect that William Wells Brown published in 1855. This letter marks the beginning of a long campaign to bring equality to the streetcars. It was reprinted in many of the antislavery papers around the country, but it brought no perceptible change to the Philadelphia streetcars. Incidents continued to occur, and the campaign for equal rights in the cars dragged on for eight years.

In 1860, Still and others formed the Social, Civil and Statistical Association of Colored People of Pennsylvania (SCSA) in order to gather data and publicize information about racial issues, including problems on the streetcars. The following year, in Still's words, "A committee was appointed to draw up a petition in favor of our rights in the cars." The committee solicited and received hundreds of signatures from prominent white members of the Philadelphia business, legal, and religious communities. They even asked the presidents of the streetcar lines themselves to sign it. Two of them did so—one on his deathbed. Two or three others said they were in favor of the petition but declined to sign it. And when presented with the signed petition in June 1862, the Board of Presidents rejected it. Still and the committee continued their work in "ferreting out individuals who had been badly treated" and "would bring them to the notice of the public, through the papers, from time to time."[37]

Meanwhile, the Civil War had begun, and Philadelphia became an important hub for the gathering and movement of troops and for the treatment of wounded soldiers. Conditions on the streetcars worsened after the summer of 1863 as Black soldiers, newly allowed to enlist for active duty, were forced off the cars by roughnecks who were all too willing to "help" the conductors eject them, and as the mothers, wives, and other relatives of wounded Black soldiers were unable to get to the hospitals where their loved ones lay ill, wounded, and dying.[38]

On December 11, 1863, Still sent a letter to the *Philadelphia Press* recounting a time in which he and a white employee of his took a morning train to Camp William Penn, the first training camp for African American soldiers in the Union army, about ten miles north of the city. Still was manager of the post exchange. Needing to get back to his business in the city, Still and his employee walked five miles to Germantown to catch the 1:00 p.m. train. They missed the train by five minutes and decided to take a streetcar. When they boarded, Still paid the fare for both of them. He would later write, "The conductor very cordially received the money, but before he took time to hand me the change that was due to me, invited me to 'step out on the platform.'" Because of his pressing business, Still reluctantly did so, but when it began to snow, the platform became "utterly intolerable," and Still decided to walk the rest of the way back. "[I felt] satisfied that no where in Christendom could be found a better illustration of Judge Taney's decision in the Dred Scott case, in which he declared that 'black men have no rights which white men are bound to respect,' than are demonstrated by the 'rules' of the passenger cars of the City of Brotherly Love."[39]

In this letter Still referred to two earlier cases, one in which a young woman was forcibly thrust out of a car, and the other in which a "venerable old minister" was killed in an accident as he stood on a streetcar platform.[40] On November 17, 1862, a prominent seventy-year-old Philadelphia AME minister, Richard Robinson (or Roberson), had been standing on the front platform of a streetcar when it collided with a hay wagon. Robinson was crushed under the car, and he died the next day. A set of resolutions written by five AME preachers opined that Robinson's death was "the result of absolute treachery existing in the white race against the colored in this city."[41]

Many papers around the country, and even the *Times* of London, reprinted Still's letter in early 1864. The reinvigorated SCSA campaign for the right to ride began to attract more attention, and hopes grew that their petition to the railway presidents would be successful. By year's end, the situation had not improved. On January 13, 1865, a meeting was held at Concert Hall, and another set of resolutions, with eighty-five signatures, was drawn up to be presented to the railroad presidents. On January 24 the Female Anti-Slavery Society sent a similar message.

Sidestepping any decision, the companies passed the buck by taking a poll of their passengers. On the very day that Congress abolished slavery with the Thirteenth Amendment, passengers on Philadelphia streetcars—all white, of course—were given ballots to answer the question, "Shall colored persons be allowed to ride in all the cars?" An overwhelming majority responded no.

By this time, however, the voice of a younger activist had begun to generate enthusiasm among a new generation of Philadelphians, that of Octavius V. Catto.

Hannibal Carter and the New Orleans Streetcar Campaign, 1862–1867

In 1835 the New Orleans & Carrollton Rail Road Company began operating three lines in New Orleans, making it the nation's second city, after New York, to put streetcars on rails. In 1860 the New Orleans City Rail Road was chartered, and additional rail lines grew up. Initially, only white passengers were allowed to ride, but in 1861 a system of "star cars" was developed. Every third or fourth car was prominently marked with a large black star, indicating that people of color were allowed to ride. In addition to the underlying inherent inequality and insult, this system provided less-frequent service for Black passengers, and often white riders would take up all or most of the available space.

Les gens de couleur libre, Louisiana's mixed-race, largely French-speaking "free people of color," had long enjoyed a degree of tolerance, though not full acceptance, in New Orleans society and had developed their own business, cultural, and social circles alongside middle-class and upper-class white society. Many, like Josephine Decuir, became quite wealthy and were themselves property owners and slaveholders. However, during the Civil War and especially afterward, the distinction between Black people, whether free or enslaved, on the one hand, and the more affluent *gens de couleur*, on the other, was disappearing. The latter found themselves experiencing increasing racial

New Orleans & Carrollton Rail Road ticket, 1868.

Hannibal C. Carter. *Appeal*, July 25, 1891. Courtesy of Floyd County, Indiana, Library.

discrimination where they had traditionally considered themselves to be in a separate category and in general had not been subject to the same degree of mistreatment and contempt as had free Blacks.

Union troops gained control of New Orleans in April 1862. Late that summer, Maj. Gen. Benjamin Butler, the military commander in the city, ordered Col. Spencer H. Stafford to form a regiment of Black troops. Among the volunteers were two brothers, Edward and Hannibal C. Carter, originally from Indiana, who left their home in Vicksburg, Mississippi, to join the new Louisiana Native Guard, where they were commissioned as captains. General Butler also gave orders allowing Black troops on the streetcars and for the star cars to be discontinued.[42]

Hannibal Carter mustered into the Second Regiment on October 12, 1862. Just five days later, he appeared in the New Orleans newspapers, though both the *Daily Picayune* and the *Daily Delta* got his surname wrong, printing it as Carty. The *Daily Delta* report provides the most detail:

> A Case of some Interest.—On the application of the driver of one of the city cars yesterday, Captain Hannibal Carty, a colored officer of the Second regiment of Colored Volunteers, was arrested by a policeman for riding on the cars. Col.

> Stafford appeared before the Provost Court to defend the Captain; and, in some very bitter and sarcastic remarks, which were delivered with the ease and grace of an old practitioner, rapped some of the thin-skins, on the subject of dark-skins, over the knuckles pretty severely. The Court decided that the Railroad Company had no right to turn colored persons out of their cars, much less to have them arrested for being on the cars.

A summary court report in the *Daily Delta* the following week clarifies the results of the case: "The Judge decided that as defendant was an officer of the United States, the Court had no jurisdiction in the matter."[43]

Subsequently, General Butler's order to integrate the cars was successfully challenged in court, and the star cars returned to service. Incidents and tension over the issue continued, however, and Butler's successor, Gen. Nathaniel Banks, again banned streetcar segregation in 1865. That ban too was overturned. Some streetcar lines began to offer cars with separate compartments for Black and white passengers; on other lines the star cars remained in service.

Hannibal Carter's confrontation with segregation, however, was not over. He resigned his commission in May 1863 and went to Tennessee, where in 1867 he was assisting in Reconstruction efforts. Then in 1868 he moved back to Vicksburg, where he would twice be elected to the Mississippi state legislature (1872–73, 1876–77). During his first term as a legislator he worked to pass the Mississippi Civil Rights Law of 1873.

On March 12, 1873, Carter and J. D. Webster, another Black legislator, put the new law to the test at the Angelo Concert Hall in Jackson, the state capital. Like Sarah Remond twenty years earlier, they were denied entry into the theater's "white" section. They sued George Donnell, who had purchased the right to sell seats for the entire floor, and he was arrested. Donnell admitted that he had refused seats to Carter and Webster, arguing that "it was to protect his pecuniary rights."[44] When Donnell was found guilty in the Mississippi Chancery Court and fined $125, he filed an appeal. The Mississippi Supreme Court heard the case in April. Carter responded to Donnell's financial argument, saying that it was a case of human rights, not property rights, and he invoked the Fourteenth Amendment, which granted citizenship rights to African Americans. The court ruled unanimously in Carter's favor.[45]

Unfortunately, over time the 1873 Mississippi Civil Rights Law "fell into desuetude," which is to say that it became invalid after a period of never being enforced.[46] After the collapse of Reconstruction and the ensuing increases in racism and segregation, Hannibal Carter left Mississippi for Chicago. In an interview in the St. Paul, Minnesota–based *Appeal* in 1891, he said that he moved north because Vicksburg had "ceased to be a healthy locality for a free man."[47]

Miles Robinson, March 11, 1865

Miles Robinson was enslaved by a Mrs. Roberts, a widow living in York County, Virginia, but he was hired out to work in Richmond, some seventy miles away, where other members of his family were also enslaved. During such leisure as he could obtain under slavery, Robinson became quite gifted as a banjo player, "but," as William Still remarks, "music in Richmond was not liberty." In 1859, at the age of twenty-two, Robinson heard that he was to be sold. Preferring to take a chance at freedom, he sought out the Underground Railroad and was directed to a woman who was a cook or chambermaid on a Richmond-to-Philadelphia steamer. She stowed Robinson away in one of the closets for pots and kitchen utensils.

Upon reaching Philadelphia, Robinson went to William Still for assistance, and after a short time he continued north to Boston and to the Twelfth Baptist Church, which, under the leadership of the Rev. Leonard Grimes, had become known as "the Fugitives' Church." Robinson worked in Boston for four years in the restaurant business, and in October 1864 he married Reverend Grimes's daughter, Emma Elizabeth T. Grimes. The couple relocated to Philadelphia, and Robinson and two friends opened a restaurant with the money he had saved.[48]

Miles Robinson's relationship with William Still stood him in good stead in two streetcar incidents. On Saturday, March 11, 1865, at about 5:00 p.m., during a pelting rain, Robinson, James Wallace, and R. C. Marshall had "an order to attend to in the eastern part of the city."[49] Four days later the *Philadelphia Press* printed a letter from the three men describing what happened to them that day. They had considered the question of taking a streetcar. "We were impressed with the idea that just now, when the impartial draft is making no distinction of color, and when, too, the tax-collectors come to our places of business as readily as to those of white persons, we might be permitted, and did enter a car of the Walnut and Chestnut streets line (to avoid the severity of the weather.)"

Robinson, Wallace, and Marshall did not set out to spark a test case, but the nature of their preliminary discussion shows that they were certainly aware of the implications and possible consequences of boarding a streetcar "while Black," to use the modern idiom. The weather may have been the immediate motivating factor, but their subsequent action, in both resisting and calling for Still's aid, demonstrates the willingness of at least one of them, when the time came, to push back against the segregation rule.

Upon entering the car, the three men were told, "You cannot ride in this car," and when they asked why not, the conductor replied simply, "Because you are not allowed." One of them responded, "We do not mean to go out; you can put us out if you choose." On that, a white passenger intervened. "In an excited manner, and with harsh language, [he] said: 'You know you are not allowed to ride in here.' 'If we are offensive to the passengers we will get up and go out,' we said. 'You are offensive to these ladies,' he responded, in a rage. The ladies rose, (but two were in the car,) and said emphatically, 'They are not offensive, but we want no disturbance.'"

At this point, the conductor summoned a policeman, who threatened to arrest them if they did not get out. "Is it against the law for us to ride in here?" they asked. The policeman replied, "It is," and one of the three said, "Then we will go out." But another one said, "It is not against the law, and you may lock me up."[50] With the help of the same white passenger and others who came in from the street to join the fray, the policeman arrested them, though not before blows were exchanged on both sides and several windows broken. Robinson and the others sent a message to William Still. Eventually around midnight Still managed to track down an alderman, pay their bail, and get them released.[51] But the wrong done to Robinson did not fade away, and he was destined to confront yet another conductor a year and a half later.

Sojourner Truth, April 1865

"I was bred and born, if I was born at all, in the State of New York, among the Low Dutch people."[52] Sojourner Truth was born into slavery in Ulster County, New York, in the late 1790s. Her parents, both enslaved by a wealthy Dutch landowner in Ulster County, named her Isabella. She spent her early life under the control of several owners, including seventeen years with the family of John Dumont. Around 1815 she was married to Thomas, a much older man enslaved by the Dumonts, and bore five children.[53]

In 1799 New York State adopted a system of gradual emancipation for enslaved people born in the state after July 4, 1799. These younger people would be nominally free but bound to indentured servitude until they reached a certain age: women at twenty-five, men at twenty-eight, and those born after 1817 at twenty-one. An 1817 state law then decreed that all enslaved people born in the state *before* 1799 were to be free by July 4, 1827. Dumont had agreed to free Isabella in July 1826, but he reneged on his promise, claiming that an

Sojourner Truth. Carte de visite, circa 1864. Library of Congress.

injury to her hand had deprived him of work she owed him. Before dawn one morning late that autumn, taking her baby Sophia and some food and clothing wrapped in a handkerchief, Isabella walked away from the Dumont estate. A friend directed her to the home of Isaac and Maria Van Wagenen, whom she also knew. When Dumont arrived to fetch her back, the Van Wagenens, who were opposed to slavery, paid him twenty dollars to allow her to work for them for the year, along with five dollars for Sophia.

Isabella had left behind her older children, who would become free only when they reached the designated age. As the end of slavery in New York drew near, many slaveholders sold their enslaved people in the hope of making a last-chance profit. In late 1826 Dumont sold Isabella's son Peter, about six years old, to one of his in-laws, who sold him to his brother, who in turn sold him to his brother-in-law in Alabama. It was illegal to sell an enslaved person beyond territory that would be free after 1827, but Isabella's pleas proved fruitless. Determined to regain her son, and in a highly unusual step for a poor, unlettered Black woman, especially one who was technically still enslaved, Isabella took the matter to court. With financial help from local Quakers and two lawyers, she won her case, becoming the first Black woman to win a lawsuit against a white man. Peter was returned to her in 1828, released from permanent slavery in the deep South and from fifteen years of servitude in New York. The judge declared that the boy "be delivered into the hands of the mother—having no other master, no other controller, no other conductor, but his mother."[54] Through this ordeal Isabella gained some knowledge and experience of the legal system and confidence in her ability to make it work in her favor.

After moving to New York City in 1828, Isabella was attracted to several Pentecostal and millenarian spiritual movements. She became a follower of Matthias the Prophet (Robert Matthews), until his commune collapsed amid allegations of murder and slander. When one of the members accused her of attempted poisoning, Isabella again returned to court, where she successfully sued for libel.

Isabella was greatly influenced by William Miller's prophesies that the end of the world would come in 1843 with the second coming of Christ. On June 1 that year she took the name Sojourner Truth and set out as an itinerant preacher, especially at various Millerite camp meetings in New York and Connecticut. When the prophesied apocalypse did not occur, Truth joined the Northampton Association of Education and Industry (NAEI), an interracial utopian community in what is now the village of Florence, Massachusetts. This community was based on complete religious freedom, the absolute abolition of slavery, full rights and citizenship for African Americans, and equal rights for women. The community supported itself through shared living, work, and ownership in its silk business, producing an alternative to cotton material based on slave labor. David Ruggles had come to the NAEI soon after its founding in 1842, as would a number of fugitive slaves, including Basil Dorsey.[55] Some years later Frederick Douglass wrote of his first visit to the Association: "The place and the people struck me as the most democratic I had ever met. It was a place to extinguish all aristocratic pretensions. There was no high, no low, no masters, no servants, no white, no black. I, however, felt myself in very high society." While there he met "that strange compound of wit and wisdom, of wild enthusiasm and flint-like common sense. . . . Sojourner Truth."[56] When the NAEI dissolved in 1846, Truth bought a house in the village. In 1850 she published *Narrative of Sojourner Truth* and began touring and speaking on both the antislavery and women's rights lecture circuits, selling copies of her book to meet her living expenses and pay off her mortgage.

There has been considerable scholarly debate over Truth's most famous speech, now known by the title "Ar'n't I a Woman?" or "Ain't I a Woman?" Truth delivered her remarks at the Ohio Woman's Rights Convention in Akron in 1851. Among several near-contemporary sources referencing the speech, the most complete appeared in Marius Robinson's *Anti-Slavery Bugle* on June 21, 1851, with a full, though perhaps not precisely verbatim transcription. The best-known and most influential version of Truth's speech, however, was not printed until twelve years later in 1863 in the New York *Independent* by Frances Dana Gage.[57]

There are significant differences between Robinson's and Gage's versions of Truth's speech. The former begins, "I want to say a few words about this matter. I am a woman's rights."[58] However, nowhere does Robinson record Truth as saying "Ar'n't [or Aren't or Ain't] I a woman?" Gage, on the other hand, whose piece was written throughout for maximum rhetorical and emotional effect, has Truth repeat "Ar'n't I a woman?" four times.[59] Furthermore, Robinson's version of the speech was printed in standard English spelling. However, Gage, who had presided over the meeting at which Truth spoke, published her version in the stereotypical, southern-inflected dialect spelling that was frequently used to represent the speech of enslaved people and uneducated African Americans. Truth's own natural dialect was much more likely to be akin to that of the Dutch-influenced English of the Hudson Valley. Though many scholars now believe that Robinson's may be closer to Truth's actual delivery, it was Gage's version that reached the largest audience and became the "canonical" version of the speech for more than one hundred years.[60]

In August 1852 Truth attended an antislavery convention in Salem, Ohio, at which Frederick Douglass was a featured speaker. Douglass had begun to doubt that slavery could be abolished by nonviolent means, thus placing him in opposition to his earlier Garrisonian insistence on nonviolent "moral suasion." As the *Pennsylvania Freeman* reported, when Douglass exclaimed "What is the use of Moral Suasion to a people thus trampled in the dust?," the voice of Sojourner Truth was heard in response: "Is God gone?"[61] In 1863, the *Atlantic Monthly* published an article by Harriet Beecher Stowe titled "Sojourner Truth, the Libyan Sibyl." This article presents somewhat mythologized portrayals of both Truth and this particular incident. Stowe, citing Wendell Phillips as her source, relocates the event to Boston's iconic Faneuil Hall, quotes Truth as saying "Frederick, is God dead?" and includes a number of additional inaccuracies. Reaching the large audience that it did, Stowe's portrait of Sojourner Truth too became "canonical." Sojourner Truth was thenceforth regularly identified as "the Libyan Sibyl" well into the twentieth century, and Stowe's version of Truth's rebuke of Douglass was frequently repeated throughout the nineteenth.

In 1856 Truth moved to Battle Creek, Michigan, to be near her daughters and other friends. For a time she lived in the nearby utopian community of Harmonia. During the war, in 1864, she went to Washington, D.C., to work with the National Freedman's Relief Association. On October 29, 1864, she met with President Lincoln, of whom she reported, "I never was treated by any one with more kindness and cordiality than were shown to me by that great and good man, Abraham Lincoln."[62]

One of the things that everyone who knew her or heard her speak agreed on is that Sojourner Truth was a powerful, effective, and charismatic speaker, couching her words in both humor and moral certainty. Her deep, determined voice, her wit, and her willingness to turn to the courts for aid all stood her in good stead, not only on the speaker's platform but on the Washington streetcars as well.[63] During 1865 Truth worked at the Freedmen's Hospital, a position that often required her to move about the city to procure supplies for the sick. The "Book of Life" appended to her *Narrative*, edited by Francis Titus in 1875, includes anecdotes about four times Truth was harassed on the streetcars. She also successfully complained to the president of the railroad about eliminating the designated Jim Crow cars before the streetcars were desegregated by federal mandate in March 1865. The new law, however, was often ignored, and the cars did not always stop for Black passengers or treat them well when they managed to board.

Truth was ready and willing to invoke the law whenever she was challenged on a streetcar. The mere hint of that threat sometimes proved successful in and of itself. On one occasion, after her signal to stop was ignored by a streetcar and then by a second one, Truth gave "three tremendous yelps":

> "I want to ride! I want to ride!! I WANT TO RIDE!!!" Consternation seized the passing crowd—people, carriages, go-carts of every description stood still. The car was effectually blocked up, and before it could move on, Sojourner had jumped aboard. Then there arose a great shout from the crowd, "Ha ha! ha!! She has beaten him," &c. The angry conductor told her to go forward where the horses were, or he would put her out. Quietly seating herself, she informed him that she was a passenger. "Go forward where the horses are, or I will throw you out," said he in a menacing voice. She told him that she was neither a Marylander nor a Virginian to fear his threats; but was from the Empire State of New York, and knew the laws as well as he did.

Several soldiers were in the car, and when other passengers came in, they related the circumstance and said, "You ought to have heard that old woman talk to the conductor." Sojourner rode farther than she needed to go; for a ride was so rare a privilege that she determined to make the most of it. She left the car feeling very happy, and said, "Bless God! I have had a ride."

Another time, after being passed by a car, Truth ran after it and boarded at its next stop, telling the conductor, "It is a shame to make a lady run so." When he threatened to throw her off if she said another word, her undaunted response again implied legal consequences: "If you attempt that, it will cost you more than your car and horses are worth." The incident was resolved when a gentleman "wearing a general's uniform" intervened on her behalf.[64]

Nell Painter relates yet another incident in which Truth attempted to enter a streetcar behind her friend Josephine Griffing. The conductor would not wait for her but signaled the driver to start. Truth was dragged for several yards. She and Griffing then brought the case to the attention of the company president, and the offending conductor was fired.[65]

Laura Smith Haviland was a white abolitionist appointed as inspector of hospitals for the Freedmen's Bureau in 1865. One day after she and Truth were tired from walking around the city, Haviland proposed that they take a streetcar. She hailed a car and boarded. According to the account given in the "Book of Life," Truth adopted a deceptive ploy to get on as well:

> "As Mrs. Haviland signaled the car," says Sojourner, "I stepped one side as if to continue my walk and when it stopped I ran and jumped aboard. The conductor pushed me back, saying, 'Get out of the way and let this lady come in.' Whoop! said I, I am a lady too. We met with no further opposition till we were obliged to change cars. A man coming out as we were going into the next car, asked the conductor if 'niggers were allowed to ride.' The conductor grabbed me by the shoulder and jerking me around, ordered me to get out. I told him I would not. Mrs. Haviland took hold of my other arm and said, 'Don't put her out.' The conductor asked if I belonged to her. 'No,' replied Mrs. Haviland, 'She belongs to humanity.' 'Then take her and go,' said he, and giving me another push slammed me against the door. I told him I would let him know whether he could shove me about like a dog, and said to Mrs. Haviland, Take the number of this car.
>
> "At this, the man looked alarmed, and gave us no more trouble. When we arrived at the hospital, the surgeons were called in to examine my shoulder and found that a bone was misplaced. I complained to the president of the road, who advised me to arrest the man for assault and battery."[66]

Truth took his advice, and the conductor was both convicted and lost his job. The case, she says, "created a great sensation," and she takes some delight in her significant role in bringing about the integration of the Washington cars: "It caused a great sensation, and before the trial was ended, the inside of the cars looked like pepper and salt. . . . A little circumstance will show how great a change a few weeks had produced: A lady saw some colored women looking wistfully toward a car, when the conductor, halting, said, 'Walk in, ladies.' Now they who had so lately cursed me for wanting to ride, could stop for black as well as white, and could even condescend to say, 'Walk in, ladies.'"[67]

After finishing her work in Washington, Truth returned to Battle Creek in 1867. She continued lecturing, and in 1870 she began collecting signatures for a petition, printed and circulated at her own expense, to be delivered to both the U.S. Senate and the House of Representatives. Recognizing the plight of many former slaves, especially the large number in the Washington area dependent on government support, the petition stated: "We, the undersigned, . . . earnestly request your Honorable Body to set apart for them a portion of the Public Land in the West, and erect Buildings thereon for the aged and infirm, and otherwise so legislate as to secure the desired results."[68] This petition ultimately proved unsuccessful.

In 1872, the same year that Susan B. Anthony was arrested for voting in Rochester, New York, Truth attempted to register to vote in Battle Creek. As a woman, especially a Black woman, she was refused. Nevertheless, on election day she showed up at the polls and asserted her right to vote, and, not surprisingly, she was again denied. The *Battle Creek Journal* stated at the time, "She was politely received by the authorities in both instances, but did not succeed in her effort, though she sustained her claim by many original and quaintly put arguments."[69]

Sojourner Truth retired from her travels in 1879 and died at her home on November 26, 1883. The following day, the *New York Times* printed a brief obituary, drawn as much from the legend of Sojourner Truth as from the facts of her life. Among other inaccuracies, it stated that she died at the age of 103. Truth herself might have enjoyed this bit of hyperbole. In 1867, addressing the American Woman Suffrage Association, she claimed, "I am above eighty years old; it is about time for me to be going. I have been forty years a slave and forty years free, and would be here forty years more to have equal rights for all."[70]

Mrs. Derry, April 1865

Philadelphia grand juries regularly declined to indict streetcar conductors on criminal charges, as in the case of Miles Robinson and his friends. However, as historian Philip S. Foner notes, there was somewhat better success with regard to a civil charge in which no grand jury was required.[71] At eleven o'clock on an April night in 1865, Mrs. Derry, whose first name is not known but who is described in contemporary records as "a very respectable woman, almost white" and as "a mulatto woman," boarded a streetcar on the Lombard and South Streets Railway in Philadelphia.[72] She was returning home from a church, where she, "with others of her race," had been attending to wounded soldiers. The description of the ensuing incident in the records of the Philadelphia Court of Common Pleas strongly suggests that the conductor's behavior in forcing her from the car was driven not simply by his wish to adhere to a company rule, but by a considerable racial animus, as well:

> After she had been seated for a few minutes, the conductor came in and told her she must get out; that no niggers were allowed to ride on that line. Mrs. Derry pleaded the lateness of the hour; that there were only two or three passengers in the car, none of whom had objected, and finally asserted her right to remain. The conductor, thereupon, called in the aid of two friends standing upon a street corner, took off his coat, seized hold of her, struck, kicked, and finally ejected her from the car with great violence, tearing her clothes and inflicting some personal injuries.

Lowry, the conductor, as we often find in these cases, claimed that he "only used force when rendered necessary by her resistance." The court record adds a telling qualification: "It appeared, however, from the testimony of officer Somers that the defendant admitted that he did kick 'the Nigger.'"[73]

We might also note a point of disagreement in surviving accounts of the affair. Where the court record says that Mrs. Derry claimed that no passenger objected to her presence, the newspaper account in the *Inquirer* states that Lowry "requested her to leave the car" after a passenger called his attention "to the fact that plaintiff, whose complexion is quite light, was in the car, by the question whether 'colored people were allowed to ride on that line?'"[74] However Lowry knew, recognized, or assumed that Mrs. Derry was "colored," it is striking that he had the car drive on to where he could get two friends to help him eject an elderly woman in the middle of the night.

In charging the jury, Judge Allison pointed out that, in fact, there was no regulation barring Black passengers from the Lombard and South Streets Railway and that "the attempt to set up the existence of such a rule enacted by the directors of the company, utterly failed." He went on to stress that even if there were such a rule, it would not serve "as a justification for the wrong complained of in the plaintiff's declaration."[75] Ultimately, the judge left little doubt as to where he stood on the whole question:

> The argument which is used as a justification for the exclusion of people of color from the cars . . . rests not on any principle of legal or moral right, but upon bald, naked prejudice alone. It is our duty, gentlemen, in the discharge of our duties, you in your sphere and I in mine, to cast aside all prejudice, that the law may vindicate its just claim to strict and impartial justice. And if, by the action of courts and juries, wrong has been done to the class of citizens to which the plaintiff belongs, it is time that such errors should be corrected.

He further charged the jury that "the instruction of a principal to a subordinate to do an illegal act, such as to commit an assault and battery upon the person of a citizen, was no justification of the subordinate for so doing; that such a plea could not shield the conductor of a car from his accountability before the law, to the person injured."[76] In other words, "I was just following orders" is no excuse.

The jury found in favor of Mrs. Derry, and the judge awarded her fifty dollars in punitive damages. The campaign for the right of Philadelphia's citizens of color to ride the cars without prejudice, however, was not yet over.

A "Colored Man," May 17, 1865

Mrs. Derry's victory in court in April 1865 may have affirmed the right of Black Philadelphians to ride the cars, but, as in the past, Judge Allison's ruling did little to ease their experience on the cars. Commenting on an editorial that appeared on May 10 in the Philadelphia *Evening Bulletin*, one of only two city papers to offer any opinion on the streetcar companies' policies, Philip Foner aptly summarizes, "In the battle against streetcar segregation, optimistic predictions invariably proved to be wrong, and the *Bulletin*'s conclusion, that conductors would now think twice about ejecting colored passengers, was no exception."[77] Indeed, a month or less after the conviction of Conductor Lowry, a conductor took a new approach precisely because of the jury's verdict and Judge Allison's imposition of a fine on the conductor. Rather than suffer Lowry's fate, on the one hand, or abandon the dictates of both his employer and his own personal prejudice by failing to expel a passenger, on the other, he tried out a new tactic to skirt the law, as reported in the *New York Times*:

> **THE RIGHTS OF COLORED CITIZENS.**
>
> **Curious Affair in Philadelphia.**
>
> Philadelphia, Wednesday, May 17–2 p.m.
>
> Last evening a colored man got into a Pine-street passenger car, and refused all entreaties to leave the car, where his presence appeared to be not desired.

> The conductor of the car, fearful of being fined for ejecting him, as was done by the Judges of one of our courts in a similar case, ran the car off the track, detached the horses, and left the colored man to occupy the car all by himself.
>
> The colored man still maintains his position in the car, having spent the whole of the night there.
>
> The conductor looks upon the part he enacted in the affair as a splendid piece of strategy.
>
> The matter creates quite a sensation in the neighborhood where the car is standing, and crowds of sympathizers flock around the colored man.[78]

A facetious poem printed in the *Philadelphia Inquirer* on June 3 refers to Mrs. Derry's victory as "The late decision of the Judge / (Which railroad men think utter fudge)," and it notes: "The colored person kept his seat, / And black folks brought him things to eat."[79] The *Times* and the *Inquirer* treat the incident with some amusement, but the derailing stratagem must have been thought effective by other conductors and street rowdies, for it was resorted to on numerous occasions in Philadelphia, as in the case of Miles Robinson a year and a half later.

Harriet Tubman, October 1865

Harriet Tubman is one of the most storied African Americans in U.S. history. Born into slavery in Dorchester County on Maryland's Eastern Shore in 1822, she was the fifth of the nine children of Benjamin Ross and Harriet Green, who was known as Rit. Tubman was originally named Araminta and was called "Minty," which is the name used in the reward notice published after her initial attempt to escape. As a child she was hired out to do household work, and she later worked as a field hand. Following her father's craft, she labored for a while on timber gangs that supplied the Baltimore shipyards with lumber. This experience not only gave her great physical strength, it also provided her with some knowledge of the world beyond the Eastern Shore, and more importantly it brought her into contact with the networks of Black and white sympathizers who stealthily assisted runaway slaves on land and by boat. Some of these may even have helped Frederick Douglass to escape from the same region in 1838.[80]

When she was about twelve or thirteen, Harriet refused to help an overseer tie up a disobedient slave to be whipped. When the slave bolted, the overseer threw a two-pound weight at the man, but he missed and hit Harriet in the head. The injury from that blow caused her to suffer throughout her life from periods of sudden, uncontrollable bouts of sleep, probably a symp-

Harriet Tubman. Carte de visite, circa 1868. Library of Congress.

tom of temporal lobe epilepsy. These seizures became a source of visions and inspiration that guided her in her later rescue missions.[81] Between the ages of seventeen and twenty-two, Harriett lived with her parents and siblings in a cabin on ten acres of land her father was given when he was manumitted around 1840.[82] At about that time, Ben Ross bought his wife's freedom but was unable to buy that of their children. In 1844 Harriett married John Tubman, who was free, and adopted her mother's first name as her own.

Between 1825 and 1840, three of Tubman's sisters—Mariah, Linah, and Soph—had been sold away from the family. Fearing the same fate when their master, Edward Brodess, died in 1849, Tubman and two of her brothers, Henry and Benjamin, decided to emancipate themselves. They left on September 17 and remained at large for two weeks, as evidenced by the $300 reward for their capture that Edward's wife Eliza advertised on October 3. Tubman's brothers, however, became fearful of the consequences of failure, and they returned, bringing their sister back with them. Undaunted, Tubman struck out on her own very soon afterward.[83] With the help of friends and Underground Railroad agents, she made her way through Maryland and Delaware and finally to Philadelphia. There she found domestic work in private homes, hotels, and guest houses, and similar work during the summers at Cape May, New Jersey.[84]

Being free herself, however, was insufficient for Tubman; she was determined to liberate as many members of her family as she could. In 1850 she traveled to Baltimore and rescued her niece and her niece's two children right from under the auctioneer's gavel. The following year she returned to Dorchester County to convince her husband to join her, but, on discovering that he had remarried, she took others with her and continued her rescue work alone. The Fugitive Slave Act of 1850 made life in the North very precarious for any escaped slave, so Tubman settled in St. Catharines, Ontario.

Altogether Tubman made about thirteen trips back to Maryland to lead her family and friends to freedom, often traveling in disguise as an elderly woman or man and in the dead of night with the North Star as her guide. Tubman's father, Ben Ross, had been given his freedom in 1840, but in early 1857 he was about to be arrested under suspicion of assisting runaway slaves (which he indeed had done). Tubman returned again and fled with her parents, now in their seventies, by means of a rudimentary, jerry-rigged, two-wheeled wagon to Wilmington, Delaware. From there the Quaker abolitionist Thomas Garrett sent them on to William Still in Philadelphia. A few weeks later Ben and Rit were able to join their sons William and John and several grandchildren and great-grandchildren in St. Catharines.[85] Among the many formerly enslaved people there, and eventually among northern abolitionists more generally, Tubman became known as "the Moses of her people."[86] In Canada she met up with the abolitionist John Brown and helped to recruit others to his cause. However, she herself did not take part in his famous ill-fated raid on the armory in Harpers Ferry, West Virginia, in October 1859.[87]

The exact number of people whom Tubman led North is unknown, but it is likely that she directly liberated seventy or eighty people and helped perhaps fifty more to escape by giving them instructions. Her bravery, ingenuity, and skill cannot be doubted, and she was fond of saying that she never lost a "passenger" on the Underground Railroad, through which she connected people to northern abolitionists and organizations that could help them find homes, support, and work in safety.

The strategic and tactical skills that Tubman developed on her journeys between 1849 and 1860 proved valuable during the Civil War. Her reputation accompanied her into the ranks of the army, where she was often referred to by the sobriquet "Moses." From 1862 to 1865 she worked as a nurse, cook, and laundress tending to Union troops in Hilton Head, South Carolina, during which time she also served as a scout or spy, slipping behind Confederate lines and collecting from slaves information about troop positions, supply depots, et cetera. In June 1863 she was one of the leaders of a military expedition up the Combahee River to rout the enemy and destroy crops and supplies. During this foray, they freed about seven hundred slaves, who were conveyed down the river by boat. Harriet Tubman thus became the first woman to lead a U.S. military operation.

Tubman spent the latter half of 1864 in New York City, in Auburn, New York, and in Boston, where she met Sojourner Truth. Though she planned to return to Hilton Head to take up a teaching position, she was convinced to go instead to the army hospital at Fort Monroe in Hampton, Virginia, in early April 1865 to care for sick and wounded Black soldiers. On April 9 Lee surrendered, and the war was over. On April 15 Lincoln was assassinated, and in a separate attack that same night, William Seward, the U.S. secretary of state, was severely wounded. After a few months at Fort Monroe, frustrated by a long-standing lack of adequate pay for many of her services, Tubman decided to return to Auburn, where she could work to support her family and repay her debt to Seward, who in 1859 had sold her the seven-acre farm in Auburn where she had built a home for her parents.

During her surreptitious career freeing slaves from Maryland, Tubman often traveled by train and certainly must have ridden in Jim Crow cars to remain inconspicuous. During the war, however, she was on numerous occasions granted a pass to travel freely at government expense. In the middle of October 1865, traveling on her hospital nurse's pass with a half-fare ticket, Tubman boarded a train from Philadelphia to New York on the Camden & South Amboy line. When the conductor came to take her ticket, he ordered her into the smoking car, saying, "Come, hustle out of here! We don't carry niggers for half fare."[88] When Tubman explained that she was a government employee and entitled to travel just as soldiers were, the conductor grabbed her by the arm and attempted to remove her from her seat. She proved stronger than he might have expected, and he called three men to help him. As she held on tightly, they forcibly wrenched her arm, breaking it. She received further injury to her shoulder and ribs when she was roughly thrown into the other car. No passengers came to her aid, although some yelled insults and shouted that she should be thrown off the train altogether. According to her friend, Martha Coffin Wright, to whom she related the incident just a few days later, Tubman called the conductor "a copperhead scoundrel, for which he choked her. . . . She told him she didn't thank anybody to call her colored person—She would be black or Negro—she was as proud of being a black woman as he was of being white."[89] (By "copperhead," Tubman was accusing the conductor of being a southern sympathizer, using a term of derision that had developed for northern Democrats opposed to the war.)

On reaching New York City, a young white man who had witnessed the incident gave Tubman his card and suggested that she should sue the railroad and that she could call on him as a witness. Tubman was treated briefly in the city before traveling on to Auburn, where she spent a difficult winter recuperating from her injuries. Martha and David Wright and others also encouraged her to sue. However, the card the young man had given her was only his visiting card and did not have his address on it. When newspaper advertisements failed to get a response from him, Tubman did not pursue the case, even though the doctor who had treated her was willing to testify on her behalf.[90]

Tubman's husband John died in Auburn in 1867. Harriet continued to struggle on the edge of poverty, and in 1869 Sarah H. Bradford wrote a short biography, *Scenes in the Life of Harriet Tubman*, with the purpose of supplying Tubman with some income. Tubman married Nelson Davis, a former soldier, in 1869, and together they ran the farm and started a brick-making business. When Bradford published a revision of her biography as *Harriet Tubman, the Moses of Her People* in 1886, Tubman reentered public life, becoming particularly active in the movement for women's suffrage, a role for which she has only recently come to be widely recognized.[91] A passage from the *Auburn Morning Dispatch*, reporting on a meeting of suffragists there in 1888, gives a clear sense of the impact Tubman could have on an audience. The newspaper quoted Tubman telling the suffragists of the "brave and fearless deeds of women who sacrificed all for their country and moved in battle when bullets mowed down men." Tubman added, the paper said, "[They] were on the scene to administer to the injured, to bind up their wounds and tend them through weary months of suffering in the army hospitals. If those deeds do not place woman as man's equal, what do?"[92]

As early as 1865, Tubman had approached Seward for his help in receiving a government pension, not only for her service as a nurse but also for her work as a scout and a spy. Her claim came to naught, and in 1887 she unsuccessfully petitioned Congress to reopen her file. Soon after Nelson Davis died in 1888, Tubman applied for a widow's pension. It wasn't until 1899, when she was seventy-seven, that she was awarded a "compromise" pension of $20 a month—$8 as Davis's widow and $12 as a nurse, but with no recognition of her service as a scout and spy.[93]

Tubman had a dream of establishing a home for elderly African Americans. With financial help and a mortgage, she added twenty-five acres to her farm in 1896, but was left with no money to proceed with her plan. Rather, she took many people into her own home. In 1903 she transferred the property to the AME Church, and eventually in 1908 the Harriet Tubman Home for Aged and Infirm Negroes was officially opened. A resident of the nursing home that bore her name, Tubman died in August 1913 at the age of ninety-one.

George Moses Horton, "Forbidden to Ride on the Street Cars," November 10, 1866

The poem "Forbidden to Ride on the Street Cars" was written by George Moses Horton, who was born into slavery in North Carolina around 1797. In his youth he composed poetry in his head, and on weekends he walked to Chapel Hill to sell fruit and recite his poems to University of North Carolina students, who would pay him twenty-five to seventy-five cents to compose love poems and acrostics for their sweethearts. In his thirties he taught himself to read, and he developed a large vocabulary by reading the Bible, Charles Wesley's hymnal, and books that he got from students.

Several of Horton's poems were published in 1828 in the *Lancaster* (Mass.) *Gazette*, in New York in *Freedom's Journal*, and in the *Raleigh Register*, and the following year he published twenty-one poems in *The Hope of Liberty*, his first book. During the Civil War he served as an aide to William H. S. Banks, a young Union captain from Michigan, who in 1865 got ninety new poems by Horton published in Raleigh under the title *Naked Genius*. Abandoned by Banks, Horton went to Philadelphia, where he was interviewed as "a poet of considerable genius" in the summer of 1866. Later that year the *Christian Recorder*, the newspaper of the AME, published "Forbidden to Ride on the Street Cars." Nothing certain is known of Horton after 1866, though he may have died in Philadelphia in 1883.[94]

Forbidden to Ride on the Street Cars

The writer, widely known as "The Slave Poet," recently saw a colored person enter a Philadelphia passenger railway car, which had stopped for a passenger, but the conductor immediately compelled her to leave. The following lines were suggested.—Ed.

Why wilt thou from the right revolt?
I wish to ride not far;
Why wilt thou fear the mild result,
Nor bid the humble horses halt,
But spurn me from the car?

And though I wish to travel fleet,
Regardless of a jar,

A short mile's journey to complete,
I dare not ride along the street,
Within a rattling car.

What retribution wilt thou meet,
When summon'd to the bar!
Wilt thou not from the call retreat?
Leave not the traveller on his feet,
Alone to watch the car.

Like thee, we bravely fought our way,
Before the shafts of war;
Lest thou shouldst fall the rebels' prey;
Why canst thou not a moment stay,
And take one on the car?

E'er long, we trust, the time will come,
We'll ride, however far;
And all ride on together home,
When freedom will be in full bloom,
Regardless of the car!

Philadelphia, *Christian Recorder*,
November 10, 1866

Emma and Miles Robinson, Fall 1866

In late 1866, Miles Robinson once again incurred the wrath of a Philadelphia streetcar conductor, as he had in the spring of 1865, and again inclement weather played a role. On their way to their home on South Twelfth Street one bitterly cold night, with deep snow on the streets, Robinson and his wife decided they should take a streetcar. As William Still relates the event, Robinson had his wife, who had a light complexion, get on the car at Third and Pine Streets, while he went ahead to board at Fourth and Pine and take a seat. This stratagem reveals that, as previously, Robinson was aware that his presence on the car might cause trouble. True to form, the conductor "straightway ordered him out, on the plea of color," on which Robinson replied: "How is this, my wife is in the car." The conductor grew angry but did not try to force Robinson out physically. Still explains, "A late decision in court had taught the police that they had no right to interfere, except in cases where the peace was actually being broken."[95] This is very likely a reference to the judgment that Judge Allison delivered in the case of Mrs. Derry.

To resolve his dilemma, the conductor resorted to the same ploy that had been used, perhaps for the first time, a year and a half earlier in May 1865, in response to the *Derry* decision. He ran the car completely off the track, "then hoisted all the windows, took out the cushions, and unhitched the horses." In doing so he was relying on the same double-edged logic as had the conductor who left a man to sit in a cold, empty, derailed car overnight and well into the next day. On the one hand, the reasoning goes, no judge could convict him if he did not use violence to throw Robinson off, and on the other hand, the company would not fire him for refusing to proceed with Black passengers. Still adds that, along with the two Robinsons, "another colored gentleman, who got on with Miles," also remained in the derailed car. The white passengers remained in the car "for a length of time, until they had sufficiently borne their testimony," before getting out to catch the next car that came along, leaving the three to make their statement alone, before a cold walk home in the snow.[96]

A somewhat different account of this incident was recorded in the *National Anti-Slavery Standard* and is summarized by Philip Foner.[97] The *Standard* version states that the Robinsons had a small child with them, a fact that, of course, would influence their decision to take a streetcar rather than walk all the way home in the cold and snow. The Robinsons' first child, Leonard, would have been between fifteen and twenty-six months old at the time of this incident. According to the *Standard*, the Robinsons boarded the car together and took seats, without an immediate objection from the conductor. The conductor later explained that he did not notice that Robinson's wife was darker than her husband until he went to collect their fares. Thus, it was Emma, not Miles, whom he initially identified as Black. The *Standard* makes no mention of an additional "colored gentleman," whereas Still says nothing about a child.

Robinson was a successful businessman, but the Philadelphia racism proved too overt and too evocative of his time enslaved. He sold their house and returned with his family to Chelsea, Massachusetts. In closing his account of Robinson, Still notes, "Instead of seeking pleasure in the banjo, as he was wont to do in Virginia, he now delights in the Baptist Church, Rev. Mr. Grimes', and in other fields of usefulness tending to elevate and better the condition of society generally."[98]

Octavius Catto and the Philadelphia Streetcar Campaign, 1865–1867

Octavius Valentine Catto was born in 1839 into a free Black family in Charleston, South Carolina, the third child of William Catto, a machinist, and his

Octavius V. Catto, circa 1871. National Portrait Gallery, Smithsonian Institution.

wife Sarah. Octavius's mother died in 1845, and his father soon remarried and moved the family north. William Catto became a Presbyterian minister and eventually settled in Philadelphia, where he became minister of the First African Presbyterian Church.[99]

Education was important to William, and his children attended public schools in Philadelphia. In his teenage years Octavius attended the Quaker-supported Institute for Colored Youth. The emphasis at the ICY was rigorously academic, including Spanish, Latin, Greek, Composition, History, Geometry, Plane and Spherical Trigonometry, and Natural Philosophy. Octavius Catto was an enthusiastic scholar, and even after graduating as valedictorian in 1858 he continued to receive tutoring in Latin and Greek.[100]

On graduating, Catto joined the prestigious Banneker Literary Institute. He became secretary of the organization and was soon delivering lectures on a variety of topics, through which he began to gain a reputation as a skilled orator. In January 1859, a month before his twentieth birthday, he was offered a position at ICY, teaching English and mathematics.[101]

When the Civil War began in April 1861, thousands of Black men served in support roles such as laborers and wagon drivers, but in spite of the need for increasing numbers of troops, neither civil nor military authorities could see their way to enlisting Black men as armed soldiers. In 1863, however, in the face of massive Union losses, President Lincoln finally approved the use of Black troops. On May 28 the first Black unit, the Fifty-Fourth Massachusetts Volunteer Infantry Regiment, under the command of white officers, was cheered as they left Boston on their way to their brave but disastrous assault on Fort Wagner, South Carolina.

That June the Confederate army was moving into Pennsylvania, and the governor put out a call for additional troops to defend the state. Posters calling for "Men of Color" to "Come Forward!" began to appear on walls and fences in Philadelphia. Eager to join, Catto and his friends took a company of ninety men to Harrisburg, but they were rejected and sent back to Philadelphia.[102]

The very day after Catto's return from Harrisburg, Lincoln's secretary of war, Edwin Stanton, gave permission and laid out the rules for recruiting three regiments of Black troops in Philadelphia. A rally was organized to encourage Black men to enlist, and Catto's name appeared at the head of the list of names on the broadside advertising the meeting. Soon a number of the earlier company had joined the Third Regiment of U.S. Colored Infantry, though not Catto.[103]

Black Philadelphians were soon bravely sacrificing their lives in battle, but race relations in the city did not improve. In July 1864, while carrying his two-year-old son, who had been suddenly taken ill, the Rev. William Alston was denied access to an empty streetcar. He sent a moving account to the *Philadelphia Press*, and the streetcar campaign took on new life. Broadsides again appeared, this time addressing "Colored citizens" and calling them to "attend a public meeting . . . to give an expression touching our exclusion from the city passenger cars." Both William and Octavius Catto were among the signatories.[104] As the war ground on, the response to the continuing discrimination at home began to change, especially among the younger generation, many of whom were risking and often losing their lives in the war. They saw the strategies of William Still and other older Black leaders as too timid or accommodating. Rather than appeal on behalf of "genteel" and "respectable" Black passengers, they insisted on the rights of the Black soldiers who fought for a country that continued to mistreat them, soldiers who were wounded, lying in hospitals where their relatives could not reach them. This new generation brought their complaints not to the railroad executives but instead directly to the state legislature.[105]

The Pennsylvania Equal Rights League was formed in January 1865, and the next month Catto headed to Harrisburg for its three-day conference. High on the list of the league's key agenda items were the right to vote and the right to ride in the cars. Catto gained notice with his careful rhetoric in couching a resolution recommending that Black students would be better served if they had Black teachers—not because of their color per se but instead because Black teachers better understood their students' lives outside the classroom. He was elected as a conference secretary and was chosen as chair of the publication committee to write up the conference proceedings. One of the persistent motifs woven throughout the fifty-seven-page report is aptly represented by a statement by Catto's fellow committee member and friend Alfred M. Green, the Philadelphia activist and soldier: "We ask that when the colored man returns from the field of battle, he will not be turned from your ballot box, your railroad cars, your hotels and schools, thereby renewing in the bosom of his white fellow soldier who has fought side by side with him, all the old prejudices which existed before the war."[106]

Following this convention, Catto spent much of his time traveling throughout Pennsylvania getting support for the Equal Rights League and encouraging people to start affiliated chapters in towns both large and small.

In 1861 the abolitionist Republican state senator Morrow Lowry had proposed a bill that stated, "It shall not be lawful for any passenger railway company, within this Commonwealth, to make or enforce any rule, regulation or practice, excluding any race of people from its passenger cars on account of color." The bill failed to pass. He presented it again in 1865, arguing so forcefully that it did pass in the senate, but it was blocked in the lower house. Especially after the disappointing outcome of such cases as that of Miles Robinson in late 1866, hope that they would ever be allowed to ride in the cars was fading among the Black citizens of Philadelphia.[107]

In early 1867 the Pennsylvania Equal Rights League, the Colored People's Union League, and the Social, Civil and Statistical Association renewed their efforts to lobby the state legislature. Octavius Catto, William Forten, and David Bowser, the Car Committee of the Equal Rights League, took it upon themselves to revise and strengthen the wording of Lowry's bill. They specified that corporations should be subject to a $500 payment for each person excluded on account of color or race, and any employee of the company who excluded, assisted in excluding, or allowed such exclusion should be subject to a fine of not more than $500 and not less than $100.

For a third time, Senator Lowry presented his bill, arguing even more passionately: "Philadelphia stands disgraced before the world, for her conduct in attempting to block up the highway of the colored man in his great and unequal contest in the battles of life."[108] The bill passed the senate in February, and late at night on March 18, in spite of fierce opposition and parliamentary strategizing to prevent a vote, it passed the lower house and was then signed by the governor.[109] Black Philadelphians now had the right to sit in the cars, but would the law change the practice in the cars themselves? The crucial first test would come from none other than Caroline R. LeCount, a Philadelphia teacher and the fiancée of Octavius Catto.

After the adoption of the Fourteenth Amendment in 1868, granting citizenship to African Americans, the Equal Rights League and other organizations increased their efforts to achieve the right to vote, and Catto threw himself into the fray. The Fifteenth Amendment granting the right to vote to Black and white men (though not to women), was ratified on February 3, 1870. Exercising that right would prove problematic across the nation. As early as 4:00 a.m. on election day in 1870, Black men began lining up to vote when the polls opened at seven at the Lombard and South Street polling station. A riot broke out when the police arrived, pushing Black voters aside, beating and arresting them. U.S. marshals finally called in fifty marines. Four of the twenty-three men charged by federal authorities with violating the Fifteenth Amendment were Philadelphia policemen.[110]

Before the election of 1871, the Fifth Brigade (Colored) of the Pennsylvania National Guard at Camp Penn was formed under the command of Gen. Louis Wagner. Octavius Catto was invited to join as brigade inspector general and given the rank of major. Officers were issued Union blue uniforms but were required to supply their own sidearms.[111] One of the duties of the brigade was to help deal with any riots that might arise in Philadelphia, especially in Black neighborhoods. It seemed likely that might happen on election day, October 10, and, sure enough, rioting again broke out as it had the previous year, once again exacerbated by the police. But this time the trouble spread for several blocks in every direction. A Black waiter, Isaac Chase, ran home to protect his family. Just outside his door, as his eleven-year-old daughter watched, he was shot by a man named Frank Kelly, who wore a blue shirt and a badge, though he was not a policeman.

Catto was teaching at ICY that morning. As the troubles increased, he and the principal, Fanny Jackson (Coppin), closed the school for the afternoon and sent the students home. Catto received a message to be on duty with the Fifth Brigade at 6:00 p.m. to protect Black residents as evening fell. He went to a pawnshop and bought a pistol; he had ammunition at home. He then

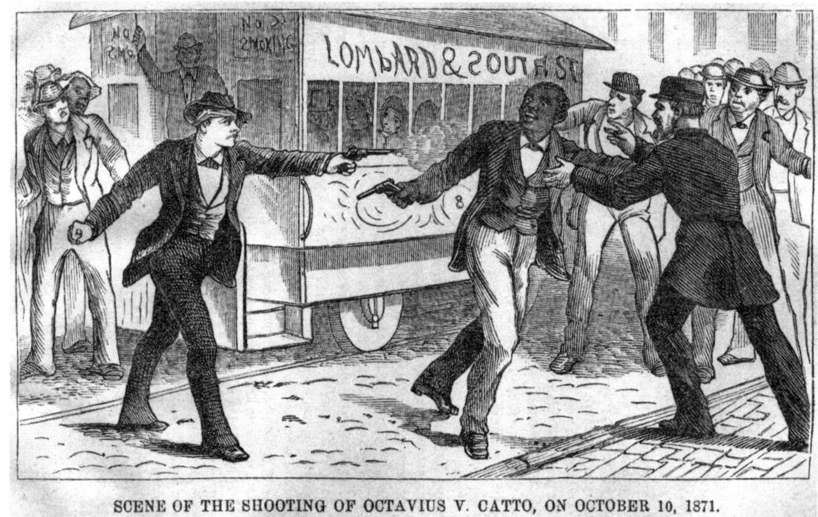

SCENE OF THE SHOOTING OF OCTAVIUS V. CATTO, ON OCTOBER 10, 1871.

The murder of Octavius Catto. From Henry H. Griffin, *The Trial of Frank Kelly*, 1877. Collection of the Historical Society of Pennsylvania.

walked down Lombard Street and over to South Street, where he lived, greeting several friends along the way. A white man passed Catto on the street, turned, crouched, pulled out a pistol, and shot him, as a neighbor yelled, "Look out for that man!" Catto ran behind a streetcar that had stopped. His assailant walked around the car, shot Catto three more times, calmly pocketed his pistol, and then ran off. Catto's biographers encapsulate the tragically ironic significance of the moment: "Five years before he had led the efforts to open up the streetcars. Now, as he lay bloodied in the middle of the tracks, Octavius Valentine Catto saw white and colored riders staring at him from a car."[112]

Because he had been on duty, Catto was accorded a full military funeral, the largest ever for a Black man in Philadelphia. Some five thousand people filed past to pay their respects as he lay in his dress uniform in the Broad Street Armory, and even more crowded the streets as the funeral procession of hundreds marched the three miles to Lebanon Cemetery. Mourners came from across the North, including Black leaders and ministers from New York, members of Congress from Washington, and state legislators from Harrisburg.

It was Frank Kelly who shot Catto. Kelly was immediately pursued and captured, but he escaped and disappeared. Five years later, in December 1876, he was captured in Chicago and returned to Philadelphia. The courtroom during his trial in late April 1877 was packed with observers both white and

Black, but the jury box held only twelve white men. After ten days and dozens of witnesses, Kelly was declared not guilty. In a shorter trial that summer he was also found not guilty of the murder of Isaac Chase.[113]

Mary Ellen Pleasant, Charlotte Brown, William Bowen, Emma Jane Turner, and the San Francisco Streetcars, 1863–1866

The facts of Mary Ellen Pleasant's life are obscured by clouds of myth, legend, gossip, and innuendo. She herself gave varying accounts of her origins and early life. She was born sometime between 1812 and 1817 in Virginia or in Philadelphia, or possibly as a slave in Georgia, where her mother was said to have been a Haitian voodoo queen. Her father may have been Asian, Native American, Kanaka (Hawaiian), or possibly a white slaveowner, John Hampden Pleasants, the son of a Virginia governor. As a girl and a young woman, Mary Ellen worked as a servant for a Quaker family on Nantucket Island, Massachusetts. After working for a while in Boston, she married a James Smith, who died in the 1840s, leaving her considerable wealth. She then married John James Pleasant (or Pleasants), formerly enslaved, a seaman and a ship's cook about whom numerous origin stories were also told, some of them well beyond belief. In one version he had been freed by the same John Hampden Pleasants. It might be nearest the truth for us to be content with the fact that Mary Ellen Pleasant constructed her own identity to suit her own purposes. She managed her money and her business relationships shrewdly and became a highly successful businesswoman.[114]

In the early 1850s, during the height of the California gold rush, the Pleasants sailed to San Francisco. Initially hiring herself out as a cook, Mary Ellen Pleasant soon established much-needed laundries in the city and later a number of boardinghouses. She diversified her investments wisely and profitably in real estate and a variety of small and large businesses and became well known among wealthy white and Black members of San Francisco society. She sheltered fugitive slaves, at times finding them positions as servants in white homes, an arrangement that provided her with a useful information network.

In 1858 Pleasant traveled with her husband to Chatham, Ontario, for a meeting of the abolitionist Chatham Vigilance Committee. There she met John Brown, to whom she gave an unknown but large sum of money to prepare for his ill-fated 1859 raid on the armory at Harpers Ferry. There is an unverified story that when Brown was captured he had a note in his pocket promising more money after "the first blow is struck," with a signature read as "W.E.P." In an interview published in 1903, Pleasant commented, somewhat

Mary Ellen Pleasant, 1857. Miriam Matthews Photograph Collection, UCLA Library Special Collections.

ambiguously, that she "had a quiet laugh . . . that my poor handwriting had given them a false trail."[115]

In the early 1860s, the rapidly growing city of San Francisco had three horse-drawn streetcar lines.[116] On March 14, 1863, the *Pacific Appeal* newspaper in San Francisco began an editorial, "Prejudice," decrying: "Two of our most respectable females were denied seats in one of the city railway cars on last Saturday." Such incidents rapidly became as problematic in San Francisco as they were at the same time in eastern cities like Philadelphia. The character of the struggle in San Francisco was largely made possible by an important legal development during that same month: African Americans in California finally won the right to testify in court.

The first person of color to take legal action against a San Francisco railway was Charlotte Brown, a schoolteacher and the daughter of a well-to-do Black businessman. After she was forcibly ejected from a horse-drawn car on the Omnibus Railroad Company line on April 17, 1863, Brown took advantage of the newly won access to the courts and sued the company for $200. In May, just a month after Brown's expulsion, William Bowen's leg was injured as he was thrown off a car, and he too took legal action.

In early June both Brown and Bowen won their cases, though Brown was awarded only $25. The *Sacramento Bee* reported, "The case will be appealed and carried, if necessary, to the Supreme Court, as the question is one of too much pecuniary importance to be allowed to stop here."[117] On appeal in county court on November 12, Brown won again, though the award was reduced to six cents, merely the cost of the fare. Meanwhile, in July, through her father, Brown had filed a civil suit against the company for $5,000, and Bowen sued for $10,000 in damages.[118] On December 21, 1864, a jury awarded Bowen the sum of $3,199.58.[119] Brown was awarded $500 in January 1865, and the company's request for a retrial was denied in mid-January 1866.[120]

In spite of these wins by Brown and Bowen and a ruling in November 1864 by district court Judge C. C. Pratt stating clearly that Blacks had the right to ride the city streetcars, passengers of color continued to be put off the cars or were simply ignored and passed by. Then in the autumn of 1866, a series of events followed one another in quick succession:

September 13—Emma Jane Turner stepped onto a car run by the North Beach and Mission Railway Company. She testified during trial that as she was holding the railing, "the conductor put his hand on her breast, . . . broke her hold on the car with his hand and pushed her off the car."[121]

September 27—Mary Ellen Pleasant, ticket in hand, hailed a North Beach and Mission car, but the driver refused to stop.

October 3—Emma Turner and Mary Pleasant each sued the North Beach and Mission Company for $5,000. In her complaint, Pleasant charged that "the agents and servants of defendant (NBMRR) acted under instructions received from said defendant requiring them to refuse to stop the cars of said defendant to allow 'colored people' or people of African Descent, to get on board."[122]

October 10—Pleasant was expelled from a car on the Omnibus line.

October 12—Pleasant sued Omnibus for $5,000.

October 17—Pleasant withdrew her suit against Omnibus, as reported in the *Daily Alta California*:

DISMISSED—Mrs. Mary E. Pleasants, a woman of color, having complained of the driver of car No. 6 on the Omnibus Railroad Company's line, for putting her off the car, appeared yesterday in the Police Court and withdrew the charge, stating as a reason for doing so that she had been informed by the agents of the Company that negroes would hereafter be allowed to ride on the cars, let the effect on the Company's business be what it might.[123]

Whether Pleasant had negotiated with the company behind the scenes or Omnibus saw the handwriting on the wall and changed its policy independently is not known. Certainly Pleasant could consider this as a victory as she awaited the outcome of her suit against North Beach and Mission. It may be, of course, that she had simply overextended herself or her resources and thus canceled the less promising suit.

There were only three passengers, all white, on the North Beach and Mission car that Pleasant hailed. One of them was a wealthy society matron, Lisette Woodworth, in whose home Pleasant had formerly worked and lived. Woodworth testified on Pleasant's behalf that she was on that streetcar and that the two of them had planned for Pleasant to join her at the Folsom Street stop. When the car did not stop, Woodworth challenged the driver and told him, "I want her to get in." When he replied, "We don't take colored people in the cars," Woodworth told him to stop so that she could get off. During her testimony, in order to convey her long relationship and familiarity with Pleasant, Woodworth also stated that she ordinarily addressed Pleasant as "Mamma." The press and San Francisco white society at large seized upon this term, transmuting it into "Mammy," with its long-standing racial overtones, thereby identifying Pleasant as a Black woman and a servant, rather than as the increasingly influential businesswoman and activist that she was.[124]

The presence of Lisette Woodworth on that streetcar was not a coincidence. The fact that Pleasant and Woodworth had arranged to meet there raises an interesting question. Might Pleasant, already known for her efforts on behalf of the Black community, have intentionally orchestrated the incident—including the presence of an unimpeachable white witness—as a test of the legality of the company's practice and the strength of the law as it had been articulated two years earlier by Judge Pratt? Charlotte Brown's suit had been successfully concluded the previous January, yet streetcar discrimination had continued. The fact that Pleasant undertook to sue for significant damages when she never even set foot on the car may indeed show that her purpose was not personal but rather to oppose the endemic racism endured by all Black San Franciscans.

In February 1867, a jury awarded Emma Turner $750. Pleasant's suit against the North Beach and Mission Railway was also initially successful, and Judge Pratt awarded her $500. On appeal, both cases were referred to the

California Supreme Court, which ruled that the awards had been excessive.[125] The court declared that Turner had not "suffered any appreciable damage in her person or estate" and that there was no proof "tending to show malice or willful injury on the part of the defendant, the railroad company" (as distinct from the conductor himself, for whose behavior the company was not held liable).[126]

The Supreme Court's judgment in Pleasant's case was similar: "There was no proof of special damage, nor of any malice, or ill will, or wanton or violent conduct on the part of the defendant."[127] The court then reversed the earlier decision in Pleasant's favor. Thus, neither Emma Turner nor Mary Pleasant was ultimately requited personally, as least not in legal or financial terms. However, the San Francisco railroad companies ceased enforcing their "no coloreds allowed" policy, and the city papers, especially Black-owned papers such as the *Pacific Appeal*, no longer had occasion to report such incidents.

In addition to defending the rights of African Americans on the streetcars, Pleasant turned her experience in court and her newly acquired knowledge of the legal system to her own advantage. She subsequently appeared frequently in court, and in the papers, particularly in matters pertaining to her dealings in real estate. Pleasant was steadfast in fund-raising and other philanthropic efforts to benefit San Francisco's growing Black community. She was frequently lauded in elite white circles. However, as a Black woman with considerable wealth, she also became a figure of notoriety and mystery. Her business dealings and her boardinghouses brought her into the orbit of many prominent white businessmen. At times, it was said, she even helped them to find wives.

For many years Pleasant lived with the family of Thomas Bell, a banker, in a thirty-room mansion on Octavia Street, which she was believed to have had built. She appeared outwardly as the Bell cook and housekeeper, but she may have functioned more as Bell's silent partner behind the scenes. It was never clear to the public whether Thomas Bell or Mary Pleasant was the true master of the house. Rumors proliferated, and the mansion itself became known in the press as "the House of Mystery."[128]

In 1883 Pleasant was involved in a long, drawn-out, sensational lawsuit that attracted national interest. Sarah Althea Hill, who was white, had become a San Francisco socialite by virtue of her relationship as the mistress of William Sharon, president of the Bank of California.[129] When Sharon stopped supporting her and had her turned out of the Grand Hotel, Hill appealed to Mary Pleasant for a house to live in. Pleasant encouraged her to take action against Sharon, and Hill sued for divorce, claiming that they had been secretly married and producing a forged marriage contract. Pleasant played a key role in the trial, testifying five times on Hill's behalf, thus occasioning much public speculation. It was widely believed, though no actual evidence indicates, that Pleasant paid Hill's legal fees.

In 1892 Thomas Bell died as the result of a fall from a second-story landing in the mansion on Octavia Street. Given the myths that had grown up around her, it is not surprising that many believed that Pleasant had murdered him. Pleasant's financial security, bound up as it was with Bell's wealth, was greatly diminished when, after considerable legal wrangling, Bell's wife and children inherited his entire estate. Pleasant's wealth and properties rapidly dwindled, and for the latter part of her life she was reduced to poverty, though she never compromised her dignity.

In a brief, albeit precise notice, the *San Francisco Chronicle* reported her death in 1904: "PLEASANT—In this city, January 11, Mary Ellen Pleasant, a native of Philadelphia, Pa., aged 89 years, 4 months and 22 days."[130]

In February 1965 the African American Cultural and Historical Society of San Francisco placed a marble marker on her grave, with an inscription that she herself had requested and that conveys the core of her own sense of identity as someone who today would be, and is, acknowledged as a civil rights leader: "She Was a Friend of John Brown."[131]

A Brief Note on "Respectability"

On March 22, 1867, the Pennsylvania governor signed a bill into law disallowing the exclusion of Black passengers from seats on trains and streetcars. Just a few days later the Philadelphia Black community held a meeting in Liberty Hall to celebrate. Octavius Catto and his compatriots on the Car Committee of the Equal Rights League were receiving much of the credit for the passage of the law, and they had indeed played a significant role in drafting the final version of the bill. However, William Still and the Car Committee of the Social, Civic and Statistical Association—the first such committee to have been formed, in 1861—felt that they were not being sufficiently recognized for their roles throughout the long effort to integrate the streetcars. Catto and the younger group of activists in the Equal Rights League criticized Still and other older Black leaders as ineffective and self-serving. The meeting became increasingly rancorous, culminating in a threat against Still, as someone in the crowd yelled, "There will be a funeral at the coal yard now!"[132] (Still was a coal merchant.)

A key factor in the discord was the perception among the younger group that Still and his committee had promoted the cause only for "respectable," well-to-do Black Philadelphians, rather than for everyone, including the very poor. Such a charge stems at least in part from the language that Still used in arguing for the acceptance of Black passengers. As early as his initial letter of August 31, 1859, he had addressed "the sore grievance of genteel colored people in being excluded . . . however unwell or aged, genteel or neatly attired." Much of that letter argues that the "degraded class" of poor Black people in one impoverished neighborhood were not representative of the city's "great mass of industrious colored people."[133] That argument itself reveals something of the class distinctions in the Black community.

Similar language was used in the resolutions passed unanimously at a meeting in Concert Hall on January 13, 1865. One began: "In the words of our venerable and respected townsman, whose name leads the call for this meeting [i.e., Still], we are 'opposed to the exclusion of respectable persons from our Passenger Railroad Cars on the ground of complexion.'" It continued: "We have heard with shame and sorrow . . . that decent women have been forced to walk long distances."[134]

It is easy to understand how the younger men could reach the conclusion they did. However, if we look at the broader historical context, we can see that there is a more generous, less elitist, interpretation available for this language. It is worth noting too that neither the petitions delivered by Still's committee to the presidents of the railway companies nor the various bills presented to the legislature make any such distinction. The petition delivered to the companies in 1862, for example, simply asks "that the various Boards of the city passenger cars rescind the rules indiscriminately excluding colored persons from the inside of the cars."[135]

As a strategy to argue for the right to ride, Still's use of the vocabulary of respectability was not innovative or unusual. Much the same terminology had been used since the very earliest years of protest against Jim Crow. This very book quotes the adjective "respectable" at least eighteen times from both Black and white commentators in reference either to specific Black individuals or to Black people in general from 1832 to 1886. Having described Emiliano Mundrucu as "noble-spirited, and highly respectable in character and manners," Lydia Maria Child in 1833 asked "why respectable colored people should not be allowed to make use of public conveyances."[136] That same year the *Boston Post* described Mundrucu as "a respectable colored man residing in this city." Elizabeth Buffum Chace, writing in 1890 about the late 1830s, references both "a few very respectable young colored women" and "a highly respectable, well-dressed colored man and his wife." The New York *Journal of Commerce* (1840) describes Thomas Downing as "an intelligent, respectable citizen." In 1841 the Cambridgeport Anti-Slavery Society lamented the mistreatment of "a highly respectable colored lady and gentleman of Boston." That same year

Isaac Bassett notes that he was traveling with "a respectable colored woman," and David Ruggles cites the case of "a respectable female." The point of these and similar comments is not to exclude any putative unrespectable passengers; it is rather to point out the fact that the discrimination is based solely on skin color, not on any other marker of social unacceptability independent of race.[137]

Anti-Black prejudice was fueled to a great extent by the ignorant but persistent "erroneous impression," as William Still called it, that people of African descent were dirty, smelly, disreputable, untrustworthy, and lived in slums.[138] It is not unreasonable, therefore, to protest against such beliefs by presenting counterexamples of people being excluded solely on account of their skin color. Indeed, not to do so would pretty much guarantee a failure to effect any change in the minds of the white people who made, enforced, or agreed with the Jim Crow rules of travel.

In their zeal and excitement at the progress and ultimate success of their effort, Catto and his friends may have overemphasized what they saw as faults and failings among their elders. On the other side, Still and his friends may have overreacted to the criticism they received. Each side had legitimate points to make. In any large social group, disagreement, dislike, and distrust can be found among subgroups—in particular, the poor may resent the rich, and the well-to-do may be wary of or even disdain the poor.

Might the latter have been true in the case of William Still? One section of Lombard Street in Philadelphia was situated in the poorest Black area of the city, while other parts were somewhat more upscale. In 1866 Still bought "a very nice house" on Lombard Street, and in a letter to his daughter Carrie, then a student at Oberlin College, he acknowledges his doubts about the neighborhood. Interestingly enough, he uses one of the same words that he was being criticized for in his writing about the streetcar problem—"genteel": "That part of Lombard St. is pretty genteel & quiet, you know, but still I have some prejudices against Lombard St. and may hesitate for some time before consenting to move there."[139] This does not mean, however, that Still's class prejudice, his elitism, was a significant factor in the arguments he presented assiduously for eight years to gain the right to ride for *all* Black train and streetcar passengers in Pennsylvania. It actually took the efforts of William Still, Octavius Catto, and all their associates to overcome massive racial prejudice to gain the simple right to sit in a streetcar. But the problem was much bigger than Philadelphia or even all of Pennsylvania.

The broad issue of respectability as a factor in helping African Americans achieve a greater degree of social acceptance became an important topic of discussion and debate among the Black elite and especially the intellectual leaders and thinkers who would come together to form the National Association of Colored Women (NACW) in 1896.[140] Among these were Ida B. Wells-Barnett and Mary Church Terrell, the NACW's first president (1896–1900), who is "considered one of the foremost proselytizers of respectability."[141] Terrell often used her own respectability as a wealthy, educated Black woman to press quite powerfully for justice.

Whatever it might have conveyed at the time, the word "respectable" appears multiple times as a determinative element in a Washington, D.C., anti-segregation law passed during Reconstruction in 1872. This municipal law stated: "Any restaurant keeper or proprietor, any hotel keeper [et cetera] refusing to sell or wait upon any respectable well-behaved person without regard to race, color, or previous condition of servitude, or . . . who refuse under any pretext to serve any well-behaved, respectable person, in the same room, and at the same prices as other well-behaved and respectable persons are served, shall be deemed guilty of a misdemeanor . . . and shall forfeit his or her license."[142] The triple repetition of the word would seem to imply that the condition of being "respectable" was independent of race, color, or any "previous condition."

Though it had been completely ignored in practice, this law was still on the books in 1950, when an integrated group including Mary Terrell, at the age of eighty-six, and three others were denied service at Thompson's Restaurant in Washington, D.C. When they filed suit against the restaurant, a municipal judge declared that the antidiscrimination law was no longer in effect. Terrell appealed, and the Municipal Appeals Court reversed the decision, stating that "because the law is not observed does not mean that it is not valid." In response, Thompson's Restaurant appealed. The U.S. Court of Appeals not only reversed the decision again, ruling that the laws were no longer valid, it even argued that where segregation was practiced and at times required by local law, it existed "for the purpose of preserving peace and good order which would likely be interfered with by racial association."[143] Appalled, Terrell and her team appealed to the U.S. Supreme Court. On June 8, 1953, the Supreme Court ruled that the anti-segregation law in question did remain valid and in effect. Terrell's case was won, and D.C. restaurants could no longer be legally segregated.[144]

But the road to justice is rough and rocky. Many theaters in D.C. remained segregated. In a clever move, the committee that mounted the case against Thompson's Restaurant announced in September that to celebrate Mary Terrell's ninetieth birthday an integrated group of four friends would be taking her out to dinner and a movie. Fearing the possibility of pickets and legal troubles, the theaters that were still segregated took the hint and abandoned their Jim Crow seating. The committee then moved on to campaign for access to hotels and to equal opportunity employment. After Terrell's death the following year, the committee disbanded.[145]

Caroline R. LeCount, March 25, 1867

Caroline Rebecca LeCount was born in Philadelphia in 1846, the daughter of James and Sarah LeCount. Her father was a cabinetmaker, a coffin maker, and an undertaker. As an agent on the Underground Railroad, according to family lore, he used his coffins, when necessary, to hide fugitive slaves on their way to freedom.[146]

LeCount graduated first in her class from Philadelphia's Institute for Colored Youth in 1863, and two years later she became a teacher and later principal at the Ohio Street School, a public school for Black students. Like her fiancé, Octavius V. Catto, LeCount firmly believed that Black children could best be taught by Black teachers. She also became active in the Ladies' Union Association, bringing aid to wounded soldiers, as well as campaigning for equal rights. The various meetings and activities this work entailed, and the fact that she and Catto attended the same church, brought her into frequent contact with Catto, and she became known as his fiancée.

A bill disallowing the exclusion or expulsion of Black passengers from Pennsylvania trains and streetcars was signed into law by Governor John W. Geary on Friday, March 22, 1867. The next day the *Philadelphia Press* noted briefly: "Harrisburg, March 22.—Gov. Geary today signed the act requiring railroad and railway companies to carry all passengers, without distinction of color."[147] But, as Black people throughout the North knew all too well, a governor's signature was no guarantee that the law would be accepted by the companies or their employees, at least not until it was successfully tested in the courts.

Three days later, on Monday, March 25, Caroline LeCount, with her assistant, Alice Gordon, signaled for a streetcar on the Tenth and Eleventh Street Railway to stop. The conductor, Edwin F. Thompson, did not stop; instead he called out to her the all-too-familiar conductor's cry: "We don't allow niggers to ride!" With remarkable self-possession for a young teacher just turned twenty-one, LeCount straightway took her complaint to a local magistrate, along with a copy of the *Press* article. The magistrate refused to recognize the law simply on the basis of a newspaper report. Undaunted, LeCount went to the Pennsylvania secretary of state, who was in the city, got from him a handwritten, certified copy of the law, and returned to the magistrate. This proved sufficiently convincing, and the judge had Thompson arrested and fined him $100.[148]

The Philadelphia campaign to integrate the cars was officially at an end. The *National Anti-Slavery Standard* summed up the new situation trenchantly:

> Henceforward, the weary school-teacher, returning from her arduous day's labor, shall not be condemned to walk to her distant home through cold and storm; henceforward invalid women and aged men shall be permitted to avail themselves of a public conveyance, even though their complexion may not be white. And their scornful brothers and sisters who cannot comfortably sit beside a colored fellow-citizen in a car, will have the right to walk, or indulge in the luxury of a private carriage, if their purses will afford it, and their prejudice is, in their estimation, worth the expense.[149]

Caroline LeCount remained a teacher and principal of the Ohio Street School until she retired in 1911. In 1878 the school was renamed the O.V. Catto School.

William Nichols and the New Orleans Streetcar Campaign, May 4–5, 1867

Following the arrest and exoneration of Hannibal Carter in 1862, conditions on the New Orleans streetcars fluctuated. Segregation was banned by the Union military commanders, but the ban was successfully challenged in court, then reinstated and challenged again. The star cars, which allowed Black passengers, returned, disappeared, and came back again. Not surprisingly, tensions just below the surface would periodically break out in protests, always with the looming specter of violence, at least in the minds of white New Orleanians.

The *New Orleans Tribune*, the nation's first African American–owned daily newspaper, founded in 1864, regularly voiced its opposition to the star cars. On April 21, 1867, it called for direct action: "All these discriminations that had slavery at the bottom have become nonsense. It behooves those who feel bold enough to shake off the old prejudice and to confront their prejudiced associates, to show their hands."[150]

On Sunday, April 28, 1867, William Nichols was arrested for riding on a streetcar that was not a star car, and he appeared in court that Tuesday. Fearing a loss, the railroad companies were reluctant to have the segregation question decided by a judge. After brief testimony was given, the corporation lawyer acknowledged that "it was evident that there had been no breach of the peace. The object, he had no doubt, was to test the question of the right to insist that colored people should ride only in star cars." The judge ruled that Nichols did not cause himself to be arrested and that the arrest had nothing to do with the question of the equal right to ride. The case was recorded: "Dismissed: there being no breach of the peace." To return the issue to a court of law, Nichols immediately countersued. The *New Orleans Republican* reported on May 1, "[Nichols's affidavit stated] that on Sunday last, between the hours of 1 and 2 P.M., whilst in city car No. 132, he was then and there assaulted and beaten by one Edward Cox."[151]

To protect themselves from lawsuits, legal costs, and setbacks in the meantime, the rail companies instructed their drivers to adopt passive resistance. If a person of color insisted on boarding a car, the driver would simply refuse to move until the protester left the car—a tactic much like that encountered by Emma and Miles Robinson just four months earlier in Philadelphia, in which the conductor derailed the car altogether.

Things were coming to a head, rumors were spreading, and Black people's hopes were being raised. On May 1, the *New Orleans Republican* published a brief notice: "The report was current on the streets last night that the President of the City Railroad had issued instructions to the various drivers that hereafter no distinction will be made, on account of race or color of their passengers, so long as their money is of the proper weight and tint."

Two days later, a notice to the opposite effect appeared in the *New Orleans Times*: "The City Railroad Cars.—The statement that drivers are permitted to allow persons of color to ride in cars not marked with a star, seems to be erroneous. No such order has been given. The cars marked with a star are expressly set apart for colored people, and all others, by a rule of the corporation, are exclusively for white persons." That same day, Philippe Duclos-Lange, a person of color and a Union veteran, boarded a city car, and he and the driver sat in a stalemate for several hours until Duclos-Lange, having made his point, left, and the empty car went on its way.[152]

Protest became more volatile on Saturday morning, May 4, as crowds of Black men gathered to surround, harass, and threaten the cars. At about 11:30 a.m., Joseph Guillaume, a veteran of the Black Louisiana Native Guard, was arrested for jumping aboard a car, seizing the reins from the driver, and leading the police on a chase. He was immediately brought before a judge "who dismissed the case and advised him to abide his time, as a similar case was [then] under advisement, which would be decided in a few days." That evening in various parts of the city, people of color began entering the cars in groups as others gathered and cheered them on.[153]

Around eight on Sunday morning, two Black women boarded a car and refused to leave when the driver told them they were in the wrong car. All the white passengers left the car as the driver prepared to outwait the women.

After a short time, however, he gave up and drove on with them to Canal Street. That afternoon larger crowds of African Americans gathered in the neighborhood of Rampart Street and Congo Square, a traditional Black gathering place, and, according to the *Daily Picayune*, "without using any violence, attempted to take possession of the cars."[154] The *New Orleans Times* gave a more detailed account of events and listed six instances in which one or more Black persons entered or attempted to enter cars in the vicinity.[155] Angry gangs of white men and boys began roaming the streets, and increasing violence seemed likely.

Fearful of another massacre like the one that had occurred the previous July at the Louisiana Constitutional Convention, during which thirty-five to fifty Black and four white people were killed and as many as 150 injured, Edward Heath, the New Orleans mayor, wisely declined to call out the police in force or request federal troops. He went to Congo Square and advised the crowd of about five hundred people to disperse and go home. "In the main, they took his advice."[156] On the following day, May 6, the chief of police sent out an order to his officers: "Have no interference with negroes riding in cars of any kind. No passenger has a right to eject any other passenger, no matter what his color. If he does so he is liable to arrest for assault or breach of the peace."[157]

Heath and the presidents of the rail companies met with the new military commander, General Philip Sheridan. The companies asked for federal troops to enforce their segregation rule, but Sheridan refused to interfere in the matter. On May 6 the streetcar companies agreed to abandon the star cars and to allow all persons to ride all the streetcars. William Nichols then dropped his assault charge.

The New Orleans streetcars were now officially integrated, but, as elsewhere, white passengers and drivers occasionally resisted the new order, and Black riders, especially working-class Black riders, generally took care not to sit next to a white passenger. In spite of some challenges, the city's cars remained integrated until 1902, six years after the U.S. Supreme Court decision in *Plessy v. Ferguson* legitimized Jim Crow across the nation.[158]

A new Louisiana constitution was adopted in 1868. Article 13 of the constitution's Bill of Rights states, in part, "All persons shall enjoy equal rights and privileges upon any conveyance of a public character . . . without distinction or discrimination on account of race or color."[159] To further codify this principle in law, the state legislature in 1869 passed Act No. 38, which spelled out the prohibition against discrimination in reverse, by enumerating the circumstances in which a driver, conductor, steamboat captain, et cetera, *would be* allowed to refuse passage to someone:

> All persons engaged within this State in the business of common carriers of passengers shall have the right to refuse to admit any person to any railroad cars, street cars, steamboats, . . . when such person shall, on demand, refuse or neglect to pay the customary fare, or when such person shall be of infamous character, or shall be guilty . . . of gross, vulgar, or disorderly conduct, or who shall commit any act tending to injure the business of the carrier, prescribed for the management of his business after such rules and regulations shall have been made known; provided, said rules and regulations make no discrimination on account of race or color.[160]

Whether such a law could withstand the pressures of entrenched racial prejudice beyond the New Orleans streetcars in Louisiana and the nation at large was soon to be tested in the person of Josephine Decuir, who had been before the war one of the wealthiest free people of color in Louisiana.

Josephine Decuir, July 20, 1872

Josephine Decuir (née Dubuclet) was a member of two of the wealthiest families among the *gens de couleur libre*, Louisiana's French-speaking "free people of color." Before the Civil War, her husband, Antoine Decuir II, presided over the Decuir family plantations in Pointe Coupée Parish, some 155 miles upriver from New Orleans, and held over one hundred people in slavery. Her brother, Antoine Dubuclet, "not only the largest free Negro slave owner in Louisiana but the richest of his class as well," was elected state treasurer in 1868 and fought against corruption in the state government until 1878.[161]

Although the social status of the *gens de couleur* diminished somewhat after the imposition of U.S. law following the Louisiana Purchase in 1803 and yet again in the 1850s, they enjoyed levels of acceptance and prosperity rarely achieved by other free Blacks. Many of the elite sent their children to be educated in France. Madame Decuir herself lived in Paris for twelve years with two of her three children. After the war and her husband's death in 1865, she returned to Louisiana only to learn that the estate was in serious financial trouble. Her husband had left considerable debts, Confederate money and bonds were worthless, and enslaved people—the economic foundation of the family's wealth—were no longer available for labor or as financial assets. Her husband had pledged his slaves as security for his debts; thus, after the Louisiana Constitution of 1864 abolished slavery, the now unsecured debts came due.

Decuir was determined to save what wealth and property she could. She was appointed executor of her husband's estate in July 1865. By 1872 the

Pointe Coupée court had finally approved the settlement of the estate, distributing the proceeds among various debtors. Most of Decuir's property had been auctioned off to pay them in 1871. She hired new lawyers from New Orleans—E. K. Washington, who was white, and S. R. Snaer, who was mixed-race and French-speaking—in the hope that they could save at least some of her property.

In due time Decuir, Washington, and Snaer prepared for the eighteen-hour trip upriver to Pointe Coupée. Washington later stated that, at this point, he did not know Decuir's racial status.[162] The three of them made plans to meet at the steamboat levee on the evening of Saturday, July 20, 1872. When Washington arrived, he booked cabins for himself and for Decuir on the *Governor Allen*. Going ashore to find her, Washington ran into Snaer, who told him that he himself was going on a different boat and that Madame Decuir would be "mortified" on the *Governor Allen*. At first Washington was puzzled as to why, but then it dawned on him that, like Snaer, Decuir was "colored."[163]

Segregation was standard practice on the Mississippi riverboats, although some captains might occasionally allow special arrangements for high-status passengers of color. Even when exceptions were permitted, women of color could not enter the first-class ladies' lounge. Doors leading into the lounge areas from their exempted rooms would be kept locked, and meals would be brought to their rooms. In the past Decuir had at times received such "special treatment." At other times she had been denied access to the first-class ladies' cabin altogether. Sleeping accommodations for people of color were usually restricted to an area below decks known as "the bureau," probably so-called as a derogatory swipe at the Freedmen's Bureau. Like the Jim Crow car on trains, the bureau, as a rule, was windowless, cramped, dirty, and unsafe, especially for women traveling alone.

When Decuir arrived at the levee, she had a porter deliver her trunk onto the *Governor Allen*, and she sat in the lounge of the ladies' cabin to wait for Washington. Perhaps she hoped to pass for white altogether. Or she may have hoped at least to be given a room in the ladies' cabin, though without access to the first-class lounges or dining area, as she had a few years before on the *Lafourche*. Alternatively, she may have known or suspected that the *Governor Allen* had a strict segregation policy and was willing to challenge it. Earlier that very summer she had refused to go into the bureau on the *Ouachita Belle*. Instead, she had sat for that entire trip in a semipublic area known as the "recess," behind the ladies' cabin. (It is worth considering too that Decuir, having been a prominent slaveholder, may not have been welcomed or tolerated by Black passengers in the bureau on any boat.)[164]

Hoping to avoid trouble, Washington asked the ship's clerk if "a person

The riverboat *Governor Allen*. Murphy Library Special Collection / ARC, University of Wisconsin–La Crosse.

of color and a very respectable person" might be given a berth in the ladies' cabin. The clerk said no. When Washington went into the ladies' lounge, he was surprised to find Decuir sitting there already. He tried to persuade her to get off the boat, until it became too late as the boat began its journey. He returned to the clerk and another ship's officer, pleading Decuir's illness, but to no avail. She was offered the use of either the chambermaid's apartment or the recess. Given this demeaning choice, she spent the night in a chair in the recess. Dinner was brought to her there—fried oysters, baked potatoes, warm rolls, and waffles.[165] She was offered a cot to sleep on but declined to use it because "the place was public and a place of passage for everyone, and she could not, on account of delicacy, disrobe herself or be exposed to the sight of every one."[166] As Decuir became increasingly distraught and despondent, Washington sought out the captain, John Benson, but Benson refused to bend his rules.

Just ten days later, on July 30, notice of a suit filed in the Eighth District Court appeared in the New Orleans *Daily Picayune*.[167] Under the headline "Action under the Civil Rights Bill—$75,000 Damages Claimed," it read: "Madame Josephine Decuir, colored, has instituted suit in this court against [John] G. Benson, captain and owner of the steamboat Gov. Allen, claiming seventy-five thousand dollars for actual and exemplary damages. . . . She therefore enters suit for the amount above stated, against Mr. Benson, under the provisions of article 13 of the constitution of Louisiana, under the laws of the United States, and under the provision act No. 38 of the General Assembly of 1869."

Article 13 of the new Louisiana constitution adopted in 1868 granted all persons "equal rights and privileges upon any conveyance of a public character . . . without distinction or discrimination on account of race or color." Act 38 similarly forbade "discrimination on account of race or color."[168] Segregation trials at the time were usually argued before a jury, and because Black jurors were not allowed, the verdicts in such cases most often went in favor of the segregationist perspective. But neither Egan nor Washington requested a jury trial, so Decuir's case was conducted as a bench trial to be decided by the judge alone. In addition to Decuir's written complaint, five witnesses testified on her behalf, and seven for Benson.

In her complaint, Decuir described the incident on board the *Governor Allen*. The complaint also outlined her status as a land-holder and said that she was well-educated and had "always demeaned herself with propriety, decorum, and respect." Significantly, she acknowledged the central importance of Article 13 and Act 38 to the case by quoting from the former in claiming her "equal rights and privileges," and by quoting Act 38 in stating that "she was not guilty of any gross, vulgar or disorderly conduct." Relevant to the matter of damages, Decuir noted that the treatment she received was not only contrary to both U.S. and Louisiana law, but that it also constituted "a gross indignity to her personally . . . [and] was such a shock to her feelings, and occasioned so much mental pain, shame, and mortification, that her mind was affected."[169]

Benson, on the other hand, was concerned that to allow persons of color into the first-class cabins would "injure the business of the carrier." His lawyers argued that it was "reasonable, usual and customary" to assign cabins on the basis of race. They did not present a clear principle of "separate but equal" per se, as would be argued twenty years later in the trial of Homer Plessy, but Decuir's trial would prove to be an important precursor to that landmark case. Benson, members of his crew, and other riverboat captains testified that the accommodations in the bureau were as good as those in the ladies' cabin and that the same food was served to both first-class passengers and those in the bureau.[170] Witnesses on behalf of Decuir strongly asserted the contrary. Decuir's cousin, P. G. Deslonde, a man of color and the newly elected Louisiana secretary of state, characterized the bureau (in general, not specifically that of the *Governor Allen*) as "a back room somewhere in the back part of the boat where they generally pen up colored passengers. . . . A dark place like a kind of prison."[171]

Benson's lawyer, Bentinck Egan, hung the bulk of his argument on three hooks: (1) that the *Governor Allen* was licensed by the federal government, and thus the Commerce Clause of the U.S. Constitution, which gives Congress the exclusive power to regulate interstate commerce, made Louisiana's antidiscrimination statute irrelevant in this particular case; (2) that the long-standing custom of segregation should (in some undefined way) override the law requiring integration; and (3) that the *Governor Allen* was private property and therefore any law abridging its owner's right to manage it as he wished was contrary to the Due Process Clause of the Fourteenth Amendment, which had gone into effect earlier that summer. In addition, Egan claimed that Decuir knew of the segregation policy on the *Governor Allen* before boarding, and therefore she could have avoided any mistreatment she received.[172]

Judge E. North Collum handed down his decision in a lengthy opinion on June 14, 1873. He ruled in favor of Madame Decuir, awarding her $1,000 in compensatory damages but no exemplary (punitive) damages. Decuir must have met this judgment with mixed emotions—pleased that the wrong done to her had been acknowledged in a court of law but disappointed in the size of the award. One thousand dollars was a substantial amount in 1873, but it was far less than the $75,000 she had asked for.

Benson might have been glad that the penalty against him was not as high as it could have been, but he and other riverboat owners remained opposed to eliminating segregation. When Judge Collum denied a retrial, Egan filed an appeal with the Louisiana Supreme Court. It was argued in late January 1874.

Chief Justice John T. Ludeling was generally sympathetic to the cause of racial equality, albeit concerned about Blacks gaining political power. The chief issue in the Decuir case as he saw it was whether Act 38 was in conflict with the Commerce Clause of the U.S. Constitution or with the Fourteenth Amendment by depriving Benson of his property without due process of law. Ludeling concluded, "[The Louisiana antidiscrimination law] does not, in any manner, affect the commercial interest of any State or foreign nation or the citizens thereof." In other words, he held that neither the Louisiana Constitution nor Act 38 violated the Commerce Clause or the Fourteenth Amendment. Upholding Judge Collum's decision, Judge Ludeling hinted that if Decuir had asked for an increase in the original judgment, it might have been granted.[173]

A rehearing was denied in Louisiana, and Benson immediately appealed to the U.S. Supreme Court. A new lawyer, Robert H. Marr, joined Benson's team to argue the case. *Benson v. Decuir* was scheduled to be heard during the October term in 1874, but on November 12 Benson died, just nine days after marrying Eliza Jane Hall. After a long delay, Hall was appointed executor of

Benson's estate and was substituted as plaintiff in his case. Redesignated *Hall v. Decuir*, the case was rescheduled for the 1877 October term.

After the war, R. H. Marr had received a pardon from President Andrew Johnson for his role as a Confederate supporter and was allowed to resume his law practice. Then in 1874 Marr was a primary instigator of the so-called "Battle of Liberty Place," an attempted coup d'état to overthrow the elected Republican government of Louisiana. Nearly a dozen city police officers were killed during the riot. The following year, as Decuir's appeal was pending, Marr argued the case of *United States v. Cruikshank*, in which the U.S. Supreme Court invalidated the convictions of nine white participants in the Colfax Massacre of 1873, during which anywhere from 60 to 150 Black people were killed. According to Reconstruction historian Eric Foner, this was "the bloodiest single instance of racial carnage in the Reconstruction era." With the collapse of Reconstruction, the new Democratic governor awarded Marr a seat on the Louisiana Supreme Court early in 1877, before Marr argued for the defense in *Hall v. Decuir* at the U.S. Supreme Court.[174]

In addition to bolstering the arguments that Egan had presented in Louisiana, Marr insisted strenuously that segregation was not only a long-standing tradition, but that it was also necessary to maintain social order, that it was ordained by God, and that it was legal in many states throughout the Union. He also placed considerable stress on the belief that the U.S. Commerce Clause preempted the Louisiana antidiscrimination law.[175]

Decuir's lawyer, E. K. Washington, argued that the Commerce Clause did not apply, because Decuir did not travel interstate, and that Congress should not legislate the segregation question, because that was a matter for individual states to decide. He also addressed the larger underlying issue: "To discriminate against anyone on account of his color, is to attack the basis-condition of his being and nature: for color is neither a moral or a legal fault."[176] A great irony in this case is that Washington was arguing to preserve the state's right to disallow segregation, while Marr, a staunch believer in states' rights, was arguing for federal control.

Hall v. Decuir was finally decided in January 1878, reversing the original district court verdict. Once again Madame Decuir suffered a further loss of dignity and a loss of the sorely needed financial award. Furthermore, she had to pay Benson's legal costs and the court costs in both state courts. In a letter to the Louisiana Supreme Court clerk, Egan stated his belief that she had "more money than God." A few days later, Washington told Egan that she was insolvent; all her money and property had been forfeited to pay her husband's debts. Having lost her plantation, she lived the rest of her life with her daughter, a seamstress, in New Orleans. She died in 1891.[177]

The social impact of the decision in *Hall v. Decuir* was immediately recognized. Boston University law professor Jack Beermann summarizes its effect: "In *Hall v. Decuir*, the Supreme Court, for the first time after the Civil War, embraced racial segregation as an acceptable practice in interstate travel. If nothing more, *Hall v. Decuir* set the tone for the Supreme Court's treatment of claims involving racial discrimination for decades."[178]

Once the Civil Rights Act of 1875 was declared unconstitutional in 1883 by the court's decision in the combined "Civil Rights Cases," which included that of Sallie J. Robinson, the gates were wide open to new Jim Crow laws throughout the nation. Even though *Hall v. Decuir* was central to the Supreme Court's 1946 decision in the case of Irene Morgan, outlawing segregation in interstate travel, it continued to be cited as justification for the right to segregate public conveyances as late as 1952.[179]

CHAPTER 3

The Ladies' Car and the Law

Immediately after the Civil War, many southern states enacted "Black Codes," laws that placed severe restrictions on African American lives in order to keep newly freed slaves in a position of servitude and dependency. Some Black Codes required Jim Crow cars where none had existed before. Most Black Codes were dismantled as the election of 1866 saw Black candidates successfully elected to local, state, and national offices, and as the Reconstruction Act of 1867 was passed. Nevertheless, with the unraveling of Reconstruction and the rise of Jim Crow in the South during the 1870s, the distinction among railway cars—the ladies' car, the smoking car, and the Jim Crow car—began to play a more visible role, particularly in legal cases in which the status of women of color was in question. In reality, of course, "ladies' car" was little more than a euphemistic name for a racially segregated, nonsmoking car, as Dickens noted as early as 1842. The more comfortable ladies' car (or ladies' cabin, in the case of steamboats) was available, at a first-class fare, to white women passengers and to white men accompanying them, but, theoretically at least, not to men otherwise. The only people of color generally tolerated in the ladies' car were Black nannies or nurses attending to a white child or other passenger, just as enslaved people had been allowed in the cars as servants prior to emancipation. Smoking, drinking, and strong language were forbidden in the ladies' car, in accord with the restrictive Victorian image of idealized womanhood, though they were allowed in the smoking car. The latter, at a lower fare, was open to all other white passengers or was partitioned into separate compartments: one open to white passengers who were free to smoke, drink, play cards, and engage in behavior that was frequently characterized as rowdy, and the other section restricted, at least nominally, for the use of Black men and women.

By and large, the segregation of Black passengers was not a matter of law but was rather enforced through custom or through the implicit or explicit policies of private railroad companies. In 1870 Anna Williams was awarded $200 for being ejected from the ladies' car on the Chicago and Northwestern

Railway. The company appealed the decision, and the Illinois Supreme Court affirmed that award on the basis that while it was reasonable to designate a car for the use of women and their male traveling companions, "in the absence of any reasonable rule on the subject, the company [could] not lawfully, from caprice, wantonness or prejudice, exclude a colored woman from the ladies' car, merely on account of her color."[1] But the stage was soon set for the introduction of just such company-instituted Jim Crow rules, followed by numerous state and municipal laws, primarily but not exclusively in the South.

On March 1, 1875, Congress approved the Civil Rights Act of 1875, which held: "It is the duty of government in its dealings with the people to mete out equal and exact justice to all, of whatever nativity, race, color, or persuasion, religious or political." It also stipulated: "All persons within the jurisdiction of the United States shall be entitled to the full and equal enjoyment of the accommodations, advantages, facilities, and privileges of inns, public conveyances on land or water, theaters, and other places of public amusement."[2]

Just three weeks later, in an attempt to circumvent this new national Civil Rights Act, the Tennessee legislature passed Chapter 130 of the Acts of Tennessee of 1875. This Tennessee law denied "any person excluded from any hotel or public means of transportation, or place of amusement" the right to take action in court, and it further stated: "Hereafter no . . . carrier of passengers for hire or conductor, driver or employee of such carrier . . . shall be bound, or under any obligation to . . . carry . . . any person whom he shall for any reason whatever choose not to carry."[3] Thus, segregation could continue on the Tennessee rails without explicitly admitting it and without fear of legal action against the companies or their employees. Significantly, although it pretends not to be defined by race, here we have, in effect, the first Jim Crow law passed by a state legislature, paving the way for a long string of contentious state and local laws and ordinances throughout the South attempting to perpetuate the segregation and oppression of African Americans.

Though there was fierce objection from white passengers to any person of color occupying the first-class cars, it was tacitly though widely acknowledged that white men from the smoking section frequently intruded into the Jim Crow section, often harassing Black women passengers in particular. It is not surprising, therefore, that a Black woman traveling alone would prefer to ride in the greater safety of the ladies' car. But any woman of color challenging the prevailing social norms, customs, or expectations on segregated railroads was at risk of a level of criticism not directed at men. Her character, her virtue, and her chastity might be impugned, no matter how well she behaved on the train. In legal terms, a passenger's character was irrelevant and should not have entered at all into her rights as a traveler, yet, when the excuse of color failed, it became the justification for excluding Black women from the cars.

Sallie J. Robinson, May 22, 1879

Sometime after midnight on May 22, 1879, Mrs. Sallie J. Robinson, who had been born into slavery, and her grown nephew, Joseph C. Robinson, boarded a train on the Memphis and Charleston Railroad at Grand Junction, Tennessee, on route to Lynchburg, Virginia. As they turned to enter the ladies' car, the conductor, C. W. Reagin, grabbed Mrs. Robinson by the arm, with sufficient force to cause a bruise that lasted for more than a week. He then blocked the doorway to the car, told them that they could not enter, their first-class tickets notwithstanding, and directed them to go into the smoking car. Mrs. Robinson replied that she did not want to go into the smoking car, for smoke made her sick, and she noted that the ladies' car was not full. Nevertheless, they went to the smoking car. Joseph Robinson went to speak to the conductor and later reported that Reagin said, "Why do you people try to force yourselves in that car?" According to Robinson's testimony, he replied that they had first-class tickets, so they were entitled to ride there, and that she was his aunt. Upon learning that, Reagin said that they could go into the ladies' car when the train reached the next station. They did so and rode there to the end of their journey, though they made a complaint to the ticket agent during a stop in Knoxville. The agent suggested that they write a letter to the superintendent, John A. Grant, in Memphis. They not only wrote to Grant, they filed a suit against the railroad company. The case was heard before a jury in the circuit court of the District of Western Tennessee before Judge E. S. Hammond.[4]

The conductor's own testimony, however, throws a different light on the case. The central argument for the company's defense begins with a remarkable sentence: "The evidence on behalf of defendant was that Sallie J. Robinson was a young good-looking mulatto about 28 years old and that Joseph C. Robinson was a young man of light complexion, light hair and light blue eyes." Reagin testified that he "supposed the said Joseph C. Robinson to be a white man traveling with a colored woman," and that "his experience as a conductor was that when young white men travelled in company with young colored women it was for illicit purposes." This justification for excluding them from the ladies' car was repeated several times during his testimony. When asked by the company's lawyer how white men traveling with colored women generally conducted themselves, he answered that "they generally laughed and drank and smoked and acted disorderly." The Robinsons' lawyer objected to such general testimony as "incompetent and irrelevant" but was overruled.

Repeating that "he suspected there were improper relations existing between them and for that reason excluded her," Reagin further explained

> that the Rail Road company had given no instructions to exclude on account of color. That any lady white or colored was entitled to go into the ladies' car, which was a car set apart for ladies and their escorts. And that Joseph C. and Sallie J. Robinson could have done nothing sexually improper in that car without being observed but might have conducted themselves so as to be offensive to passengers. And that it was a part of the business of the conductor to see that nothing improper was done by them or the other passengers.

The jury handed down a verdict in favor of the railroad. The Robinsons appealed on the basis that Hammond had erred in allowing the jury to consider the question of Sallie Robinson's character in their deliberations, and the case moved up to the U.S. Supreme Court.

At the Supreme Court, *Robinson v. Memphis & Charleston Railroad Company* was consolidated, under the heading "Civil Rights Cases," with four other cases in which the application of the Civil Rights Act of 1875 was at issue. Those four cases, however, were cases of exclusion from two inns or hotels and two theaters; *Robinson* was the only transportation case. The court determined that the primary matter to be considered was whether the Civil Rights Act itself was constitutional, for, if it was unconstitutional, then none of those prosecutions decided in the light of that act were valid.

After considerable delay, on October 15, 1883, Chief Justice Joseph P. Bradley publicly delivered a lengthy opinion stating that the first two provisions of the Civil Rights Act were, indeed, unconstitutional, and the court mandated that the Robinsons repay the company's $20 costs. In his decision, Bradley argued at some length that Sallie Robinson's former enslaved status had no bearing on her case—in other words, the Thirteenth Amendment, which abolished slavery in 1865, did not provide any "special status" that might help her case toward a favorable verdict. At the very heart of his decision, with which seven justices concurred, was a narrow interpretation of the first section of the Fourteenth Amendment to the Constitution, which states in part, "No State shall make or enforce any law which shall abridge the privileges or immunities of citizens of the United States." While the Fourteenth Amendment forbids states to make discriminatory laws, Bradley argued, it does not apply to the actions of private individuals or businesses. As a consequence, he declared the Civil Rights Act of 1875 unconstitutional because it impinged on the rights of private citizens and corporations. Therefore, the Memphis and

Charleston Railroad had the right to seat passengers where they, and not the passengers themselves, pleased.

As soon as Bradley finished his hour-long reading to the press, the sole dissenting justice, John Marshall Harlan, announced that he would be making his opposing opinion public as soon as possible. Even before writing it he began receiving accolades from around the country for his bravery in dissenting. As one Ohio correspondent said, "You, sir, have won a place in the hearts of my race that shall never be usurped by another."[5] Judge Harlan was now on his way to becoming known as "the Great Dissenter," especially in the cause of civil rights. A month later Harlan filed a 13,300-word dissent, twice as long as Bradley's opinion, presenting detailed arguments against each of Bradley's points.

Harlan based much of his response to Bradley on the principle, often quoted subsequently, that "it is not the words of the law but the internal sense of it that makes the law. The letter of the law is the body; the sense and reason of the law is the soul." Addressing Bradley's narrow interpretation of the Thirteenth Amendment, Harlan asserted, "The thirteenth amendment . . . may be exerted to the extent at least of protecting the liberated race against discrimination in respect of legal rights belonging to freemen where such discrimination is based upon race."[6] As to the Fourteenth Amendment, Harlan similarly argued that an exemption from discrimination is contained within it: "[A] denial . . . of that equality of civil rights . . . is a denial by the State within the meaning of the Fourteenth Amendment. If it be not, then that race is left, in respect of the civil rights under discussion, practically at the mercy of corporations and individuals wielding power under the States."

He further argued that, whereas the other members of the court agreed that the amendment, by granting equal citizenship, only gave Congress the right to legislate against discriminatory state laws, he believed that, by granting equal citizenship to all persons born in the United States or naturalized as such, the amendment contains within it the right of Congress to legislate proactively in defense of those rights. Thus, he maintained, the 1875 Civil Rights Act was constitutionally sound.

While the outcome of their case was, naturally, disappointing to the Robinsons, it led to Judge Harlan's important analysis and articulation of the case for defending the right of Black citizens to be free from discrimination and to have those rights protected by the federal government. That such a powerful dissent should have come from the only southern judge on the court is one of the ironies of the perennial complexities of life in the United States.

The response to Harlan's dissent was widespread and varied. Some newspapers published it in full. Others criticized it to varying degrees. Public opinion in much of the country, North and South, saw things differently than Justice Harlan. The *New York Times* praised Bradley's decision as flowing "clearly and easily from the obvious meaning and purport of the fourteenth amendment" while describing Harlan's response as "laboring to give a forced construction to the amendment."[7] On the other hand, Harlan received laudatory messages from Frederick Douglass and from President Rutherford B. Hayes, who wrote, "The people who made the amendment meant by it all you claim."[8] William Howard Day, who had lost his own case in 1855, wrote to thank him on behalf of "thousands of the Colored Citizens" and for himself.[9]

Judge Harlan's role in the campaign for equal rights was by no means over. With the voidance of the Civil Rights Act, railroads and other businesses were now free to institute discriminatory rules, and state legislatures, especially in the South, were keen to find ways around any remaining federal restrictions. Nevertheless, intrepid travelers of color continued, often at great personal risk and expense, to challenge those rules and customs. The "Great Dissenter" would raise his voice again in the consequential case of *Plessy v. Ferguson*.

Jane Brown, October 1880

In October 1880 Jane Brown bought a first-class ticket from Corinth, Mississippi, to Memphis, Tennessee, on the Memphis and Charleston Railroad, and sat in the ladies' car. Court records note that "her behavior while in the car was lady-like and inoffensive."[10] Nevertheless, the conductor told her to move to the smoking car, described as "crowded with passengers, mostly emigrants, travelling on cheap rates, with many women and children." Having paid for a first-class ticket, she refused. When the conductor and others tried to remove her forcibly, she held on tightly and, like Frederick Douglass, hooked her feet under the seat. In the ensuing struggle her thumb was dislocated, and she suffered abrasions on her neck from being choked. Having been forced from the car, she sued for damages, and the case went to the U.S. circuit court for the Western District of Tennessee, with Judge Eli S. Hammond on the bench, the judge who presided over the case of Sallie Robinson.

The railroad company initially made the familiar claim that Brown was "a woman of color" and that "the company had a regulation excluding persons of color from the ladies' car, but providing equal accommodations in another car, which she refused to accept." The court, however, determined that no such regulation existed, that the company "as a matter of fact made no distinction as to color on its cars." Thus, any defense on the basis of color was disallowed, and the jury was "charged that the case was to be tried precisely as if the plaintiff were a white woman excluded under similar circumstances."

The Tennessee Chapter 130 law enacted on the heels of the Civil Rights Act of 1875, allowing railroads to refuse a passenger "for any reason whatever," would have allowed Jane Brown to be ejected from the ladies' car simply at the whim of the conductor. Judge Hammond, however, declared Chapter 130 unconstitutional at least in regard to cases involving interstate travel, for the regulation of interstate commerce was under the purview of the federal government, not individual states.

Having been denied the argument of exclusion based on color, and rather than admit Jane Brown's right to ride in the ladies' car, the company lawyers argued instead that "the plaintiff was a notorious and public courtesan, addicted to the use of profane language and offensive habits of conduct in public places; that the ladies' car was set apart exclusively for the use of genteel ladies of good character and modest deportment, from which the plaintiff was rightfully excluded because of her bad character."[11] More pointedly they argued, "We submit that nothing could be more repulsive and annoying to ladies, and their fathers, husbands, and brothers, than to know that whores will be entitled to be seated by them in railroad cars."[12]

Brown responded with testimony that she had frequently traveled in the ladies' car on the same road with other conductors without being excluded, but that the conductor in this instance had twice before ejected her, "and that this conductor had been seen talking familiarly with white women known in the town where plaintiff lived, and all along the road, as belonging to the denounced class."[13] To be explicit, "denounced class" here means prostitutes.

Judge Hammond considered the company's argument to be "wholly unsound," and he continued, "Nor do I see why it should not be applied to men as well as women. . . . But the experience of every man who travels demonstrates, as a fact, that no such classification is attempted." Nor were there any precedents showing that a claim based on a woman's character had ever been made either, and the judge instructed the jury accordingly: "The carrier is bound to carry good, bad, and indifferent, and has nothing to do with the morals of his passengers, if their behavior be proper while travelling." To exclude women on the basis of character "would put every woman purchasing a railroad ticket on trial for her virtue before the conductor as her judge."[14]

The judge further charged the jury that, because she had purchased a first-class ticket, Jane Brown was entitled to alternative accommodations that were "equal in all respects to the best which the company offered on that train to other female passengers travelling alone as the plaintiff was," and noted that the smoking car did not meet that standard.[15] The jury returned a verdict in Brown's favor and awarded her the considerable sum of $3,000.

The following year the railroad company presented a motion for a new trial, having found an additional witness who had been present at the incident and was willing to testify in their favor. After reviewing the case in considerable detail, Judge Hammond let the jury's settlement stand, and on April 25, 1881, he delivered a lengthy opinion overruling the railroad's motion for a new trial.[16] Whoever Jane Brown was in her private life in Corinth and Memphis, she endures in the annals of law as a determined woman insisting on her rights and the principle that women and men, Black or white, should be treated equally and according to law.

The four Black members of the Tennessee legislature at the time twice proposed but failed to pass a bill nullifying the objectionable Chapter 130 law. Instead, on April 7, less than three weeks before the April 25 decision on Jane Brown's case, the legislature overwhelmingly passed a bill stating: "[Railroad companies] shall furnish separate cars, or portions of cars . . . in which all colored passengers who pay first class passenger rates of fare, may have the privilege to enter and occupy, and such apartments shall be kept in good repair, and with the same conveniences, and subject to the same rules governing other first class cars, preventing smoking and obscene language."[17]

The doctrine of "separate but equal" was on its way to being defined, refined, and embedded in numerous state laws across the South.

Ida B. Wells-Barnett, September 15, 1883

Ida Bell Wells, the most influential late nineteenth-century and early twentieth-century African American investigative reporter (before that term was even coined), was born into slavery in Holly Springs, Mississippi, on July 16, 1862. Ida's father, James Wells, and his wife Elizabeth were enslaved by Spires Boling, a successful house designer and builder, and James became a skilled carpenter.[18] By 1878 the family had grown to include seven children.

A "colored school" had been founded in Holly Springs in 1866, and it was apparently there that Ida began her formal education.[19] At the same time, Shaw University (now Rust College) was founded in Holly Springs to educate former slaves. There Ida's mother learned to write and to read the Bible. Ida too studied there prior to 1878. In addition to literacy and literature, a good part of the Shaw curriculum was of a practical bent, including teaching such domestic skills as washing and ironing. Ida may not have relished this menial curriculum, but Paula Giddings notes, "She had not only devoured the Shakespeare, Dickens, Oliver Optic stories for boys, and Alcott and Brontë books found in the Shaw and Asbury [Methodist Church] libraries, but had, as she wrote in her autobiography, 'formed her ideals' on them."[20]

In September 1878, a yellow fever epidemic swept through the southeast-

Ida B. Wells, circa 1893. National Portrait Gallery, Smithsonian Institution.

ern United States, killing as many as twenty thousand people, among them Ida's parents and her nine-month-old brother. Relatives and friends made a plan to have the surviving two boys, eight and twelve, apprenticed as carpenters, her youngest sisters, five and two, fostered in different homes, and her disabled fourteen-year-old sister committed to a paupers' institution. Ida, only sixteen herself, was determined to keep the family together. She quit her studies and took a teaching job for twenty-five dollars a month in a school some six miles away, traveling there by mule. In her absence during the week, her grandmother looked after her siblings. On weekends she came home to wash, iron, and cook for the family. In 1880 Ida accepted her widowed Aunt Fannie's invitation to bring the girls, then seven and four, to live with her and her own three children in Memphis, Tennessee, and Ida found a job teaching primary school in Woodstock, a ten-mile train ride away.

On September 15, 1883, an incident on the train to Woodstock changed the course of Wells's life. The handwritten transcript of the court proceedings resulting from this incident includes her first-person testimony as taken down by the court reporter, giving a concise and clear account of what happened.[21]

> I am 20 years of age and unmarried, my profession is that of School Teacher, and during September 1883 I was teaching [in] a public school at Woodstock, a station on defendant's road, ten miles North of Memphis. My salary was $30.00 a month. On 15th September 1883, I was in Memphis and started to return to Woodstock. [I] took a seat in the car of defendant's passenger train that left Memphis about 4 o'clock that afternoon. When I went in the car, some half hour before leaving time, the ticket office was not open. I afterwards went and bought a ticket which read as follows: Chesapeake, Ohio & Southwestern R.R. / one continuous trip / Memphis / to / Woodstock / 1010.
>
> I returned to my seat in the rear car. There were only two passenger cars in the train, two passenger car [*sic*], and one baggage car. I saw one drunken white man in the front coach. I had before this time ridden in said rear car, once about July 1883. Rougher people ride in the front car than in the rear car. There was no person in the seat with me and I was the only colored person in that car. The car was not crowded.
>
> When a mile or so from Memphis, the conductor came collecting tickets, he took mine, looked at me, and returned it to me, saying he could not accept it in that car, and passed on. I was reading a newspaper at the time. Directly the conductor returned to me and said that I would have to go to the coach in front, that I was in the wrong car. That he had the rear car for white people alone, and that colored people must ride in the forward coach. To this I replied that I would not ride in the forward car, that I had a seat and intended to keep it. He said to me that he would treat me like a lady, but that I must go into the other car, and I replied that if he wished to treat me like a lady he would leave me alone.
>
> When we reached Fraziers, the first station, the train stopped, and the conductor again came to me and said he would again ask me politely to go into the other car, and I refused to do so. He then took hold of me to carry me to the other car. I resisted him—holding on to my seat—when he called for help, and two white passengers helped him to carry me out. I resisted all the time, and never consented to go. My dress was torn in the struggle, one sleeve was almost torn off. Everybody in the car seemed to sympathise with the conductor and were against me.
>
> The conductor had carried my bag and parasol, etc., into the forward coach before carrying me out, and when they got me onto the platform between the cars, I got off the train refusing to go into the forward coach. The conductor asked me not to get off, but I said that I would not ride in the forward coach.

> There were several colored passengers in that car. I paid 30¢ for my ticket and still hold it. The train was known as the Covington accommodation, and only run between Covington and Memphis. I also noticed smoking going on in the forward car. This car was used for colored people and white men, too. There never was any smoking and drunkenness in the rear coach, and sometimes colored people also rode in it.

Outwardly, the railroad company had followed the letter of the 1881 Tennessee law requiring "equal accommodations" in the ladies' car and the car for Black passengers and white men not in the company of a woman. Indeed, on this particular branch the "ladies' car" in one direction became the "colored car" in the other. William Murray, the conductor that day, testified that he did not allow smoking and drinking in the forward car and that smoking was only allowed in a third car—the "front" or "combination" car, which was a baggage car with a section partitioned off for second-class passengers and smokers. However, in spite of Murray's repeated assertions to the contrary, those rules and distinctions were not always enforced. G. H. Clowers, a Black minister and magistrate, testified on Ida's behalf, "The people in said forward coach where I was were rough. They were smoking, talking and drinking, very rough. It was no fit place for a Lady . . . I know that I smoked in that car that afternoon." Similarly, another witness testified, "There were drunken persons in there, and some smoking. . . . It was not a fit place for a lady to be." A third man admitted that he too "rode in the forward car, and smoked in it."[22]

When Murray tried to remove Wells forcibly from the ladies' car, tearing her dress in the process, she scratched him with her nails and drew blood when she bit him on the hand. Two passengers turned the seat in front of her around, so that she could not hook her feet under it, while two others helped Murray drag her to the platform between the cars. Wells got off the train rather than ride in the "colored car."[23]

Murray testified that he had recognized Wells, having encountered her previously "with two other colored women" boarding the train in Woodstock, and that he told them to go into the forward car. Murray said that all three of them rode in the forward car and that Wells told him "that she had rode in that rear car, and that she intended to do it again."[24] In her rebuttal, Wells said that "she had never got on the train at Woodstock, with two other colored women, and had no such conversation as conductor Murr[a]y had detailed regarding her wanting to ride in rear coach a week before she was ejected."[25] Sam Owsley, a resident of Woodstock who knew Wells, identified the others as Mrs. Wells, Ida's aunt, and her friend Miss Ragland, and he testified that

Wells "did not go on the train. She did not go on the step or platform of the cars."[26]

Wells sued the railroad for $1,000 in damages for ejecting her on September 15, and she engaged Thomas Cassels, a Black former legislator and assistant attorney general, to handle her case. Before the suit came to court, however, the U.S. Supreme Court, on October 15, declared key portions of the Civil Rights Act of 1875 to be unconstitutional, in particular arguing that Congress did not have the power to prohibit discrimination in private businesses (see Sallie J. Robinson above). This decision sparked outrage among African Americans, and it may have been what led Wells to challenge segregation on the trains yet again by sitting in the ladies' car.

The precise date of this second incident is uncertain, but the principal witness, Allene Kimbrough, placed it "sometime in November or the first of December 1883," as did her husband.[27] On this second occasion, Wells boarded the train at Woodstock, en route to Memphis, took a seat in the ladies' car, then left it briefly, leaving her bag behind. When she returned, a white woman, Allene Kimbrough, was sitting in that seat, and Ida's bag was missing. Kimbrough's husband had initially assumed that Wells "was the nurse of another white woman on the car."[28] According to long-standing custom, nurses and nannies were the only Black passengers openly tolerated in the ladies' car. After Ida demanded her seat back, she was escorted off the train. Denied a seat a second time on account of her color, Ida in turn sued a second time.

The two cases were tried together. Witnesses to the September 15 incident gave their testimony in January 1884. Progress on the second case, however, was delayed, and pleas to the first case were not filed until May 1. Frustrated with the delays, Wells engaged James Greer, a prominent white lawyer, to take over the case. Depositions from the Kimbroughs were taken on October 8, 1884, shortly before the trial finally got under way that November.

The non-jury case was decided not on the basis of racial segregation per se, but rather on the basis of the Tennessee Act of 1881, chapter 155, which forbade compelling the holders of first-class tickets "to occupy second class cars where smoking is allowed and no restrictions are enforced to prevent vulgar or obscene language," and the Act of 1882, chapter 6, which stressed that first-class ticket holders were entitled to "accommodations equal in all respects to the first-class cars on the train, and subject to the same rules governing other first-class cars."[29] Though the court was satisfied that the two cars were equal in their material fittings, Judge James O. Pierce, a former Union officer from Minnesota, ruled that because of the smoking, drinking and rowdy behavior in the "colored car," it was not of the same first-class quality as the ladies' car.

Accordingly, on December 24, 1884, he decided the case in favor of Wells and awarded her $500 in damages.

The railroad company's lawyers filed an appeal. The case was submitted to the Tennessee Supreme Court on March 31, 1885, and within five days Chief Justice Peter Turney, formerly an avid secessionist and a colonel in the Confederate army, delivered the court's opinion. The case summaries of Judge Pierce and Chief Justice Turney are noticeably different. Judge Pierce issued his verdict citing only the facts of the September 15 incident, without mentioning the second one. Conversely, Justice Turney reversed Pierce's decision in the light of the second, less dramatic incident, without mentioning the first. Neither judge clarified that Wells had twice sat in the ladies' car and been removed against her will. Nevertheless, Turney concluded, "We know of no rule that requires railroad companies to yield to the disposition of passengers to arbitrarily determine as to the coach in which they take passage. . . . We think it is evident that the purpose of the defendant in error [Wells] was to harass with a view to this suit, and that her persistence was not in good faith to obtain a comfortable seat for the short ride."[30] The judgment was reversed, and Wells was ordered to pay the court costs.

The question arises, as her case was being scheduled for court in the fall of 1883, why would Wells run the risk of sitting again in the ladies' car, albeit with a different conductor on duty? A summons for the railroad company's representatives to appear in court in January was issued on November 28 and executed on November 30. The Kimbroughs testified that the second incident had occurred at that very same time or close to it.[31] Was Wells intentionally challenging Jim Crow in response to the repeal of the Civil Rights Act a month earlier? Or might she perhaps have hoped to ride once more in the ladies' car unmolested in order to be able to say that she had done so when she gave her testimony? Ida B. Wells's temperament and determination were such that either explanation is plausible.

On Monday, April 11, 1885, Wells movingly recorded her reaction to the reversal of the decision in her private diary:

> The Supreme Court reversed the decision of the lower court in my behalf, last week. Went to see Judge G. this afternoon & he tells me four of them cast their personal prejudice in the scale of justice and decided in the face of all the evidence to the contrary that the smoking car was a first class coach for colored people as provided for by that statute that calls for separate coaches but first class, for the races. I felt so disappointed because I had hoped such great things from my suit for my people generally. I have firmly believed all along that the law

was on our side and would, when we appealed to it, give us justice. I feel shorn of that belief and utterly discouraged, and just now if it were possible would gather my race in my arms and fly far away with them. O God is there no rest, no peace, no justice in this land for us? Thou hast always fought the battles of the weak & oppressed. Come to my aid at this moment & teach me what to do, for I am sorely disappointed. Show us the way, even as thou led the children of Israel out of bondage into the promised land.[32]

The most important result of this case, far outweighing either the original decision or its reversal, was the effect it had on Wells herself. Sometime during 1884 she published an account of her mistreatment on the trains in the *Living Way*, a Baptist weekly newspaper published in Memphis. Thus began the career of one of the country's great journalists. Unfortunately, no known copies of this article have survived, but she continued writing about issues of racial inequity for the *Living Way* and for other Black newspapers. Under the pen name "Iola," she became nationally known as a forthright critic on matters of the rights of people of color and of Black women, in particular. T. Thomas Fortune, editor of the *New York Age*, wrote of meeting her,

I met 'Iola' at the conference. She has become famous as one of the few women who handles a goose quill with diamond point as handily as any of us men in newspaper work. Her name is Ida B. Wells. She teaches school in Memphis. She is rather girlish looking in physique, with sharp, regular features, penetrating eyes, firm set, thin lips and a sweet voice. . . . she is as smart as a steel trap, and she has no sympathy for humbug.[33]

Shortly after her court victory in December 1884, Wells was offered a teaching job in Memphis. In 1885 she was elected editor of the *Evening Star*, a Black paper published by the Memphis Lyceum, a social and literary group begun by Black teachers in the city. Then in 1889 she became editor of and a partner in the *Memphis Free Speech and Headlight*.

In 1891 Wells wrote a letter to Fortune, who published it in the *New York Age* under the heading "The Jim Crow Car: A Woman's Opinion of the Infamous Thing." In this letter she speaks of the need for a national organization to represent African American interests, citing as a model the "tireless zeal" of the abolitionists, and she reproves the apparent indifference of those who tolerate segregation in public transportation while she encourages them to resist:

As to my journey to Chattanooga, I rode (as I anticipated) in the Jim Crow car; I waited (as I had to) in the Negro waiting room, with a score or more of the men of my race looking on with indifferent eyes. Yes, we will have to fight, but the

> beginning of the fight must be with our own people. So long as the majority of them are not educated to the point of proper self-respect, so long our condition here will be hopeless.[34]

Soon after that letter was published, an editorial in *Free Speech*, probably written by Wells, drew the ire of white Memphians because it directly expressed sympathy toward the Black men in Georgetown, Kentucky, who did fight back by setting fire to a number of buildings in their angry response to a lynching: "Not until the Negro rises in his might and takes a hand in resenting such cold-blooded murders, if he has to burn down whole towns, will a halt be called in wholesale lynching."[35] Commenting in the *New York Age* on the harsh reaction to this editorial by two white-owned southern newspapers, Wells articulated a simpler, deeper, self-evident truth: "The way to prevent retaliation is to prevent the lynching."[36] Wells now found herself in a field that was to define her life, and when she lost her Memphis teaching job, she turned to journalism full time.

The following year, a close friend of Wells was lynched, along with two others, in a riot that stemmed from an argument between a Black boy and a white boy over a game of marbles. Wells began collecting stories and data about lynchings, both Black and white, from around the country. She used this data to dismantle the myth that most lynchings were the result of Black men raping white women. In 1892 she published *Southern Horrors: Lynch Law in All Its Phases.* In 1895 she wrote *A Red Record: Tabulated Statistics and Alleged Causes of Lynchings in the United States, 1892–1893–1894*, which sardonically notes on its title page: "Respectfully submitted to the Nineteenth Century civilization in 'the Land of the Free and the Home of the Brave.'" Five years later, under her married name, Ida B. Wells-Barnett, she published *Mob Rule in New Orleans: The Story of Robert Charles and His Fight to the Death—The Story of His Life, Burning Human Beings Alive, Other Lynching Statistics.*[37] These works, still often consulted and cited well into the twenty-first century, established the evidence-based model for what is today known as investigative reporting.

In 1895 Wells married Ferdinand L. Barnett, an attorney and the founder of Chicago's first African American newspaper, the *Conservator*, which Wells-Barnett herself then bought from its stockholders. She had four children while she continued her work indefatigably, presiding over Chicago's Ida B. Wells Club, cofounding the Frederick Douglass Club, working alongside the settlement activist Jane Addams to prevent segregation in the city's public schools, and protesting lynchings in Illinois and elsewhere. After a riot in 1908 in Springfield, Illinois, she became one of the "Founding Forty" members of the National Association for the Advancement of Colored People (NAACP), though she later grew impatient with the organization's moderate methods. In 1913 she cofounded the first Black women's suffrage club in Chicago. She was accused of treason when she protested the court-martial and hanging of twelve Black soldiers alleged to have taken part in a riot in Houston, Texas, in 1917. She published investigations of the East St. Louis Massacre in 1918. She encouraged Black people to testify after a 1919 riot in Chicago killed twenty-three Black residents and fifteen white ones. She worked for years along with the NAACP to defend victims of the horrific race riot in Elaine, Alabama, in 1919, in which an indeterminate number of African Americans were killed, one thousand sharecroppers imprisoned in a stockade, sixty-seven given long prison sentences, and twelve sentenced to death (but eventually freed). The year before her death in 1931, she ran unsuccessfully as an independent for a seat in the Illinois state senate.[38]

Had she not been dragged out of that ladies' car in 1883, Ida B. Wells-Barnett's career may never have drawn the world's attention. But that seems unlikely; she was not one to remain quiet in the face of oppression. Her lifelong work as a teacher, a skilled researcher, a fearless writer, a club and community organizer, a suffragist and women's rights activist, and an undaunted moral voice during the nadir of U.S. race relations has placed her indisputably in the pantheon of African American heroes.

On May 4, 2020, the Pulitzer Prize Board awarded Ida B. Wells-Barnett a special citation: "For her outstanding and courageous reporting on the horrific and vicious violence against African Americans during the era of lynching."[39] On March 29, 2022, 130 years after *Southern Horrors* appeared and after more than two hundred failed attempts to get a bill passed through Congress, President Biden signed into law the Emmett Till Antilynching Act, which the U.S. Senate passed unanimously after a vote of 422 to 3 in the House of Representatives.

Martha, Mary, Lucy, and Winnie Stewart, August 15 and September 2, 1884

Martha, Mary, Lucy, and Winnie Stewart were raised near Kinsale, in Westmoreland County, Virginia. In the early 1880s they moved to Baltimore to work. Each summer they would travel home to visit their mother on the steamship *Sue*, which sailed regularly down Chesapeake Bay from Baltimore, then up the Potomac to Washington, with stops along the way.[40]

On August 15, 1884, the Stewart sisters and their aunt, Pauline Braxton, purchased round-trip first-class tickets for three dollars each from Baltimore to Kinsale Landing, near the mouth of the Potomac. After boarding the boat, they took their wraps down to the rear first-class cabin and selected bunks. They then went up to sit in the saloon or lounge area. Shortly afterward one of the chambermaids brought their wraps to them, saying that she did so on the captain's orders and that the cabin below was now locked. They spent the night on chairs in the saloon. On the return trip on September 1, they were told immediately upon boarding that the first-class cabin was locked and the captain had given orders "not to let any colored passengers go down there." Again they spent the night in the saloon. After arriving home, the sisters sued the Baltimore, Chesapeake, and Richmond Steamboat Company.

The case was heard by Judge C. J. Morris in the District Court of Maryland on September 18, 1884. The chronology regarding earlier trips taken by the Stewarts is unclear in the surviving court transcript of testimony, but three or four different occasions are described. Sometime earlier they had purchased second-class tickets for $2.50. This consigned them to the forward segregated cabin belowdecks, with sleeping accommodations that were so unacceptable that they spent the night in the public saloon above deck. It may have been in reference to that trip that Winnie Stewart testified that "about three years ago" she had a second-class ticket and went down to the segregated cabin:

> When I goes down there it was not fitten for a dog to stay in. I goes right to the bunks and I hushed up the sheets to see the condition the mattress was in, and it was just as black as could be, and I didn't undress to get in there. I just got two chairs and put [them] together, and borrowed the cooks overcoat and spread [it] over my head and passed the night that way, and I said then at that time "if money will ever prevent me from staying in that hole I will never go in there again." When I went home the next summer I paid $3.00 for a first class ticket and goes down in the white ladies cabin. It was doubly superior to this place. There was white spreads, white blankets, white sheets, wash-bowl, pitcher, comb and brush, looking-glass, towels; nice carpet on the floor, nice chairs and everything down there. I was just getting ready to undress to go to the bed and the clerk himself came down and drove me out, and then I had to go up into the upper saloon and pass the night sitting there.

On one occasion Mary, Lucy, and their aunt, Pauline Braxton, successfully managed what in the 1960s might have been termed a "sleep-in." When asked, "Did you ever know of colored persons being permitted to occupy the after cabin?" Mary Stewart Johnson testified, "Yes sir; once before I had gone down in that cabin, and then it was the captain's orders for us all to come out that night; but we were undressed and wouldn't come out." Lucy Stewart Jones and Pauline Braxton similarly testified that they had boarded with first-class tickets, gone down to the first-class cabin, undressed, and got into bed. When the ship's clerk sent the chambermaid down to say "Every colored person must come out of there," they refused. As Pauline Braxton stated bluntly, "I told her I had undressed and gone to bed, and wasn't coming out by any means."

The court transcript adds further explicit detail about the conditions in the segregated cabin. After describing the first-class cabin in almost exactly the same glowing terms as Winnie's statement above, Martha was asked by her lawyer about the second-class area she had refused to sleep in the previous year:

> **Tell the court w[h]ere that is on the steamer, and what accommodations you saw there?**
> That is in the forward end of the boat.
>
> **Where?**
> Underneath where all the cattle and horses is tied; right over the cabin. It isn't hardly respectable; it isn't nice enough for a respectable person to go in. One half the time there is no sheets on the bunks. I haven't seen nary blanket down there; I haven't seen any glass, and I haven't seen any wash-bowl and pitcher down there; never no water; and it is kept very dirty, as much as I have seen of it.
>
> **Was that place underneath the forward part of the boat, where the cattle were, appropriated to women alone?**
> Women and men went down the same flight of steps, and there is only a little partition in between that divides the men's part and the women's. They both goes down the same flight of steps, and there is no key to the door. The door between is thrown open all the time. They talk right out of the window, or the door, into the women's part.

In his written opinion, delivered on February 2, 1885, Judge Morris, citing the Supreme Court decision in *Hall v. Decuir*, ruled that, in the absence of any legislation by Congress on the matter of regulations concerning the separation of passengers in interstate travel, private companies were free to establish their own regulations. He stressed, however, "One of the restrictions which the common law imposes is, that such regulations must be reasonable and tend to the comfort and safety of the passengers generally, and that accommodations equal in comfort and safety must be affordable to all alike who pay the same price." Regarding the testimony he had heard, Morris stated, "I am quite convinced that no disinterested person would have gone into the forward cabin in its actual condition in August, 1884, who had the option of the other one, irrespective of all questions of color or race." He ruled in favor of the Stewarts and awarded each of them $100. This decision in its turn was cited ten years later in the case of *Plessy v. Ferguson*, which brought the debate over the "separate but equal" principle to a head as a matter of law.

Lola Houck, September 21, 1886

It is one thing to pass laws separating travelers on the basis of color. It is quite another thing to determine to whom such laws apply. Who is "white"? Who is "Black"? How does one know? The above example of Sallie Robinson's nephew Joseph is a good case in point, for in that case the train conductor had simply assumed that the light-skinned, fair-haired, blue-eyed young man was white. From the earliest days of steamboats and railroads, Jim Crow rules were applied arbitrarily or at times ignored. If no one complained, some train conductors were content to let people of color ride in the "long car," "ladies' car," or "first-class car." On rare occasion, as in the case of Basil Dorsey, a conductor might even rule against the objections of white passengers. And there were undoubtedly many times when a "colored" passenger passed as "white" without notice, as Lola Houck admitted she had.

On September 21, 1886, Lola and her husband, Leon, were living in Victoria, Texas, when she received a telegram saying that her infant child, at the time with Lola's mother in Galveston, was very ill. Houck, who was "to some extent pregnant," immediately booked a first-class ticket on the Southern Pacific Railway to Rosenberg, Texas, where she would then, presumably, make a connection to Galveston.[41]

There were two passenger cars on the train. The rear car was "for the accommodation exclusively of white passengers; the front car, was known in Texas as the 'Jim Crow Car,' and it was for the use of colored people, though white people often rode in it." This particular Jim Crow car was a "combination car," partitioned into two unequal sections with a door between them. In one section "passengers, white or colored, were allowed to smoke," and the benches there were not upholstered. The other section was for "colored" passengers; it had cushioned seats and "smoking was forbidden by the rules, but these rules were often violated."

Lola Houck and her husband were both very light-complexioned, so that, as the court report puts it, "casually looking at her or her husband it would be difficult to distinguish either of them from white persons." Nevertheless, the Houcks "were known at their home in Victoria, Tex., as respectable colored people." The legal issue being tried in this case, however, was not whether Lola Houck was "colored." It was agreed by all parties that she was. But her ability to pass as white becomes relevant insofar as she acknowledged that "she had previously ridden in the rear car of the train, or one reserved for white people by the company on the defendant's line; and she has since then ridden there without any question."

On that day, however, Houck was denied access to the car reserved "exclusively" for white passengers. She boarded the train, and while still on the platform between the two cars she was challenged as she was about to enter the rear car: "The brakeman, meeting her at the door, forbade and denied her entrance thereto. He shut the door in her face, and locked it from the inside, and, holding the keys up against the door-glass, told her that he was inside and she was outside, and she could not come in because she was a negro."

That sneering taunt with the keys is more than enough to give a sense of the brakeman's character and attitude. The conductor came along, took her ticket, and told her to go into the front car. Lest she try to follow him into the rear car, he passed his ticket punch to the brakeman through a window and told him to punch people's tickets, take their fares, et cetera. He himself went into the front car, leaving her on the platform.

At the next stop the brakeman left the door locked and allowed new white passengers in through the car's rear door. Mrs. Houck got off the train and followed those passengers to the rear platform, where the brakeman once again refused to let her enter. The train started up, leaving her on the car's rear platform until the next stop, where she returned to the front of the car and tried unsuccessfully to enter again. The conductor told her to go into the Jim Crow car, but she refused and remained on the platform until the train reached Rosenberg, even though it was "an ugly, rainy September day."

Following this ordeal, Mrs. Houck became ill, was confined to her bed for a number of weeks, and suffered a miscarriage. She and her husband then sued the Southern Pacific Railway for $7,500 for personal damages, and a verdict was delivered in a jury trial in the U.S. circuit court, Eastern District of Texas, on December 11–12, 1888. In the course of the trial, Mrs. Houck testified to a number of points that the brakeman denied. She said that he had spoken roughly to her, that he had "called the attention of men about the train to the fact that he had a negro riding on the platform," and that he had pushed her so that she was in danger of falling off the train and in doing so he had torn her dress. She also explained that "the front car had a rough lot of white and colored people in it, and some of them were boisterous and drinking; that the attention of those people had been directed to her by the language and acts of the brakeman, and she was afraid to go in among them."

The brakeman testified that "when she had travelled before with him he did not know that she was a negro, and he only knew that she was a colored woman after the bootblack on the train told him about her being a colored woman." The railway company, for their part, contended, "The evidence shows that the front car, which was set apart by the company for colored people, was as safe, and was substantially equal in its conditions to the rear car, to which she was denied entrance." The judge instructed the jury that the railway company's Jim Crow rule was legally justified and that if they determined that the safety and comfort of the two cars were substantially the same, "the plaintiff cannot complain of any injury coming to her because she was denied entrance to the rear car."

The Houcks' lawyers argued that Mrs. Houck's illness and miscarriage were the result of her mistreatment by the railway company's employees, but the jury was further instructed that the company should only be charged with any injuries resulting directly from the actions of the brakeman or conductor:

> [If] she remained on the platform in the rain, and became sick in consequence thereof, she, by her own negligence, in not going to a better place for protection against the rain and weather was at fault; that if the miscarriage and illness was caused, not by the mental irritations, humiliations, annoyances and rude acts caused by the faults and wrongs of the brakeman, but by the physical discomforts and fatigue which her ride, unseated, on the platform, gave her, she could not recover for the injury inherent in the illness of the miscarriage.

The all-white jury seems not to have been satisfied as to the equality of accommodations, for they found in favor of the plaintiff, Mrs. Houck, and awarded her "Two thousand Dollars for exemplary damages and Three thousand Dollars for actual damages."[42]

Judge Aleck Boarman himself acknowledged that the Jim Crow car was "nothing like as comfortable to ride in," that it "was occupied by boisterous passengers, both white and colored, who were smoking and drinking, as is usually the case in such cars," and that "the brakeman treated [the] plaintiff, who 'acted all the time in a ladylike manner,' rudely, wrongfully, and, in some degree, maliciously." Yet he wrote in response to the verdict: "I do not think the jury were warranted by the facts in allowing $3,000 for actual damages, for it was not at all clear that the miscarriage or illness was of a serious nature; nor was it made sufficiently clear that either the miscarriage or illness came to Mrs. Houck proximately in consequence of the acts of the brakeman, or of the conductor, in denying her admission to the rear car." Thus, he reduced the award for actual damages to $2,500, at the same time denying the Southern Pacific's motion for a new trial unless the Houcks refused to accept the reduced award within ten days. (It is unclear whether he let stand the $2,000 exemplary damage award, for he does not mention it again.) The most striking aspects of the judge's opinion are his doubt that Mrs. Houck's illness and miscarriage were "of a serious nature," and the belief that it was not "sufficiently clear" that they were caused by the actions of the brakeman and conductor.

Tangential as it was to Lola Houck's lawsuit, the larger question remains: what difference does color make? Mrs. Houck had ridden in first-class cars before and after September 21, 1886, and no one was any the wiser; no one suffered a whit of harm because of her presence. The only harm done on that particular day was done to Mrs. Houck—first, as the judge acknowledged, by the wrongful and malicious treatment of the brakeman, and secondly, by the fear and suffering she endured during the ride and her subsequent illness and miscarriage. The jury apparently recognized the latter, though Judge Boarman did not.

William H. Council, May 1887

William Hooper Councill was born into slavery in Fayetteville, North Carolina, in 1848. His father escaped to Canada in 1854 but was unable to secure the freedom of his wife and children. In 1857 Councill, his mother (Mary Jane), and his brother Cicero were sold at the slave market in Richmond, Virginia, to a plantation owner in northern Alabama. Two other brothers were sold separately. During the Civil War, Councill, with his mother and brother, escaped in 1863 to a U.S. Army camp in Chattanooga, Tennessee. Returning to Alabama after the war, Councill was educated in a freedmen's school and was tutored in Latin, chemistry, physics, and mathematics in the evenings. In 1867 and 1869 he founded schools for freedmen in Jackson and Madison Counties. His political ambitions led him to a two-year stint (1872–1874) as chief enrolling clerk for the state legislature and to a failed bid for a seat as a legislator.[43]

Councill left the Republican Party for the Democratic Party in 1875, a move that lost him many supporters but gained him a position as the first principal of the State Normal and Industrial School (now Alabama A&M University) near Huntsville. While there he simultaneously published the *Huntsville Herald* from 1877 to 1884 and read law. He was admitted to the Alabama bar in 1883, though he never practiced law. In 1885 Councill was acquitted of charges of rape and assault, but as a result of the notoriety of that and because of his accommodationist views in matters of race relations, a significant amount of philanthropic donations to the school shifted to Booker T. Washington's rival Tuskegee Institute.[44]

On April 7, 1887, Councill held a first-class ticket to travel on the Western & Atlantic Railroad from Chattanooga into Georgia. On boarding the train he sat in the first-class coach, where he was assaulted by another passenger and violently forced into the Jim Crow section of the smoking car.[45] Councill was not opposed to segregation per se, but he firmly believed that the accommodations offered to segregated Black first-class passengers should be the same as those for white first-class passengers.

A new agency had just come into being that allowed someone to register a complaint without going through the court system. The Interstate Commerce Act was signed by President Grover Cleveland in February 1887, establishing the Interstate Commerce Commission (ICC) to regulate domestic commerce and transportation. Section 3.1 of the act states unequivocally: "It shall be unlawful for any common carrier subject to the provisions of this act to make or give any undue or unreasonable preference or advantage to any particular person . . . in any respect whatsoever, or to subject any particular person . . . to any undue or unreasonable prejudice or disadvantage in any respect whatsoever."[46]

On May 31 Councill became the first person to file with the ICC a complaint about the mistreatment he suffered as a result of the railroad company's Jim Crow rules, asking "that the Commission award him $25,000 in damages, and such other relief as it may deem proper."[47] The ICC report outlines the case in some detail, describing Councill as "an intelligent colored man, well dressed, self possessed and of good address." It is particularly remarkable that, by way of contrast, the Commission quotes verbatim the deposition of Councill's assailant, Charles Whitsett:

> I walked forward to the front end of the car and told Mr. Bivins, the flagman, that I wanted his lantern a minute. I took it out of his hand, then turned and walked back to where Council [*sic*] was sitting and told him there was to be no more foolishness, that I did not want to hurt him, but he had to go. He replied very insolently that he would not go, and then I grabbed him in the collar and struck him over the head with the lantern. I knocked him out of his seat and pulled him out. He fell to the floor and as he raised up he came toward me, and I let him have it again with the lantern. I hit him several times before I conquered him and then rushed him right out of the car into the darkies' car. He was willing to go by the time I got through with him.[48]

Whitsett's comment that "he came toward me," of course, suggests that Whitsett was claiming that he was being attacked and acting in self-defense.

The ICC chairman declined to rule on the matter of damages as beyond the purview of the commission, agreeing with the railroad that the company did have the right to classify passengers "on the color line." Councill's lawyers conceded that point but argued further that first-class facilities and conveniences had to be equal for both races. On December 3, 1887, the commission ruled in Councill's favor, stating, "There is no **undue prejudice or unjust preference** shown by the railroad companies in **separating** their **white and**

colored passengers by providing cars for each, **if** the **cars** so provided are **equally safe and comfortable**."[49] Any damages, fees, or expenses for which the company may have been liable, they determined, had to be decided in a court of law. Twelve days later the ICC turned to the similar case of William Heard.

In late 1887, when several State Normal and Industrial School students attempted to sit in the first-class coach on a trip from Huntsville to Decatur, Georgia, Councill was accused of "forcing social equality" and pressured to resign as principal, though he was reinstated in 1888. After this time Councill became more openly accommodationist, accepting Jim Crow as he worked to support the school, even while also addressing questions of race in his writing.[50]

William H. Heard, Spring 1887

William H. Heard was born into slavery in Elbert County, Georgia, in 1850. His mother died when he was nine, and at ten William was set to work as a plowboy and to care for his younger siblings. After the Civil War, William lived with his father, George W. Heard, a skilled blacksmith, wheelwright, and carpenter. William seized every available opportunity to get the education forbidden him as an enslaved person. "I secured the services of a 'Poor white' boy named Billee Adams and paid him ten cents a lesson and studied in Webster's Blue Back Spelling Book. I studied spelling, reading, and arithmetic all in this one book."[51] By the age of seventeen he had earned a second-grade teaching certificate.

Heard became a high school teacher in Mount Carmel, South Carolina, and in 1876 was elected to the South Carolina state senate. He attended the University of South Carolina until the following year, when Reconstruction ended, federal troops were withdrawn, and the Democratic Party took over the South Carolina legislature and barred Black students from the university. Heard returned to Georgia and briefly attended both Clark College and Atlanta University. In 1879, however, he had a religious awakening and became a licensed preacher, serving African Methodist Episcopal churches in Georgia, South Carolina, Pennsylvania, and Delaware for the next fifteen years.[52]

While a minister in Charleston, South Carolina, Heard had occasion to travel north in the spring of 1887, returning by train on a first-class ticket from Cincinnati. He rode undisturbed all the way to Atlanta, but on the last leg of his journey he was ejected from his first-class seat on the train to Charleston and moved to the "colored car," really just a partially partitioned section of the smoking car, in which the "seats were not upholstered, and there was no carpet on the floor." Heard described the car as "dusty and dirty, and at times as full of smoke as the adjoining compartment." Furthermore, while no Black passengers were allowed in the first-class cars, white men did go into "the colored compartment with whiskey and drank it from the glass used by the passengers for water, and indulged in rude and profane language." Only when Heard requested did the conductor ask them to leave.[53]

The Interstate Commerce Commission was established that April, and on July 6, less than a week after William H. Councill filed his complaint with the ICC, Heard filed one of his own on the same grounds—that "undue or unreasonable preference or advantage" and "undue or unreasonable prejudice" were unlawful. A common tactic employed by defendants charged with prejudicial treatment of passengers was to deflect attention away from the discriminatory nature of segregation itself. The response to Heard's complaint by the Georgia Railroad Company is a classic example of the lengths to which segregationist arguments were stretched, albeit couched in legalese. On July 30, the *New York Times* illustrated this in a short piece under the heading "*No 'Jim Crow Cars.'* The Georgia Railroad Demands Relief of the Commission." In his complaint Heard had used the term "Jim Crow car," and, in response, Joseph B. Cummings, general counsel to the Georgia Railroad Company, argued that "Jim Crow car" was not a term used or even heard of by the company. As printed in the *Times*, the ICC case report states,

> Petitioner claims that he was not permitted to ride in the first class coach of respondent, but was required to ride in what is known on said Georgia Railroad as the "Jim Crow car."
>
> Respondent replies that it has in no way given or authorized such designation of any car on its road; and if, when complainant says that the car on which he rode is "known as the Jim Crow car," he means to say that respondent is in any way responsible for this designation and implied contempt for its inmates, respondent denies such allegation. . . . If any of respondent's cars have been spoken of by evil disposed persons as "Jim Crow cars" respondent is not aware of it.

In reality, the term "Jim Crow car" had been in common use for at least fifty years. David Ruggles had used it in 1838 and 1841, as had the white abolitionist William C. Coffin on the first day of 1841 and Mary Newhall Green the following September. Cummings went on to argue with blatant mendacity that "the cars provided for the colored passengers are equally as safe, comfortable, clean, well ventilated, and cared for as those provided for whites." He claimed, "[The difference,] if any, relates to matters aesthetical only, and consist in higher ornamentation and matters of that sort rather than in those which affect the substantial conditions of safety, comfort, and convenience."[54]

The ICC recognized that "educated and reputable colored persons" had "reason for complaining under such conditions" and that Black passengers were "not furnished with the just and equal accommodations for which they [paid] and to which they [were] entitled under the Law." However, it did not—nor would it for a long time—acknowledge that segregation itself was a prejudicial violation of the law. It recommended (ineffectively and without the authority to enforce such a recommendation) some such solution as dividing cars into first- and second-class sections so that white and Black passengers in their respective cars could choose the conditions under which they would like, or could afford, to travel.[55]

Four years later, a brief notice in the *New York Age* on August 8, 1891, headed "A Pullman Sleeper Outrage," recorded a more violent attack against Heard on the Louisville & Nashville Railroad:

> On the night of July 20, Rev. W. H. Heard, D.D., was forcibly ejected by three ruffians from a PULLMAN sleeper, on the L. & N. R.R. He had bought lower berth No. 11, and the ruffians had his ticket, clearly showing a conspiracy between the sleeping car conductor and them. He was also by the railroad officials forced into the car for "colored people," after being driven from the PULLMAN sleeper. . . . An investigation is being made by the attorney of the [Afro-American] League . . . and a vigorous prosecution will be instituted against both companies, if the facts warrant it.

In 1895 Heard was appointed as the U.S. minister to Liberia for a three-year term. He then returned to church work, serving from 1904 to 1908 as secretary-treasurer of the Connectional Preachers' Aid and Mutual Relief Society. In this position he traveled widely throughout the country, "two and three nights in a week curled up on a bench in a 'jim crow' car."[56] In 1908 he was elected bishop of the AME church and ultimately became bishop of the First AME District, encompassing New York, New England, New Jersey, Pennsylvania, and Delaware. At the age of eighty-seven Bishop Heard attended the 1937 World Conference on Faith and Order in Edinburgh, Scotland. While there he was asked to leave the hotel where he and his niece were staying. Such a demand seems contrary to Scottish traditions of liberalism and hospitality, but apparently some American tourists at the hotel had an "antipathy to Negroes." Sir John Simon, the Chancellor of the Exchequer, and his wife, Lady Simon, expressed their regrets and invited him to the hotel where they were on holiday, and the archbishop of York asked Heard and his niece to stay with him. The bishop replied with thanks but said that he was "comfortably installed" in the hotel where he was staying.[57] He died just three weeks after returning home.[58]

CHAPTER 4

Jim Crow across the South

Segregated travel had been imposed, generally by company rules, throughout the South after the war and Reconstruction, but during the last two decades of the nineteenth century numerous southern states adopted statutes *requiring* segregated railroad cars. Tennessee had passed a separate car law in 1881 and strengthened it in 1891. The Mississippi Separate Car Law was enacted in 1883 and upheld in the U.S. Supreme Court in 1890—though not without strong opposition from the Great Dissenter himself, Justice John Harlan.[1] These laws were followed by similar ones in Florida (1887), Texas (1889 and 1891), Kentucky (1890 and 1892), Arkansas (1891), South Carolina (1898 and 1900), Virginia (1900), and Maryland (1904). To provide a veneer of legal logic and respectability, and perhaps to ease the legislators' consciences, the new Jim Crow laws invariably stated that separate white and Black first-class accommodations had to be equal, though that requirement was rarely met or enforced.

The persistence of William Nichols and others during the spring of 1867 had successfully resulted in the integration of the New Orleans streetcars. Railroad trains, however, were another matter, and throughout Louisiana, as elsewhere in the South, the Jim Crow car held sway. The U.S. Supreme Court's 1878 reversal of the Louisiana Supreme Court ruling in favor of Josephine Decuir meant that Article 13 of the 1868 Louisiana Constitution and Act 38 of 1869, both barring discrimination in travel, no longer carried the force of law, even for travel entirely within the state boundaries. In 1883 the U.S. Supreme Court decision in the five combined "Civil Rights Cases," which included the Tennessee case of Sallie J. Robinson, resulted in the elimination of the public accommodation protections in the 1875 Civil Rights Act. The stage was set for one of the most contentious and far-reaching decisions to face the U.S. Supreme Court.

Homer Plessy, June 7, 1892

In May 1890, as the post-Reconstruction proliferation of Jim Crow laws spread across the country, a legislator introduced House Bill No. 42 in the

Louisiana House of Representatives. Officially titled the Louisiana Railway Accommodations Act, it became widely known as the Separate Car Act. The full 166-word title of the bill begins on a pleasant-sounding note: "An Act to promote the comfort of passengers on railway trains." But this congenial tone is misleading. The title continues, at some length, clarifying its real purpose. Since the act is the focal point of one of the most significant—and notorious—U.S. Supreme Court decisions, and because the title alone encapsulates many of the points against which the people profiled throughout this book were struggling, it is worth quoting it in full:

> An Act to promote the comfort of passengers on railway trains; requiring all railway companies carrying passengers on their trains, in this State, to provide equal but separate accommodations for the white and colored races, by providing separate coaches or compartments so as to secure separate accommodations; defining the duties of the officers of such railways; directing them to assign passengers to the coaches or compartments set aside for the use of the race to which such passengers belong; authorizing them to refuse to carry on their train such passengers as may refuse to occupy the coaches or compartments to which he or she is assigned; to exonerate such railway companies from any and all blame or damages that might proceed or result from such a refusal; to prescribe penalties for all violations of this act; to put this act into effect ninety days after its promulgation, and to repeal all laws or parts of laws contrary to or inconsistent with the provisions of this act.[2]

In 1889 a group of prominent Black and mixed-race Louisiana businessmen had formed the American Citizens' Equal Rights Association (ACERA), led by Louis Martinet, editor of the *Louisiana Standard* and founder of the *New Orleans Crusader*. In their fight against Louisiana's move to enshrine Jim Crow in law, they presented a petition to the state legislature on May 24, 1890, decrying the bill as "unconstitutional, un-American, unjust, dangerous and against sound public policy."[3]

On the very day that Martinet presented the ACERA petition in Baton Rouge, an article in the New Orleans *Times-Democrat* celebrated the passage of a separate coach act in Kentucky. The article exults, "Were Virginia now to follow suit, the phalanx of States insisting upon such a separation would be complete and unbroken." It then makes explicit the underlying extent of the "comfort" to which the Louisiana bill merely alluded in its opening. Noting that the Kentucky vote had been attended by many "leading ladies" of that state who enthusiastically applauded the bill's passage and showered its advocates with their "grateful and gracious attentions," the article editorializes: "This feature of the discussion told more eloquently than any words could tell the absolute need that exists for such a measure, and the quarter in which the need is most urgently required. The male portion of the traveling public can always take care of itself in indiscriminate travel; but the protection that is afforded only by a statutory separation of cars for the races is peremptorily demanded in the interest and for the safety, let alone the comfort, of white women."[4]

This so-called "absolute need" had long been, and would long continue to be, a specious excuse for deeply held racist beliefs, behaviors, and cruelty. The comfort of Black women and men, of course, was not a matter of concern at all.

Some members of the Louisiana legislature opposed the separate car bill, but it passed in the lower house on June 3, 1890, by a vote of fifty-six to twenty-three, with fifteen absent. In early July it easily passed in the senate. In haste, Martinet sent a telegram to the governor on July 10, stating simply, "Governor, thousands good and true men petition you to veto separate car bill." Unmoved, the governor signed the bill the same day. In the next edition of the *Crusader*, Martinet promised, "We will make a case, a test case, and bring it before the Federal Courts. No such case has been fairly made or presented."[5]

To challenge the new law, Martinet and others formed the Citizens' Committee to Challenge the Constitutionality of the Separate Car Law, known among French-speaking people of color in New Orleans simply as the Comité des Citoyens. In August a member of ACERA, Eli Freeman, wrote a letter seeking advice from Albion Tourgee, a prominent white author, lawyer, and activist from upstate New York who wrote a widely read syndicated column on civil rights under the pseudonym "The Bystander." Martinet and the Citizens' Committee were greatly encouraged when Tourgee not only agreed to lead their effort but also to do so free of charge, in partnership with a leading New Orleans criminal lawyer, James C. Walker.

Tourgee, Walker, and the Citizens' Committee began to strategize. The goal was to get the Separate Car Act tested in the U.S. Supreme Court, where, if the outcome was in their favor, the Jim Crow car would be outlawed. This, in turn, would challenge segregation in other venues such as schools and theaters. To that end, they agreed that the best way to get to the highest court would be through a criminal case. They would need to arrange a situation in which someone would be arrested and convicted under this clause of Section 2 of the Act: "Any passenger insisting on going into a coach or compartment to which by race he does not belong, shall be liable to a fine of twenty-five dollars or in lieu thereof to imprisonment for a period of not more than twenty days in the parish prison."[6] However, should a struggle or a fight break out, and the passenger be arrested for a breach of the peace, the purpose of the test case would be defeated, for the Separate Car Act would not be the law under which charges would be brought.

To insure the right sort of arrest, Martinet met with representatives of the Louisville & Nashville Railroad. Railroad companies on the whole were opposed to separate car laws for the simple reason that running separate cars cost them money. On the other hand, they did not want to run the risk of angering their white clientele by openly supporting integration. Thus, the L&N agreed to make a car quietly available at a predetermined time. A preselected passenger with an interstate ticket would then politely refuse to leave the car when his presence was challenged by a selected member of the train crew. At Tourgee's suggestion, the committee also decided that that person should have a light complexion, so as not to draw the attention of the other passengers until the time came for the arrest. Daniel Desdunes, the twenty-year-old son of Rodolphe Desdunes, one of the leaders of the Comité des Citoyens, was chosen to be that person.

On the morning of February 24, 1892, Desdunes boarded an L&N train in New Orleans with a ticket to Mobile, Alabama.[7] As the train left the station, the brakeman asked Desdunes to move to the car designated for people of color. Desdunes refused. The conductor was summoned, and as Desdunes insisted on his right to stay seated, the train was stopped. As planned, a police captain just "happened" to be on board, and Desdunes was arrested and taken to court. There he was charged under the Separate Car Act, and the treasurer of the Citizens' Committee paid a $500 bond to keep the young man out of jail before his trial.

The plan was to have Desdunes convicted, after which he would refuse to pay the fine and be sentenced to twenty days in prison. The putative crime was too minor to allow for an appeal, and thus Tourgee could move the case immediately to the U.S. circuit court on a writ of habeas corpus to determine whether his detention was legal. If the conviction were upheld there, as was likely, Tourgee and Walker could then appeal to the U.S. Supreme Court. The judge appointed to the case was none other than R. H. Marr, the segregationist who had successfully argued for the reversal of the original verdict in favor of Madame Decuir, and who had earlier orchestrated the "Battle of Liberty Place," a coup attempt to overturn the election of the Louisiana governor. Desdunes's trial was considerably delayed when Marr disappeared on April 19, never to be seen again. The case could not proceed until Marr was found or declared dead and a new judge appointed.

Meanwhile, on May 25, the Louisiana Supreme Court ruled in an unrelated case that the Separate Car Act could not be enforced in instances of interstate travel.[8] This meant that Desdunes could not be convicted under the act. When Judge John H. Ferguson was appointed in Marr's place, he ruled on June 9 that the case against Desdunes was not valid in his court. The district attorney agreed and dropped the case. There was no more path to the Supreme Court. But Tourgee and Walker had a backup plan—another "passenger" was already challenging the Separate Car Act.

Once the Separate Car Act could no longer be challenged on interstate trains, the Citizens' Committee made another arrangement with a different railroad—the East Louisiana Railroad, which ran entirely within the state, providing excursions north around Lake Pontchartrain to popular vacation spots away from the stifling heat of the city. The Citizens' Committee also enlisted a private detective, Captain C. C. Cain, manager of the Cain Detective Bureau, to arrest and sign a complaint against the "offending" passenger.

That passenger, Homer Adolph Plessy, was a married, twenty-nine-year-old shoemaker from a family long recognized among the New Orleans *gens des couleur*. His great-grandmother on his father's side had been granted her freedom from slavery in 1779. His maternal grandfather had served with other freemen of color in the War of 1812 and had later signed a petition to President Lincoln demanding equal rights. Homer himself had considerable political interests and was friends with Rodolphe Desdunes and other members of the Comité des Citoyens.[9]

At the Press Street station on Tuesday, June 7, two days before Judge Ferguson dismissed the charge against Daniel Desdunes, Homer Plessy took a seat in the first-class coach of an East Louisiana train, with a first-class ticket to Covington.[10] The *Times-Democrat*, unaware that the encounter had been prearranged, reported, "The conductor, on discovering the presence of the negro, accosted him and inquired: 'Are you a colored man?' 'Yes,' was the reply."[11] Martinet's *Crusader* couched that question in reverse terms:

> As the train was moving out of the station, the conductor came up and asked him if he was a white man. Plessy, who is as white as the average white southerner, replied that he was a colored man. Then, said the conductor, "you must go in the coach reserved for colored people."
>
> Plessy replied that he had a first-class ticket and would remain in the first-class coach.
>
> The conductor insisted that he retired [*sic*] to the Jim Crow coach. Plessy determinedly told him that he was an American citizen and proposed to enjoy his rights as such and to ride for the value of his money.

Captain Cain was summoned and told Plessy that "he would have to go into the coach or to jail. Plessy said he would go to jail first before relinquishing

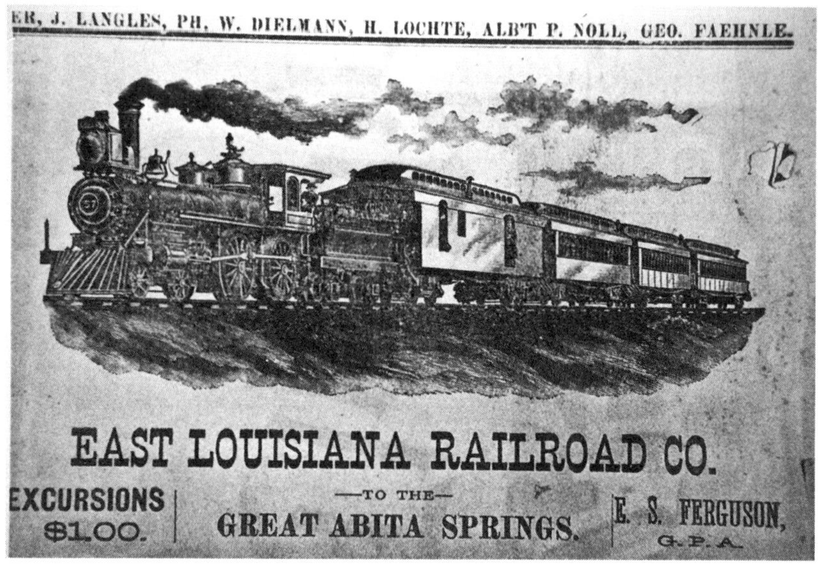

East Louisiana Railroad advertisement, circa 1891. Courtesy of the Plessy & Ferguson Initiative.

his right as a citizen."[12] The train, which had been moving slowly, stopped at the Rampart Street intersection, and Plessy was duly taken to the Fifth Precinct police station by Cain "and a couple of citizens, who apparently had volunteered their aid to make the arrest."[13] At the station Plessy was charged with violating Section 2 of the Separate Car Act.

By referencing his own status as a U.S. citizen, Plessy was insisting on his rights under the Fourteenth Amendment to the Constitution, which reversed that portion of the *Dred Scott* decision denying citizenship to African Americans and requiring the equal protection of the law to all. This amendment was an important pillar of the case that Tourgee planned to bring to the Supreme Court.

Tourgee and Walker filed a plea presenting their arguments regarding the denial of Plessy's constitutional rights. Their hope was that Ferguson would overrule their plea and set a date for a trial, which would lead to Plessy's conviction, followed by appeals to the Louisiana Supreme Court and then to the U.S. Supreme Court. Judge Ferguson delivered his decision on this plea on November 18, 1892, and it was printed in full the following day in the New Orleans *Daily Picayune*. Walker had argued that the lengthy title of the Separate Car Act, "An Act to promote the comfort of passengers on railway trains [etc.]," did not express the act's true aim: "its purpose [instead] is to legalize a discrimination between classes of citizens based on race and color." Ferguson countered this by stating bluntly, "This law is free from all ambiguity, and the letter of it is not to be disregarded, under the pretext of pursuing its spirit." Both Ferguson and the state's attorney agreed with Plessy's lawyers that the section of the law claiming that railway companies were exempt from liability was unconstitutional, but Ferguson stressed that this part of the law might be rejected as unconstitutional and the remainder yet stand: "Eliminate the clause which is objected to and then remains a perfectly valid and constitutional enactment."[14]

Ferguson also dismissed Walker's claim that Plessy was denied due process of law when the conductor was allowed to make the determination of Plessy's race. The judge sidestepped the question of a train conductor's ability to decide someone's race and countered by simply declaring, "It would be impracticable, in fact almost impossible, to organize and utilize a circuit court or any tribunal with special jurisdiction to instanter [i.e., at that moment], on the train, try and determine the color of a passenger, when the question was specially put at issue."[15]

Turning to the question of equality, Judge Ferguson cited five cases, including the Maryland case of Martha Stewart and her sisters on the steamboat *Sue* in 1884, each time stressing the requirement of equal accommodations. He spent the most time reviewing a Tennessee case from 1885, which determined that the railroad did have the right to deny an Alabama woman access to the ladies' car, even though she had often ridden there before, as long as she was offered equal accommodations, though noting, "Equal accommodations does not mean identical accommodations."[16]

While acknowledging that Plessy's lawyers "displayed great research, learning and ability," Ferguson concluded, "The plea herein filed by defendant should be dismissed, and it is further ordered, that defendant plead over." In other words, the trial of Homer Plessy could now proceed. But Tourgee and Walker faced another problem—Ferguson had not yet set a trial date, and without a trial there would be no conviction to appeal. There was, however, an alternative path to the U.S. Supreme Court. Walker filed for a "writ of prohibition," which would stop the case from proceeding until the Louisiana Supreme Court ruled on the constitutional issues touching on the case. On December 19, 1892, the Louisiana court did just that.[17]

The decision was written by an associate justice on the Louisiana Supreme Court, Charles E. Fenner. Fenner, a former Confederate officer, had delivered a fulsome eulogy for Confederate General Robert E. Lee at the dedication of a monument to Lee in New Orleans in 1884.[18]

After setting aside Tourgee's arguments referencing the Thirteenth Amendment as irrelevant to this particular case, the court addressed the question of equal protection under the Fourteenth Amendment, pointing out that many laws, such as those requiring separate schools or banning interracial marriage, had been found constitutional. The justices acknowledged that if the Louisiana railroad law was found to be unconstitutional, then all those other laws would be nullified as well: "All are regulations based upon difference of race, and if such difference cannot furnish a basis for such legislation in one of these cases, it cannot in any." In other words, though they did not say so explicitly, the long-standing sociocultural hierarchy of the South, founded as it was on racial difference, was being threatened. The five justices ruled unanimously that the Separate Car Act was valid within state borders because "it impair[ed] no right of passengers of either race" and "the penalty would be the same whether the accused were white or colored."

In a passage of seriously blindered logic, the Louisiana justices betray their inability to understand the intangible effects of segregation. They could not, or at least did not, even state outright which race was being legislated into separate status. Rather they saw only that an unspecified "portion of the people" was unhappy with the law. They maintained the pretense that "equal" accommodations and enforcement of the law meant that the law was not prejudicial, for a white passenger could (theoretically) be arrested for going into a car "to which by race he does not belong," as the statute put it. Nor could the court fully acknowledge that Jim Crow laws were indeed based on prejudice; the closest they dared to come to such an admission was their conditional "Even if it were true":

> We have been at pains to expound this statute because the dissatisfaction felt by a portion of the people seems to us so unreasonable that we can account for it only on the ground of some misconception. Even were it true that the statute is prompted by a prejudice on the part of one race to be thrown in such contact with the other, one would suppose that to be a sufficient reason why the pride & self respect of the other race should equally prompt it to avoid such contact, if it could be done without the sacrifice of equal accommodations. It is very certain that such unreasonable insistence upon thrusting the company of one race upon the other, with no adequate motive, is calculated, as suggested by Chief Justice Shaw, to foster and intensify repulsion between them, rather than to extinguish it.[19]

On receiving the court's judgment, Walker filed for a rehearing the day after Christmas. He and Tourgee modified their original plea, this time stating Plessy's race explicitly "in the proportion of seven-eighths Caucasian and one-eighth African blood." They argued that race is a matter of law as well as of fact, and since Louisiana, unlike some other states, had no legal definition of race, Plessy could not be classified by law as "colored." The court, however, denied a rehearing.

The door was now open for Tourgee and Walker to file for a writ of error and a chance to get the U.S. Supreme Court to make a decision as to the constitutionality of the Separate Car Act and all that such a decision would imply. The case sent to the Supreme Court was now known as *Homer Adolph Plessy v. J. H. Ferguson, Judge of Section "A" Criminal District Court for the Parish of Orleans,* or more briefly, *Plessy v. Ferguson.* Plessy, Tourgee, and Walker on one side and Judge Ferguson on the other had all initially hoped for an early hearing and ruling, but in the summer of 1893 fate intervened when Justice Samuel Blatchford of New York died. In the spring of 1864 President Cleveland nominated, and the Senate confirmed, Justice Edward White, a Louisiana Democrat who had served in Confederate forces as a lieutenant. Tourgee could now count on only one vote for certain and possibly three others, with a vague hope that, given enough time, one of the five remaining justices might be swayed to their side by public opinion.[20]

Tourgee, Walker, and Samuel F. Phillips, their colleague and liaison in Washington, had prepared a lengthy brief, each writing a separate section, bringing to bear every argument against segregation that they could think of. The case was finally scheduled for early April 1896, and all three lawyers planned to present their arguments before the court in person. Their presentation was curtailed somewhat, however, when Walker took ill and was unable to attend.

Only eight justices took the bench to hear *Plessy v. Ferguson.* Justice David Brewer, an uncertain but possible vote in Plessy's favor, missed the hearing because his daughter was ill, and after she died he declined to take part in the case. Tourgee presented his arguments with his considerable oratorical skills. Among other challenges to the constitutionality of the Separate Car Act, he questioned how a mere railroad train conductor could determine the race of someone who may have looked white, but who was one-eighth or one-sixteenth of African descent, especially when the state provided no legal guidance on the matter.

On May 18, 1896, the court delivered its opinion, agreeing with Louisiana justice Fenner's understanding of the case. The majority opinion, shared by seven of the justices, was written by Justice Henry Billings Brown, who summed up the arguments with what in twenty-first century terms could be called blaming the victim: "We consider the underlying fallacy of the plaintiff's argument to consist in the assumption that the enforced separation of the two races stamps the colored race with a badge of inferiority. If this be so, it is not by reason of anything found in the act, but solely because the colored race chooses to put that construction upon it."[21]

There was only one dissent—once again from John Harlan. Harlan made an important distinction between the requirement of equal accommodations and the legislation by government of the "civil conduct" of citizens, highlighting the possible, and patently unreasonable, consequences such laws could lead to:

> It is one thing for railroad carriers to furnish, or to be required by law to furnish, equal accommodations for all whom they are under a legal duty to carry. It is quite another thing for government to forbid citizens of the white and black races from traveling in the same public conveyance, and to punish officers of railroad companies for permitting persons of the two races to occupy the same passenger coach. If a State can prescribe, as a rule of civil conduct, that whites and blacks shall not travel as passengers in the same railroad coach, why may it not so regulate the use of the streets of its cities and towns as to compel white citizens to keep on one side of a street and black citizens to keep on the other? Why may it not, upon like grounds, punish whites and blacks who ride together in streetcars or in open vehicles on a public road or street? Why may it not require sheriffs to assign whites to one side of a courtroom and blacks to the other? And why may it not also prohibit the commingling of the two races in the galleries of legislative halls or in public assemblages convened for the consideration of the political questions of the day? Further, if this statute of Louisiana is consistent with the personal liberty of citizens, why may not the State require the separation in railroad coaches of native and naturalized citizens of the United States, or of Protestants and Roman Catholics?[22]

Despite Harlan's dissent, the "separate but equal" doctrine was now firmly embedded in law. Following the court's decision, Homer Plessy and his lawyer, James Walker, on January 11, 1897, once again appeared for trial in New Orleans Criminal Court A, this time before a new judge, Joshua Baker. Plessy changed his plea to guilty and the Comité des Citoyens paid the required twenty-five-dollar fine.

In later years, Plessy may have taken the determination of his personal race into his own hands. In the 1880 census, he had been recorded as "Mu" for "Mulatto." In 1900, perhaps because "Mu" was not an option on the 1900 census forms, he was listed as "B" for "Black." In 1910 he was also categorized as "B," even though "Mu" had been restored as a possibility. In 1920, however, Homer Plessy and his wife Louise are both recorded as "W" among their "Mu" neighbors.[23]

In his dissent, Justice Harlan predicted, "The judgment this day rendered will, in time, prove to be quite as pernicious as the decision made by this tribunal in the *Dred Scott Case*."[24] Plessy, Tourgee, Walker, and, presumably, a large majority of African Americans also considered that decision pernicious on the very day it was delivered, yet it would be another fifty-eight years before the U.S. Supreme Court could bring itself to the same conclusion, with the decision in *Brown v. Board of Education* that finally overturned *Plessy v. Ferguson*.

In November 2021, the Louisiana Board of Pardons voted unanimously to recommend that Plessy's record be cleared. Jason Williams, the Orleans Parish district attorney, told the board, "There is no doubt that he was guilty of that act on that date. . . . But there is equally no doubt that such an act should have never been a crime in this country."[25] On January 5, 2022, Louisiana governor John Bel Edwards granted Homer Adolph Plessy a full gubernatorial pardon.[26]

Alice A. Bowie and Streetcar Boycotts across the South, June 6, 1896

The 1896 Supreme Court decision in *Plessy v. Ferguson* meant that "separate but equal" had become a doctrine sanctioned by law, but that did not make it right, nor did it mean that it was acceptable to or accepted by African Americans throughout the country. Just five and a half weeks after the *Plessy* decision was handed down, Alice A. Bowie, a Sunday school teacher accompanying a large group of children to a picnic, was injured when she was violently forced off one of the new electric streetcars in Birmingham, Alabama. There was no law or local ordinance requiring segregation on the cars—only, as so often, a company-imposed rule. In *Bowie v. Birmingham Railway & Electric Co.*, the Alabama Supreme Court dwelt particularly on the question of whether the company had a right to establish a rule separating the races and, if so, whether such a rule was reasonable. While the company argued at length that the races should be separate because God made them that way, the court ruled that the right to establish such a rule had already been determined in earlier cases, including *Hall v. Decuir* and *Plessy v. Ferguson*. As to the question of the rule's reasonableness, the court declared simply: "The carrier's right of property . . . and the public interest are best subserved by a separation of negro and white passenger; . . . their separation tends to secure order, promote comfort, preserve the peace and maintain the rights of both carrier and passengers." With that they affirmed the lower court's verdict that the railway company's rule segregating passengers was legal and reasonable and that the company was not liable for damages suffered by Alice Bowie.[27] After *Plessy*, other cases challenged the constitutionality of segregation, but all were unsuccessful. Many lower courts declined to hear segregation cases at all.

As Jim Crow laws spread through the South, many cities enacted segregated streetcar laws. The railway companies were often opposed to such laws, because of both the expense and the trouble they caused. If company rules were not considered adequate or sufficiently effective, city councils and mayors, encouraged by white citizens, would push for local ordinances requiring separation. Nor were all Black citizens opposed to racial separation. Some saw it as a way to avoid trouble and were willing to accommodate to white rules and practices. When Montgomery, Alabama, instituted a separate car rule in 1900, Rev. Titus Weathington, pastor of the Old Ship Church, published an open letter to the city council, stating in part,

> This ordinance is doubtless an inspiration looking forward to the peace and harmony of the two races hitherto observed in this city.
>
> Again allow me, as pastor of one of the most historic and leading negro churches of this city, representing a membership of nearly 2,000 communicants, to thank you for this wise and timely legislation. . . .
>
> I wish also to assure the Street Railway Company that we take no exception and no boycott will be practised on our part.[28]

Rev. Weathington was certainly wrong about one thing—a boycott. Many of the city's African Americans held the opposite opinion, and a boycott was mounted that lasted for two years, one of the very few that were even temporarily successful. One of the compromises that helped end the Montgomery boycott was the inclusion of a "vacant seat" provision, by which a Black passenger could not be required to give up a seat for a white passenger if there was no other vacant seat in the "Black" section for the Black passenger to move to. Though it was soon being ignored by drivers, this provision remained in the Montgomery City Code and would play a role in the cases of Claudette Colvin and Rosa Parks in 1955.

There was similar opposition throughout the South, and boycotts became common. Drawing largely on contemporary newspaper accounts, August Meier and Elliott Rudwick documented twenty-nine boycotts in twenty-six Southern cities between 1891 and 1907 (plus five more with weakly attested boycotts, indicated below with question marks). They acknowledge too: "[This] is probably an undernumeration, for there are serious lacunae in the surviving evidence."[29]

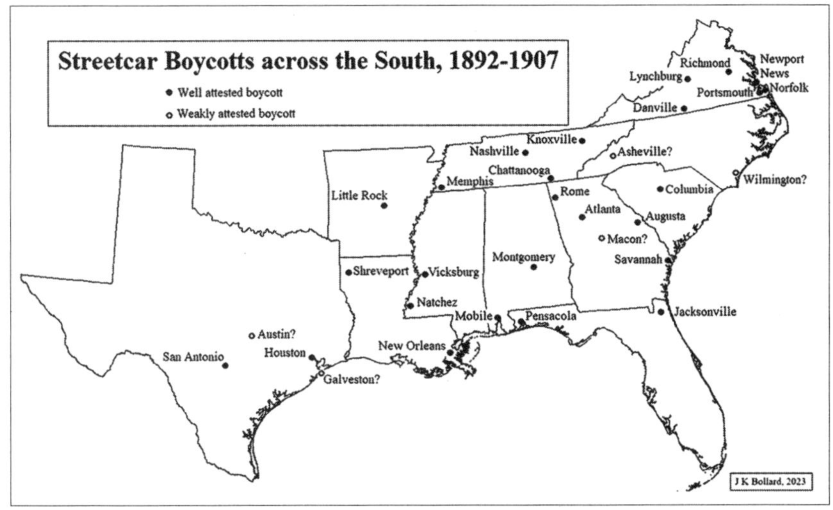

Map of streetcar boycotts, 1892–1907. J. K. Bollard.

1892–93	Atlanta
1898	Augusta, Ga.
1899	Macon, Ga. (?)
1900	Atlanta; Rome, Ga.
1900–2	Montgomery, Ala.
1900–3	Augusta, Ga.
1901	Jacksonville, Fla.
1902	Mobile, Ala.
1902–3	New Orleans; Shreveport, La.
1903	Little Rock, Ark.; Columbia, S.C.
1903–5	Houston
1904	Vicksburg, Miss.; Natchez, Miss.
1904–5	San Antonio; Richmond, Va.
1905	Memphis; Chattanooga, Tenn.; Knoxville, Tenn.; Pensacola, Fla.; Jacksonville, Fla.
1905–6	Nashville
1906	Danville, Va.; Lynchburg, Va.; Portsmouth, Va.; Norfolk, Va.; Austin, Tex. (?); Galveston, Tex. (?)
1906–7	Newport News, Va.; Savannah, Ga.
1907	Wilmington, N.C. (?); Asheville, N.C. (?)

A simple list and a map are perhaps sufficient to reveal the geographical scope and suggest the scale of discontent. Place names and dates, however, do not convey the human cost of segregation and the racism underlying it. Nor do they reveal the central role of transportation in the social drama of urban life in the South, especially as streetcars were becoming more common throughout the country.

The New Orleans Streetcar Boycott, Summer 1902

Thanks to the efforts of Hannibal Carter, William Nichols, and others, streetcars in New Orleans had been successfully integrated in 1867. As the century drew to a close, however, pressure to segregate the cars once again was increasing, especially from people who might not have been familiar or comfortable with the long-standing gradations of racial attitudes and interactions among city residents. By 1900 all the city's streetcars were electric, faster, and more efficient, and as the number of both white and Black passengers rose, the status of passengers of color became increasingly tenuous. A brief paragraph at the end of the *Daily Picayune*'s legislative summary on May 26, 1900, reported, "Mr. Wilson, of Tangipahoa, gave notice of a bill in the house to compel street railroads in cities of 50,000 or over to provide separate cars for white and colored people. This is a measure which bobs up at every session of the legislature and is killed with the regularity of clockwork. The railroads make the plea that it would entail too much expense upon them to comply with such a law, and that it would lead to endless complications."

There was only one city of that size in the state: New Orleans. Wilson's bill, containing language nearly identical to that in the Separate Car Act of 1892, passed the House in June.[30] Isaiah B. Scott, editor of the *Southwestern Christian Advocate*, the city's only Black newspaper at the time, called for a boycott, and Black leaders increasingly voiced protests against the bill. While some people stopped riding in protest, others continued to ride. Walking long distances to and from a long, grueling day's work was not always practical or even possible.

Any plans for an organized, effective boycott were suddenly thrown into disarray by events that were not initiated by trouble on a streetcar but in which streetcars played an important and tragic role. Whatever racial tensions permeated the hot summer streets of New Orleans, they exploded on July 24, 1900, in the murderous riots chronicled by Ida B. Wells-Barnett in *Mob Rule in New Orleans: Robert Charles and His Fight to the Death*.[31] While resisting an unprovoked attempt to arrest him on the evening of Monday, July 23, Robert Charles, a laborer, shot a white policeman in an exchange of gunfire. Wounded in the leg, Charles escaped to his home. In the small hours of Tuesday morning, he shot two of the police who attacked the house before he escaped again.

Encouraged by the offer of a $250 reward and a general order to shoot Charles on sight, enraged mobs of white men and youths roamed the streets, terrorizing the Black community. Streetcars were particularly easy targets. By the time he was killed on Friday, July 27, Charles had killed four policemen and three civilians, and wounded about twenty others. But the riots took a much heavier toll. On Wednesday evening a crowd of about five hundred white men and youths gathered around the Robert E. Lee statue and grew to about seven hundred as it made its way to Douglas Square (now A. L. Davis Park). There they were egged on by a man from nearby Kenner, Louisiana, who said (among other things equally appalling), "The only way you can teach these Niggers a lesson and put them in their place is to go out and lynch a few of them as an object lesson. String up a few of them, and the others will trouble you no more."[32]

After looting a pawnshop of its weapons and ammunition, as well as jewelry, the crowd rushed to the Parish Prison in a failed attempt to seize and lynch Leonard Pierce, Charles's roommate, who had been arrested with him. The mob then split up, going in different directions and continuing to riot through the night. Streetcars were stopped and searched for Black passengers. Thomas P. Sanders was beaten by numerous attackers and shot in the knee.[33] Another man was pulled off a streetcar, chased, beaten, and then shot to death. There was little to no police presence on the streets to quell the violence that night. Even the white-owned *Daily Picayune* opined, "And there was NOT A SINGLE ARREST made by the police."[34]

Rioting continued through the week, even after Charles was killed. All told, six white people and over twenty Black people were murdered, including seventy-five-year-old Baptiste Philo on his way to work in the French Market at 2:30 a.m. Hannah Mabry was killed in her bed when a mob pulled the shutters off her house and shot about twenty times through the windows.[35] Many more were beaten, hospitalized, and traumatized.

Well after the death of Robert Charles, violence against people of color persisted sporadically throughout the summer and into the autumn. In the face of strong opposition from both African Americans and white business interests, Harry Wilson's bill to segregate the streetcars failed in the legislature. The boycott of the streetcars proposed by Isaiah Scott never gained momentum. And, understandably, many in the Black community became wary of open dissent of any kind.

Once again, in 1902 Harry Wilson, who represented Tangipahoa Parish ("[It] hasn't a street-car in it"), introduced his Jim Crow bill, this time into a more sympathetic legislature.[36] In 1896 the number of African American men registered to vote in Louisiana had been 130,334. (No women of any color had yet gained that right.) In 1898 the state adopted a new constitution that instituted a poll tax and other requirements making it difficult for Black citizens to register and vote.[37] As a result, in 1900 there were only 5,320 Black registered voters, and by 1904 the number was a mere 1,342.[38] With a legislature in 1902 chosen by such an overwhelmingly white electorate, there were few members who were sympathetic to Black interests, and in June of that year the Separate Streetcar Act was passed, the first such law making segregation mandatory on streetcars throughout a state.[39]

Even as larger and better-equipped electric cars came into service, conditions on New Orleans streetcars rapidly deteriorated for Black riders. In accordance with the new law, movable screens were put up on seat backs to separate the rear seats designated for Black passengers. These screens inclined to the rear, perhaps accommodating the hats of white women and men, but making it difficult for a passenger to sit behind the screens without bumping into them. The screens could be moved farther back to accommodate additional white passengers, but they were not always moved forward again to provide seats when needed for additional Black passengers. On a crowded car, white men standing in the aisle would often put their feet on the rear seat, thus blocking Black riders from sitting. Blair Kelley reports one instance in which "a white man refused to remove his foot from the empty colored seat even when his wife directly asked him to do so." Black riders were frequently injured under crowded conditions, and sometimes deliberately pushed off the rear platform.[40]

In the hope that white business interests would oppose a separate car movement, even Isaiah Scott's enthusiasm for a boycott had tempered. The increasing number of white passengers meant that a Black boycott might have insufficient economic impact on the railway companies. Scott hoped that the companies themselves would bring a test case to the courts, claiming a loss of income from empty "Black" seats no longer available for white passengers. While Scott and other Black clergymen consulted and negotiated with the companies and were thus reluctant to mount an all-out protest against them pending such a test case, streetcar riders grew impatient in the face of increasing humiliation and mistreatment. Some stopped riding the cars on their own initiative, but others felt the need for an organized response.

A group of Black clubwomen called a meeting of the leaders of Black organizations: "[This gathering is] for the purpose of determining upon some concerted course of action which will in some way free us from being separated from other civilized races in street cars by means of wire screens."[41] Over two hundred leaders from some sixty organizations responded, and a more formal boycott was initiated. Some Black organizations canceled large events that would require streetcar rides to attend. Most notably, William H. Penn, president of the Longshoremen's Protective Union, canceled a memorial service that would have drawn about three thousand members.[42]

In an ironic reversal of the usual course of events, H. H. Pearson, president of the newly consolidated New Orleans Railway Company, and two vice presidents and the general manager were arrested for failing "to provide wire or wooden screens to separate the white and colored races in the cars of the company." In their defense, Pearson's lawyers argued that the law unduly burdened conductors who were required to determine a passenger's race. The criminal court judge, Auguste Alcoin, found the segregation law unconstitutional and dismissed the case. The prosecutors appealed to the Louisiana Supreme Court. In March 1903 the Supreme Court declined to address the question of a conductor's right or duty to decide a passenger's race on the grounds that the matter was "not considered properly raised in the instant case." Rather, the defendants were charged simply with failing "to provide separate accommodations for the white and colored races, as the statute commands." In those portions of the law relevant to the case at hand, the court found the Separate Streetcar Act to be constitutional and reversed Alcoin's original decision.[43]

With the constitutionality of the Separate Streetcar Act thus confirmed, and with the precedents of the 1890 Separate Car Act and *Plessy* in 1896, screens remained to segregate the cars. The New Orleans streetcar law went into full effect in early November 1902. Though some people kept riding, especially over long distances as necessary for their livelihood, the boycott continued, and many "Black" seats were thus left empty. This, of course, raised the ire of white passengers who were no longer allowed to occupy those seats on otherwise crowded cars. The New Orleans boycott lasted for eight months or more, well into 1903, but ultimately proved unsuccessful.[44]

Georgia Edwards, August 31, 1906

In the 1870s and 1880s challenges to Jim Crow in the form of the "separate but equal" doctrine increasingly focused on "equality" rather than the essential fact of separation. Numerous complaints, beginning with those of William Councill and William Heard in 1887, came to the Interstate Commerce Commission (ICC) about inequities in the facilities made available to white and Black passengers by railway companies. Unfortunately, the 1896 Supreme Court decision in *Plessy v. Ferguson* granted such firm legal status to the "separate" component of "separate but equal" that it seemed unassailable—segregation was declared constitutional. As a result, except in cases of personal injury, subsequent debate was almost entirely about the details of Black versus white accommodations. Precisely how equal must equal be? The case of Georgia Edwards reveals how the ICC managed to pay lip service to the ideal of equality though it lacked the ability to enforce that ideal in practice.

Georgia Edwards bought a first-class ticket from the Nashville, Chattanooga and St. Louis Railway Company on August 31, 1906, to travel from Chattanooga, Tennessee, to Dalton, Georgia, a distance of some thirty-eight miles. When she boarded the train she took a seat in a first-class coach. A railway flagman told her that she was in the wrong car and requested her "to go forward to that portion of another car set apart . . . for the use of people of her race." Edwards refused, and the flagman summoned the company's assistant station agent, who had her removed to the forward car "using only such force as was necessary for that purpose." Edwards then took her case to the ICC, complaining that the car in which she was put was very dirty, "and not as clean as the car first occupied by her," to which the ICC report adds, "but this claim is not supported by the record."[45]

The ICC report, issued on June 24, 1907, then goes into considerable detail enumerating the conditions of both the first-class car for white passengers and the compartment in the forward car designated for Black passengers. The report states that before the train left Nashville "all the cars in the train were thoroughly cleaned inside," and "they were again cleaned to some extent at Chattanooga." It then declares that the two cars were of the same quality, with upholstered seats and "with exactly the same quality of goods." Aside from the question of cleanliness and the fact that the section of the forward car for Black passengers was partitioned off by a swinging door separating it from the smoking section, there were some additional notable differences between them. The car for white passengers was equipped with washbowls and towels, whereas the forward car had neither. The forward car had just one toilet, whereas the other car had two, one marked for use by men and the other for women, "but such restriction is only partially enforced." This last qualifying remark aims, it would seem, to help justify the further explanation: "The principal reason for providing two toilets in one case and only one in the other is that the number of passengers carried in the negro compartment is very much less than the number contemporaneously transported in the other car."[46]

In 1905 the city of Nashville mandated that all its streetcars be segregated. The Black-owned *Nashville Globe* began publishing in January 1906 with the express purpose of promoting "a boycott of the city's streetcars and to combat racial discrimination and social inequalities."[47] Commenting in a front-page article on the "Interstate Commission's Important and Far-Reaching Decision," the *Globe* noted that Edwards "protested that it was anything but human to put her into the smaller of two compartments of the same coach with white men using the other as a dram shop and a smoking rendezvous." They then gave their own assessment of the use of the Jim Crow car by white passengers:

> It is a universally known fact throughout the South that the white men who frequent the smoker end of the car, the other end of which is set aside for first-class Negro passengers, have a fiendish penchant for using the private room in the Negro's part. They deliberately leave their part and take possession of the Negro's, preferring it, it seems. This small compartment, which comprises the Negro's smoker, chair car, dining-car, observation car and sleeper, is usurped by that class of whites that squawks the loudest about the intermingling of the races, yet is always found courting the society of Negroes.[48]

In general, the printed ICC report very much gives the impression that it has drawn heavily on information provided by the railway company. It even goes so far as to state, "On the whole, defendant's Nashville-Atlanta passenger trains are among the best in the country so far as equipment is concerned." No further details of Edwards's complaint are given other than the comment that the car was dirty, as quoted above. Based on earlier Supreme Court decisions, such as *Hall v. Decuir* and especially *Plessy v. Ferguson*, the commission reiterated the railway's right to segregate passengers by race. Nevertheless, in at least a token bid for equality, the ICC found in Edwards's favor, insofar as it ordered the company "to cease and desist, and during a period of at least two years thereafter abstain, from failing to furnish and provide on said railroad a washbowl and towels and a separate smoking compartment for colored passengers, where the same accommodations [were] provided for white passengers paying the same fare."[49]

Though it did specify the principle of material equality, the ICC, unfortunately, had little power—and, to be sure, not much will—to see that its rulings were carried out. Railway companies simply persisted as before. By early 1908, complaints had reached the desk of President Theodore Roosevelt, who wrote on April 2 a letter to the Justice Department noting the failure to enforce the ICC order:

> To the Department of Justice:
>
> I forward herewith the report of the Interstate Commerce Commission containing its order of June 27, 1907, and the report of the failure of the railroad company to obey this order. . . . It appears that the Nashville, Chattanooga & St. Louis Railway Company has not complied with the order of the Commission to

> furnish the same facilities to colored passengers paying first class fare that are furnished to white passengers paying first class fare. From time to time various complaints have been made to me by reputable colored people to the effect that the accommodations furnished to colored persons on certain railways are filthy and inadequate compared to the same accommodations furnished to white passengers paying the same fare. . . . In this particular case where the railway has neglected to comply with the order of the Commission it is important that compliance with this order be immediately obtained. I suggest that you proceed to enforce the order by injunction proceedings, unless in your judgment some other course is preferable.
>
> Theodore Roosevelt[50]

Whatever course Attorney General William H. Moody found preferable, the president's letter too had little effect, and Jim Crow cars remained as objectionable as ever.

Mary Church Terrell, June 26, 1908

President Lincoln issued the Emancipation Proclamation on September 22, 1862, stating that on January 1, 1863, "all persons held as slaves within any State or designated part of a State, the people whereof shall then be in rebellion against the United States, shall be then, thenceforward, and forever free." Three and a half million slaves became nominally free that day, but only in parts of the South that were still under Confederate control. Abolishing slavery throughout the country would run the risk of encouraging Delaware, Maryland, Kentucky, and Missouri—the four slave states that had not seceded from the Union—to join the Confederacy and thus make the war much harder to win. It was also hoped that the proclamation would increase the moral justifications for the war being waged in the rebellious areas, as well as allow formerly enslaved southerners to join the Union army, which was badly in need of soldiers. Had the Confederate states chosen to cease fighting and rejoin the Union in late 1862, the proclamation might never have gone into effect.

Tennessee had joined the Confederacy in June 1861, but by early 1862 the Union army had gained control of the state capital, Nashville, and large parts of the state. Tennessee was put under the military governorship of Andrew Johnson, a pro-Union senator, former Tennessee governor (1853–57), later Lincoln's second vice president (March 4–April 15, 1865), and then president. Thus Tennessee was no longer considered to be in rebellion, and as a result slaves in Tennessee were not included under the terms of the Emancipation Proclamation.

Mary Church Terrell, circa 1880–1900. Library of Congress.

Both of Mary Church Terrell's parents, Robert Reed Church and Louisa Ayres, were the children of wealthy white fathers and enslaved mothers. After his mother died, Mary's father, Robert, at about the age of twelve, was sold to his own father, Charles B. Church. Mary's mother, Louisa, was both daughter and slave of T. S. Ayres. Neither C. B. Church nor T. S. Ayres granted freedom to their enslaved children before the end of the war. When Mary Church was born in Memphis on September 23, 1863, nine months after the Emancipation Proclamation went into effect, her parents were still enslaved, and as the daughter of an enslaved woman, so was Mary, at least until Andrew Johnson finally declared the slaves of Tennessee to be free on October 24, 1864. Both of Mary's parents continued to live and work closely with their respective families, though not openly acknowledged as actual family members. As Terrell's biographer, Alison Parker, deftly puts it, "Their status was likely a fluid and contradictory mix of free and unfree."[51]

After the Civil War, each of Mary Church's parents established successful businesses. Her mother opened her own store as a hairdresser in an elite part of Memphis, selling wigs and hair extensions to white women. It was she who initially provided financial security for the family. Mary's father ran a number of saloons and brothels (though the latter were unknown to Terrell until much later in her life). He eventually became very wealthy, investing in profitable Memphis real estate, and a key figure in the development of Beale Street, now famous as the home of the blues.[52]

Mary Church first became aware of the "race problem" when her father took her into the white coach on a train from Memphis. The train had a Jim Crow car, though there was no Jim Crow law in Tennessee at the time. As Terrell describes the traumatic incident in her 1940 memoir, *A Colored Woman in a White World*, her father soon went by himself to the smoking car, leaving five-year-old Mary on her own. When the conductor came to collect tickets, he asked what she was doing in that car. Whatever she said in reply, the conductor determined to move her to the Jim Crow car:

> As he pulled me roughly out of the seat, he turned to the man sitting across the aisle and said, "Whose little nigger is this?"
>
> The man told him who my father was and advised him to leave me alone. Seeing the conductor was about to remove me from the car, one of my father's white friends went into the smoker to tell him what was happening. My father returned immediately and there ensued a scene which no one who saw it could ever forget.
>
> In that section at that time it was customary for men to carry revolvers in their pockets. Fortunately, no one was injured and I was allowed to remain with my courageous father in the white coach.

Assuming, as children often do, that the trouble was somehow her own fault, Mary did not understand what she had done wrong, but her father refused to talk about the incident afterward. Her mother did, however. "My mother patted me on the head and comforted me by saying she was sure I was behaving myself, but she explained the incident by telling me that sometimes conductors on railroad trains were unkind and treated good little girls very badly. Seeing their children touched and seared and wounded by race prejudice is one of the heaviest crosses which colored women have to bear."[53]

Mary's parents separated around 1870 and divorced in 1874. Mary lived with her mother for a while, then at age eight she was sent to an integrated school affiliated with Antioch College in Yellow Springs, Ohio. At age twelve she was sent to public school in Oberlin, Ohio. Graduating at seventeen, she then attended Oberlin College, enrolling in the full "gentlemen's course," rather than the two-year course usually taken by women. Her mother had moved her business to New York City, but, after graduating from Oberlin with a BA in 1884 and an MA in 1888, Mary returned to Memphis to live with her father.

Mary was not content, however, with a life of leisure as the daughter of a wealthy businessman, and in 1885 she accepted a position teaching at Wilberforce University, just south of Yellow Springs. Two years later she began teaching Latin at the Preparatory High School for Negro Youth (the renowned M Street High School) in Washington, D.C. There she met Robert H. Terrell, a Harvard graduate who was head of the Greek and Latin Department at M Street while studying law at Howard University. From 1888 to 1890 Mary Church took a leave of absence from teaching in order to travel and study in Europe, where she became fluent in French, German, and Italian.

Upon her return, Mary agreed to marry Robert, who was then working for the Treasury Department. Female schoolteachers were not allowed to continue teaching once they married, and Mary reluctantly reconciled herself to sacrificing her career for her husband. When an invitation to become the registrar at Oberlin College arrived just before the wedding, she was sorely tempted but regretfully declined the offer, and they were married in 1891.

After recovering from a late-term miscarriage brought on by kidney disease the following year, Terrell threw herself into the growing anti-lynching campaign. After introducing a speech by Ida B. Wells, Terrell was named chair of a committee to arrange further speaking dates for Wells. This led to speaking engagements of her own, and she began to dedicate herself to the principle that educated African Americans had a duty to work for the betterment of their race. As the only available Black female college graduate, Terrell was asked to return to the M Street School as a substitute teacher, and the unmarried teacher rule was waived. Not long afterward she was elected as the first Black woman to serve on the district school board.

Terrell's work as one of the founders of the Colored Women's League in Washington eventually led to the formation in 1896 of the National Association of Colored Women (NACW). She was elected as the first president and was subsequently reelected twice before being named honorary president for life. In addition to establishing day-care nurseries, free kindergartens, and clubs to support Black mothers, Terrell encouraged NACW members to fight for the whole range of civil rights for African Americans and to join the struggle to gain the vote for all women, Black and white. In February 1898 she was the only woman of color to speak before a meeting of the National American Woman Suffrage Association, on a slate of speakers that included Susan B. Anthony, Elizabeth Cady Stanton, and Frances Willard. In a letter to her father, Terrell's husband wrote, "Several white women went so far as to hug and kiss her when the meeting closed. . . . When white women publicly embrace a colored woman you know the reason for it must be strong."[54]

As privileged as she was, and as successful as she became, Mary Church Terrell was by no means exempt from the racial abuse that other Black women and men suffered. But she was well educated, an accomplished speaker, and had developed something of a sense of confidence and self-possession that wealth, class, and public acclaim can provide. All these qualities combined to allow her to maintain the image of "genteel respectability" that she fostered, while simultaneously refusing to back down or hold her tongue in the face of racism. By many of her peers she was "considered one of the foremost proselytizers of respectability."[55]

A streetcar encounter in Washington on June 26, 1908, illustrates the forthright determination and insistence on equal treatment that Terrell exercised throughout her life. She describes the incident briefly in her memoir, but a more detailed account appears in her personal diary entry written the day after it happened:

> Last night on the little streetcar . . . I had a very disagreeable experience. I had my dress suitcase, my old hammock, and a tennis racket in my hand. There was plenty of room for me to have a seat by a white man who refused to move. I asked him to make room for me, but when he did not do so, I simply sat down. He said something to me, and I replied, "When I tell you to move, you move." "I won't be sassed by a nigger," he growled. Before I knew it, I hit him in the face, not very hard to be sure, for I tried to restrain my hand and I partially succeeded, but I had slapped him just the same. A tall poor white fellow whose clothes almost hung off him rose and said, "Jim you are not going to let a nigger hit you are you?" "You had better not try to protect him," I replied. Then the white man sitting next to me began to brandish his umbrella threatening to strike me. "Hit me," I said, "Just hit me, if you think best." But he didn't strike me.

A Mrs. Dyson, whom Terrell did not know, reacted. "[She] jumped up when the man brandished the umbrella and said 'Oh, don't let him hit you, Mrs. Terrell.'"[56] According to the shorter version printed in Terrell's memoir, "[She] remonstrated with him and warned the men they would 'get into a lot of trouble' if they struck me."[57]

A Black woman slapping a white man and another Black woman intervening on her behalf would put both women into considerable danger, of course, but in retrospect Terrell was mostly disturbed by the fact that the only person who came to her defense was not only a woman but also one of her own race. Neither source records the final outcome, though this silence in the record suggests that no further overt harm, at least, was done to either of them.

A further indication of Terrell's unwavering persistence in challenging racist attitudes can be seen in the later admission in her diary that she had chosen to "sit by [a] hard-looking customer in street car purposely."[58]

The following year, Mary Terrell and Ida B. Wells-Barnett were the only Black women on the committee, chaired by W. E. B. Du Bois, that created the National Association for the Advancement of Colored People. When the NAACP was incorporated in 1912, Terrell was a member of its first board of directors, speaking frequently for the organization.[59]

On March 3, 1913, Terrell, Wells-Barnett, other NACW members, and numerous additional Black suffragists insisted on taking part in an important march in Washington organized by the National American Woman Suffrage Association, in defiance of attempts to ban African American women from the parade or to force them into segregated positions.[60] After women won the right to vote in 1920 with the ratification of the Nineteenth Amendment, Terrell continued to campaign for an Equal Rights Amendment to further improve women's legal rights and status.

Terrell worked on various Republican Party campaigns to elect candidates, Black and white, who would work actively to promote issues of importance to African Americans. Throughout her life she was proud to be as outspoken as necessary in her opposition to segregation and other forms of racial inequality. Well into her late eighties she brought a lawsuit against Thompson's Restaurant (see page 141), even picketing in the streets in protest.

Charlotte Hawkins Brown, Fall 1920

Charlotte Hawkins Brown was born in Henderson, North Carolina, in 1883, the daughter of Caroline Frances Hawkins. After Charlotte's father, Edmund H. Hight, left them, her mother married Nelson Willis, and in 1888 they and their extended family moved to Cambridge, Massachusetts. Willis worked odd jobs, and Caroline Hawkins boarded Black Harvard University students and operated a laundry. In a brief undated memoir, Brown wrote, "Knowing the surroundings as I now do, it is hard to believe that I cannot recall a single instance in my grammar-, high-, or normal-school days in which I was, by gesture or word, made to feel or realize that I was any different from anybody else. . . . I went where I wanted to go, sat where I wanted to sit, and had scores of intimate friends, young and old, in both races."[61]

In this memoir, however, she includes a brief anecdote "of strange importance" about segregation during her high school years. She and some friends organized a dance for Black students at Cambridge High and Cambridge Latin School. The event was a great success, with nearly two hundred

Charlotte Hawkins Brown. Courtesy of North Carolina State Historic Sites.

couples attending, and it received a glowing report in the next morning's *Boston Herald*. Summoned the next day to come immediately to see the wife of the *Herald*'s editor, Hawkins expected to be lauded for her accomplishment. "Imagine my surprise when this woman told me in a strong forceful way that I had committed a terrible error. She told me of the fight they were making to include Negroes in all things and that never again must we be guilty of having anything separate and apart in our school. 'It will defeat our purpose,' she said. Here was I in the lead of a segregated movement and didn't know it—doing then what I have been forced to do for forty years since."[62]

In her last year of high school, Hawkins had met, by chance, Alice Freeman Palmer, a former president of Wellesley College, who not only gave her a letter of recommendation to the Salem Normal School (now Salem State University) in 1900, she offered financial assistance as well. As Hawkins began her second year at Salem, however, in another chance meeting she so impressed a representative of the American Missionary Association that she was offered a position running a one-room school in Sedalia, North Carolina. Hawkins accepted and taught there until the school was suddenly shut down at the end of the 1901 school year. She returned north, determined to raise enough money to start her own school in Sedalia. Alice Palmer, ill at the time, gave Hawkins the names of some possible benefactors. With about $400 and a gift of eleven acres of land in Sedalia, Hawkins opened her school in an old blacksmith shop in October 1902. Alice Palmer died near the end of that year, and Hawkins named her school the Palmer Memorial Institute. Through assiduous fund-raising and the support of the American Missionary Association, Hawkins managed over the years to accrue a permanent endowment of some $250,000.

Hawkins improved her own education by taking courses at Simmons College, Temple University, and Harvard. At Harvard, she met Edmund S. Brown. They married in 1911, and she took his surname. Her husband returned with her to Sedalia, but after five years he left to teach in South Carolina, and they later divorced. Charlotte Brown remained at the Palmer Institute, which eventually expanded to three hundred acres with fourteen buildings, as it shifted its focus toward college preparatory work. By 1960 Palmer had an enrollment of over two hundred students. In addition, Brown was one of the founders (later president) of the North Carolina State Federation of Women's Clubs in 1909, and she worked with the Commission on Interracial Cooperation. She retired as president of Palmer in 1952 and as its financial director in 1955. She died in January 1961.

Fund-raising and lecturing, naturally, required a good bit of travel, and Brown fought against racism and Jim Crow as she went. Among her papers is an undated, twelve-page typescript, quoted from above. It is written in the first person and titled "Some Incidents in the Life and Career of Charlotte Hawkins Brown Growing out of Racial Situations, at the Request of Dr. Ralph Bunche." In this paper, perhaps delivered as an address in the late 1930s, Brown recounts some of her experiences, including her willingness to sue in response to mistreatment. She notes, "For years I was put out of Pullman berths and seats during all hours of the night. Stranger than fiction is the fact that each time my southern lawyer, taking no percent of the recovery, sued and won."[63] She recounts:

> The most tragic of these Pullman escapades occurred in the fall of 1920. The local agent almost always arranged the trip. I had slept from Greensboro, North Carolina, to within twenty miles of Anniston, Alabama, had dressed and undressed in the berth to avoid trouble and contact in the dressing room. Doing ones [*sic*]

toilet was out of the question. No sooner had I descended the ladder and occupied an empty seat than I was surrounded by twelve husky young white men who evidently had been told of my presence by a cowardly conductor (a northerner I afterwards found out) who shut himself up in the dressing-room of the coach. One of the men leaned down and said, "Madam, this is God's country. Negroes can't ride in coaches with white people. You will have to go back to the Jim Crow car." I remonstrated, said I had bought my ticket, etc., but they assured me that I could take my choice between the car and being put off in the hands of a mob at the next stop. Dying at the hands of those hoodlums (though in dress and speech they seemed, as I afterwards learned, to be college boys) would not have made me a martyr. So in humiliation and some resentment I gathered up my bags as they with march step led the way through three coaches to the Negro coach.

> I was on my way to that first famous International Meeting at Memphis, Tennessee. And the shame of the whole affair was that southern white women passing for Christians were on that very car and bound for that same meeting where they declared their purpose was to make the Negro woman unashamed and unafraid.[64]

But trains and streetcars were not the only form of transportation in which African Americans were segregated, even in the North. Especially in large cities there was considerable vertical traffic in very close quarters. Brown explains that "there are still in New York floor directors who order all colored people to the freight elevators, and I have without knowing found myself landing in the back entrance."[65] Again she provides, with some humor, an example from her personal experience on a fund-raising trip:

> In metropolitan New York I had an elevator ride that netted the school $75,000. In one of the "swanky" hotel lobbies, I attempted to enter the elevator and was told, "Around the other way." But having traveled that way before, I had the cue. Another elevator started up. It was empty. I walked in. The starting porter said, "Carry her down to the cellar." With arms folded I smiled and said, "Young man, I am here for the rest of the day. I am not getting out here." Up and down, as people came and went, we rode. I impressed him that I wanted to go to the eleventh floor. I had a very important engagement with a trustee and large contributor to our school.
>
> Finally realizing that my friend was waiting, I got off at the tenth floor as some one else did and inquired of the hall clerk for the eleventh floor. "This way," said she, and to my surprise I found myself going up the back stairs.
>
> However, I reached my destination, and in spite of the fight in my heart, I smiled. As a part of my argument for education for Negroes I used the incident as illustration that most white people looked upon every Negro, regardless of his

appearance, modulated tones that reflected some culture and training, as a servant and happened to say, "If some person who had faith in the race would make a gift of $50,000 or $75,000 to (and I needed just that amount then to carry out a building project) to some Negro woman, it would raise all Negro womanhood in the estimation of people." My friend thought I was exaggerating that it could have any such appeal, but in less than forty-eight hours after consultation with other members of the family, there was flashed over the wires a gift of $75,000 to this Negro woman for a building project at the Palmer Memorial Institute at Sedalia, North Carolina, and the Associated Press carried it to the remote places of America.[66]

Brown was well educated, and a lover of books, art, and music who greatly appreciated the advantages life in Massachusetts had afforded her. Nevertheless, she chose to live and work in the segregated South:

> My people who need what I have to give live in larger numbers in the land of segregated ideals. . . . I sit in a Jim Crow car, but my mind keeps company with the kings and queens I have known. I sit in a theatre gallery and hear Heif[e]tz, Kreisler and Lily Pons. I am even segregated in my own town to hear the Negroes, Roland Hayes and Marian Anderson. . . . But my mind is rejuvenated by their music to strive harder to build a race that will some day rise in majesty and break down every wall of segregation in American life.[67]

Benjamin J. Davis, Summer 1923

Like Ida B. Wells-Barnett before him and Dovey Johnson Roundtree after him, Benjamin J. Davis became a professional advocate for human rights after taking a seat in the "wrong" section of a trolley in Atlanta. Davis was born in Atlanta in 1903, the son of Willa Porter Davis and Benjamin Davis Sr., a wealthy, self-made businessman, the publisher of the *Atlanta Independent* newspaper. Though the family was well-off, they did not consider themselves members of Atlanta's Black elite. Indeed, Davis describes his father as "a bitter foe of every type of social exclusiveness."[68]

Davis attended public grade school, but there were no high schools for African American students in Atlanta at the time. In their stead, the city's Black colleges were required to provide a high school education for those who qualified, and some included lower grades. As a result, Davis became a boarding student at Morehouse College through seventh and eighth grade, high school, and one year of college. The Morehouse students were largely the sons of workers, sharecroppers, and tenant farmers. "Here . . . I learned more about my people, their potentialities and talents. . . . Along with my studies,

I learned human warmth. I also learned . . . that Negro students—far from being 'shiftless,' as the slanderous white supremacists maintained—were full of ambition and high purpose."[69]

In 1922, following a year of college at Morehouse, Davis was accepted at Amherst College in Massachusetts. Back home during the summer after his first year at Amherst, Davis was riding an Atlanta trolley when a pregnant Black woman boarded the car. He gave her his seat toward the back and took a seat himself farther forward in the "white section"—with predictable results: "The rednecked cop grabbed me by the belt of my pants and yanked me off the trolley in the white business section of the city, as if I were a desperado. The Negro women on the trolley screamed. They were all called disorderly, ejected from the car, and shooed away as if they were chattels."

The next morning found Davis and his father sitting in another Negro section, this time in the rear of the court waiting for his case to come up.

> The police court provided a form of entertainment, of sport, for the petty officials, at the expense of the hapless, humble Negro workers caught in the complicated toils of jim-crow laws. The vulgarity of the tin-horn magistrate was repellent, while the police and their hangers-on stood around making merry. One Negro woman was virtually stripped bare by the lewd language and gestures of the magistrate. The clerks and bailiffs fingered the woman's breasts as she stood there helplessly, her face bathed in tears of shame and agony.
>
> I remarked to my dad that I had never seen such obscene behavior. I was boiling. He said: "That's why I want you to be a lawyer. Maybe you can defend your people some day from this sort of thing."

When Davis's own case came up, the magistrate cut off Davis's attempt to explain and turned instead to his father, who asked the judge "to excuse him this time and parole him into my custody." The magistrate then gave a sharp, blatantly racist lecture to his father, addressing him as "Ben" (as Davis explains, "Negroes were never addressed as Mr. or Mrs.") and castigating him. "You're starting your boy off on the wrong track. You sent him up no'th to school and he comes back thinking he's as good as a white man. . . . I'm gonna let him off this time, but I warn you we ain't gonna have no niggers down here sitting down with white people. Ten days or ten dollars. As a favor to you, Ben, pay the ten dollars and I'll suspend sentence."

His father paid the fine and they left, but Davis's reaction was understandably strong: "I was furious. At the same time I felt ashamed and humiliated—not so much for myself as for my father and my people. If this could happen to me—the son of a well-to-do Negro—what, indeed, would have been the fate of a Negro who had failed to get himself born into a 'well-to-do' family."[70]

After graduating from Amherst, Davis went to Harvard Law School and received his law degree in 1928. However, not sure that he wished to follow the law as a profession, he worked for a while in the African American newspaper industry in Chicago and Baltimore. In 1931 he returned to Atlanta, passed the Georgia bar exam, and opened a law practice, "challenged by the thought of what could be done if one put up a really tough fight for the constitutional rights of Negroes in a Georgia court and was himself a Negro lawyer."[71] Soon he formed a partnership with John Geer, a Black lawyer of working-class origins.

In the summer of 1932, Davis read about the arrest of Angelo Herndon, a Black nineteen-year-old union organizer and member of the Communist Party. Herndon had been sent from Alabama to revitalize the Atlanta chapter of the party's Unemployed Council. On June 30, 1932, Herndon organized a racially integrated protest of over a thousand workers at the Fulton County Courthouse in reaction to cuts in relief payments. The protest was successful in that it scared the county commissioners into restoring some of the funds, but it also brought Herndon to the attention of authorities. Under an 1866 anti-insurrection law that had been repurposed from an 1833 law prohibiting slave revolts, Herndon was arrested for "attempting to incite insurrection against the state of Georgia," a charge that carried the death penalty.[72]

Benjamin Davis offered his services and the International Labor Defense wing of the Communist Party engaged him as chief trial counsel in Herndon's case, even though he had only been a member of the bar for six months, had no experience, and had never tried a case in court.[73] During his discussions with Herndon and educating himself in preparation for the trial, Davis became attracted to Communist theory, tenets, and beliefs, and during the trial he joined the party himself. Herndon was found guilty by an all-white jury, and the verdict was upheld by the Georgia Supreme Court. In an appeal, the U.S. Supreme Court overthrew the verdict in 1937.

Davis moved to New York in the mid-1930s, editing and writing for a number of Communist journals, including the *Daily Worker*, and he worked with other Black leaders to form the National Negro Congress to work against racial discrimination. He forged a close friendship with the Rev. Adam Clayton Powell, who became a New York City councilman in 1941. When Powell left the council in 1943 to run for Congress, Davis was elected to succeed him, and he was reelected in 1945. There he worked for rent control, better pay for teachers, low transit fares, and other issues to the benefit of his constituents in Harlem.[74]

By 1949 the Cold War with the Soviet Union had begun and a "Red Scare" was in full swing. Davis was expelled from the city council that year when he was convicted along with nine others of violating the Alien Registration Act, known as the Smith Act, a charge stemming from his association with the Communist Party. While serving a five-year prison sentence in Terre Haute, Indiana, from 1951 to 1955, he filed suit and won a case that curbed segregation in federal prisons. Davis became a frequent speaker on college campuses during the 1960s, extolling the principles of equality that were espoused by the Communist Party. Like him, many other African Americans during the twentieth century were drawn to the party, which respected no color line and was often, as in the cases of "the Scottsboro Boys" and Angelo Herndon, the first—and sometimes the only—organization to come to their defense.[75]

Samuel Wilbert Tucker, June 1927

Samuel Wilbert Tucker, known as Wilbert as a boy and later as S. W., is credited with saying, "I got involved in the civil rights movement on June 18, 1913, in Alexandria. I was born black."[76] There is no reason to doubt that he did indeed say this succinct, wry observation on the stark reality of African American lives. But there is a date not too much later that might more precisely have ignited the spark that kindled Tucker's quiet but stellar career.

In June 1927, Wilbert (aged fourteen), his older brother George (sixteen), younger brother Otto (eleven), and a friend were heading home on a streetcar in Washington, D.C., from Twelfth and D Streets Northwest. In order for Wilbert and Otto to be able to sit facing the others, Otto switched the reversible seat back. A white passenger, Lottie May Jernigan, considered that seat to be in the "white section," and once the car entered Virginia, with its stringent segregated seating laws, she told Otto to move. Otto did not move until the car reached Patrick and King Streets in Alexandria, where the boys got off. Jernigan too got off, followed them, and relayed her complaint to a policeman.[77]

Because of Otto's age, he was not charged, but George and Wilbert were summoned to police court on charges of disorderly conduct, assault, and abusive language. A neighbor, who knew that their parents were out of town, ran to alert Thomas Watson, a Black lawyer who shared an office with Samuel A. Tucker, Wilbert's father, a real estate agent. The court fined Wilbert $5.03 plus court costs. George, being older, was fined $50 plus costs. Watson appealed the case.[78]

The appeal was heard by Judge Howard W. Smith, who three years later would be elected to Congress to become a leader of the Conservative Coalition of Democrats and Republicans. With a Black attorney before a conservative judge and five white male jurors, the Tuckers did not have high hopes, but surprisingly the jury found the boys innocent. In S. J. Ackerman's words, "The shock of unexpected justice electrified S. W. He vowed to follow in Watson's footsteps."[79] A legal career was in the offing.

At that time, Alexandria had no high school for Black students. Thus, Tucker "bootlegged an education," as he put it, by taking the trolley every day into Washington and then walking twenty-two blocks to Armstrong High. Years later Tucker noted, "We knew that something was wrong with it, there was a public high school within sight of my home that white children attended as a matter of course."[80]

Tucker attended Howard University and then, unable to attend Virginia's "whites only" law schools, he studied law under Tom Watson while researching cases for him at the Library of Congress. He passed the Washington bar exam at the age of twenty—too young to get his law license. When he turned twenty-one he was called to the bar, coincidentally at the same court in which he had been tried at fourteen. He became a clever and dogged champion of civil rights.

In 1939 Tucker had petitioned unsuccessfully for a court order to require that George Wilson, a retired Black army sergeant, be given a library card at the Alexandria public library. Inspired by Gandhi's campaign of nonviolent protest, and perhaps by the memory of Otto's quiet refusal to leave his seat when they were boys, Tucker arranged a unique event to bring attention to the issue of segregation before a separate library branch could be built for Black Alexandrians.

On a hot Monday morning in August, five well-dressed young Black men approached the librarian's desk one at a time and politely asked for an application for a library card. The five were all turned away, but, instead of leaving, each of them went over to the stacks, picked out a book, sat down at a table, and began to read. The head librarian went to city hall and appealed to the city manager and the chief of police. When they all arrived at the library, they were surprised to find about three hundred observers out front, including members of the press. The five aspiring library patrons were arrested peacefully and publicly, while a sixth ran off to tell Tucker how his plan was working. Stories in the *Washington Post*, the *Times Herald*, and the *Washington Tribune* used the new vocabulary of nonviolent protest, calling the incident a "sit-down strike."[81]

The city attorney repeatedly delayed the trial, knowing that it would not look good to come down hard on young men asking for library cards, and he eventually dropped all charges. The judge acknowledged that George Wilson was indeed qualified for a library card, though he denied Tucker's petition on a specious technicality. Rather vaguely he recommended that, in the absence of "a separate library for the colored race," the librarian should accommodate the city's Black residents. When Wilson and Tucker once again showed up with applications in January, the librarian gave them cards for the not-yet-completed "Colored Library." Tucker refused. When the new branch opened that spring, with "shorter hours, cast-off books, and a hand-me-down typewriter," the press saw it as a victory, but, as Ackerman emphasizes, "S. W. Tucker was disgusted."[82]

During World War II, Tucker served in Italy with the rank of major in the all-Black 366th Infantry Regiment in the U.S. Army. Upon returning, he set up a law practice in the town of Emporia, Virginia. As the only Black lawyer in an area with "no black judges, no black prosecutors, no black lawyers and no black jurors—only black defendants," Tucker worked as hard to oppose the racially biased system as he did to defend his individual clients.[83]

On April 23, 1951, sixteen-year-old Barbara Rose Johns orchestrated an unauthorized school assembly and led a walkout of 450 fellow students at R. R. Moton High School in Farmville, Virginia, to protest the crowded conditions and dilapidated buildings. The students appealed to the NAACP for help. NAACP lawyers Spottiswood Robinson and Oliver Hill agreed on the condition that the students sue not simply for a better school for Black students but also for fully integrated schools for the county. The resulting case, *Davis v. County School Board of Prince Edward County*, became one of the five cases eventually bundled together as *Brown v. Board of Education*, in which the Supreme Court in 1954 declared segregation in schools unconstitutional.[84] Tucker subsequently became the NAACP's lead lawyer overseeing the campaign to desegregate Virginia schools.

Opposition to integration was fierce, and through the 1950s, 1960s, and well into the 1970s, Tucker worked assiduously in opposition to efforts to keep schools racially segregated in spite of the court's decision in *Brown*. In 1969, when the district court ordered the recently incorporated city of Emporia to end its "freedom of choice" agreement with the county, the city adopted a new tactic: establishing its own independent school system. This plan was challenged, and the case made its way to the Supreme Court in 1972. Tucker argued that by separating city schools from the county schools, the former would have a higher proportion of white students and the latter would be left with a correspondingly higher percentage of Black students. In a 6–3 decision the court concluded that the city had not decided to establish its own school system "until the [district] court's order prevented the county from continuing its long-maintained segregated school system," and that "a separate school system would impede the process of dismantling the segregated school system."[85] By the mid-1970s, local and state governments in Virginia and elsewhere ended their concerted attempts to avoid the integration of public schools.

Tucker died in October 1990. "On November 16, 1999, the Alexandria School Board voted to name a new elementary school, its first new school building in 30 years, the S. W. Tucker School."[86]

Bigger Thomas No. 5, circa 1927

It may seem odd to include a fictional character in a book such as this, on a topic for which there are so many incidents and stories of real people who simply wanted to ride a bus or train in peace, people who suffered insult, injury, and even death through the cruelty of Jim Crow. But it is often the artist, the writer, who can express the truth and the complexities of our deeds and misdeeds, when actual events are not allowed the public scrutiny they deserve.

Richard Wright published his most famous novel, *Native Son*, in 1940, and it quickly generated considerable controversy with its dark portrayal of life in the Black ghetto and its suggestion of interracial sex. Though the latter was expurgated at the insistence of the Book of the Month Club, the book was a huge success, and it made Wright the first African American best-selling author. His protagonist is Bigger Thomas, a tough criminal, portrayed as the product of the harsh world in which Wright himself grew up. However frightening and cruel Bigger Thomas may be, James Baldwin, in spite of his criticisms of Wright's book, acknowledged his own belief that "no American Negro exists who does not have his private Bigger Thomas living in the skull."[87]

Wright published a brief article, "How 'Bigger' Was Born," in the *Saturday Review of Books* (June 1, 1940), to explain what he could about the origins of his tale:

> I shall sketch the outline of how I *consciously* came into possession of the materials that went into "Native Son," but there will be many things I shall omit, not because I want to, but because I don't know them. . . .
>
> The birth of Bigger Thomas goes back to my childhood, and there was not just one Bigger, but many of them, more than I could count and more than you suspect.

As Wright describes him, Bigger No. 1 was a bully who terrorized Wright and his friends when they were young boys, taking from them their balls, bats, tops, and marbles. Sometime later Wright met Bigger No. 2, a young man of about seventeen, whose hardness "was not directed toward me or the other Negroes, but toward the whites who ruled the South." Bigger No. 3 was of a type "the white folks called a 'bad nigger.' He carried his life in his hands in a literal fashion." Wright gives the example of a man who would simply walk into a Negro movie house without paying.

> "Did he pay?" the proprietor would ask. "No, sir," I'd answer. The proprietor would pull down the corners of his lips and speak through his teeth: "We'll kill that Goddamn nigger one of these days." And the episode would end right there. But later on . . . he was shot through the back by a white cop.
>
> And then there was Bigger No. 4 whose only law was death. The Jim Crow laws of the South were not for him. But as he laughed and cursed and broke them, he knew that someday he would have to pay for his freedom.

Most relevant to the topic of the present book, however, is the man Wright describes as "Bigger No. 5." Wright's phrase, "I remember one morning," suggests the possibility that this passage is based on an actual event, perhaps one that he witnessed. It is not unreasonable, therefore, to date the Bigger No. 5 incident sometime before November 1927, when Wright left the South to live in Chicago for ten years.

> Then there was Bigger No. 5 who rode the Jim Crow street cars without paying and sat wherever he pleased. I remember one morning his getting into a street car . . . and sitting in the white section. The conductor went to him and said: "Come on, nigger. Move over where you belong. Can't you read?" Bigger answered: "Naw; I can't read." The conductor flared up: "Get out of that seat!" Bigger took out his knife, opened it, held it nonchalantly in his hand, and replied: "Make me." The conductor turned red, blinked, clenched his fists, and walked away, stammering: "The Goddamn scum of the earth!" A small angry conference of white men took place in the front of the car and the Negroes sitting in the Jim Crow section overheard: "That's that Bigger Thomas nigger and you'd better leave 'im alone." The Negroes experienced an intense flash of pride and the street car moved on its journey without incident. I don't know what happened to Bigger No. 5. But I can guess.

Bigger No. 5 is able to face down the streetcar conductor and thus express his own sense of manliness, self-worth, and dignity, though not without the threat of violence. Yet the most telling aspect of Wright's account is not so much Bigger's intrepid self-assurance as it is the "intense flash of pride" experienced by the other Black riders when one of their own successfully opposes the abuse so familiar to them all. This reaction reveals a great deal about the weight of the oppressive burden that would, out of necessity, rise to the conscious awareness of all Black people whenever they found themselves in unavoidably close quarters with whites on a streetcar, train, or bus, and which they were seldom able to resist without harsh consequences. At the same time, Wright's "But I can guess" suggests that Bigger No. 5, like the fictional Bigger Thomas he helped inspire, may have ultimately come to a bad end.

Arthur Wergs Mitchell, April 21, 1937

Arthur Wergs Mitchell was born in Roanoke, Alabama, in 1883, the son of formerly enslaved Taylor and Ammar Patterson Mitchell. Mitchell had a varied career that eventually led in 1934 to him becoming the first African American member of the Democratic Party to be elected to the U.S. House of Representatives.

At eighteen Mitchell enrolled in Booker T. Washington's Tuskegee Institute, but he left after a year. Soon afterward he founded the West Alabama Normal and Industrial Institute, which offered training in agriculture, blacksmithing, wheelwrighting, carpentry, sewing, cooking, housekeeping, and laundering. However, according to his biographer, Dennis S. Nordin, Mitchell's motives were not entirely altruistic: "The school was in reality a scheme to attract poor blacks to farms and woodlots in need of cheap labor."[88] While students received a rudimentary education, they were worked very hard in the school's gardens and other activities.

When the school's main building burned down in 1911, Mitchell opened another operation in Geiger, Alabama, in which workers were hired with promises of education for their children. During the summers Mitchell attended nondegree programs at Harvard and Columbia University to improve his future prospects and his command of English. In early 1915, the school at Geiger too was shut down by a fire. Mitchell then took an administrative position at the Armstrong Agricultural Institute in West Butler, Alabama, but in 1919 lawsuits began to be filed against him for defrauding people of their land.

To avoid arrest Mitchell moved to Washington, D.C., invested in some apartments, and began to study law on his own. After passing the D.C. bar exam, he joined and in 1926 became national president of Phi Beta Sigma, a Black fraternity founded at Howard University in 1914. Through the connections this gained him, Mitchell accepted a position in 1928 directing the presidential election campaign in Chicago for the Republican nominee, Herbert Hoover.

Mitchell launched his own political career in Chicago, encouraged in part by the 1929 election of Oscar DePriest, the first African American elected to Congress from a northern state. Because most African Americans in Chicago were affiliated with the Republican Party, Mitchell determined that he stood a better chance to gain personal recognition in the Democratic Party. When the white Democratic nominee for the Illinois First Congressional District died, Mitchell was selected as the replacement candidate. Party leaders made it clear to Mitchell, however, that to retain the support of party leaders, he had to become an advocate for Roosevelt's New Deal policies and recognize their importance for improving conditions for African Americans. He narrowly unseated Oscar DePriest and entered the 74th Congress in January 1935.

In Congress, Mitchell distanced himself from the NAACP's anti-lynching campaign and other issues that would be resented by southern Democratic congressmen. In a speech given in Chicago in May 1936, Walter White, the president of the NAACP, strongly criticized Mitchell for his failure to help bring the anti-lynching bill to a vote in the House. According to the *Atlanta Daily World*, "White pointed out that not a single congressman from the State of Illinois has signed the petition which would bring the anti-lynching legislation to the floor of Congress and declared that nearly all of these Democratic Congressmen indicated that they were being guided by 'their cooperation with Mr. Mitchell.'"[89] How genuine such "cooperation" with Mitchell might have been, is, of course, open to question. They may have simply been glad to use his position to justify their own. White also noted in this speech that many congressmen from the deep South "commend Rep. Mitchell for his lack of enthusiasm, if not actual opposition" and that "there were definite reasons to believe that the legislation would pass if it were brought to a vote." According to Dennis Nordin, Mitchell adopted a stance that "promoted the mythology that African Americans in the rural South were more fortunate than their counterparts who lived in the urban North," though that may rather be an interpretation of Mitchell's desire, as the only African American in Congress, not to offend too openly his southern Democratic—and segregationist—colleagues.[90]

Mitchell entered Congress saying, "I don't plan to spend my time fighting out the question of whether a Negro may eat his lunch at the Capitol or whether he may be shaved in the House barber shop." But this suggestion that he would not be a strong congressional advocate for racial equity was put to the test during his second term. In the spring of 1937 Mitchell planned a trip to Hot Springs, Arkansas, and on April 20 he took a train from Chicago on the Illinois Central Railroad as far as Memphis, and thence on the Rock Island line. Mitchell initially wished to purchase a ticket for a berth in a Pullman sleeper car, but none were available, so he bought a first-class round-trip ticket at a rate of three cents a mile and was seated in a compartment in the sleeper car bound for New Orleans. Just before reaching Memphis, he moved to the Pullman car destined for Hot Springs, where a seat was now available, though at the increased rate of ninety cents per mile. When the train left Memphis on the morning of April 21 and crossed into Arkansas, the conductor came through to collect tickets. He accepted Mitchell's Memphis to Hot Springs ticket but would not accept payment for the increased Pullman fare. Rather, he said that Mitchell had to move to the car reserved for colored passengers, because of an Arkansas segregation law requiring "equal but separate and sufficient accommodations." Under threat of arrest, Mitchell complied. The conductor later returned the portion of the ticket he had taken, saying that Mitchell could get a refund, because the coach rate for that portion of the trip was only two cents a mile.

Rather than apply for a refund of a penny per mile (in effect, less than two dollars), Mitchell filed a complaint with the Interstate Commerce Commission alleging unjust discrimination in the furnishing of accommodations to colored passengers. The ICC dismissed the suit, and Mitchell appealed to the U.S. District Court of Northern Illinois. That court, claiming it was without jurisdiction, also dismissed the case, thus affirming the ICC's decision, and the case was appealed directly to the Supreme Court, which heard arguments on March 13, 1941.

On April 28, the court handed down its decision in Mitchell's favor:

> The undisputed facts showed conclusively that, having paid a first class fare for the entire journey from Chicago to Hot Springs, and having offered to pay the proper charge for a seat which was available in the Pullman car for the trip from Memphis to Hot Springs, he was compelled, in accordance with custom, to leave that car and to ride in a second class car, and was thus denied the standard conveniences and privileges afforded to first class passengers. This was manifestly a discrimination against him in the course of his interstate journey, and admittedly that discrimination was based solely upon the fact that he was a Negro. The question whether this was a discrimination forbidden by the Interstate Commerce Act is not a question of segregation, but one of equality of treatment. The denial to appellant of equality of accommodations because of his race would be an invasion of a fundamental individual right which is guaranteed against state action by the Fourteenth Amendment . . . , and, in view of the nature of the right and of our constitutional policy, it cannot be maintained that the discrimination as it was alleged was not essentially unjust.[91]

Mitchell did not challenge the right of states to legislate segregation. Rather his case hinged on defining more precisely the principle of "separate but equal" as laid down in *Plessy v. Ferguson* and the 1907 ICC ruling in the case of Georgia Edwards, which also went into the details of furnishings and conveniences. In such a light, the certainly "separate" but hardly "equal" accommodations described in some detail in the court's decision is revealing:

> The Commission further found that the Pullman car contained ten sections of berths and two compartment drawing rooms; that the use of one of the drawing rooms would have amounted to segregation under the state law, and ordinarily such combinations are available to colored passengers upon demand, the ninety cent fare being applicable. Occasionally they are used by colored passengers but, in this instance, both drawing rooms were already occupied by white passengers. The Pullman car was of modern design and had all the usual facilities and conveniences found in standard sleeping cars. It was air-conditioned, had hot and cold running water, and separate flushable toilets for men and women. It was in excellent condition throughout. First class white passengers had, in addition to the Pullman sleeper, the exclusive use of the train's only dining car and only observation parlor car, the latter having somewhat the same accommodations for day use as the Pullman car.
>
> The coach for colored passengers, though of standard size and steel construction, was "an old combination affair," not air-conditioned, divided by partitions into three main parts, one for colored smokers, one for white smokers and one in the center for colored men and women, known as the women's section, in which appellant sat. There was a toilet in each section, but only the one in the women's section was equipped for flushing, and it was for the exclusive use of colored women. The car was without wash basins, soap, towels or running water, except in the women's section. The Commission stated that, according to appellant, the car was "filthy and foul smelling," but that the testimony of defendants' witnesses was to the contrary.[92]

As part of their defense, the railroad companies had also argued that the frequency with which colored passengers requested Pullman accommodations was insufficient to warrant the necessity of including them—"the conductor estimated that this demand did not amount to one per year"—and they further pointed out that about three months after Mitchell's journey they replaced the old cars with new ones that were better equipped.

The court declared, however, that neither of these arguments was sufficient or relevant in regard to the question of discrimination against Mitchell. The ruling stressed that "equal" accommodations under the "separate but equal" principle had to truly be equal: "Colored persons who buy first-class tickets must be furnished with accommodations equal in comforts and conveniences to those afforded to first-class white passengers."[93] The court further stipulated that infrequent demand was insufficient cause for an exception: "The comparative volume of traffic cannot justify the denial of a fundamental right of equality of treatment, a right specifically safeguarded by the provisions of the Interstate Commerce Act."[94]

Though he adopted a cautious, nonconfrontational stance in Congress, Arthur Mitchell was inevitably looked to in matters of race. He nominated several Black candidates to the U.S. military academies and supported legislation to eliminate poll taxes. During the war he spoke out against discrimination in the armed services and in the civil service. Predictably, however, the Chicago Democratic political machine was not happy with Mitchell's complaints against prominent Chicago-based companies or with his speeches in the House of Representatives against discrimination by government defense contractors. In 1942 the party decided to back another candidate, and without party support Mitchell chose not to run. He retired to a small estate in Virginia, where he built a mansion that some have compared to Tara, the O'Hara plantation in *Gone with the Wind*. He spent his retirement raising prize-winning cattle and prize-winning roses until his death in 1968.

Pauli Murray, March 23, 1940

Pauli Murray was born Anna Pauline Murray in Baltimore in 1910. Murray's mother, Agnes Fitzgerald Murray, died in 1914, and Murray was adopted by an aunt, Pauline Fitzgerald Dame, in Durham, North Carolina. Murray's father, a public school teacher, was murdered in a state hospital in 1923. After finishing the eleventh grade, Murray went to live with relatives in New York City and graduated from Richmond Hill High School in 1928.

The following year Murray entered Hunter College and took on the gender-neutral name Pauli. Gender identification was a lifelong concern for Murray. The Pauli Murray Center for History and Social Justice notes,

> We don't know how Pauli Murray would identify if they were living today or which pronouns Murray would use for self-expression.
>
> Murray self-described as a "he/she personality" in correspondence with family members. . . . Later in journals, essays, letters and autobiographical works, Murray employed "she/her/hers" pronouns and self-described as a woman.
>
> . . . Respectability politics, widespread homophobia and transphobia, and federal and state policies likely constrained Pauli Murray's ability to publicly and thoroughly explore their gender. As Naomi Simmons-Thorne writes, "Given the rigid enforcement of the gender binary, we do not, nor will we ever know, Murray's true gender identity."[95]

Murray was briefly married in 1930 and graduated from Hunter in 1933 with a degree in English and ambitions to become a writer.[96] After graduation

Pauli Murray. Inscribed "To mother with love—1941, Pauli." Schlesinger Library, Harvard Radcliffe Institute.

Murray worked for a year as a field agent for the National Urban League's *Opportunity* magazine and from 1936 to 1939 taught reading under the Works Progress Administration (WPA) and the Workers' Education Project.

In November 1938 Murray applied for postgraduate studies at the University of North Carolina, which Murray's white great-grandfather had attended and where his father before him had been both a university trustee and a member of Congress. On December 12, the U.S. Supreme Court handed down its decision in the case of Lloyd Gaines, requiring the State of Missouri to provide Gaines with a law school education in the state equal to that which white law students received, rather than offering him the possibility of attending a law school in another state.[97] While this decision gave Murray some hope, a letter of rejection from the UNC graduate school dean came as no great surprise, though it carried a sharp sting, especially given the close ties to the university forged by Murray's white forebears: "Under the laws of North Carolina . . . members of your race are not admitted to the University." He suggested, pointing to a vague future, that the next session of the state General Assembly was expected to take "positive action" toward making "provision for graduate instruction for Negroes."[98]

Murray wrote to the president of the university, stating clearly, "It would be a victory for liberal thought in the South if you were favorably disposed toward my application instead of forcing me to carry the issue to the courts." The dean replied for the president, "The important matter you raise is for the State to decide. . . . In the meantime, I suggest that you file with this office a transcript of your undergraduate record and information concerning your citizenship and residence." Murray, in turn, sent copies of all this correspondence to the NAACP, where it was referred to the office of the assistant special counsel, Thurgood Marshall.[99]

The news of a Black applicant broke in the campus newspaper, the *Daily Tar Heel*, and quickly spread to local, state, and national papers. When Murray's name was revealed in some of the Black newspapers, Murray and especially Aunt Pauline—who, after all, lived right in Durham—became apprehensive, though Murray received no direct threats. By early March, the state legislature had adopted an act that "provided for graduate courses and professional training for Negroes when and as they were required, or became necessary, or were demanded." But the white-owned *Durham Morning Herald* noted, "It takes more than a law authorizing graduate facilities for Negroes to bring them into existence."[100]

In the end Murray was bitterly disappointed to hear from Thurgood Marshall that the NAACP had decided not to use Murray's rejection as a test case. Murray's academic record was perfectly sound, but residency in New York would have added a new complication to the *Gaines* decision, thus jeopardizing the outcome. As the first such application to attract wide publicity, however, Murray's efforts did have a positive effect. A note of well-deserved pride can be detected in Murray's statement that "within a month Negroes had filed applications with officials of the universities of Georgia, South Carolina, Kentucky, Arkansas, West Virginia, and the School of Journalism at the University of Missouri."[101]

Not long after finishing work with the WPA in 1939, Murray became executive secretary for National Sharecroppers Week, an organization supporting tenant farmers nationwide. In early 1940, after a successful campaign culminating in a banquet at which Eleanor Roosevelt was the featured speaker, Murray decided to spend the Easter holiday with relatives in Durham. Murray invited a housemate, Adelene McBean, to come as well. Murray would write, "[McBean] was a peppery, self-assertive young woman of West Indian parentage who had never been confronted with segregation law and believed that southern Negroes were altogether too timid about their rights. . . . Increasingly, my own resentment against segregation was becoming difficult to control." Murray notes, "I had read . . . a study of Gandhi's method of Satyagraha—nonviolent resistance coupled with good will—and had pondered the possibility of applying the technique to the racial struggle in the United States." They took a bus to Washington, D.C., hoping to avoid problems with Jim Crow by borrowing a car from Murray's sister and driving the rest of the way to Durham. Unfortunately, the car was unavailable.[102]

On March 23, the day before Easter, Murray and McBean took a bus to Richmond without incident. The connecting bus to Durham was filled, and they were told to wait for a relief bus. There were empty seats near the front of the relief bus, including two side by side right behind the driver. They, however, were obliged to take the only remaining seats, two rows from the rear, seats that were cramped because of the wheel well intruding into the space. The bus raced to catch up with the regular bus. Sitting so awkwardly, McBean began to feel ill, with a sharp pain in her side. She suggested that they move to the two front seats. Murray knew that would be disastrous and asked the driver, Frank W. Morris, if he would move two white children from the rear to those front seats, but he curtly refused. According to an article in the African American *Carolina Times*, Murray then "appealed to the mother of the children, explaining the situation. The mother refused to reseat her children stating that the driver would take care of it."[103] Writing a memoir later, Murray acknowledges, "It was foolish of me to expect humane treatment within the segregation system; to make the system work fairly would threaten the entire structure of white supremacy which Jim Crow was designed to reinforce."[104] Within this system, of course, it would be unthinkable for a driver to ask white passengers to move in order to accommodate Black passengers.

At Petersburg a number of passengers left the bus, and before about twenty Black people boarded the bus, Murray and McBean moved forward two rows, still remaining behind all the white passengers. As soon as Morris saw them move, he yelled at them to go back, on the basis of the regulation that "black passengers fill the bus from the rear and white passengers from the front." In actual fact, that "regulation" was not embedded in Virginia segregation law; rather it was a rule that the company adopted in order to keep Black passengers as far from white passengers as possible. Murray explained that the seat behind them was broken, yet Morris persisted. When they declined to move, he threatened to have them arrested.

McBean insisted that she was ill and could not ride over the wheel or in a broken seat, and that she was willing to leave the bus if her money and her baggage were returned to her. Morris angrily went into the station to call his superiors. As the tension on the bus mounted, Murray gave Aunt Pauline's name and address to a Black passenger who was going to Durham and asked him, if they were arrested, to tell her to wire Walter White, the executive secretary of the NAACP.

Forty-five minutes later Morris reentered the bus with two policemen with arrest warrants. McBean was "peppery" indeed, saying, "If you're looking for me, here I am. But you needn't think that your big brass buttons and your shiny bullets are going to scare me, because I have rights, they're substantial, and I'm sitting on them."[105] She argued that if she were white they would treat her differently, and she put to them her own version of David Ruggles, Frederick Douglass, and Lydia Maria Child's core question, asking "why they couldn't give her the same consideration even though she was colored."[106] The officers were stymied. On the one hand, it was not clear whether McBean and Murray were defying any Jim Crow laws; on the other hand, McBean had publicly ridiculed two police officers representing the racist authority that instituted those laws.

After another consultation with the driver, one policeman returned to ask them simply to move back one row. Morris repaired the broken seat, and Murray and McBean moved back. The matter was resolved, and two white passengers boarded to take the newly vacated seats. "Morris then distributed witness cards to all white passengers, pointedly ignoring the seven or eight Negro passengers in the rear of the bus."[107] Murray would write, "Up to this point my role in the ludicrous affair had been relatively minor, but this final damning implication that black people were *nobodies* and did not have to be taken into account was more than I could bear." Murray called out to Morris, asking why he did not hand out cards to the people in the back. Morris's response was to jump out of the bus yet again, returning with the policemen. The warrants were read, and Murray and McBean were arrested for "disorderly conduct and creating a public disturbance."[108]

Murray was leaving the bus when there was a commotion from behind. Adelene McBean, ill and not having eaten since noon, had fainted. She was "half-carried, half-dragged" to the door and then laid on a stretcher on the ground, as Murray stood in the cold and dark, "almost rigid with fear." Murray and McBean were driven to the Petersburg hospital, where McBean was examined and treated for "hysteria" and minor bruises. They were then taken to the Petersburg City Prison, where they spent the Easter weekend in a foul, bug-ridden cell with three local women. Though they were treated harshly by the prison officials and even regarded with suspicion by other inmates, they were careful always to reply quietly and politely.[109]

That Sunday evening they were visited by two NAACP lawyers who had been alerted to their plight after a Black man at the bus station reported their arrest to the president of the local branch of the NAACP. When court opened to a large crowd on Tuesday morning, McBean and Murray were quickly convicted of the original charges, as well as of violation of sections of segregation law. They were fined five dollars each and court costs, and their attorneys filed an appeal. Released on bond, they caught the 2:00 p.m. bus to Durham, driven by none other than Frank Morris, who was accompanied by two uniformed Greyhound guards. Under such company scrutiny, "Morris was the essence of new-found courtesy."[110]

Murray's sister had sent a telegram to Eleanor Roosevelt, which was answered by her secretary about ten days late: "Mrs. Roosevelt . . . asked the Governor of Virginia about it, which was all she could do, and he says that Miss Murray was unwise not to comply with the law. As long as these laws exist, it does no one much good to violate them." Murray was disappointed, of course, and felt that Mrs. Roosevelt "had little understanding of what it meant to be a Negro in the United States at that time."[111]

The NAACP decided to defend the case and challenge the constitutionality of state segregation laws in interstate travel. A powerful team of lawyers included Thurgood Marshall, Link Johnson Jr., and William H. Hastie. However, when the case came to court on May 10, the judge found Murray and McBean guilty of creating a disturbance, though not of violating any segregation laws, and fined them ten dollars and costs. Rather than pay the fine, they decided to go back to jail. Their second stay in the prison proved to be better than the first; they were given a better cell, clean mattresses, and the bedbugs were exterminated with a blowtorch. Several days later the Workers Defense League (WDL) paid their fines and they were released.[112]

In *Song in a Weary Throat,* Murray articulates for the twentieth century the pain of traveling under Jim Crow as clearly as did Frederick Douglass for the nineteenth in his comments about his treatment on the *Cambria*:

> The bus was the quintessence of the segregation evil, because there the separation of the races was merely symbolic. The intimacy of the bus interior permitted the public humiliation of black people to be carried out in the presence of privileged white spectators, who witness our shame in silence or indifference.
>
> It was not the fact of separation that hurt so much; it was, as everybody knew, the fact that the overriding purpose of segregation was to humiliate and degrade colored people. Even if one quietly accepted being forced to sit in the back of the bus, there was apt to be some white driver whose contemptuous treatment of Negro passengers, combined with his uniform and swaggering manner, gave him a striking resemblance to a Nazi storm trooper.[113]

After being released from Petersburg Prison, Murray was asked to join the administrative committee of the WDL. That August the case of Odell Waller came to the League's attention. Waller, a sharecropper, had shot his landlord, Oscar Davis, in a dispute over Waller's portion of their wheat crop, which Davis had locked in his own barn. Waller fled to Ohio but was extradited back to Virginia, and in September he was convicted of first-degree murder by an all-white jury (predominantly farmers who employed sharecroppers) and sentenced to die on December 27. The WDL hired Murray to go to Richmond to raise money to try to prevent Waller's execution and later to work full-time raising money and support for Waller's appeal. In December Waller received a stay of execution, and during the following year, 1941, Murray traveled across the country with Annie Waller, Odell's wife, fund-raising and educating people about the complexities of the case and the pernicious effects of the Virginia poll tax on the course of justice for African Americans and poor whites alike.[114] Waller was executed in July 1942.

Personal experiences with Jim Crow and the Waller case drew Murray to an interest in the law. Murray earned a law degree from the Howard Law School in 1944, graduating first in the class. Applying to Harvard Law School for further study, Murray was rejected, not on the basis of race but rather on the basis of gender. The following year, however, Murray received an LLM from the Boalt Hall School of Law at the University of California at Berkeley, with a thesis on "The Right to Equal Opportunity in Employment."[115]

Passing the bar in both states, Murray served for a short while as deputy attorney general in California and in April 1949 opened a private practice in New York. Running in Brooklyn as a Liberal Party candidate for the New York City Council that year, Murray lost but did much better than anyone expected. While doing a study on segregation for the Methodist Women's Division of Christian Service, Murray received a query about states' laws. Researching the law codes of all forty-eight states and the District of Columbia, in 1951 Murray published *States' Laws on Race and Color*, a 746-page volume that remains an indispensable resource for the study of racial history and the law.

Leaving the practice of law in 1960, Murray taught for a year at the Ghana Law School in Accra. Returning to the United States, Murray was accepted at Yale Law School and became the first African American Doctor of Juridical Science in 1965. After serving for a year as vice president of Benedict University in South Carolina, Murray taught for five years at Brandeis University in Massachusetts, during a time of intense racial debate, protest, and turmoil.

Among many contributions in the continuing struggle for women's rights, Murray served on the Committee on Civil and Political Rights in the President's Commission on the Status of Women established by President Kennedy in 1961, a committee that was instrumental in adding a ban on sex discrimination to the 1964 Civil Rights Act.[116] Coining the term "Jane Crow" to draw parallels between the evils of racism and sexism, Murray coauthored a groundbreaking article, "Jane Crow and the Law: Sex Discrimination and Title VII," published in the *George Washington Law Review* in 1965.[117] From 1965 to 1973 Murray served on the board of the American Civil Liberties Union, and in 1966 Murray became one of the twenty-eight founding members of the National Organization of Women.[118] Over time, however, disappointed with the ways in which NOW failed to address adequately issues pertaining to Black and poor women, Murray refrained from taking a leadership position in the organization.[119]

In the late 1960s and early 1970s Murray's practice of religion began to strengthen, despite bridling against the Episcopal Church's denial to women of full participation in the priesthood and ministry. After many doubts and much soul searching, and moved by the death of a close friend, Murray entered General Theological Seminary in New York. On January 8, 1977, Murray was ordained as an Episcopal priest and later wrote about that: "All the strands of my life had come together. Descendant of slave and of slave owner, I had already been called poet, lawyer, teacher, and friend. Now I was empowered to minister the sacrament of One to whom there is no north or south, no black or white, no male or female—only the spirit of love and reconciliation drawing us all toward the goal of human wholeness."[120]

In 2024 Pauli Murray became the eleventh person whose image was included on the reverse of a U.S. coin in the American Women Quarters series.

Elmer W. Henderson, May 17, 1942

Elmer W. Henderson was a Black lawyer who worked for the federal Fair Employment Practices Committee. Traveling in the course of his work on a first-class ticket from Washington, D.C., to Birmingham, Alabama, via Atlanta, he was denied a seat on the Southern Railroad. Unlike the earlier case of Congressman Arthur Mitchell, however, the issue became not what car he had to sit in, but rather where, or even if, he could sit and eat in the train's dining car. On the Southern Railroad all of the seats in the dining car were available for white passengers, but the two tables at the end closest to the kitchen—which is to say, the noisiest and hottest tables—were "conditionally reserved for Negroes."[121] "Conditionally reserved" meant that when both of the end tables were empty, Black diners could be seated at one or both, and a curtain was drawn to hide them from the view of the white diners. If it happened that the other tables were full and no Black diners were present, additional white passengers wishing to eat would be seated at the end tables. Any Black passengers who arrived subsequently would have to wait until the white diners at the end tables had left.

Around 5:30 p.m., at the first call for dinner, Henderson quickly went to the dining car only to find that it was already almost full, and the end tables were partially occupied by white passengers. Although there was at least one place empty, Henderson was denied a seat there. The steward told him that he would be glad to bring Henderson's dinner to his regular Pullman seat at no extra charge. When Henderson declined this offer, the steward assured him that he would send word when the tables were free. No word came. Twice Henderson returned to the dining car without getting a seat, and at 9:00 p.m. the dining car was detached from the train.

Like William H. Councill and William H. Heard forty-five years earlier, Henderson filed a complaint that October with the Interstate Commerce Commission, arguing that the Southern Railroad was in violation of Section 3.1 of the Interstate Commerce Act of 1887, which stated, "It shall be unlawful for any common carrier subject to the provisions of this part to make, give, or cause any undue or unreasonable preference or advantage to any particular person . . . in any respect whatsoever; or to subject any particular person . . . to any undue or unreasonable prejudice or disadvantage in any respect whatsoever." The ICC ruled that Henderson had indeed received "undue or unreasonable prejudice or disadvantage," as it had similarly determined in the case of Arthur Mitchell. However, the commission concluded that rather than being a systematic prejudice embedded in the railroad's policies in violation of the Interstate Commerce Act, it was "a casual incident brought about by the bad judgment of an employee." This reasoning allowed the commission to sidestep the Supreme Court's clarifying statement in *Mitchell v. United States* that infrequent demand was insufficient cause for abrogating the legal requirement for "equality." The commission declined to give any order regarding the future practice of the Southern or other railroads.

Henderson appealed to the U.S. District Court for the District of Maryland, which held that the railroad was, indeed, in violation of the Interstate Commerce Act. In February 1946 the court sent the case back to the ICC for "further proceedings." On March 1 the railroad changed its policy to state that henceforth there would be "ten tables, of four seats each, exclusively and unconditionally for white passengers and one table, of four seats, exclusively and unconditionally for Negro passengers." The curtain separating them remained, sometimes replaced by a wooden partition. Presumably the repeated "exclusively and unconditionally" was meant to satisfy the "equal" part of "separate but equal." The commission accordingly stated that the company's new rules did not violate the Interstate Commerce Act, and that "no order for the future [was] necessary."

The case was returned to the Maryland District Court. This time the court sustained the commission's argument "on the ground that the accommodations [were] adequate to serve the average number of Negro passengers and [were] 'proportionately fair.'" This decision, once again, seemed to ignore the prohibition against the "insufficient demand" argument. Henderson appealed his case to the Supreme Court. Citing the *Mitchell* case as a foundational precedent, the justices overturned the district court's decision and dismissed the ICC's ruling, even adding a specific stipulation: "The curtains, partitions and signs emphasize the artificiality of a difference in treatment which serves only to call attention to a racial classification of passengers holding identical tickets and using the same public dining facility." While the court did not rule against segregation altogether, as Henderson's lawyer had strenuously argued it should, it did define and constrain "separate but equal" more tightly. This provided the legal background for Dovey Roundtree to sue the ICC for breach of contract in the case of her grandmother's mistreatment, also on the Southern Railroad, just a week before the *Henderson* decision was handed down on June 5, 1950, and again in the case of Sarah Keys.

Bayard Rustin, Summer 1942

Though his name is unfamiliar to many, Bayard Rustin was one of the most influential civil rights activists of the twentieth century. He was a superb and indefatigable organizer who worked both behind the scenes and on the front lines resisting segregation laws, racism, and intolerance altogether with his fervent commitment to nonviolence.

Rustin's career as a protester began at an early age, perhaps in grade school when he successfully resisted his teachers' attempts to make him write with his right hand instead of his left. As a high school student in West Chester, Pennsylvania, he was refused service at a restaurant in Media, Pennsylvania, while traveling with the school football team. "I sat there quite a long time, and was eventually thrown out bodily. From that point on, I had the conviction that I would not accept segregation," he later recalled.[122] On another occasion he refused to take part in an out-of-town track meet unless he and another Black team member would be allowed to stay at the same hotel as their white teammates. They were. The first of his many arrests also came while he was in high school. The West Chester movie theater was segregated, and African Americans had to sit in the balcony. Much as Sarah Remond had

Bayard Rustin, circa 1950. Courtesy of Walter Naegle.

done in 1853 and Hannibal Carter in 1873, Rustin attempted to integrate the orchestra seats, and though he did not succeed in the short run, this failed gesture further strengthened his determination and resolve to resist injustice.

Rustin's grandmother had been raised as a Quaker, and from her he learned the principles of pacifism and nonviolence. He attended Wilberforce University for a year, but he was dismissed because he refused to join the ROTC program and because he was gay. He then attended Cheyney State Teachers College back in West Chester and became active in the Society of Friends. When he was dismissed from Cheyney State in 1937, he went to Manhattan to attend City College of New York. In the city he became affiliated for a time with the Young Communist League because, as he later said, "They seemed the only people who had civil rights at heart."[123] It should be noted that the African American experience of the Communist Party in the mid-twentieth century was quite different than white experience, not least because the International Labor Defense (ILD) wing of the U.S. Communist Party came to the defense of the nine "Scottsboro Boys," who had been falsely accused of rape in Alabama in 1931, and of Angelo Herndon, who was defended by Benjamin J. Davis and the ILD against the charge of attempting to incite insurrection in 1932. Rustin left the party when he became disillusioned with its support for joining the war in Europe.

Rustin was a fine tenor, and, in addition to singing at civil rights protests, he was a member of the chorus in the musical *John Henry*, starring Paul Robeson, in 1940. He also performed with the blues and folk singers Lead Belly and Josh White at the Café Society Downtown in Greenwich Village.

In 1941 Rustin worked with A. Philip Randolph to organize the March on Washington Movement in order to convince President Roosevelt to integrate the armed forces and end discrimination in the defense industry. The week before the march was scheduled, the president signed Executive Order 8802: Fair Employment Practice in Defense Industries, and, to the disappointment of Rustin, Randolph canceled the march. During this period Randolph introduced Rustin to the thinking and writings of Mohandas Gandhi and A. J. Muste, which coalesced with Rustin's own religious and pacifist background.

The United States entered the Second World War after the Japanese attack on Pearl Harbor in December 1941, and Rustin began traveling throughout the country as the youth secretary of the Fellowship of Reconciliation, recruiting pacifists to the cause and speaking out against the internment of Japanese Americans. On a trip from Louisville to Nashville, Rustin decided to sit near the front of the bus. His own description of the ensuing events, published in the July 1942 issue of *Fellowship*, is an eloquent example of the effectiveness of nonviolent action. Rustin presents us today, as much as he did the original readers of *Fellowship*, with a powerful and explicit model for the practice of nonviolent resistance, as he balanced the very real threats, risks, and dangers of the moment against his deep sense of moral justice and right. In "Non-Violence vs. Jim Crow" he begins his protest with his own version of the question posed by Lydia Maria Child, David Ruggles, Frederick Douglass, and many others: "Why?"

> Recently I was planning to go from Louisville to Nashville by bus. I bought my ticket, boarded the bus, and, instead of going to the back, sat down in the second seat. The driver saw me, got up, and came toward me.
>
> "Hey, you. You're supposed to sit in the back seat."
>
> "Why?"
>
> "Because that's the law. Niggers ride in back."
>
> I said, "My friend, I believe that is an unjust law. If I were to sit in back I would be condoning injustice."

Angry, but not knowing what to do, he got out and went into the station. He soon came out again, got into his seat, and started off.

This routine was gone through at each stop, but each time nothing came of it. Finally the driver, in desperation, must have phoned ahead, for about thirteen miles north of Nashville I heard sirens approaching. The bus came to an abrupt stop, and a police car and two motorcycles drew up beside us with a flourish. Four policemen got into the bus, consulted shortly with the driver, and came to my seat.

"Get up, you ___ nigger!"

"Why?" I asked.

"Get up, you black ___!"

"I believe that I have a right to sit here," I said quietly. "If I sit in the back of the bus I am depriving that child"—I pointed to a little white child of five or six—"of the knowledge that there is injustice here, which I believe it is his right to know. It is my sincere conviction that the power of love in the world is the greatest power existing. If you have a greater power, my friend, you may move me."

How much they understood of what I was trying to tell them I do not know. By this time they were impatient and angry. As I would not move, they began to beat me about the head and shoulders, and I shortly found myself knocked to the floor. Then they dragged me out of the bus and continued to kick and beat me.

Knowing that if I tried to get up or protect myself in the first heat of their anger they would construe it as an attempt to resist and beat me down again, I forced myself to be still and wait for their kicks, one after another. Then I stood up, spreading out my arms parallel to the ground, and said, "There is no need to beat me. I am not resisting you."

At this three white men, obviously Southerners by their speech, got out of the bus and remonstrated with the police. Indeed, as one of the policemen raised his club to strike me, one of them, a little fellow, caught hold of it and said, "Don't you do that!" A second policeman raised his club to strike the little man, and I stepped between them, facing the man, and said, "Thank you, but there is no need to do that. I do not wish to fight. I am protected well."

An elderly gentleman, well dressed and also a Southerner, asked the police where they were taking me.

They said, "Nashville."

"Don't worry, son," he said to me. "I'll be there to see that you get justice."

I was put into the back seat of the police car, between two policemen. Two others sat in front. During the thirteen-mile ride to town they called me every conceivable name and said anything they could think of to incite me to violence. I found that I was shaking with nervous strain, and to give myself something to do, I took out a piece of paper and a pencil, and began to write from memory a chapter from one of Paul's letters.

When I had written a few sentences, the man on my right said, 'What're you writing?' and snatched the paper from my hand. He read it, then crumpled it into a ball and pushed it in my face. The man on the other side gave me a kick.

A moment later I happened to catch the eye of the young policeman in the front seat. He looked away quickly, and I took renewed courage from the realization that he could not meet my eyes because he was aware of the injustice being done. I began to write again, and after a moment I leaned forward and touched him on the shoulder. "My friend," I said, "how do you spell 'difference'?"

He spelled it for me—incorrectly—and I wrote it correctly and went on.

When we reached Nashville, a number of policemen were lined up on both sides of the hallway down which I had to pass on my way to the captain's office. They tossed me from one to another like a volleyball. By the time I reached the office, the lining of my best coat was torn, and I was considerably rumpled. I straightened myself as best I could and went in. They had my bag, and went through it and my papers, finding much of interest, especially in the *Christian Century* and *Fellowship.*[124]

Finally the captain said, "Come here, nigger."

I walked directly to him. 'What can I do for you?" I asked.

"Nigger," he said menacingly, "you're supposed to be scared when you come in here!"

"I am fortified by truth, justice, and Christ," I said. "There's no need for me to fear."

He was flabbergasted and, for a time, completely at a loss for words. Finally he said to another officer, "I believe the nigger's crazy!"

They sent me into another room and went into consultation. The wait was long, but after an hour and a half they came for me and I was taken for another ride, across town. At the courthouse, I was taken down the hall to the office of the assistant district attorney, Mr. Ben West. As I got to the door I heard a voice, "Say, you colored fellow, hey!" I looked around and saw the elderly gentleman who had been on the bus.

"I'm here to see that you get justice," he said.

The assistant district attorney questioned me about my life, the *Christian Century*, pacifism, and the war for half an hour. Then he asked the police to tell their side of what had happened. They did, stretching the truth a good deal in spots and including several lies for seasoning. Mr. West then asked me to tell my side.

"Gladly," I said, "and I want *you*," turning to the young policeman who had sat in the front seat, "to follow what I say and stop me if I deviate from the truth in the least."

> Holding his eyes with mine, I told the story exactly as it had happened, stopping often to say, "Is that right?" or "Isn't that what happened?" to the young policeman. During the whole time he never once interrupted me, and when I was through I said, "Did I tell the truth just as it happened?" and he said, "Well . . ."
>
> Then Mr. West dismissed me, and I was sent to wait alone in a dark room. After an hour, Mr. West came in and said, very kindly, "You may go, Mister Rustin."
>
> I left the courthouse, believing all the more strongly in the non-violent approach. I am certain that I was addressed as "Mister" (as no Negro is ever addressed in the South), that I was assisted by those three men, and that the elderly gentleman interested himself in my predicament because I had, without fear, faced the four policemen and said, "There is no need to beat me. I offer you no resistance."[125]

In 1940 Rustin had registered as a conscientious objector. However, in 1943, when he received a conscription notice from his local draft board in New York City, he realized that even serving as a noncombatant entailed implicit support for war and the divisions among people that war relies on. He returned the notice to the draft board, along with a letter setting out his reasons, both religious and philosophical, concluding, "Though joyfully following the will of God, I regret that I must break the law of the State. I am prepared for whatever may follow."[126] What followed in 1944 was a prison sentence that lasted until June 1946, well after the war's end. While serving his sentence in the penitentiary in Ashland, Ohio, he organized hunger strikes with other conscientious objectors to desegregate recreation areas, the chapel, and the prison dining hall. This activity landed him in solitary confinement, before being transferred to a prison in Lewisburg, Pennsylvania. After he was released, Rustin joined protests in Washington, D.C., to advocate for the release of other imprisoned war objectors.[127]

During 1946 Rustin "functioned as a one-man civil disobedience movement in his travels across the United States," as Jarvis Anderson memorably puts it. "He occupied 'white only' railroad compartments, sat in at 'white only' hotels, and refused to budge unless he was forcibly ejected."[128] Returning to work for the Fellowship of Reconciliation (FOR) and the newly formed Congress of Racial Equality (CORE), Rustin came up with the idea of the Journey of Reconciliation, a bus tour of the Upper South to test compliance with the Supreme Court ruling in the case of Irene Morgan, delivered on June 3, 1946. He worked particularly closely with Jim Peck, a white union organizer and CORE volunteer from New York, and George Houser, the executive secretary of CORE, to plan the innovative—and indisputably dangerous—journey, which began on April 9, 1947 (see pp. 270–81).

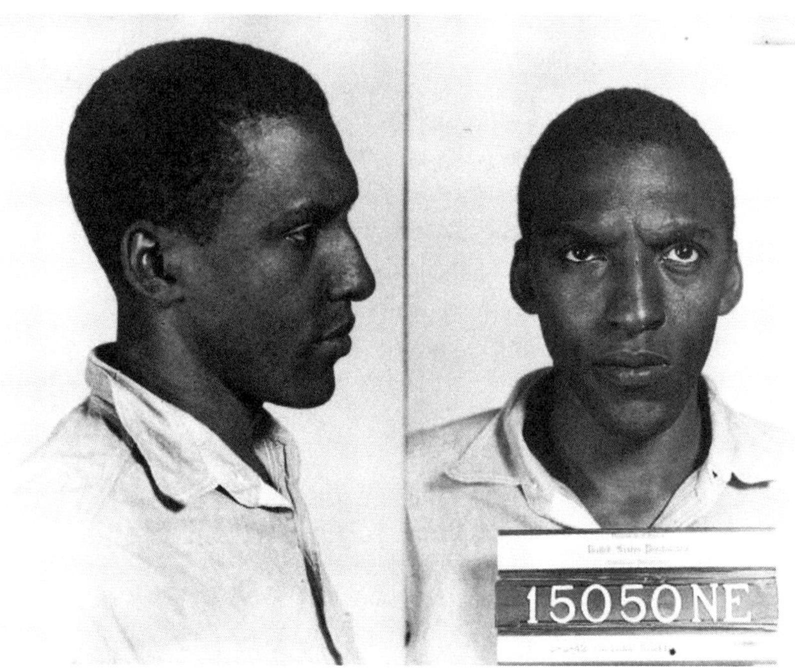

Bayard Rustin, Lewisburg Penitentiary, August 3, 1945.

Hugh M. Gloster, August 22, 1942

Hugh Gloster was born in Brownsville, Tennessee, in 1911, and his family moved to Memphis in 1915. Both of Gloster's parents were teachers, so it is not surprising that he too became an educator. He received a junior diploma from LeMoyne College (now LeMoyne-Owen College) and in 1931 a bachelor's degree in English from Morehouse College in Atlanta, followed by a master's degree from Atlanta University two years later. He began teaching at LeMoyne in 1933, and in 1937 he and eight professors from other Black colleges founded the Association of Teachers of English in Negro Colleges, which later became the College Language Association. He served as the organization's first president, a position that gave him considerable visibility among Black educators early in his career. In 1941 Gloster became a professor of English at Morehouse while he was simultaneously studying for a PhD from New York University.

At about 10:15 p.m. on Saturday, August 22, 1942, Prof. Gloster was on his way from Atlanta to Memphis. He changed trains at Birmingham and boarded the "Sunnyland" on the St. Louis–San Francisco (Frisco) Railway, which should have taken him to Memphis. L. O. Swingler wrote for the *Atlanta Daily World* a detailed account of what happened before Gloster reached home. Around

3:00 a.m. on Sunday morning the train left Amory, Mississippi, by which time the Jim Crow car was filled to overflowing, with standing room only. The next coach had only two white people in it, so Gloster asked the conductor if they could be moved to another "white" coach to allow the Black passengers more room. A dispute ensued between them but did not seem to lead to trouble, and Gloster returned to his seat. However, a few miles before Tupelo, about twenty-five miles down the road, the conductor came and took Gloster's ticket check out of the window shade. When asked why he did this he told Gloster that "he merely wanted to make some corrections in his report."[129]

In Tupelo, the conductor left the train and soon returned with several policemen. A reporter for the Black *Atlanta Daily World* described what followed:

> "When the policemen, three of them, reached the colored coach, they asked, 'Where is the nigger?'" Prof. Gloster stated. "The conductor, pointing me out, said, 'There he is.'"
>
> The prominent educator was then seized by the three officers, and the conductor, and pitched off the train. Afterwards, right in front of the door of the colored coach, Mr. Gloster was severely assailed for about five minutes. They took him to the squad car, and all the way to the police station, they beat their victim, cursed him, and asked if he had forgotten that he was a "nigger." Another suggested that he be taken out to the lake and beaten some more.[130]

Gloster spent the night in a filthy, roach-infested jail cell that, as he described it, was "foul-smelling with blood, mercurochrome and body waste," much like that occupied by Pauli Murray and Adelene McBean in Virginia two years earlier. That night and the next day he was denied an opportunity to call his family. The second time he asked, the officer said, "So you're the nigger that sassed the conductor this morning. Don't you know you're in Mississippi? Have you ever been here before? If I'd been one of the arresting officer [*sic*], I'd have beat your G . . . . D . . . . brains out."[131]

Later on Sunday a Frisco line agent asked Gloster to sign papers confessing that he was wrong and "regretted recommending better riding accommodations to the conductor."

> The agent tried to impress upon Mr. Gloster that he had committed a grave wrong for which he could be kept in jail or put in the chain gang for disturbing the peace and trying to break the Jim Crow law.
>
> "So under duress, and because I didn't know of any way to reach my people and didn't want to be further exposed to beating, I set down in my own handwriting a letter which he dictated and signed," Mr. Gloster continued.[132]

The agent was even careful to tear off the company letterhead from Frisco stationery that Gloster was given to write on. Gloster was then given the choice to remain in the Tupelo jail or be returned to Amory to stand trial there, where the incident originated. By this time Gloster's brother-in-law and his sister had arrived from Atlanta, and they accompanied Gloster and the agent to Amory. Instead of being taken to the jail, however, they were brought to the railway office. From there, "realizing that he had some cash money on him, the Frisco agent took Mr. Gloster in the Chief of Police's car to the home of the mayor," where Gloster was fined $10 and told the "case was a closed book."[133]

In a compendium of race-related items published later that year, Sterling A. Brown included a more detailed account of the Amory mayor's comments, without naming Gloster:

> Young Negro professor . . . closes his narrative of how he was thrown off the train and badly beaten in Tupelo, Miss. "He told me that I looked like a smart boy, that I ought to know better than to sass a white man in Mississippi. That he would fine me $5 for breaking the peace and $5.40 for costs of court, or else he would bind me over for the next court session. He advised me to pay the fine. After I paid it he said to me that he hoped I would profit by my experience."[134]

Soon after this traumatic episode, Gloster completed his PhD in 1943. He was drafted into the army and served with the Tenth Cavalry, Buffalo Soldiers, in Arizona. After the war he taught at Hampton Institute in Virginia, where he published a definitive study of Black literature, *Negro Voices in American Fiction* (1948). He was a Fulbright professor of English at Hiroshima University in Japan from 1953 to 1955, and he taught in the international program at the University of Warsaw in Poland. In 1967 he left Hampton Institute and became highly successful as president of Morehouse College. At Morehouse, he expanded the college's physical plant with twelve new buildings, doubled the size of the faculty while doubling their salaries, added new majors in international studies, business, and engineering, and developed the Morehouse School of Medicine before he retired in 1987. He died in 2002 at the age of ninety.[135]

CHAPTER 5

World War II and the Black Soldier

Life for African American men and women in the armed forces during World War II was fraught with tension. Many white soldiers and civilians, especially but by no means exclusively in the South, did not like to see Black soldiers in uniform, insisting that the uniform represented a level of status, equality, and respect that should have been reserved for white soldiers. Black and white army units had always been segregated, but interracial contact, both on the post and off, was inevitable and often led to conflict and at times to death. As early as 1941, just months after the first "Negro selectees" entered the army under a plan to increase the ratio of Black to white soldiers, the body of Pvt. Felix Hall was found hanging with his hands tied behind him at Fort Benning, Georgia. While most of the Black population believed he was lynched, some post authorities suggested that his death might have been a suicide, and an official investigation found no proof of foul play.[1]

There are numerous accounts of Black servicemen, from the North as well as the South, running afoul of Jim Crow laws governing public transportation. A letter from Pvt. Bert B. Babero in February 1944 to Truman K. Gibson, civilian aide to the secretary of war, describes the conditions that Black soldiers endured while traveling to and from their bases:

> We have buses which are local and those that run to and from camp, on the local buses we are compelled to sit in the back, threaten by the drivers if we refuse. Despite the fact that buses run all day back and forth to camp at regular one half hour entervals, we have only three in which we may ride. Our buses are crowded to the extent that it is practically impossible to close the doors and yet extra buses has been refused us. The camp provides army buses that carry soldiers to town but we aren't allowed to ride them.[2]

Pvt. Charles J. Reco, July 27, 1942

In 1941 rapidly expanding wartime production in the shipyards and other industries in and around Beaumont, Texas, resulted in an increase in racial tension as the growing population, both white and Black, quickly overwhelmed the city's housing and transportation facilities. On the morning of July 27, 1942, just a few weeks after a string of altercations between Black and white citizens on Beaumont's overcrowded buses, Pvt. Charles J. Reco was beaten and shot by city policemen for violating the Jim Crow laws, though he may not have actually done so.[3] Although he survived his wounds, an investigation into the case by the U.S. Justice Department came to naught. Steve M. King, the U.S. district attorney overseeing the case, stated that it was "lacking in those elements promising a successful prosecution."[4]

Pvt. Henry Williams, August 15, 1942

Less than three weeks after Private Reco was attacked, on August 15, while getting off a bus in Mobile, Alabama, after an argument with the armed bus driver, Pvt. Henry Williams was shot by the driver three times and died. A bus boycott planned by the Mobile NAACP was canceled when the bus company agreed to a number of demands, including the disarming of city bus drivers. The driver was charged with murder, but the case was never brought to trial and the grand jury records have not been located.[5]

Lt. Nora Green, September 12, 1942

A brief item in the November 1942 edition of the *Crisis* records an incident that demonstrates that animosity toward African Americans in the military was not limited to what one might think of as the "typical Black soldier." The article, headlined "Army Nurse Beaten," is sufficiently revealing to be worth quoting in full.

> On October 2, the attention of the Department of Justice was called to the mystery surrounding the beating and jailing of Second Lt. Nora Green of the Tuskegee Army Air Corps School medical detachment, September 12. The NAACP told Victor Rotnem, chief of the DOJ's Civil Rights Section, that "it becomes more and more apparent that strong forces are at work trying to hush up the matter" and demanded immediate investigation.
>
> Lt. Green was badly beaten by Montgomery, Alabama, police and jailed for several hours following a dispute over a bus seat for which she had already paid her fare. The Army nurse was returning to Tuskegee from a shopping tour in Montgomery, made following her selection for overseas duty.
>
> Colored officers and men at the Tuskegee base, it is reported, are under military orders not to talk.[6]

According to J. Todd Moye, Lieutenant Green was dressed in civilian clothes. On being told that the bus was for whites only, she refused to get off, telling the driver that she was due back at Tuskegee and that a later bus would make her late. She was then arrested and beaten before being turned over to authorities at the Tuskegee Army Air Field.[7]

Capt. Dovey Johnson Roundtree, Winter 1943

Dovey Mae Johnson was born in Charlotte, North Carolina, in 1914. After her father died in the flu epidemic of 1919, Dovey, her mother, and her two sisters lived with her mother's parents. Her grandmother, Rachel Bryant Graham, was a strong-willed woman whose example and teaching played a considerable role in establishing Dovey's own character. In her memoir, Roundtree records her first encounter with Jim Crow at the age of six or seven. Her grandmother decided to take Dovey with her on an errand into town for the first time, and they walked up the block to catch a trolley. As the trolley opened its doors, Dovey, exuberant and delighted in anticipation of her first trolley ride, ran up the steps and sat in the empty seat right behind the driver, "with a perfect view of just about everything worth looking at." When he saw her there the driver shouted, "Get that pickaninny out of here! You know she can't sit there." Her grandmother yanked the signal cord, and as soon as the trolley stopped, she took Dovey firmly by the arm and pulled her down the steps and out the back door. In spite of her grandmother's painfully crippled feet—the result of a white man's attempt to rape her as a young woman—they walked determinedly into town that day and all the way home again.[8] Dovey could not know it at the time, but it would seem that her pathway through life was already mapping itself out.

After completing school, Dovey initially intended to become a doctor, and, with the help of her grandmother's friend, the renowned educator, activist, and stateswoman Mary McLeod Bethune, she enrolled at Spelman College in Atlanta. After studying at Spelman from 1934 to 1938 and unable to afford medical school, she taught seventh and eighth graders for three years in South Carolina.

But Dovey Johnson had bigger dreams. As the buildup to war was taking place, A. Philip Randolph, the influential founder of the Brotherhood of Sleeping Car Porters union; Walter White, head of the NAACP; and other Black leaders convinced President Roosevelt to issue Executive Order 8802. That order, signed in early July 1941, reaffirmed: "It is the policy of the United States to encourage full participation in the national defense program by all citizens of the United States, regardless of race, creed, color, or national or-

Dovey Johnson recruiting for the WAAC in Akron, Ohio, 1943. Opie Evans Papers, University of Akron Archives & Special Collections.

igin."[9] It was Johnson's hope, therefore, that she could find one of the jobs for women that would become available as a result, so she went to Washington, D.C., to ask Mary Bethune for help. "'No,' [Bethune] said enigmatically, 'I have something else in mind.'"[10] For the time being she set Dovey to work in her (Bethune's) own office. Mary Bethune had been campaigning arm in arm with Eleanor Roosevelt for the establishment of a military unit for women. Their efforts proved successful, and in May 1942 the first class of women was inducted into the Women's Army Auxiliary Corps (WAAC). Bethune's plan was then revealed: Dovey Johnson became one of the forty African American women in that group of 440—the first female officers in the U.S. Army. The following year, "Auxiliary" was dropped as the Women's Army Corps (WAC) was assigned to active duty.

Many of the white and Black women officers who trained alongside Johnson in Fort Des Moines got along perfectly well, but the army was still segregated. In addition to the constant degradations, large and small, wrought by Jim Crow, there was, not surprisingly, a heavy layer of a more general misogyny throughout that hitherto exclusively male organization.

In the winter of 1943, Johnson was sent on a recruiting trip throughout the South. In Miami, while traveling alone and in uniform, she boarded a bus and, as the "colored" section in the rear of the bus was full, she took a seat in the "white" section:

> "What do you think you're doing?" [the bus driver] called to me. "Don't you see there's somebody waiting for that seat?"
>
> I turned to see a white soldier standing looking down at me, unsmiling. I was reduced . . . in the space of a single moment, to a six-year-old child, the one who'd been called a "pickaninny" so many years ago in Charlotte. And then I remembered who I was: a captain in the WAAC, a member of the United States military.

Ignoring her attempts to explain herself, the driver insisted that she yield her seat to that white marine, get off the bus, and go to the end of the line of boarding passengers, mostly military men.

> The black passengers in the rear went quiet. They knew, as I did, that this was how "incidents" started—the kind that got you killed or landed you in jail, where you could languish indefinitely, whether you were military or not. In fact, my status as a WAAC—a WAAC already branded a "walking NAACP" by my superiors—placed me in the gravest danger. . . .
>
> I looked at the driver and at the white soldier, both silently daring me to challenge them, and I picked up my duffel bag and climbed off the bus. As I took my place in the line of white army and navy personnel, not a single one saluted, or offered a hand, or even spoke. They filed into the bus and it roared out of the station, leaving me behind. . . .
>
> That night I wrestled with hatred deeper than I had ever known, hatred of Jim Crow, hatred of the army that had cast me adrift in hostile territory, and most of all, hatred of these people who had treated me as an interloper in my own country.[11]

But Dovey Johnson rose above her hatred and continued her recruiting mission, though she never whitewashed her explanations of what life would be like for Black women in a predominantly white male army.

When the army shut down its recruitment of African Americans in June 1943, Johnson was reassigned to Fort Des Moines. There she was pleased to learn that the Black and white women had been organized into an integrated

WAAC officers training regiment, "the shining exception to the grotesqueness of Jim Crow that still existed among the enlisted women on our base and among all women on other bases." But just a week before the WAAC officers were scheduled to take their oaths as members of the fully activated Women's Army Corps (WAC), the new Des Moines base commander, Col. Frank U. McCoskrie, issued a memo announcing that the integrated unit was to be disbanded and new separate training regiments would be formed for white women and Black women. Responses among the Black women were mixed. Some saw the change as a better way to get an actual command and a quicker path to promotion; others were opposed to the segregation on principle. The latter group appointed Johnson to be their spokesperson in a meeting with the colonel.

At that meeting Colonel McCoskrie presented the segregated plan as a fait accompli. As he turned to go, leaving any further details to his subordinates, Johnson called out, "Sir, may I ask whether questions are in order?" McCoskrie remained in the room as Johnson's companions outlined their perspective to him. Most of the Black officers were opposed to a segregated regiment, and they asked what would happen if any one of them refused to take the reenlistment oath? The answer, of course, was obvious—that would be the end of her army career.

Dovey Johnson made a quick decision. She stood up, looked McCoskrie in the eye, and unpinned the captain's bars from her shoulder. "Sir, you are setting us back a hundred years. . . . Can you actually believe that the advantages of this proposal can outweigh the damage it will cause?" Silence filled the room. Not even her companions stood in her support. But four days later another memo came from Colonel McCoskrie revoking the plan for a Jim Crow regiment. Soon afterward the army, including Capt. Dovey Johnson, resumed its program of recruiting Black women. "I was deeply changed by having seen the way in which a single voice—my voice—could make a difference," Roundtree later wrote.[12]

Johnson was discharged from the army in August 1945, and she took a nine-month position traveling on the West Coast in an effort to help A. Philip Randolph save the Fair Employment Practice Commission and thus provide protection for African American jobs in the tight postwar job market. In the course of that work she met Pauli Murray, who convinced her that she could best serve the cause of racial equality by studying law rather than medicine.

In late 1945 Dovey married her college sweetheart, Bill Roundtree, whom she hadn't seen for seven years. However, the marriage failed within a year as they realized that they had different goals in life. Dovey, in particular, was not willing to abandon her commitment to fighting for civil rights and an end to segregation. (Following the general practice of the time, she kept her married name after their divorce.)

Like the military, the practice of law at the time was a heavily male-dominated culture, and the Howard University Law School was no different in that respect from the rest of the profession. Roundtree entered Howard in 1947 as one of only five women law students. Howard was as exciting as any place could be right then for any African American aspirant to the law. The university's president invited Thurgood Marshall and other members of his team from the NAACP Legal Defense Fund to use the law school's library, rooms, and resources to prepare themselves for presenting *Brown v. Board of Education* before the U.S. Supreme Court. At Howard they held moot courts, trying out their arguments on the law faculty and students and developing their strategies for dismantling the long-standing policy of "separate but equal." This gave Roundtree a front-row seat for one of the most important legal struggles of the twentieth century—the assault on *Plessy v. Ferguson* and its social consequences.

Roundtree sent train tickets to her mother and grandmother so they could come from Charlotte to see her receive her law degree in May 1950. Throughout that train journey all the seats in the Jim Crow car were full, and her mother and grandmother had to stand the entire way, even though there were plenty of seats in the "white" cars. On reaching Washington, it was necessary for her grandmother to get medical help for her injured feet. The following week the U.S. Supreme Court delivered its decision in *Henderson v. United States*, stating that a failure to provide truly equal accommodations in a railway dining car was a violation of the Interstate Commerce Act. At that moment Roundtree began her career as a lawyer. Drawing on the *Henderson* decision, she sued the Southern Railway on her grandmother's behalf for breach of contract, since they had sold her reserved seat tickets. Rather than subject her grandmother to a court battle—and yet more travel—Roundtree was willing to settle the dispute. Although the settlement of several hundred dollars was far too low, it was still a minor victory over Jim Crow, and soon that experience was to strengthen her determination in a later important case of segregation in transportation.

After she qualified for the bar in Washington, Roundtree and a former Howard classmate, Julius Robertson, opened a practice together to serve the people of Southeast Washington and Anacostia—two Black lawyers among just a few others, "interlopers in a legal establishment that excluded us as surely as if they had put up ropes."[13] And as if decreed by the Fates themselves, in September 1952 a case was referred to her that replayed a scene from her own life. Pfc. Sarah Louise Keys, a WAC traveling through Virginia by bus, alone and in uniform, had been arrested "for disorderly conduct" after refusing to move to the back of the bus.[14]

The church was always an important part of her life, and in 1961 Roundtree was ordained as one of the first women ministers in the African Methodist Episcopal Church, achieving full ministerial status in 1963. She served for thirty-five years as associate pastor of the Allen Chapel AME Church in Washington. In 1962 she scored another first: she was the first African American woman admitted into the Women's Bar Association of Washington, D.C. For the rest of her long career she fought at the bar and from the pulpit for equal rights, for women's rights, and for family rights, becoming one of the most respected lawyers in Washington. She retired from practicing law in 1996 and died in 2018 at the age of 104.

Pvt. Edward Green, March 14, 1944

With military bases located near towns and cities, the disquiet and turmoil generated by racially motivated violence on streetcars and buses were liable to spread farther afield than the bus route and the specific incident. On March 14, 1944, Pvt. Edward Green was shot by a bus driver in Alexandria, Louisiana. Tensions remained high at nearby Camp Claiborne, and soon thereafter a Black soldier was lynched after being accused of raping a white woman. In August riots and mutiny along racial lines broke out at the camp.[15]

Lt. Jackie Robinson, July 6, 1944

On Friday, April 11, 1947, in an exhibition game between the Brooklyn Dodgers and the New York Yankees, Jackie Robinson became the first African American to play major league baseball since the 1880s. Well before that day, however, he had achieved fame throughout the United States as an outstanding athlete in baseball, basketball, football, and track. His success and promise in these several sports ensured that he was destined for a notable career.

Robinson was born in Cairo, Georgia, on January 31, 1919. A year and a half later, his mother took the family to join her half-brother in Pasadena, California. There she worked as a maid for wealthier white families and was the primary breadwinner for the extended family. They lived in a largely white, working-class neighborhood. Pasadena was founded with abolitionist and liberal tendencies and had integrated schools, but like the rest of the country racial and ethnic prejudice were endemic.[16]

Robinson's early athletic career has been well documented and much written about. In the mostly white John Muir Technical High School, he became

Jackie Robinson, 1947. Photo by Harry Warnecke. National Portrait Gallery, Smithsonian Institution.

Pasadena's star football player and acting captain of the basketball team. At Pasadena Junior College he broke his brother's national junior college long jump record, jumping 25 feet, 6½ inches. On the baseball team he batted .418, and he scored 131 points for the football team in their 11–0 season. In the summer of 1939, he won the singles and doubles titles in the Western Federation of Tennis Clubs, an organization for Black players. At UCLA that fall he gained notice as one of the country's top football players and became the first UCLA athlete to letter in four sports in the same season—football, basketball, baseball, and track.

Frustrated by the impediments of racism, Robinson left UCLA in March 1941 without graduating. After playing with an all-star college football team in a charity game against the Chicago Bears at Soldier Field, he went on to play briefly with the mixed-race Los Angeles Bulldogs before signing on with the Honolulu Bears—a position that also included a construction job near Pearl Harbor.

Robinson left Hawaii on December 5. Two days later Pearl Harbor was attacked and the country was at war. President Roosevelt's Executive Order 8802, signed earlier that summer, encouraged people to seek work in the national defense program, "regardless of race, creed, color, or national origin." To help support his family, Robinson took a defense industry job for $100 a month as a truck driver with Lockheed Aircraft.

In March 1942 Robinson was drafted and sent for basic training at Fort Riley, Kansas. His college education qualified him for officer candidate school (OCS), but his application was denied without explanation. Secretary of War Henry L. Stimson had said, "Leadership is not imbedded in the negro race yet, and to try to make commissioned officers to lead men into battle—colored men—is only to work a disaster to both."[17] Instead, Robinson was assigned to take care of the horses at the base's stables.

Not surprisingly, Jim Crow extended beyond the duty roster, and when Robinson tried out for the camp's baseball team, he was rejected there as well. Joe Louis, who had famously beat the German boxer Max Schmeling in 1938, was also at Fort Riley for basic training, and the two became friends. Louis wrote to Truman K. Gibson, an assistant to William Hastie, the Black aide to Secretary Stimson, regarding Robinson's OCS denial. Gibson came to Fort Riley to investigate and meet with Louis, Robinson, and other Black soldiers, and Robinson was then admitted into the first integrated OCS class of about eighty.

On January 28, 1943, Jack Robinson became a second lieutenant in the U.S. Cavalry and was assigned to a truck battalion in the Black Second Cavalry Division at Fort Riley. His rank, however, was still insufficient to get him onto the camp baseball team. Disappointed certainly, but undaunted, he took to a new sport and soon became the U.S. Army table tennis champion.

The summer of 1943 was plagued by race riots in New York, Los Angeles, Detroit, Beaumont, and Mobile. A riot in Harlem was sparked on August 1 when a white policeman shot and wounded a Black soldier, Robert Bandy, and six people were subsequently killed. In the midst of this national atmosphere, Robinson was asked to join the Fort Riley football team, and he agreed to practice with them. As the season was about to start, with the team's first game against the University of Missouri, he was unexpectedly given an unrequested two weeks' leave. The university, it turned out, had refused to play against a team with a Black player on it. Robinson went home, and when he returned he showed up at practice only to resign immediately from the team.

In April 1944, Robinson and other Black officers were sent to Camp Hood, Texas, to join the 761st Tank Battalion. Camp Hood had rapidly expanded to accommodate some sixty thousand soldiers, all of whom lived in a highly segregated environment. Robinson was given command of a tank platoon, and when the orders were given for the battalion to prepare to ship overseas in late July and early August, the battalion commander, Lt. Col. Paul L. Bates, appointed him as battalion morale officer.

But Jim Crow was determined that it was not to be. On July 6, Robinson was a patient at McCloskey General Hospital in nearby Temple, Texas, being treated for bone chips in his ankle. That evening he took a city bus back to camp, where he spent a few hours at the "colored officers club." Around eleven o'clock he boarded a camp bus to take him back to Temple. Fortunately, we have Robinson's letter, written July 16 on McCloskey General Hospital stationary, to Truman Gibson describing the ensuing event in his own words and asking for Gibson's advice:

> Sir:
>
> I am sorry to bother you again, but under the circumstances there seems to be no alternative.
>
> On or about the 7th of July I was at Camp Hood, Texas visiting the colored officers club and upon leaving I took a shuttle bus from the club to the central station. As I moved to the rear I noticed one of the officer's wife [*sic*] and sat down beside her. The lady is very fair and to many looks to be white. It is evident that the driver seemed to resent my talking to her and told me to move to the rear. He didn't ask the lady to move so I refused. When I did he threatened to make trouble for me when we reached the bus station. Upon reaching the bus station a white lady tells me that she is going to prefer charges. She said she heard the driver tell me to move to the rear. I told her I didn't care if she prefered [*sic*] charges against me and she went away angry. That was the last that was said to the lady and the next thing I hear is that I've cursed a white lady out. I feel now that I should have but I have never cursed one out and I certainly didn't start with her.[18]

Unlike other soldiers who had similar encounters with bus drivers, however, that wasn't what got Robinson into the most trouble, though it provided the initial spark. Tempers began to flare, and the driver, Milton N. Renegar, told the depot dispatcher to call the military police. While Robinson was being escorted to the MP guard room, several enlisted men and officers became involved in the incident, as did a white female stenographer and another white woman. Robinson became particularly incensed when he was referred to as a "nigger" by a Pvt. Ben Mucklerath.

As Capt. Gerald Bear, the MP commander, questioned the white soldiers to get their account before hearing Robinson's version, he insisted that Robinson remain at ease out of the room. Robinson objected, and Bear later characterized Robinson's attitude as "disrespectful and impertinent to his superior officers, and very unbecoming to an officer in the presence of enlisted men." Robinson in turn testified, "[Bear] did not seem to recognize me as an officer at all. But I did consider myself an officer and felt I should be addressed as one."[19] He repeatedly asked if he was under arrest, and Captain Bear told him that he would be considered "under arrest in quarters" at the hospital, where he was taken in a police pickup truck. A doctor at the hospital told Robinson that he had heard rumors of a drunken Black lieutenant causing trouble, so he recommended that Robinson take a blood alcohol test, which he did to prove he had not been drinking.

Captain Bear intended to have Robinson court-martialed, and when the battalion commander, Lieutenant Colonel Bates, refused to bring charges, Bear requested to have Robinson transferred to a different battalion—one with a more willing commander. On July 24 he was transferred to the 758th Tank Battalion of the Fifth Armored Group, and the commander there signed orders for his prosecution.

Racial tensions in and out of the army were already heightened, and they were further exacerbated by a highly publicized incident in early 1944 in which Joe Louis and Sugar Ray Robinson, who were stationed at Camp Sibert, were harassed by white MPs at an Alabama bus depot as they waited for a taxi.[20] Robinson's visibility as a famous Black athlete in uniform was enough to justify the intensity and cynicism of the message Col. E. A. Kimball, commander of the Fifth Armored Group, delivered in a telephone conversation with Col. Walter Buie, chief of staff of the Twenty-Third Corps, on July 17: "This is a very serious case, and it is full of dynamite. It requires very delicate handling. . . . This bus situation here is not at all good, and I am afraid that any officer in charge of troops at this Post might be prejudiced."[21] Kimball may have been referring specifically to the bus situation at Camp Hood, but the murder of Pvt. Booker T. Spicely by a bus driver in Durham, North Carolina, just two days after the incident with Robinson, made the atmosphere throughout the army, especially among Black soldiers, even more volatile.

Robinson was formally arrested by the military police on July 24, and that same day he wrote to the NAACP in New York to ask for help and advice. Not until after the court-martial did he get a reply saying that they could not give him an attorney, but that if he were convicted they would write to the adjutant general on his behalf.

The trial began on August 2, with Lt. William A. Cline, a young lawyer from Wharton, Texas, as Robinson's defense attorney of record, with two assistant defense counselors, 1st Lt. Joseph C. Hutcheson and 1st Lt. Robert H. Johnson. According to Robinson's biographer, Arnold Rampersad, it was probably Johnson (from Michigan) who did most of the real work.[22] Five charges had been leveled against Robinson:

1. A violation of Article of War No. 63, accusing him of "behaving with disrespect toward Capt. Gerald M. Bear, CMP, his superior officer, . . . by contemptuously bowing to him and giving him several sloppy salutes, repeating several times 'OK Sir,' 'OK Sir,' or words to that effect, and by acting in an insolent, impertinent and rude manner toward the said Captain Gerald M. Bear."
2. A violation of Article of War No. 64, accusing him of "willful disobedience of lawful command of Gerald M. Bear, CMP, his superior," in that "having received a lawful command . . . to remain in a receiving room and be seated on a chair on the far side of the receiving room, [he] did . . . willfully disobey the same."
3. A second violation of Article 63, charging him with disrespect towards the officer of the day, Captain Peelor Wigginton, while complaining about the treatment he was receiving by saying, "Captain, any Private, you or any General calls me a nigger and I'll break them in two, I don't know the definition of the word," and by speaking to Wigginton, too, "in an insolent, impertinent and rude manner."
4. A charge of "abusive and vulgar language" towards the bus driver, "in the presence of ladies."
5. A charge of saying to a white woman on the bus who threatened to bring charges against him, "'You better quit fuckin with me' or words to that effect."[23]

For reasons not entirely clear, charges 3, 4, and 5 were dropped from the case. One significant effect of this was that the court-martial was no longer about what happened on the bus. Robinson's defense team, therefore, had to focus on the treatment he had received after being brought to the guard room. Rather than defend Robinson's insubordination per se, his lawyers stressed Captain Bear's poor management of the entire situation, which had understandably drawn Robinson's ire.

In his discussion of the trial, Rampersad makes a very telling statement: "Clearly, almost all of the whites involved were genuinely mystified that Robinson disliked being badly treated."[24] It may seem obvious that he—or anyone—would dislike being badly treated, but this actually cuts to the heart of the matter and brings us to that complicated and most heavily charged of all the words in the modern American vocabulary of race. Though Private Mucklerath denied using that word, one of the MPs, Corporal Elwood, testified: "[Mucklerath] asked me if I got that nigger Lieutenant. Right then the Lieutenant said, 'Look here, you son-of-a-bitch, don't you call me no nigger.'" The bus dispatcher too, participated in this language, which was all too frequent in the everyday speech of white Americans: "I told him [Corporal Elwood] that the trouble was with a nigger Lt. The nigger Lt., hearing the remark, resented being called so." In other words, though they undoubtedly knew it was an insult, many white speakers at the time used this word as their everyday designation for Negroes (to use Robinson's preferred term), refusing to acknowledge, often even enjoying, the depth of an insult intended to cause deep pain.

Robinson took the stand in his own defense, and his comments on the word give a nuanced response that lays out the complexity of connotation and emotional weight that the word carries, most especially when spoken by a white person. He evoked the memory of his grandmother, Edna Sims McGriff, who was born into slavery in Georgia in 1858. When asked at the trial, "Do you know what a nigger is?" he gave a fulsome and elegant response:

> I looked it up once, but my grandmother gave me a good definition, she was a slave, and she said the definition of the word was a low, uncouth person, and pertains to no one in particular; but I don't consider that I am low and uncouth. I looked it up in the dictionary afterwards and it says the word nigger pertains to the negroid or negro, but it is also a machine used in a saw mill for pushing logs into saws. I objected to being called a nigger by this private or by anybody else. When I made this statement that I did not like to be called nigger, I told the Captain, I said, "If you call me a nigger, I might have to say the same thing to you. . . . I do not consider myself a nigger at all, I am a negro, but not a nigger."[25]

The testimony of a number of character witnesses, including Lieutenant Colonel Bates, provided further support to Robinson's defense, who noted in their closing argument that the case stemmed from "simply a situation in which a few individuals sought to vent their bigotry on a Negro they considered 'uppity' because he had the audacity to seek to exercise rights that belonged to him as an American and as a soldier." The jury consisted of nine men, one of whom was Black and another a former UCLA student. Six votes would be necessary to convict him. The votes were secret and written, and Robinson received in his favor at least the four votes necessary to avoid conviction, for he was found "not guilty of all specifications and charges."[26]

Robinson's court-martial, along with the complications caused by his injured ankle, had dampened his enthusiasm for the army. He was reassigned first to a different tank battalion and then to an infantry regiment, rather than to the Special Services Division as he had hoped, where he could apply his athletic expertise in the area of recreation, much as Joe Louis and Sugar Ray Robinson were assigned to entertaining the troops with exhibition boxing matches. His disappointment and reassignment led Jack Robinson to leapfrog over the chain of command in a letter to the adjutant general in Washington asking for relief from active duty. He was honorably discharged in November 1944 "by reason of physical disqualification," a remarkable designation for one of the country's finest athletes, one who would soon change the shape—and color—of the entire sports world in America.

As he left the army, Robinson decided to explore his possibilities in the Negro Leagues, and by Christmas he had an offer to play for the top-flight Kansas City Monarchs. He also accepted an interim job offer from his friend, the Rev. Karl Downs, to teach physical education at Samuel Huston College in Austin, Texas, a position that allowed him to join the Monarchs for spring training. Life in the Negro Leagues was hard, but he was there to gain experience as much as anything, and he soon became the regular Monarchs shortstop.

The Negro leagues also gave Robinson a chance to play with and against, and to learn from, some of the greatest ballplayers ever, among them Satchel Paige, Josh Gibson, and Cool Papa Bell. Before long there grew up an expectation (surely not entirely welcome among some of the veteran Negro Leaguers who had similar hopes of their own) that Jackie Robinson would become the first Black player to play major league baseball since the brief careers of Moses Fleetwood Walker and Weldy Walker in 1884, just before the color line was drawn in seemingly indelible ink. And, sure enough, in August 1945, Branch Rickey, president and general manager for the Dodgers organization, began courting Robinson as much for his strength of character as for his athletic prowess.

Robinson signed with the Dodgers in October, and the following January he married his long-time sweetheart, Rachel Isum. He was due to report for spring training in Daytona Beach, Florida, by noon on March 1. Rather than endure a long train ride from California, the Robinsons decided to fly on February 28. The first leg of the journey landed them in New Orleans at seven in the morning, but then they were bumped from the eleven o'clock flight to Pensacola. Though they were promised seats on a twelve o'clock flight, that one too left without them. At seven that evening they finally got on a flight to Pensacola. Once there they were again bumped off their connecting flight with more feeble, transparent excuses. Ultimately, after further humiliations, they decided to take a bus to Jacksonville. During that sixteen-hour ride, even as they sat exhausted near the rear of the bus, the driver made them move even farther back to the very last row. On the last leg of the trip, a bus got them to their destination late in the afternoon of March 2. That nightmare journey was Rachel Robinson's introduction to the Jim Crow South.[27]

Robinson led the minor league Montreal Royals to the International League championship in 1946, and he opened as the Brooklyn Dodgers' first baseman in April 1947. Some of the team's players initially threatened a boycott if he were to be on the field with them, but Rickey made it clear that anyone who refused to play would simply be traded or let go. By the time Robinson's .297 batting average, his aggressive and masterful base running, and his league-leading stolen bases got him named Rookie of the Year and helped win a spot for the Dodgers in the World Series, baseball had changed forever. Jackie Robinson retired from the Dodgers in 1956, but he never retired from a job he had held since his school days—as a determined and vocal opponent of prejudice, racism, and inequality. Much of his time in retirement was spent raising funds for the NAACP and encouraging Black-owned businesses.

Pvt. Booker T. Spicely, July 8, 1944

Two days after Jackie Robinson was arrested on a bus at Camp Hood, Texas, Pvt. Booker T. Spicely was similarly challenged in Durham, North Carolina. Rather than being arrested, however, he was shot and killed—not by a policeman, MP, or other officer of the law, but, like Pvt. Henry Williams in Alabama two years earlier, by the bus driver himself, and again like Williams, *after* he got off the bus.

Spicely grew up in Blackstone, Virginia, and enlisted in the army in December 1943 at the age of thirty-four. In the segregated army, many Black soldiers were assigned to menial, noncombat roles, and Spicely was trained as a cook. In the summer of 1944 he was stationed at Camp Butner, North Carolina. On the evening of July 8, in uniform but unarmed, along with another Black soldier and an African American woman and child who were at the same bus stop, he boarded a bus in Durham on his way back to camp.

According to the woman's later testimony, they sat in the next-to-last seat on the bus.[28] When two white soldiers entered the bus, the driver, Herman Lee Council, told the woman and Spicely to move to the rear seat. The woman and her child moved, but Spicely remained where he was. One of the white soldiers testified that Spicely asked why he had to move and that he said something like "I thought I was fighting this war for democracy." He did finally move to the rear seat, but continued complaining until the driver ordered him off the bus. Still wanting to talk with or complain further to

Council, Spicely exited through the rear door and walked toward the front door, whereupon Council got off the bus, shot Spicely twice, got back on the bus, and continued his route.

After finishing his route Council turned himself in to the police. He was subsequently charged with second-degree murder. The case was prosecuted by Thurgood Marshall, at the time head of the NAACP Legal Defense Fund. On September 15 the all-white jury returned a verdict of not guilty on the grounds of self-defense.[29]

On December 1, 2023, a state highway marker was erected in Durham, reading, "Booker T. Spicely, 1909–1944. Black U.S. Army soldier shot nearby in 1944 for resisting Jim Crow laws on a bus. Aftermath of killing helped revitalize North Carolina's NAACP."

Irene Morgan, July 16, 1944

A week after the death of Pvt. Booker T. Spicely and ten days after Lt. Jackie Robinson declined to move to the back of a bus at Fort Hood, Texas, Irene Morgan, on her way home to Baltimore, was told to give up her seat on a bus in Virginia. Though she had nothing like the fame that Robinson had earned as a nationally known athlete, the legal case resulting from her actions had profound implications.

Irene Amos was born in 1917 and raised in Baltimore, where she had to leave high school to help support the family of eleven by doing cleaning, laundry, and childcare during the Great Depression. In 1939 she married Sherwood Morgan in Springfield, Massachusetts, and they lived briefly in Hartford, Connecticut, before returning to Baltimore where they lived with their two sons.[30] During World War II, Sherwood worked on the Baltimore docks and Irene had a job with the Martin Company helping to build B-26 bombers.

In the summer of 1944, Morgan suffered a miscarriage, and she went to recover at her mother's family home near Hayes Store, a small, poor, rural hamlet in Gloucester County, Virginia, where their forebears had been held in slavery in the early nineteenth century.[31] On July 16 she was heading back to Baltimore for a doctor's appointment and hoping to return to her work and home life. When she boarded the Greyhound bus from Norfolk it was already crowded, with a number of African Americans standing in the aisle at the rear. Seeing Morgan looking for a seat, a young woman offered to let her sit on her lap. After about twenty-six miles the bus arrived at the town of Saluda, and Morgan took a seat left vacant as a passenger disembarked. Unfortunately, though she was only three rows from the rear and sitting next to a Black woman with an infant, Morgan's seat happened to be in front of seats occupied by a white couple. In Virginia, this was not merely contrary to custom: a Virginia statute (4097dd) enacted in 1930 embedded that custom in law, making it a misdemeanor to disobey the driver "pursuant to any lawful rule, regulation, *or custom* in force . . . as to assigning separate seats or other space to white and colored persons."[32]

Two more white people entered the bus, and the driver told Morgan and the woman next to her to give up their seats. The woman with her child went to stand in the aisle. Morgan, however, offered to change seats with one of the white passengers behind her, and she explained that she was unable to stand for a long time. The driver repeated his order, and when Morgan, in turn, repeated her refusal, he went to find the local sheriff. Morgan was taken off the bus, but not easily. The sheriff and a deputy testified that they did not use force until Morgan ripped up their arrest warrant and threw it out the window. The deputy said that she kicked him three times in the leg. In a later interview, however, Morgan gave a more graphic account: "He touched me. . . . That's when I kicked him in a very bad place. He hobbled off, and another one came on. He was trying to put his hands on me to get me off. I was going to bite him, but he was dirty, so I clawed him instead. I ripped his shirt. We were both pulling at each other. He said he'd use his nightstick. I said, 'We'll whip each other.'"[33] Morgan was dragged off the bus, arrested, and charged with resisting arrest and breaking the Virginia transit law. Her mother posted $500 bail later that afternoon.

A hearing was scheduled for October 18 in Middlesex County Circuit Court, perhaps with the expectation that Morgan, like many other African Americans charged before her, would forfeit the bail money, return to Maryland, and fail to show up in court, rather than risk going to jail or something even worse. Morgan had never been an activist or a member of the NAACP, but as she came to realize the significance of her case, she was determined to stick up for her rights. At the hearing, Morgan represented herself. She pled guilty to the charge of resisting arrest and paid the $100 fine. However, on being found at fault for disobeying the segregation law, she refused to pay the $10 fine. Rather, she declared that she would appeal the case to the Virginia Supreme Court and even to the U.S. Supreme Court, if necessary.[34] For several years the Virginia NAACP had been looking for a case to challenge the Virginia Jim Crow laws, and, after consulting with Thurgood Marshall and the national organization, they took up Morgan's appeal.

Morgan's lawyers argued that no state law, such as the Virginia statute in question, could apply to the regulation of interstate travel, which fell under the jurisdiction of the interstate commerce clause of the U.S. Constitution.

The U.S. Supreme Court had established that principle in 1877 in the case of Josephine Decuir.[35] In reversing a Louisiana Supreme Court opinion that had been in Decuir's favor, *Hall v. Decuir* rejected the validity of an 1869 Louisiana law that prohibited segregation in travel because it represented an unconstitutional regulation of interstate commerce. Ironically, in citing *Hall v. Decuir*, Morgan's lawyers applied the precedent of the interstate commerce argument to rejecting the validity of laws *requiring* segregation. As expected, the Virginia Supreme Court, zealous to protect their understanding of their own state's rights and maintain its culture of strict segregation, voted unanimously to uphold Morgan's conviction. The statute was "a reasonable police regulation," the court ruled. "It applies to both intrastate and interstate passengers. It is not obnoxious to the commerce clause of the Constitution."[36]

This decision played right into the hands of the NAACP, and in January 1946 the U.S. Supreme Court agreed to hear Morgan's appeal. In *Morgan v. Virginia*, Thurgood Marshall and the NAACP legal team were able to present, for the first time, the case against segregation in transportation before the nation's highest court. They argued that the Virginia statute did violate the commerce clause, adding that it thereby limited congressional authority and that it threatened the long tradition of free travel across state lines. The Virginia attorney, Abram Staples, had argued nine cases before the Supreme Court and won every one of them; nevertheless, he was no match for Marshall and his team.[37] Because of the death of Justice Harlan Fiske Stone and the absence of Justice Robert Jackson, who was serving as a prosecutor at the postwar Nuremberg trials in Germany, Morgan's case was heard by only seven justices. The 6–1 majority opinion reversed the judgment of the Virginia court, concluding, "It seems clear to us that seating arrangements for the different races in interstate motor travel require a single uniform rule to promote and protect national travel. Consequently, we hold the Virginia statute in controversy invalid."[38]

Segregation in interstate bus travel was now clearly stated to be unconstitutional, even when traveling between two states in which internal travel was segregated by state law. Unfortunately, the air of celebration among those who hailed the court's decision faded fairly rapidly. The opinion mentioned only "motor vehicles," "motor buses," "interstate motor travel," and the like; nothing was said about other forms of transportation. Nor did it contain any guidance as to how the ruling might be enforced. For the most part, the *Morgan* decision was ignored, and segregation remained common on both intrastate and interstate buses throughout the South.[39]

The following year, however, the challenge to segregated travel was given new impetus outside the courts by Bayard Rustin and others who set out on

The Price of the AFRO Is 7 Cents In D.C.—Pay No More

WASHINGTON AFRO-AMERICAN

COMING! COMING! Two new serials that you'll enjoy — Starting June 22.

WASHINGTON, D.C., JUNE 8, 1946

JC Bus Travel Outlawed

Supreme Court Votes 6-1 in Morgan Case

Jurists Rule State Laws Place Undue Burden on Interstate Travel

Jim crow on Southern busses is dead.

Reversing the opinion of the Supreme Court of Appeals of Virginia in the Irene Morgan case, the United States Supreme Court on Monday, by a 6 to 1 vote, ruled that State jim-crow laws are not applicable to interstate bus transportation.

The majority opinion, which was read by Justice Stanley F. Reed, held that State segregation laws imposed "an undue burden on interstate commerce."

Chronology of Morgan Case

Uphill Fight Took Two Years

1. Arrested July 16, 1944.
2. Fined $10 by Trial Judge, Oct. 18, 1944.
3. Conviction Upheld by Virginia Court, June 6, 1945.
4. Petition for Rehearing Denied September 4, 1945.
5. Appealed to Supreme Court, March 2, 1946.
6. Decision Reversed, June 3, 1946.

Interstate passengers coming from the North were not being segregated Wednesday, on either the Greyhound or Trailways bus lines running into Richmond. Those coming from the South were still seated from the rear, it was learned.

Managers of the Richmond terminals told the AFRO they were awaiting advice from their home offices before instructing drivers not to enforce the outlawed Virginia Statute.

The law calling for the segregation of passengers on buses in Virginia was enacted in 1930, while the statute applying to trains was put on the books in 1902.

Fined $10 for Refusing to Move

The validity of the Virginia statute was challenged by Mrs. Irene Morgan of Baltimore, who appealed from a Virginia Supreme Court decision upholding the imposition of a $10 fine on her by a Middlesex County circuit court judge for refusing to move to the rear of the bus.

Mrs. Morgan had been arrested on a warrant on July 16, 1944, after she refused to move to the rear of the bus

Her Fight Ends Bus Jim Crow

MRS. IRENE MORGAN

Cases of Bus Jim Crow Show Barbarity of Policy

Pickets March in Protest; Choir Sings

U. S. Sues Klan for Unpaid Taxes

Georgia's Governor Also Cracking Down on Order

FBI PROBE ASKED

Organization Big Factor in Gubernatorial Drive

By CARDELL W. McVICKERS

(See Campbell Cartoon on Editorial Page)

ATLANTA— The United States Government Thursday entered the arena in the growing battle to squelch the revival of the Ku Klux Klan when suit was filed against the hooded order seeking recovery of $685,305 in back income taxes.

The suit, admittedly a blow to the organization efforts of Dr. Samuel Green, the Klan's grand dragon, was filed in Fulton Superior Court by Marion H. Allen, U.S. Collector of Internal Revenue.

Treasury Department officials disclosed that the order owed the

the week

'Metamorphosis' of the Colonel

By VINCENT TUBBS

NEW YORK—Col. B. O. Davis Jr., commander of Lockbourne (Ohio) Army Air Field and the 477th Composite Group, is emerging as one of the better twin-engine pilots in the air forces.

He flew into Manhattan recently to have a word to say at a meeting of the Citizens' Committee on Harlem—the fourth such meeting at which he has appeared in recent weeks and which puts him in the forefront as an emerging racial leader as well.

In both instances the metamorphosis is noteworthy.

Colonel Davis earned his wings in single-engine craft and flew fighter planes during the war. The switch from fighter craft of P-40, P-51 and P-47 types to twin-engine B-25's is no joke—as any flyer will tell you.

The Old Days

The pursuit planes, in which

(Continued on Page 23 Col. 3)

Hundreds Ignore Line to Hear Tuskegee Concert

Dr. Patterson Refused to Cancel Date at DAR Constitution Hall

Although a group of some 60 colored and white persons picketed Constitution Hall, Monday night, in protest of the DAR's jim-crow policy, a near capacity audience passed the line and went in to hear the famed Tuskegee Choir concert.

Organized by the Committee for Racial Democracy, the protest was against a statement made by Mrs. Julius Talmadge, DAR president, approving the concert on the grounds that the proceeds would be used to aid colored schools and not mixed schools.

Refuses Proceeds

Proceeds of the concert, which originally were to have been accredited to the Washington committee of the United Negro College fund, will now be sent direct to national headquarters in New York because the local refused to accept them.

Dr. Frederick D. Patterson, president of Tuskegee, refused to yield to demands of the Washington committee that the concert either be cancelled or moved to Watergate, and derided the demonstration as "a commotion about nothing."

It is estimated that some 25 per cent of those who came to the concert refused to go into the hall when they were met suddenly by pickets who carried placards and chanted "Jim Crow must go, stay out, save your self-respect."

Endorsing Groups

Organizations which endorsed the picket line were the Washington Industrial Union Council, CIO, Henry Brascher, president; Washington Chapter, Southern Conference for Human Welfare, Dr. Joseph L. Johnson, chairman;

Washington Council, National Negro Congress, Charles Hill, president; local NAACP, George E. C. Hayes, president; Washing-

(Continued on Page 21, Col. 4)

The Supreme Court outlaws segregated interstate travel, June 3, 1946. Courtesy of AFRO American Newspapers.

their Journey of Reconciliation through the Upper South to draw attention to the fact that segregation in interstate travel was illegal. While planning this precursor to the Freedom Rides of the 1960s, Rustin and fellow activists wrote the song "You Don't Have to Ride Jim Crow," celebrating Morgan's victory.[40] The first two stanzas:

> You don't have to ride Jim Crow!
> No, you don't have to ride Jim Crow!
> On June the Third the high court said,
> When you ride interstate, Jim Crow is dead!
> You don't have to ride Jim Crow!
>
> And when you get on the bus,
> And when you get on the bus,
> Get on the bus, sit anyplace
> 'Cause Irene Morgan won her case.
> You don't have to ride Jim Crow!

Before the Supreme Court decision, Morgan had moved to New York City, where she worked as a practical nurse. Her husband, Sherwood, died in 1948, and with her second husband, Stanley Kirkaldy, she ran a childcare center. In 1985, at the age of sixty-eight, Irene Morgan Kirkaldy earned a bachelor's degree in communications from St. John's University, and five years later she gained a master's degree in urban studies from Queens College.[41]

Viola White, 1944

During World War II Viola White, a mother of three, worked at Maxwell Air Force Base in Montgomery, Alabama. On one occasion in 1944, while riding a Montgomery bus, White refused to give up her seat at the driver's command. She was arrested, beaten by the police, charged, convicted, found guilty, and fined ten dollars. White immediately appealed, though city officials delayed putting the case on the court calendar.

In a sadistic act of retaliation for White's repeated attempts to get her appeal heard, a white Montgomery policeman, A. A. Enger, kidnapped her sixteen-year-old daughter, took her to a cemetery, and raped her. As she was being attacked, Mrs. White's daughter memorized the license number of Enger's car. The very next day she bravely reported the attack to E. D. Nixon, president of the Montgomery chapter of the NAACP. With such specific evidence Nixon was able, though only after several tries, to convince a judge to issue a warrant for Enger's arrest. When he learned of the warrant, the police chief tipped off Enger, who left town to avoid any charges or being fired.[42]

As for White's appeal, E. D. Nixon recounted, "The city of Montgomery knew that they couldn't win . . . and we couldn't get on the Court calendar."[43] By the time Viola White died in 1954, her appeal had been languishing for ten years without being referred by the city to a state circuit court. The case became moot after her death, but it served as an important inspiration for E. D. Nixon, Fred Gray, and others in planning a more promising legal strategy during the 1956 Montgomery bus boycott following the arrest of Rosa Parks.[44]

Langston Hughes, May 1945

In October 1942 Elmer W. Henderson filed a complaint about the prejudicial treatment he had received the preceding May in a Southern Railroad dining car. Not receiving a satisfactory decision from the Interstate Commerce Commission, Henderson appealed to the U.S. District Court in Maryland, where the case lingered until it was returned to the ICC in 1946 and then went back to the court, which again upheld the ICC ruling. Henderson's lawyer took the case to the Supreme Court, but it was not heard or decided until 1950, when the court ruled in Henderson's favor.

Meanwhile, however, the trains kept running—and Black passengers continued to be denied service in the dining cars. In May 1945, three years after Henderson's experience, the poet Langston Hughes was lecturing throughout the South, traveling by train from city to city. In one of his weekly columns in the *Chicago Defender*, Hughes describes his own experience in dining cars under the heading "Adventures in Dining": "On some trains heading southward from Washington through Virginia, I have been served without difficulty at any table in the diner, with white passengers eating with me. Further South, I have encountered the curtain, behind which I had to sit in order to eat, often being served with the colored Pullman porters and brakemen. On other trains there has been no curtain and no intention for Negroes to eat."

On a train out of Chattanooga, Hughes was simply ignored by the white steward, so he sat himself at an empty table in the middle of the car. When three white passengers joined him, the steward gave them menus but continued to ignore Hughes. Finally, however, the steward whispered in his ear, apparently looking for some excuse to serve him without getting into trouble himself. Hughes negotiated their exchange without compromising his own integrity:

> "Say, fellow, are you Puerto Rican?"
>
> "No," I said, "I'm American."
>
> "Not American Negro, are you?" he demanded.
>
> "I'm just hungry," I said loudly.
>
> He gave me a menu! The colored waiters grinned. They served me with great courtesy, a quality which I have always found our dining car waiters to possess.

While Hughes notes the arbitrary and unpredictable ways in which Jim Crow was exercised, this very inconsistency might be taken as a sign that change was in the air. Some white passengers, at least, were willing to dine publicly with a Black stranger. Hughes strikes a somewhat lighthearted tone in closing this article, but the advice he delivers with a smile is no less significant:

> Certainly there is great variation in railroad dining for the race these days in the South. Just exactly what to expect still remains a mystery for Negroes—but it has the aura of adventure.
>
> I would advise Negro travellers in the South to use the diners more. In fact, I wish we would use the diners in droves—so that whites may get used to seeing us in diners. It has been legally established that Negro passengers have a lawful right to eat while travelling. If we are refused service or ejected on grounds of color, we can sue. Several cases have been won and damages assessed recently.

So, folks, when you go South by train, be sure to eat in the diner. Even if you are not hungry, eat anyhow—to help establish that right. Besides, it will be fun to see how you are received.[45]

Sarah Elizabeth Ray, June 21, 1945

Sarah Elizabeth Ray was born in 1921 and raised as one of thirteen children in Wauhatchie, Tennessee. Soon after getting married she and her husband may have assumed they had escaped Jim Crow by moving to Detroit, and in many ways they had. As early as 1885 Michigan had enacted a civil rights law, amended by 1937 to guarantee: "All persons within the jurisdiction of this State shall be entitled to full and equal accommodations, advantages, facilities and privileges of inns, hotels, restaurants, eating houses, barber shops, billiard parlors, public conveyances on land and water . . . and all other places of public accommodation, amusement, and recreation."[46]

Sarah Ray worked for the Detroit Ordnance District, which oversaw the production of tanks during World War II. She took a secretarial course under the auspices of the district in June 1945, shortly before the district sponsored an excursion for the class to Bois Blanc. Bois Blanc, Ontario, is a small island in Canadian territorial waters on the Detroit River about eighteen miles south of Detroit, Michigan. Over the years, the pronunciation of the French name Bois Blanc was Americanized, and the people of Detroit came to call the island Bob-Lo (often spelled "Boblo"). During the summer season for much of the twentieth century, people could enjoy day trips to the island on one of the two privately owned steamships of the Bob-Lo Excursion Company, which owned most of the island and operated a popular amusement park there. But only *some* people could enjoy that trip. The company, according to the testimony of an assistant general manager, "adopted the policy of excluding so-called 'Zoot-suiters,' the rowdyish, the rough and the boisterous and it also adopted the policy of excluding colored."[47] The reference to "Zoot-suiters" itself had racial overtones, for the zoot suit became especially popular in the 1930s and 1940s among African Americans in urban settings such as Harlem, Chicago, and Detroit and among Mexican Americans and Filipino Americans in California, leading to the "Zoot Suit Riots" of 1943.[48]

Sarah Ray, twelve of her classmates, and their teacher arrived at the Bob-Lo ticket office on June 21, where one of them collected the money and purchased the tickets—eighty-five cents round trip—and handed them out. Thus, it is possible that the ticket agent was not aware that one of their number belonged to that long-excluded class of "colored," though the ticket taker as they passed through the gate to board the ship might have. Nevertheless,

Sarah Elizabeth Ray, 1974. Photo by Ronald Ernst, Detroit News.

the group boarded the ship, checked their coats, and found chairs on the upper deck.

Soon a Mr. Devereux, the Bob-Lo assistant general manager, and a ship's steward named Fox appeared and told Ray that she would have to leave the ship. More than a hundred years after the steamboat protests of David Ruggles and others, and ninety years after William Howard Day was refused a cabin on that very same Detroit River, African Americans were still forbidden to ride the steamers. Like Ruggles, Sarah Ray refused to leave, but it soon became clear that they would use force to remove her, and she reluctantly allowed herself to be escorted off the ship. Once ashore, Devereux and Fox offered to return her fare, "saying the company was a private concern and could exclude her if it wished."[49] She angrily refused the return of the eighty-five cents, but she also had the presence of mind to take their names before she left, and she followed that up by taking her story to the NAACP, whose lawyers filed a complaint with the Detroit Recorder's Court for violation of the Michigan Civil Rights Act.

The *Columbia*, one of the Bob-Lo steamers. Library of Congress.

Ray and her lawyers waived her right to a jury trial. The company reiterated in court their argument that as a privately owned company they did not operate a public conveyance and were thus not subject to the Michigan civil rights law. The Detroit court, however, ruled that the company was "guilty as charged." The offense is classified in the Michigan Civil Rights Act as a misdemeanor, for which a guilty party "shall be fined not less than 25 [$25.00] dollars or imprisoned for not less than 15 days or both such fine and imprisonment in the discretion of the court" and in addition "shall be liable to the injured party, in treble the damages sustained."[50] The court fined the Bob-Lo Company the minimum, $25. The company appealed to the Michigan Supreme Court, which, in its turn, also affirmed, "There is no escape from the conclusion that defendant herein is engaged in the business of operating 'public conveyances' by water."[51] The Supreme Court upheld the earlier conviction.

By this point, of course, pursuing the case had cost the Bob-Lo Company far more than the $25 fine it would have to pay. Nevertheless, in the hope to retain the legal (if not the moral) right to exclude African Americans from their business, they appealed to the U.S. Supreme Court. Sarah Ray's case was argued by the Michigan solicitor general, and an amicus curiae ("friend of the court") brief was filed by Thurgood Marshall and other NAACP lawyers. In their carefully constructed opinion, the court dismantled in some detail the company's implied argument that Michigan law did not apply because their business took place primarily in Canada. The court agreed with and affirmed the ruling of the Supreme Court of Michigan. "Holding the provisions of the Michigan statute effective and applicable in the instant case results only in this, defendant will be required in operating its ships as 'public conveyances' to accept as passengers persons of the negro race indiscriminately with others."[52]

With that U.S. Supreme Court decision, two and a half years after she had been barred from travel and participation in the simple joys of a day at an amusement park, Sarah Ray became one of a growing number of men and women who successfully challenged the insidious persistence of Jim Crow, not only in the South but in the North as well. As in many other instances, the experience that Sarah Ray endured also changed the course of her life. After Ray married her second husband, Rafael Haskell, they became noted community activists and ran the Action House on Detroit's east side, in order to foster better understanding among the Black and white residents of their community. Sarah Ray (Lizz Haskell) died in poverty in 2006.[53]

Laws prohibiting racial segregation and discrimination laws, in and of themselves, do not eliminate either the discrimination or the racism that lies behind it. Sarah Ray's right to participate freely in public activities had been embedded in Michigan law for sixty years. While it should not have been necessary for her to invoke that law in order to exercise her rights, doing so led to the courts disarming yet another specious argument exploited by the Bob-Lo Company to suit its own wishes. Her boldness in challenging the company's blatant racism in a northern city revealed at a crucial time that the Supreme Court in 1947 may have been more willing than in the past to rule in favor of protecting the civil rights of African Americans. Matters were coming to a head and pressure on the courts increased as the nation moved inexorably into the 1950s.

Sgt. Isaac Woodard, February 12, 1946

Isaac Woodard, the son of sharecroppers in Fairfield County, South Carolina, entered the U.S. Army in October 1942. He was assigned to the 429th Port Battalion and shipped out to New Guinea, in the Pacific, where he worked as a longshoreman, loading and unloading ships, at times under heavy fire, during a long and fierce campaign. By the end of the war, at the age of twenty-seven, he was a Technician Fourth Grade, with a sergeant's stripes on his shoulder and three service medals and a good conduct medal on his chest. In January 1946, Woodard was sent to Camp Gordon, Georgia, where he received an honorable discharge on February 12.[54]

That same day, while still in uniform, Woodard boarded a bus in Augusta, bound for Columbia, South Carolina, to join his wife, Rosa, in Fairfield County. He planned to take her to New York, where his parents and siblings had moved. The bus was largely filled with Black and white soldiers in a jovial mood, for they too had just been discharged after enduring the war in the Pacific. Racial tension was first introduced into the bus when the driver, Alton Blackwell, asked a white soldier nicknamed Montana, who was sitting next to Woodard, to move to the front of the bus.[55] According to Woodard's later testimony, he then had an angry exchange of words with Blackwell after requesting time at a stop in a small town to go to the restroom. Greyhound drivers were instructed to honor such requests from passengers, but Woodard stated that Blackwell responded, "Hell, no. God damn it, go back and sit down. I ain't got time to wait." Woodard replied, "God damn it, talk to me like I am talking to you. I am a man just like you." Blackwell then told him to "go ahead then and hurry back," which Woodard did.[56] Blackwell later claimed that Woodard repeatedly asked to leave the bus at each stop and that this put the bus behind schedule. He also said that Woodard was sharing a bottle of whiskey with a white soldier sitting next to him and was becoming increasingly intoxicated. A Black soldier and a white soldier both testified to the drinking but denied that Woodard was disruptive. A white woman also testified that Woodard was drinking and "using language not becoming to a gentleman."[57] Determined to get Woodard off the bus, when they reached Batesburg, South Carolina, Blackwell went to find a policeman.

Batesburg was a small town with only two police officers: Chief Lynwood Shull and Elliot Long. Blackwell told them that a soldier had been causing a disturbance. Woodard was taken off the bus, and as he was explaining what had happened, Shull hit him over the head with a blackjack and told him to "shut up." Both a Black soldier and a white one testified to this during the subsequent FBI inquiry. Shull initially said that he did not hit Woodard until they were some distance from the bus, and then only because Woodard was resisting him. Later, however, he admitted that he "may have" struck Woodard while still near the bus.[58]

Shull arrested Woodard and led him down the street toward the jail. Officer Long remained behind. Out of sight of the bus stop, Shull asked Woodard if he had been discharged from the army. When Woodard said "Yes," Shull struck him in the head again and said the correct answer was "Yes, sir." Woodard grabbed the blackjack from Shull. At this point Long appeared, drew his gun, and told Woodard, "[Drop it, or] I will drop you." After Woodard complied, Shull picked up the blackjack and began beating Woodard with it until Woodard fell to the ground unconscious.

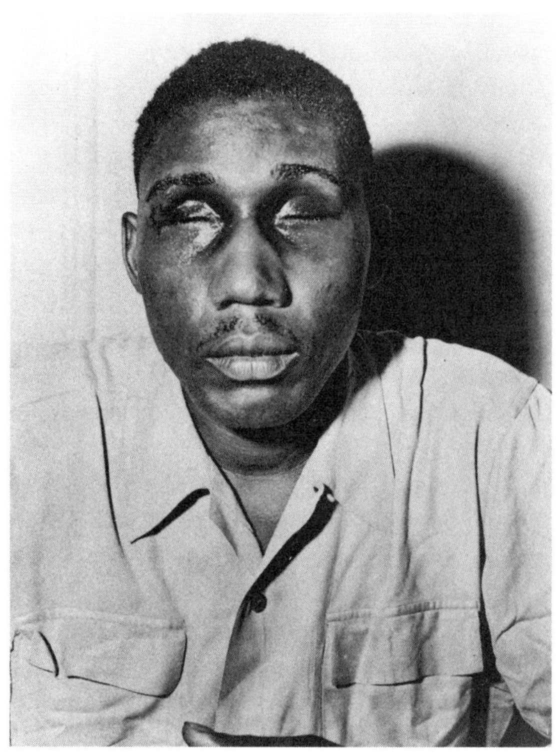

Isaac Woodard, 1946. Photo by J. DeBisse. Library of Congress.

When he came to, Shull told Woodard to get up. "When I started to get up, he started punching me in my eyes with the end of his billy."[59] Shull hit him with such ferocity that the handle of his blackjack broke. Woodard was then taken to a jail cell and left alone overnight. In the morning he discovered that he could not see. Shull led him to a sink to wash the dried blood from his face, and then took him to the town judge and mayor, H. E. Quarles, to face a charge of drunk and disorderly conduct.

Quarles found Woodard guilty and fined him fifty dollars or thirty days hard labor. Woodard had only forty-four dollars in cash and his mustering-out check for $694.73. The judge agreed to accept the forty-four dollars. Woodard was free to go, but feeling ill he returned to the jail to lie down. That afternoon the town doctor saw Woodard and recommended that he be taken immediately to a hospital. Shull then drove Woodard to the Veterans Administration Hospital in Columbia, South Carolina, where he was diagnosed as totally and permanently blind. He was treated there for two months. He was allowed only partial VA disability benefits because he had been discharged from the army five hours before he was injured.

Woodard's wife did not want to live with a disabled husband, so two of

Woodard's sisters came down from New York and brought him home. Hearing about the attack against Woodard, the NAACP took up his case in the hope that it would raise awareness of attacks against returning Black soldiers. Walter White, executive secretary of the NAACP, wrote to Robert Patterson, the secretary of war, requesting an investigation. Patterson replied six weeks later, saying that the War Department had no jurisdiction over the matter because Woodard was "a civilian at the time of the incident."[60] The NAACP issued a press release demanding an investigation by the Department of Justice and offering a $1,000 reward for the arrest and conviction of the policeman responsible. The resulting press coverage led to numerous complaints and letters to the White House, the Departments of Justice and War, and the NAACP. An FBI investigation was conducted during the summer of 1946. White sent a copy of Woodard's FBI affidavit to Orson Welles, the famous radio broadcaster and film director. Welles's reading of Woodard's affidavit on his weekly broadcast in late July prompted a further flood of outraged responses from Black veterans and citizens.[61]

That August, C. B. Powell, the publisher of the *Amsterdam News,* organized a benefit concert for Woodard in New York. Twenty-three thousand people filled Lewisohn Stadium in Harlem to hear Joe Louis, the heavyweight champion boxer, speak on Woodard's behalf. As many as ten thousand more were turned away. There were performances by such notable Black musicians as Cab Calloway, W. C. Handy, Carol Brice, and Nat King Cole. Woody Guthrie sang his new song, "The Blinding of Isaac Woodard," which ends,

> It's now you've heard my story, there's one thing I can't see,
> How you could treat a human like they have treated me;
> I thought I fought on the islands to get rid of their kind;
> But I can see the fight lots plainer now that I am blind.[62]

Because of the case's notoriety, J. Edgar Hoover was hesitant to shut down the FBI investigation prematurely, though the investigators were not inclined to think that Shull had done anything wrong. However, a group of civil rights, labor, and religious leaders comprising the National Emergency Committee Against Mob Violence had been granted a meeting with President Truman in September to discuss racial unrest. Richard Gergel summarizes the outcome of that meeting:

> Truman's closest ally in the room, Walter White, sensed that the president did not appreciate the gravity of the situation. Rather than continuing the discussion on proposals for presidential action, he began sharing with Truman, in graphic detail, the beating and blinding of Isaac Woodard. As the story unfolded,

Truman sat riveted and became visibly agitated and angered. One observer later described his face as "distorted in horror." Casting his staff's advice aside, an obviously distressed president responded, "My God! I had no idea it was as terrible as that! We have got to do something."[63]

The president agreed to establish a blue-ribbon committee to make recommendations before the next Congress convened in January 1948.

Just three business days after that meeting, the Civil Rights division of the Department of Justice opened criminal charges against Lynwood Shull. Bringing the case before a federal grand jury in South Carolina would take a long time, and there was good reason to believe that an all-white, sixteen-person grand jury would not deliver the necessary twelve votes to indict a white police officer for violating the civil rights of a Black man. To avoid the necessity of a grand jury, Shull was charged with a misdemeanor, which would only carry a punishment of a year or less, but could go straight to trial.

The NAACP organized a fall tour of over two dozen cities to raise money for Woodard and to focus attention on the plague of postwar racial violence. While it drew considerable interest, the tour was cut short when it was announced unexpectedly that the trial was about to begin, under the gavel of Judge J. Waties Waring. Woodard was sent immediately to Columbia, South Carolina, with just one day to prepare.[64] The selection of the all-white jury began at 10:30 a.m. on November 5. After brief opening statements, Woodard was led to the stand to tell his version of events, and he was followed by the Batesburg doctor and two VA doctors who had treated him. Then, to the surprise of the NAACP observers, the prosecutor rested his case at 12:35 p.m., without calling two white witnesses who were willing to testify that Woodard had not been disruptive on the bus. That afternoon, Blackwell and Officer Long gave their versions of events, followed by Shull's own testimony. Not surprisingly, their accounts differed from Woodard's, with considerable confusion generated by Shull's claim that he had only hit Woodard once, a claim inconsistent with the injury to both of Woodard's eyes.[65]

In his closing argument one of the defense lawyers argued, "If a decision against the government means seceding, then let South Carolina secede again." He characterized Woodard as belonging to "an inferior race that the South had always protected" and asked the jury to return a verdict of not guilty. The U.S. attorney, Claud Sapp, made a brief closing argument for the prosecution, oddly concluding with the statement that "whatever verdict you gentlemen bring in, the government will be satisfied with." He did not even ask them, as prosecutors generally do, to find the defendant guilty.[66]

Judge Waring sent the jury out to deliberate at 6:28. To forestall the travesty of a five-minute verdict, he left the courthouse to take a walk around town; the jury could not return in his absence. After twenty-five minutes, he was told that the jury had been incessantly banging at the jury room door. In court three minutes later they delivered their unanimous decision: not guilty.[67]

While a not-guilty verdict in such a case in South Carolina was not a great surprise, the attack on Isaac Woodard ultimately had a lasting effect on race relations throughout the country. Walter White's moving narrative to President Truman woke the president to civil rights issues. The President's Committee on Civil Rights, composed of a wide range of white and Black leaders, was established. As it began its work, Truman became the first president to address a meeting of the NAACP. In a nationally broadcast speech, he stated, "It is my deep conviction that we have reached a turning point in the long history of our country's efforts to guarantee freedom and equality to all our citizens. Recent events in the United States and abroad have made us realize that it is more important today than ever before to insure that all Americans enjoy these rights. When I say all Americans, I mean all Americans."[68]

In October 1947 the President's Committee delivered its final report, *To Secure These Rights*. This report was frank and forthright, identifying lynching as "a terrorist device" and highlighting the "widespread" problems of police brutality, disenfranchisement, and discrimination in the armed forces, schools, and federal offices, especially through government-enforced segregation. Truman upset many southern politicians when he fully endorsed the report in a "special message" to Congress in February 1948. He announced too that he would issue an executive order to end discrimination in the armed forces.[69]

Despite the opposition of a large majority of Americans to his civil rights program during an election year, Truman remained firm, even throughout a Democratic Convention that became contentious over the issue of civil rights. In July Truman called a special session of Congress. On the day that session opened, Truman issued two executive orders. Executive Order 9980 prohibited segregation in federal offices and facilities. Executive Order 9981 declared, "It is hereby . . . the policy of the President that there shall be equality of treatment and opportunity for all persons in the armed services without regard to race, color, religion or national origin."[70] Some members of Congress refused to stand when Truman entered the House chamber, and he wrote to his wife, "They sure are in a stew and mad as wet hens. If I can make them madder, maybe they'll do the[ir] jobs."[71] Nevertheless, Truman famously, and surprisingly, won the 1948 election over Thomas Dewey. Post-election analysis attributed his win to the high turnout of African American voters in the key states of Illinois, Ohio, and California.[72]

The blinding of Isaac Woodard had even further profound, if indirect, impact on U.S. racial and judicial history. Judge Waring, an eighth-generation Charlestonian, had long been a gradualist opponent of Jim Crow, believing that racial disparities could be dealt with incrementally to achieve the equality promised by the 1896 *Plessy* doctrine of "separate but equal." Woodard's testimony in Waring's courtroom, however, forced the judge to face the horrors of racism. After the trial, shunned by the white Charleston elite, Waring and his wife, Elizabeth, became friends with Black and white civil rights leaders in South Carolina and around the nation and began to educate themselves on issues of racial justice. Waring worked to achieve more rapid and meaningful change in his court.[73]

A 1949 case on Waring's docket was *Briggs v. Elliott*, in which a group of African American parents from Summerton, South Carolina, sued the local school board to provide a school bus for their children. Thurgood Marshall undertook the case for the NAACP and expanded it to address unequal educational opportunities and facilities more generally. Waring cleverly convinced Marshall to bring the case before a three-judge panel, including Waring himself. In the likely event that the case would be lost by a 2–1 vote, it could then be appealed directly to the U.S. Supreme Court. Waring also convinced Marshall not to argue for greater, albeit segregated, equality, which had been prior NAACP strategy, but to challenge the "separate but equal" doctrine itself as unconstitutional. To do this, Marshall called an expert witness, Dr. Kenneth Clark, a psychology professor at City College in New York, to testify about his research using otherwise identical Black and white dolls to assess the effects of segregation on Black children. Clark's experiments demonstrated that under segregation children suffered from a sense of inferiority and long-term psychological injury.

As expected, the judges ruled 2–1 that, while the school district had violated the Constitution by not providing equal educational services, the state had the right to segregate schools, a right with which "the federal courts are powerless to interfere." In his dissent Waring articulated the principle that "segregation is per se inequality."[74] Marshall and the NAACP took their appeal to the Supreme Court, where it became the first in the cluster of five education-related cases known as *Brown v. Board of Education*. In its unanimous opinion in May 1954, the Court overthrew *Plessy* with an echo of Waring, stating, "The doctrine of 'separate but equal' has no place. Separate educational facilities are inherently unequal."[75] Segregation had been struck the severest blow yet.

After Shull was found not guilty, Woodard sued the Atlantic Greyhound Company, but that suit also failed. He bought a house from the proceeds of the *Amsterdam News* concert, but the city then took it by eminent domain to build a housing project. He faded into obscurity, living in near poverty on his partial pension and a small income from a Bronx commercial building, and sharing his five-room apartment with a son, an adopted son, and his elderly parents. His situation improved in the 1960s when Congress granted full disability rights to servicemen injured on their way home after being discharged. He bought a home with a VA loan in 1978, where he died in 1992. Woodard never learned of the effect his story had on President Truman or on Judge Waring, and, by extension, on the larger struggle for civil rights.[76] In June 2018, the town attorney of Batesburg-Leesburg reopened Woodard's case and, after seventy-two years, Sergeant Woodard's conviction was expunged from the record.[77]

CHAPTER 6

"You Don't Have to Ride Jim Crow"

While white local, city, and state officials might have wanted to suppress the spread of news of any "trouble" they saw as threatening their own superior social status, improvements in communication, especially at the dawn of the television age, made it increasingly difficult to keep the public uninformed. Across the country dedicated activists like E. D. Nixon, Ella Baker, Bayard Rustin, Jo Ann Robinson, Rosa Parks, Fred Shuttlesworth, Martin Luther King Jr., and lawyers with the stature of Thurgood Marshall, Pauli Murray, Dovey Johnson Roundtree, and Fred Gray rose up to confront segregation in travel and in education. Through their efforts and those of hundreds like them, the two postwar decades have come to be known as the Civil Rights Era.[1]

Bayard Rustin and the Journey of Reconciliation, April 9–23, 1947

The 1946 Supreme Court decision in the case of *Morgan v. Virginia* established that segregation was illegal in interstate travel, at least on buses. The decision specified "motor vehicles," "motor buses," and "interstate motor travel" but did not mention trains or other modes of travel. Nevertheless, even on buses the court's ruling had little effect on actual practice. Bayard Rustin's experience on a bus from Louisville to Nashville in 1942 had confirmed for him the power of resisting segregation law and authority with nonviolent protest, while it simultaneously demonstrated the very palpable risks of doing so. Never one to shrink from danger in the face of oppression, Rustin made a proposal to George Houser, a white staff member of the Fellowship of Reconciliation (FOR) and a fellow cofounder in 1942 of the Congress of Racial Equality (CORE) to undertake an interstate journey to test the effectiveness of the *Morgan* decision.

Rustin and Houser developed a plan to be supported jointly by FOR and CORE, calling it the Journey of Reconciliation. Groups of riders, both Black and white, would travel together, with designated members occupying forbidden seats—Blacks in the front, whites in the back, and sometimes Black and white sitting together. Others, sitting "in a segregated manner," would not challenge the seating laws but would serve as witnesses and provide any necessary assistance. After some discussion, they decided not to travel through the deep South, where severe violence would have been inevitable, possibly putting other Black passengers at risk. Rustin and Houser had initially planned to include both women and men in the experiment, but it was ultimately decided that on this initial foray, at least, only men would take part, in the belief that "mixing the races and sexes would possibly exacerbate an already volatile situation." This decision was met with considerable opposition from the women involved in the planning, especially Ella Baker and Pauli Murray, who had themselves fought back against Jim Crow on buses and trains.[2]

Sixteen participants—eight Black and eight white—went on the trip. The group met beforehand in Washington to train in nonviolent resistance and take part in role-playing exercises approximating situations that might arise. Rustin and Houser wrote up a set of guidelines:

> WHEN TRAVELING BY BUS WITH A TICKET FROM A POINT IN ONE STATE TO A POINT IN ANOTHER STATE
>
> 1. If you are a Negro, sit in a front seat. If you are white, sit in a rear seat.
> 2. If the driver asks you to move, tell him *calmly and courteously*: "As an interstate passenger I have a right to sit anywhere in this bus. This is the law as laid down by the United States Supreme Court."
> 3. If the driver summons the police and repeats his order in their presence, tell them exactly what you said when he first asked you to move.
> 4. If the police tell you to "come along," without putting you under arrest, tell them you will not go until you are put under arrest. Police have often used the tactic of frightening a person into getting off the bus without making an arrest, keeping him until the bus has left and then just leaving him standing by the empty roadside. In such a case this person has no redress.
> 5. If the police put you under arrest, go with them peacefully. At the police station, phone the nearest center of the NAACP, or one of their lawyers. They will assist you.
> 6. If you have any money with you, you can get out on bail immediately. It will probably be either $25 or $50. If you don't have bail, anti-discrimination organizations will help raise it for you.
> 7. *If you happen to be arrested the delay in your journey will only be a few hours. The value of your action in breaking down Jim Crow will be too great to be measured.*[3]

Specific roles were designated on each leg of the Journey—who would sit where, who would take care of bail if necessary, who would abide by Jim

Journey of Reconciliation members (*left to right*) Worth Randle, Wallace Nelson, Ernest Bromley, Jim Peck, Igal Roodenko, Bayard Rustin, Joseph Felmet, George Houser, and Andrew Johnson, Richmond, Virginia, April 10, 1947.

Crow to make sure that they did not all get arrested at the same time. To guarantee their right to travel freely under the law as determined in *Morgan v. Virginia*, any tickets purchased included a destination in another state. When possible, two groups would travel separately, one on Trailways buses and the other by Greyhound. This would ensure that they were not simply testing the practices of just one company. As it turned out, however, all the arrests made on the trip were on Trailways. To spread the word more widely among local communities, meetings were scheduled at various stops, during which the riders would explain their purpose. At the conclusion of the Journey, Houser and Rustin produced a pamphlet titled *We Challenged Jim Crow! A Report on the Journey of Reconciliation.*[4] Unless otherwise noted, the following chronology is based on that pamphlet.[5]

APRIL 9: WASHINGTON, D.C.–RICHMOND, VA.

To begin the Journey, two groups of riders boarded buses in Washington, D.C., bound for Richmond, Virginia. Rustin, on a Greyhound bus, sat down in the third seat from the front. Seeing him in one of the forward seats may have motivated a white couple not in the group to sit in the back seat next to two Black passengers, and an elderly Black woman took Rustin's seat when he moved farther forward to sit next to a young white boy in the front seat right behind the driver. Despite this, there were no incidents on either bus that day.

APRIL 11: PETERSBURG, VA.–DURHAM, N.C.

The second leg of the journey, from Richmond to Petersburg, Virginia, on April 10, was similarly uneventful. The following morning, however, on the Greyhound from Petersburg to Durham, North Carolina, Rustin and Jim Peck, a white member of FOR, cofounder of CORE, and editor of the Workers Defense League *News Bulletin*, sat together toward the front of the bus. The driver ordered Rustin to move to the rear. Rustin refused, calmly and courteously, as his guidelines stated. After a change of buses in Clarksville, Virginia, another driver called the police in Oxford, North Carolina, but the police decided not to arrest him. Although one Black passenger, a schoolteacher, pleaded with Rustin to move, others were supportive. One even threatened to sue the bus company over the delay.

PETERSBURG, VA.–RALEIGH, N.C.

The journey's first arrest took place that same morning after group members boarded a Trailways bus to Raleigh. Before leaving Petersburg, the driver told Conrad Lynn, a Black civil rights lawyer from New York City, to move to the rear. When Lynn attempted to explain the Supreme Court's *Morgan* decision, the driver insisted that he worked for the bus company, not the Supreme Court, adding, "Personally, I don't care where you sit, but I have my orders." After an hour and a half delay, during which an ominous crowd began to gather, Lynn was arrested on a charge of disorderly conduct. "The magistrate in Petersburg would not sign the warrant until the bus company attorney in Richmond had been called, and dictated the statement of the warrant over the telephone. . . . The bus operator apologized for having to arrest Lynn."[6] Lynn paid the $25 bail, and violence was averted.

As in the case of the teacher on Rustin's bus, opposition to the Journey of Reconciliation was at times voiced by African Americans. For some, Black ambivalence or even distrust of the protest was based on fear or concern that drawing attention to the problem would put regular passengers or local residents at risk or would rile local white racists. Houser and Rustin address this opposition in response to the three Black persons during the journey who, separately but "in very emotional terms," urged the protesters to comply with the Jim Crow laws: "Their request was in part the result of fear, or in the case of the Negro porter, an attempt to ingratiate themselves with white authorities. Such reactions are to be expected in a caste system and represent the kind of personal degradation which ought to spur us on to eliminate caste."[7]

Other Black observers had genuine concern for the protesters themselves. One Black passenger warned Houser and Igal Roodenko, a white activist from New York, that a Negro might be able to get away with riding up front in Virginia, but some bus drivers were crazy: "And the farther South you go, the crazier they get."[8]

APRIL 12: RALEIGH, N.C.–CHAPEL HILL, N.C.

On a crowded Trailways bus en route to Chapel Hill via Durham, Conrad Lynn and Wally Nelson, a Black CORE member from Cincinnati, sat in the next-to-last row. A Black woman sitting opposite them moved to the rear seat when a white woman got on the bus. As two white college students entered the bus, the driver asked Lynn and Nelson to move back, but they declined. A white passenger offered to "help" the driver—implying the use of force. The driver said he would handle things in Durham, but when they arrived there he did nothing.

DURHAM, N.C.–CHAPEL HILL, N.C.

That same day, Rustin and Andrew Johnson, a Black college student from Cincinnati, sat in the second row of a Trailways bus in Durham, headed for Chapel Hill. Within five minutes or so, they were arrested "for refusing to move when ordered to do so," whereupon Jim Peck volunteered, "If you arrest them, you'll have to arrest me, too, for I'm going to sit in the rear." He was detained as well, but when an attorney arrived to represent them, all three were released. A Trailways official acknowledged that the company was aware of the protest: "We know all about this. Greyhound is letting them ride. But we are not." The bus then took them on the twelve-mile trip to Chapel Hill.

APRIL 13: CHAPEL HILL, N.C.–GREENSBORO, N.C.

Chapel Hill was and remains one of the most liberal towns in North Carolina, yet it was only there that the Journey of Reconciliation met with physical violence. On the morning of April 13, Andrew Johnson and Joseph Felmet, a white representative of the Southern Workers Defense League who lived in Asheville, sat together at the front of the bus to Greensboro. They were quickly arrested. When Felmet caused a momentary delay by asking the policeman if they were under arrest, he was pulled from his seat and shoved off the bus. As the driver began to distribute witness cards to other passengers, one white woman responded, "You don't want me to sign one of those. I am a damn Yankee and I think this is an outrage." Seeing that at least some of the passengers were sympathetic to their cause, Rustin and Igal Roodenko moved forward and sat in the seats vacated by Johnson and Felmet. They too were arrested. A southern white woman on the bus gave Rustin her name and address as he left the bus. At the police station, conveniently located across the street, Johnson and Rustin were charged with "disorderly conduct for refusing to obey the order of the bus driver," and Felmet and Roodenko were charged with "interfering with arrest."

As the delay stretched to two hours, a group of taxi drivers around the bus station became agitated. "One hit Peck a hard blow to the head, saying, 'Coming down here to stir up the niggers.' Peck stood quietly looking at them for several moments, but said nothing." One of the cab drivers, who went into the courthouse ostensibly to get a drink of water, was heard to say, "They'll never get a bus out of here tonight."[9] Peck later wrote, "I recalled how of the 31 indicted two months ago in Greenville, S.C., for lynching a Negro, 28 of them were cab drivers."[10] (In that case, all thirty-one were acquitted of the charge of killing twenty-four-year-old Willie Earle, whom they believed had stabbed another cab driver to death.)

After the four men were released on $50 bail, Rev. Charles Jones, a white Presbyterian minister, drove them to his house. As they reached the porch, two taxis pulled up, and men got out and approached the house, armed with sticks and rocks. Fortunately, one of them called the others back, but a few moments later Reverend Jones received an anonymous phone call saying, "Get those damn niggers out of town or we'll burn your house down. We'll be around to see that they go." Rustin and the others decided it would be wise to leave town before nightfall, and they were driven to Greensboro in two cars.

APRIL 14: GREENSBORO, N.C.–WINSTON-SALEM, N.C.

Conrad Lynn and Wally Nelson sat near the front on two separate Greyhound buses from Greensboro to Winston-Salem. There were no arrests or incidents, but on Lynn's bus a passenger from South Carolina told Ernest Bromley, a white minister from North Carolina and a member of FOR, "In my state he would either move or be killed."

APRIL 15: WINSTON-SALEM, N.C.–ASHEVILLE, N.C.

The trip to Asheville began on a Greyhound bus, and no one commented on the two Black men in the second row. In Statesville, however, the group changed to a Trailways bus. Some miles farther down the road, the driver told Wally Nelson to move to the rear. Nelson said that he was traveling interstate, and the driver responded that it was not an interstate bus. Nelson then explained that, even so, his ticket was interstate, thus the Supreme Court ruling applied. The driver returned to his seat and drove on. A couple of passengers complained, but the driver simply blamed the Supreme Court and said there was nothing he could do.

APRIL 17: ASHEVILLE, N.C.–KNOXVILLE, TENN.

Dennis Banks, a Chicago musician, and Jim Peck sat in the second seat of a Trailways bus. While still in the Asheville station, a passenger asked the driver to tell Banks to move to the rear. "Banks replied, 'I'm sorry. I can't,' and explained that he was an interstate passenger. The police were called and the order repeated." After twenty minutes Banks was arrested. Once again Jim Peck insisted that he should be arrested too because they were traveling together. Peck was arrested for sitting in the rear, and they were charged with violating Jim Crow laws. They were released on $100 bail, with the trial to be held the following day.

KNOXVILLE, TENN.–NASHVILLE

That same evening in Knoxville, when he boarded a bus to Nashville, a white soldier asked the driver to move Nathan Wright, a Black social worker from Cincinnati. The driver asked Wright politely, "Would you like to move?" After Wright declined, the driver disappeared into the station for fifteen minutes, presumably to consult his superiors. When he returned, he simply drove off "without raising any more questions."

APRIL 18: ASHEVILLE, N.C.

The trial of Banks and Peck was held in the Asheville police court. Their NAACP lawyer, Curtis Todd, was the first Black lawyer to appear in the Asheville court, a fact made even more striking in that he was defending a Black man and a white man together. The driver and the policeman both testified that Banks and Peck had not been disorderly. Neither the judge nor the prosecutor had heard of the *Morgan* case and had to borrow Attorney Todd's copy. In spite of this testimony and the evidence of the *Morgan* decision, the judge sentenced them to the maximum, thirty days each, and released them on $250 bond pending appeal. After the trial, Jim Peck reported what he called "the most fantastic extreme of segregation in my experience—Jim Crow Bibles," one for Black witnesses and a separate one for whites. He later learned that this was a common southern phenomenon.[11]

KNOXVILLE, TENN.–LOUISVILLE, KY.

That same day, William Worthy, a Black journalist from New York, and Igal Roodenko sat near the front of a Greyhound bus from Knoxville to Louisville.

No one objected until they reached the town of Corbin, Kentucky, where Worthy was asked to move. "The driver hinted that there would be violence from the crowd if Worthy did not move. A white woman from Tennessee talked with the officials in the bus station and to the bus driver, protesting threatened arrests. The bus driver received orders to drive on."[12]

APRIL 19: WEAVERVILLE, N.C.–BRISTOL, VA.

An event on another Greyhound bus further illustrates the pettiness of Jim Crow and the lengths that people would go to minimize even the slightest hint of racial equality. According to Jim Crow "rules," no white person was ever to sit behind a Black person. Dennis Banks was the only Black person on this particular bus. Being without a companion witness, he sat in the rear seat, which could accommodate five people. "The bus was extremely crowded. The driver asked Banks to move from the rear seat to the double seat in front of the rear seat so that only one white person, and not four, would have to sit beside him. Banks complied. He had a friendly conversation with a young white farmer who sat beside him."[13]

NASHVILLE–LOUISVILLE

Nathan Wright and Homer Jack, a white minister from Cincinnati, took their reserved seats on a train in Nashville, headed to Louisville. As he was collecting their tickets, one of the conductors asked Jack if Wright was his prisoner. If so, then the Black man could remain in the white coach—one of the long-standing Jim Crow exceptions. On learning that they were friends, the conductor invoked the company's rule consigning Wright to the Jim Crow car. Wright refused to move, and the conductor left. When he returned, he said to Wright, "If we were in Alabama, we would throw you out the window," and he threatened to have him arrested in Bowling Green. After the conductor left, a woman a couple of seats behind them gave her name and address. Bowling Green came and went with no arrest.

APRIL 22: LYNCHBURG, VA.–WASHINGTON, D.C.

Wally Nelson and George Houser rode at the front of a Trailways bus from Lynchburg back to Washington, D.C. A few miles out of Lynchburg the driver stopped and asked Nelson to move to the rear. When Houser explained that they were traveling together, the driver said they could ride in the rear. Houser asked whether that would not also be breaking the rules, since he was white. The driver replied that Houser would have to sit in the rear, but one row in front of Nelson. As they refused to move, the bus was delayed for an hour until an arrest warrant was obtained. Nelson was then taken to the small town of Amherst, Virginia, and held on $50 bail. Houser noted that when he left the bus to pay Nelson's bail, the driver "apologized profusely for his action."[14]

After posting Nelson's bond, Houser and Nelson took a Southern Railway train from Amherst to Washington. When they asked the conductor where they could sit together, the conductor asked if Nelson were Houser's prisoner. Upon learning that they were merely friends, he said, "I'll turn you over to the officials at Charlottesville if you sit together." They sat together in the Jim Crow car, whereupon the conductor threatened to have Houser arrested in Charlottesville if he refused to leave that car. Houser did not move, but no arrests were made.

APRIL 23: CHARLOTTESVILLE, VA.–WASHINGTON, D.C.

On a Trailways bus to Washington, Dennis Banks sat alone near the front. Jim Peck and Worth Randle, a white biologist from Cincinnati, both sat on the rear seat. About two hours into the trip, in the town of Culpeper, Banks declined to move to the rear, and the bus waited for about two hours until an arrest warrant was obtained. Nothing was said about Peck and Randle breaking the company rule in the rear. A Black woman who had a concession selling bus tickets in Culpeper came onto the bus and offered to help Banks in any way she could. Banks was released on payment of a $25 bond.

Throughout the Journey of Reconciliation, there were twelve arrests in six separate incidents.[15] Most of these were dealt with quickly, as charges were dismissed or the accused were acquitted. The arrests of Johnson, Felmet, Rustin, and Roodenko in Chapel Hill on April 13, however, were not so easily resolved. The trial of Rustin and Roodenko came up first, on May 20, with a staunch segregationist judge, Henry Whitfield, presiding. The prose-

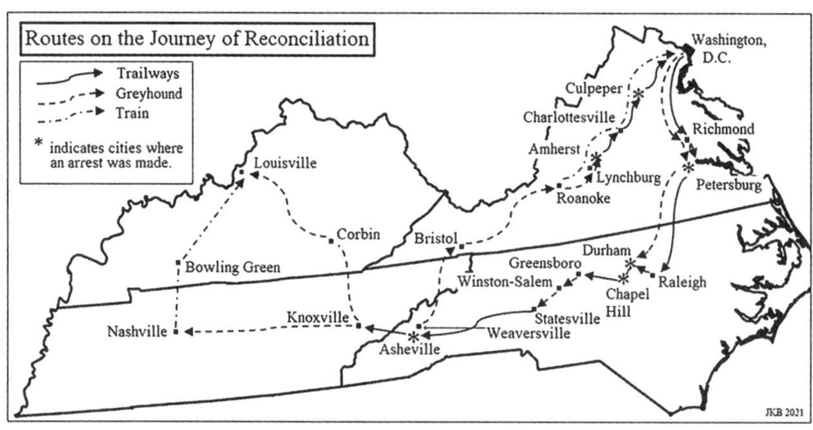

Map of the Journey of Reconciliation. J. K. Bollard.

cutor, T. J. Phipps, presented a long screed to justify segregation, summed up neatly by James Peck: "He went on to state that the Negroes had been brought over from Africa as savages and had been civilized by the whites. Then came a lengthy argument to show that the Negroes really wanted jimcrow."[16] Whitfield found both Rustin and Roodenko guilty and sentenced Rustin, whom he described as "a poor misled nigra from the North," to pay the court costs. He sentenced Roodenko, on the other hand, to thirty days on a chain gang, saying, "I presume you're Jewish, Mr. Rodenky. Well, it's about time you Jews from New York learned that you can't come down here bringing your nigras with you to upset the customs of the South."[17] The NAACP attorneys filed an appeal at the state superior court level.

A month later, Whitfield sentenced Felmet and Johnson. He initially fined Johnson $50 and sentenced Felmet, a white native North Carolinian, to six months on a road gang. When he was told that the maximum sentence allowed was one month, Whitfield changed Felmet's sentence to thirty days and reduced Johnson's fine to $25 plus court costs. On appeal in superior court in March 1948, Judge Chester Morris declared that the four men arrested on that bus were not interstate passengers, and he gave them all sentences of thirty days on the road. Following a further appeal, in January 1949 the North Carolina Supreme Court adhered to Morris's ruling that the men were riding intrastate, not interstate, and ordered Rustin, Peck, Felmet, and Roodenko to serve their sentences.[18]

Rustin and Houser were in favor of taking the case to the U.S. Supreme Court, but the NAACP had been reluctant all along to defend direct action approaches such as the Journey of Reconciliation (JOR) and was not willing to carry the case further. The Fellowship of Reconciliation could try to convince the North Carolina governor to overturn the decision, but that might imply an admission that the men were actually guilty of a crime, which they were not. Ignoring the order in the hope that the state might not extradite the four would mean abandoning the group's moral high ground. The JOR committee and the FOR executive council decided that the best and most honorable solution would be to serve the sentences.

Rustin, Felmet, and Roodenko surrendered themselves at the Orange County Courthouse in Hillsboro, North Carolina, on March 21, 1949. Andrew Johnson, about to graduate from the University of Cincinnati and enter law school in the autumn, told FOR that he would be neither physically nor mentally able to serve his sentence and so he did not show up. The three prisoners were released after twenty-two grueling days, with eight days off for good behavior. Rustin wrote a memoir titled "Twenty-Two Days on a Chain Gang," which was serialized in both the *New York Post* and the *Baltimore Afro-*

American. This straightforward and searing account not only woke readers to the harsh realities and cruelty of prison life, it also led to an investigation of the North Carolina prison camps by the state legislature.

Among the "General Observations" with which Houser and Rustin concluded their pamphlet *We Challenged Jim Crow!* is a brief paragraph that gives a new perspective on the objections of Ella Baker and Pauli Murray to the exclusion of women from the Journey of Reconciliation. On a larger scale it reminds us of the prominent roles played by women throughout the long history of protest against Jim Crow—not only Irene Morgan, whose determination gave rise to the JOR itself, but also women as diverse as Mary Newhall Green, Elizabeth Jennings, Mary Church Terrell, Lt. Nora Green, Claudette Colvin, and, of course, Rosa Parks.

> **The Importance of Women**
> It appeared that women were more intellectually inquisitive, open for discussion, and liberal in their sentiments than men. On several occasions women not only defended those who broke with Jim Crow, but gave their names and addresses in offering to act as witnesses. In appealing for aid in the psychological struggle within the bus one might do well to concentrate on winning over women.[19]

While the Journey of Reconciliation did not significantly reduce Jim Crow travel in the South, it proved invaluable as a prototype for protests in the future, especially the Freedom Rides of 1961, during which John Lewis and the other Freedom Riders brought the issue to a head, five years after the arrest of Rosa Parks and the Montgomery bus boycott.

Bayard Rustin continued his struggle against injustice, becoming an important advisor to Martin Luther King Jr., always insisting on the importance of nonviolent protest. Rustin was the principal organizer of the 1963 March on Washington for Jobs and Freedom, during which Dr. King delivered his iconic "I Have a Dream" speech. A pacifist, a lifelong socialist, a strong proponent of workers' rights, and a supporter of labor unions, Rustin was also a figure of controversy. As a gay man, he frequently worked behind the scenes in order to avoid the potential of sensationalist distractions from the goals of the civil rights movement. In the 1980s, however, he openly promoted gay rights, though he declined to identify himself as being in the forefront of the gay rights struggle: "While I have no problem with being publicly identified as homosexual, it would be dishonest of me to present myself as one who was in the forefront of the struggle for gay rights. . . . I fundamentally consider sexual orientation to be a private matter. As such, it has not been a factor which has greatly influenced my role as an activist."[20]

In Rustin's later years, many were disappointed or angered by his shifting political and economic views, but there is no doubt that he is among the first rank of civil rights leaders in the twentieth century. The *New York Times* page one obituary of Rustin, August 25, 1987, quoted Roy Innes, the national chairman of CORE, on Rustin's significance: "Bayard Rustin was a planner, a coordinator, a thinker. He influenced all of the young leaders in the civil rights movement, even those of us who did not agree with him ideologically."

On June 17, 2022, the convictions of James Felmet, Andrew Johnson, Igal Roodenko, and Bayard Rustin were vacated by North Carolina superior court judge Allen Baddour in the same courtroom where the four men were sentenced seventy-five years earlier. "We failed their cause and we failed to deliver justice in our community," Baddour said. "And for that, I apologize. So we're doing this today to right a wrong, in public, and on the record."[21]

Jo Ann Robinson, December 24, 1949

Jo Ann Gibson was the youngest of twelve children born to Owen B. Gibson, a Georgia farmer, and his wife, Dollie Welsh. In 1918, when Jo Ann was six, her father died. Her mother kept the farm running until 1926, when she moved with her younger children to live with one of her sons in Macon. After graduating at the top of her high school class, Jo Ann began teaching school in Macon while attending Fort Valley State College (now Fort Valley State University), about thirty miles away. She received a BS degree in 1936, and in 1943 she married Wilbur Robinson. Following the loss of an infant child born the following year, however, she and Wilbur divorced in 1946. She went to Atlanta for further study and was awarded an MA at Atlanta University in 1948. After a brief stint as chair of the English Department at Mary Allen College in Crockett, Texas, Robinson accepted an offer to join the English faculty at Alabama State College (now Alabama State University) in Montgomery in the fall of 1949.[22]

In the prologue to her memoir, *The Montgomery Bus Boycott and the Women Who Started It*, Robinson narrates a key event in her life at the end of her first term at Alabama State. Robinson writes, "I was as happy as I had ever been in my life that Saturday morning . . . as I prepared to leave the campus . . . for the holidays." After boarding a bus to meet a friend before going to the airport, she closed her eyes and anticipated a two-week vacation with family and friends in Ohio. There were two other passengers on the bus, a white woman in the third row from the front and a Black man near the rear. Robinson took a seat in the fifth row. As she sat immersed in pleasant daydreams about her upcoming vacation, she gradually became aware that the bus had stopped and the driver was speaking to her:

> "If you can sit in the fifth row from the front of the other buses in Montgomery, suppose you get off and ride in one of them!" I heard him, but the message did not register with me. My thoughts were elsewhere. . . .
>
> Suddenly the driver left his seat and stood over me. His hand was drawn back as if he were going to strike me. "Get up from there!" he yelled. He repeated it, for, dazed, I had not moved. "Get up from there!"
>
> I leaped to my feet, afraid he would hit me, and ran to the front door to get off the bus. I even stepped down to the lower level, so that when the door was opened, I could step off the bus and hide myself, for tears were falling rapidly from my eyes. It suddenly occurred to me that I was supposed to go to the back door to get off, not the front! However, I was too upset, frightened, and tearful to move. I never could have walked to the rear door. Then the driver opened the front door, and I stumbled off the bus and started walking back to the college. Tears blinded my vision; waves of humiliation inundated me; and I thanked God that none of my students was on that bus to witness the tragic experience. I could have died from embarrassment.
>
> My friends came and took me to the airport, but my holiday season was spoiled. I cried all the way to my destination and pretended to have a headache when my relatives met me at the airport in Cleveland five or six hours later. In all these years I have never forgotten the shame, the hurt, of that experience. The memory will not go away.[23]

On returning to campus, Robinson became active in the Women's Political Council, an organization of Black women that had been founded at the college in 1946 by the chair of the English Department. Somewhat analogous to the all-white League of Women Voters, the WPC worked to inspire African American women and men to take leadership, register to vote, and improve the quality of their lives. As Robinson described the group, "We were 'women power,' organized to cope with any injustice, no matter what, against the darker sect." In 1950 Robinson was asked to become the WPC's second president. "I had suffered the most humiliating experience of my life when that bus driver ordered me off the fifth row seat from the front and threatened to strike me when I did not move fast enough. Thus, I was ready to take over the WPC when the time came."[24] As the treatment of African Americans worsened on the Montgomery buses in the early fifties, the WPC received many complaints and tales of mistreatment. When possible, members met with the mayor and other Montgomery officials—though with little substantive effect.

One day in September 1955, Robinson realized that "*six long years* had gone by" since she had been so humiliated. "Yet not one thing had been done to improve the conditions under which black citizens were forced by law to ride public transportation lines."

> "How long will this go on?" I asked myself aloud, and was startled when the answer came as though someone else was in the room. The answer seemed to come from all corners and from many voices: "As long as black Americans will allow it!" I turned and looked to see if anyone else was in the room, but I knew I was alone. . . .
>
> "What must we do? What *can* we do?" I asked, half aloud, half to myself. And the answer seemed to come from everywhere at once: "Boycott! Boycott! Boycott! BOYCOTT!" I did not have the slightest idea how—without involving others who might get hurt—to begin a boycott against the bus company that would put that company out of business. But the Women's Political Council took the idea under advisement.[25]

A plan for organizing a boycott was drawn up for when the time came. Ways to distribute information were discussed, and telephone lists prepared. Jo Ann Gibson Robinson was ready. The time would come just two months later with the arrest of Rosa Parks.

Pfc. Thomas Edward Brooks, August 12, 1950

On July 26, 1948, President Harry Truman signed Executive Order 9981, which required the desegregation of the U.S. armed forces. But while declaring such a policy and establishing a commission to oversee its implementation was a necessary and helpful step in moving toward that ideal, it could not, and indeed did not, eliminate the problem of racial animosity within the military. A Black soldier in uniform remained a conspicuous target when out in public, especially in a venue as fraught with the lengthening history of Jim Crow as public transportation.

On August 12, 1950, Pfc. Thomas Edward Brooks (or Hilliard Brooks, according to some accounts) got on a bus on the Cloverdale route in Montgomery as he headed towards his parents' home, where his wife Estella also lived, in West Montgomery. Brooks was a twenty-year-old private first class in the U.S. Army and, like Charles Reco, Henry Williams, Edward Green, and Booker T. Spicely, he was in uniform. According to some accounts, Brooks had been drinking that day. However, even if true, this is in essence a trivial fact that does not justify the enormity of subsequent events. After Brooks deposited his bus fare, he started down the aisle toward the rear of the bus. Doing so ran counter to an intentionally demeaning "custom" enforced in

Montgomery and elsewhere. Black passengers were required to get on the bus through the front door, pay their fare, then get off, go to the rear door, and get on again. And depending on his mood or whim, a driver might just close the doors and drive off with the fare but without the passenger.

Based largely on their interviews with several other passengers, both Black and white, Donnie Williams and Wayne Greenhaw reconstructed the exchange that then took place when Brooks got on the bus. The following account draws on theirs but only quotes verbatim the words of reported speech:[26]

The driver, C. L. Hood, called Brooks back: "Hey! Get off the bus up here and enter through the back doors. You know the routine."

Brooks smiled and turned toward Hood, who rose from his seat and said, "Get off up here, nigger! Then go to the back door."

"Ain't nobody blocking my way," Brooks replied, meaning the aisle was clear to the back.

"You don't need to be riding this bus. Git off now!"

Brooks shrugged, "Gimme back my dime."

"I ain't giving you a goddamn thing. Now git your black ass off, or I'm calling the cops."

The driver then called through the open front door to a white policeman nearby, "Hey! I got a nigger on here who won't act right. I need your help."

The policeman, M. E. Mills, got on the bus and said, "Git down here, nigger!"

Brooks didn't move, though his smile faded. Officer Mills drew out his billy club and swung it, hitting Brooks in the head. Brooks fell to his knees, and Mills pulled him down the aisle toward the front door, where Hood helped pull him toward the steps. Brooks shook himself free, stood, and jumped out the door. As he did so, the policeman yelled, "Stop!," then he drew his revolver and shot and killed Brooks.

Not all accounts of this incident agree either in the details or even in broad outline. J. Mills Thornton presents a different scenario, drawn from the *Montgomery Examiner* (August 17, 24, 31, 1950) and the *Birmingham World* (August 18, 29, 1950). In this version of the incident Brooks was drunk and cursing, and the driver refused to admit him onto the bus. Mills first knocked Brooks to the sidewalk and then shot him when he got to his feet. Mills stated that Brooks was moving toward him when he shot, though others reported that he was standing with his hands at his side. A police review board judged the killing to be "justifiable homicide." Thornton adds that a Black and a white bystander were also wounded.[27]

Pfc. Sarah Louise Keys, August 2, 1952

Not long after Dovey Johnson Roundtree and Julius Robertson established their law practice in Washington, D.C., memories of the past were unexpectedly revived in their office when an NAACP lawyer recommended that Sarah Louise Keys take her case to them. Sarah Keys grew up under the shadow of Jim Crow in the Keysville section of the small town of Washington, North Carolina. After graduating from high school, she went to New Jersey to live with her sister, but in 1951 she enlisted in the Women's Army Corps. She was trained at Fort Lee, Virginia, and after a short tour in Texas she was posted to Fort Dix, New Jersey, with the rank of private first class.

Sarah was proud to be a WAC, and she was proud of her two brothers stationed at the time in Korea. In the small hours of the morning of August 2, 1952, she was in uniform on a Safeway Trails bus on her first furlough, heading to Washington, N.C., to visit her family. In 1946 the Supreme Court had ruled in *Morgan v. Virginia* that segregation was illegal in interstate travel, and in order to avoid conflict with any in-state Jim Crow laws, Keys's father

Pfc. Sarah Louise Keys. Courtesy of Sarah Keys Evans, via Cornelia Keys Hargrave.

had reminded her to make sure that her trip would not require changing buses in Virginia or North Carolina. While case records suggest that she had to transfer to a different Carolina Trailways bus in Washington, D.C., Keys maintained in later interviews that she did not. In either case, she was sitting in the fifth seat from the front and had fallen asleep, when she was wakened by the driver asking for her ticket at a stop in Roanoke Rapids, North Carolina. At the time she did not recognize that he was not the same man who had been driving when they left D.C. He told her to move to the back of the bus so that a white marine seated in the Jim Crow section could take her seat.[28]

When Keys declined to move, the driver collected everyone else's ticket, saying to Keys, "I'm not taking your ticket." He went into the station, presumably to get instructions on how to handle the situation, and returned about fifteen minutes later to announce, "All passengers get off the bus except the lady who refused to move to the rear. She can stay here until this moves out, but it's not going any place tonight." Nevertheless, Keys exited with them. The other passengers were transferred to a different bus, which Keys was not allowed to board.

Sarah Keys was left alone in the middle of the night, not knowing when or even whether there would be another bus—or whether she would be allowed to get on it if there were. She went into the station where the ticket seller and the dispatcher ignored her, so she turned to a police officer for help. Instead of being helped, she was arrested. "I said, 'Why are you taking me to the police station?' They said, 'We're putting you in jail tonight. We're arresting you.' I said, 'For what?' They said, 'Oh, we can get you for something. We can get you for disorderly conduct.' I said, 'But you were there. And . . . there was nothing disorderly going on.' They said, 'Well, we don't have to get you to the police station.' That's sort of like when my whole body—everything froze. . . . I kept quiet."[29]

The similarities of this incident to the mistreatment Roundtree had received nine years earlier—being threatened and then stranded at night in a deserted bus station—were enough to convince Roundtree and Robertson to take on Sarah Keys's case. As an opening strategy they decided to claim a breach of contract against Safeway Trails, who had promised a "through-line" ticket that guaranteed "uninterrupted passage over its various connecting bus lines."[30] This was essentially the same claim that Roundtree had lodged against the Southern Railway before the Interstate Commerce Commission on her grandmother's behalf.

The Supreme Court's 1946 decision in *Morgan v. Virginia* ostensibly disallowed segregation in interstate travel, but it did not forbid the segregation of travelers altogether, nor did it dismantle or weaken the broader "separate but equal" principle embodied in *Plessy v. Ferguson*. Thus, southern carriers felt free to exploit a loophole through which private companies could establish their own rules for separating passengers—internal company rules that were not subject to federal oversight. The effect, as Roundtree notes, was that "the humiliation and the upheaval and the degradation continued, unabated, across the South, where the individual bus drivers and train conductors remained, for all practical purposes, the law of the land."[31] The driver who carried Sarah Keys from Washington, D.C., to Roanoke Rapids, seems to have been content to leave well enough alone; trouble arose when a new driver who had not crossed any state line took the wheel.

Keys and Roundtree drew on the Supreme Court's ruling in *Mitchell v. United States*, which linked the Interstate Commerce Act, which prohibits "undue and unreasonable prejudice," and the Fourteenth Amendment to the Constitution, which stipulates, "No State shall make or enforce any law which shall abridge the privileges or immunities of citizens of the United States." But where the *Mitchell* case and the *Henderson v. United States* decision in 1950 focused on the railroad cars and service, the external trappings of a visible "equality" implied in "separate but equal," Roundtree hoped, by more firmly and explicitly linking the Interstate Commerce Act and the Fourteenth Amendment, to challenge the true core of that doctrine, the requirement that people be "separate." She argued instead for "true equality, the kind that could only be realized in an integrated society."[32] Rather than risk losing their case and perhaps even encountering violence in the face of virulent racism in a North Carolina court, Roundtree and Robertson decided to file the case against both Safeway Trails and Carolina Trailways in Washington, D.C., where Sarah Keys had made the connection from one to the other.

Meanwhile, the teams of lawyers who were preparing the five cases that ultimately coalesced under the umbrella of *Brown v. Board of Education* were, at the demand of the Supreme Court itself, bringing the implications of the Fourteenth Amendment to bear on the question of segregated schools. On December 10, 1952, Thurgood Marshall completed his argument in *Brown* before the Supreme Court, his most famous appearance there until he himself became a Supreme Court justice nine years later. The legal battle against Jim Crow was fully engaged on several fronts.

That same day, however, word came to Roundtree and Robertson that Carolina Trailways had refused their summons, arguing that they were a Virginia corporation based in North Carolina with no connection to Safeway Trails, and that the summons was improperly served. Safeway Trails, in turn, argued that they bore no responsibility for what had happened on another line. The only viable option that Sarah Keys's lawyers saw—and it was not an encouraging option—was to take her case to the Interstate Commerce Commission, in spite of the fact that throughout its existence the commission had been so consistent in its negative rulings on complaints against segregation in transportation that it had come to be known as "the Supreme Court of the Confederacy."[33]

Until the case of Sarah Keys, the ICC had dealt with cases involving Jim Crow on trains but never on buses. And the commission also interpreted the Supreme Court decisions in *Mitchell*, *Morgan*, and *Henderson* so narrowly that there was very little, if any, change in daily practice on the railroads. A victory for Keys seemed hopeless, except possibly for the fortunate coincidence that Jim Crow and the Fourteenth Amendment were now under such close scrutiny in the Supreme Court and in the public news.

When the bus driver, M. E. Taylor, testified before the ICC, he said that Keys sat not in the fifth seat from the front, but in the third seat, and on the other side of the bus than she said. Such differences were of no legal consequence whatsoever—no one disputed that both seats were in the "white" section. But such comments, as can be seen throughout this history, are aimed at casting doubt on the truthfulness and honesty of the complainant, at discrediting a defendant's character. This disparagement continued as the Carolina Trailways attorney cross-examined Keys: "about how she'd behaved when she was barred from boarding the second bus. Hadn't she, in fact, cursed? Hadn't she shouted, as the driver and dispatcher contended? Hadn't she threatened to make a test case of her situation? Sarah, calm and exquisitely polite and ever so military in her WAC dress uniform, quietly made a mockery of the bus company's characterization of her, as much by her manner as by the content of her answers."[34]

But all of that was beside the point. In her effort to dismantle Jim Crow altogether, Roundtree compressed the case into three relevant facts:

> Carolina Trailways had a Jim Crow rule . . . ; their drivers were authorized [by the company] to impose it; Sarah had been directed to move to the back of the bus solely because she was a Negro. . . . Carolina Trailways' Jim Crow rule and the hundreds of carrier rules just like it rested on the lie that segregation did not constitute discrimination, that the notion of inferiority was a delusion, that the law was powerless to guarantee true equality. That was the lie we sought to destroy in *Sarah Keys v. Carolina Coach Company*.[35]

Five days after Roundtree and Robertson presented their case to the ICC, Chief Justice Earl Warren announced the Supreme Court decision in *Brown v. Board of Education* and related cases. As of May 17, 1954, "separate but equal" was no longer law. *Plessy v. Ferguson* had been overthrown at last. Though there was much turmoil yet to come, Justice Warren asked and answered the key question: "Does segregation of children in public schools solely on the basis of race, even though the physical facilities and other 'tangible' factors may be equal, deprive the children of the minority group of equal education opportunities? We believe it does."[36]

The Supreme Court quickly followed the *Brown* decision with a series of decisions nullifying segregation in other public places, such as golf courses, public housing, and amusement parks. Meanwhile, in September, a decision was made in Sarah Keys's case, not by the full panel of ICC commissioners but rather by the administrative hearing examiner, Isadore Friedson, who ruled that *Brown* was restricted to the field of public education and had no relevance to segregation in private business, such as travel on private carriers.

Roundtree and Robertson filed an exception to this decision, and in October they submitted a brief to be reviewed by the full commission. They invoked *Brown*, arguing, "[It can] no longer be doubted that any regulation requiring segregation of passengers in interstate commerce on the basis of race is not only unreasonable but unlawful."[37] Of course, the Supreme Court had already come to that conclusion in *Morgan v. Virginia*, but the ICC had often resisted or ignored such decisions. However, the times were changing, and the *Keys* decision became the first unequivocal ruling from the ICC identifying segregation itself as discriminatory and hence unlawful:

> We conclude that the assignment of seats in interstate buses, so designated as to imply the inherent inferiority of a traveler solely because of race or color, must be regarded as subjecting the traveler to unjust discrimination, and undue and unreasonable prejudice and disadvantage. . . .
>
> We find that the practice of defendant requiring that Negro interstate passengers occupy space or seats in specified portions of its buses, subjects such passengers to unjust discrimination, and undue and unreasonable prejudice and disadvantage, in violation of Section 216 (d) of the Interstate Commerce Act and is therefore unlawful.[38]

The ICC delivered its decisions on *Keys v. Carolina Coach Co.* and on the railway case, NAACP *v. St. Louis-San Francisco Railway Company* on Thursday, November 7, 1955.[39] The order was published on November 25, directing that by January 10 all segregated seating on interstate trains and buses had to end, and that all signs designating "colored" and "white" sections in terminals serving the affected carriers had to be removed. The following day the *New York Times* published a front-page article under the headline "ICC Orders End of Segregation on Trains, Buses."[40] Sarah Keys had earlier moved to Brooklyn, and the *New York Post*, in an article headed "Balky Dixie Keeps Jim Crow in

States," quoted her: "This is just the greatest thing for me and my people. It's a wonderful thing for the whole American people as well."[41]

Max Lerner, also writing in the *Post* in praise of the landmark ICC ruling, concluded his article, "We Walk Together," saying, "The name of Sarah Keys is now added . . . as a symbol of a movement that cannot be held back."[42] He could hardly have guessed how soon and how inexorably that movement would march on, as another inspiring symbol presented herself to the entire nation. Less than a week after the *Keys* decision was published, Rosa Parks was arrested on a city bus in Montgomery, and the struggle for racial equality shifted its focus to state and local segregation laws, as yet another determined woman stood up against the insult, indignity, and injustice of Jim Crow.

In 1958 Sarah Keys married George Evans; she died on November 16, 2023.

Martha White, T. J. Jemison, and the Baton Rouge Bus Boycott, June 1953

As in other cities in the South in the 1950s, the front ten seats on buses in Baton Rouge, Louisiana, were reserved for white people. The ten rear seats were also nominally reserved for Black people. Like the streetcars in New Orleans in 1902, the Baton Rouge buses had screens to mark the boundary, forward of which Black passengers could never sit. Even if there were no white riders on the bus, if all the other seats were full, and if the aisle was crowded with people standing, those ten front seats were to remain empty. About eighty percent of the bus ridership in Baton Rouge was composed of African Americans, so when buses got crowded, especially at the end of a hard day's work, resentment and tension were bound to rise.[43]

In January 1953 bus fares were raised from ten cents to fifteen cents. In response, Rev. T. J. Jemison, pastor of Mount Zion First Baptist Church, met with the Baton Rouge City Council to address the basic inequity. While Black passengers had to pay the same increased fare, many of them were forced to stand while seats remained empty. Jemison was sufficiently convincing that the council decided to abandon the ten-seat rule while maintaining a segregated system. They unanimously passed City Ordinance 222, which stated that Black riders should fill the bus from the rear, while white riders should fill seats from the front. The border between Black and white would thus be determined by the number of passengers of each race at any given time. This would benefit both Black passengers, more of whom would be able to sit, and the bus company, for they would not have to drive past waiting Black customers even though they had empty seats. Ordinance 222 went into effect on March 19, and the drivers were duly instructed. The bus drivers, however, refused to enforce the new law, complaining of "incidents in which Negroes seated in front seats have refused to make room for white passengers."[44]

In mid-June, assured by the city authorities that the law would be enforced, Jemison and the head of the local chapter of the NAACP distributed fliers explaining Ordinance 222 and what to do if you were challenged. That same month Martha White, a weary housekeeper, entered a crowded bus and took a seat behind the driver, explaining that she would get up if a white passenger got on the bus. When the driver told her to get out of that seat, Black passengers in the rear encouraged her to stay and another Black woman sat down next to her in solidarity. The driver threatened to have them both arrested and called the police.

T. J. Jemison was downtown at the time, and, seeing the police at the bus, he went to find out what was happening. He told the policeman that Martha White had a right to sit there, whereupon the driver had Jemison removed from the bus. The manager of the Baton Rouge Bus Company arrived and told the driver to comply with the ordinance. When the driver refused, he and another driver who similarly refused were suspended. Martha White was also put off the bus, but Reverend Jemison's intervention kept her from being arrested. In a 2005 interview with the *Southern Digest* she said, "It seemed like every police in town was there, and the head of the bus commission. . . . I vowed never to get back on the bus."[45]

In the small hours of Monday morning, June 15, the Employees Association of the Baton Rouge Bus Company, the union representing about one hundred drivers, voted to go out on strike. They claimed that Louisiana state law required "a portion of each bus to be reserved for whites" and that by failing to enforce that law they would be subject to a state fine. They also objected on more racially charged grounds: "Drivers are forced to pass up white passengers when routes through Negro sections fill up the busses with Negro passengers."[46] On Thursday the state attorney general ruled that Ordinance 222 was in conflict with state segregation law and thus invalid. The drivers ended their strike the next day.

Jemison and other Black leaders formed the United Defense League (UDL) to organize a response. Overnight word was spread through the African American community not to ride the buses. A "Fair Lift" ride-sharing system was organized, in which Black car owners would give free rides to get people to and from work. This was an important development as both a clever strategy and a powerful indication of Black solidarity across economic and class boundaries. As Taylor Branch notes in his discussion of the early stages of the

1955 Montgomery bus boycott, "The automobile was still among the prime status symbols in the United States, and therefore to volunteer one's car as public transportation was a radical act of togetherness."[47]

When buses pulled up at a bus stop, people turned their backs and waited for a Fair Lift car. Boycotts were illegal in Louisiana; thus, at a meeting Jemison announced, "We're not boycotting the buses . . . that's illegal . . . we're just not riding."[48] The UDL held open meetings each evening. By Monday, June 22, these meetings had inspired so much enthusiasm that the venue had to be moved to the municipal stadium to accommodate an enthusiastic crowd of 7,000.

The loss of a majority of their riders—15,000 or more fares per day—put the bus company at serious risk of collapse, especially after a five-day strike. The city council, under pressure from the company and from the state attorney, replaced Ordinance 222 with Ordinance 251, which stipulated a return to reserved seats for white passengers. Though fewer seats were reserved than previously, Black passengers were once again barred from sitting there even if all other seats were filled.

To the surprise and consternation of many, Jemison announced on June 23 that he had reached an agreement with the city, and he recommended disbanding the Fair Lift free rides, which had grown from some one hundred cars to more than three hundred in just a few days. He did add, "But if you have cars and want to help people, that's your business."[49] By the end of the week Black patrons were returning to the buses, and the boycott was over.[50]

The Baton Rouge bus boycott was brief and yielded disappointing results, but it took on a greater significance two and a half years later, when Rev. Martin Luther King Jr. called Reverend Jemison to get advice on how to organize the rideshare pool that became a key factor in the Montgomery, Alabama, bus boycott following the arrest of Rosa Parks.[51]

Along with Dr. King, T. J. Jemison became one of the founders of the Southern Christian Leadership Conference in 1957, and he was president of the National Baptist Convention, USA, from 1982 to 1984.[52]

Martha White also remained in Baton Rouge, where she died at the age of ninety-nine on June 5, 2021.

Claudette Colvin, March 2, 1955

Claudette Colvin was raised by her great-aunt and great-uncle, Mary Ann and Q. P. Colvin, whom she called Mom and Dad, in the little town of Pine Level, Alabama, and then in Montgomery, where they moved when she was eight. Growing up in Alabama, Colvin was aware of, and often puzzled by, the racially complex attitudes and rules of behavior that must be learned at a young age by every African American child. That she also grew up with a strong sense of self-respect, and maybe a bit of a temper, is revealed by her account of a childhood incident:

> Once, I went into a store with my mom and saw a beautiful Easter hat I really wanted. None of the other kids had that hat. But the saleslady kept bringing out different hats. For some reason she didn't want me to have the hat I wanted. I got madder and madder. She kept saying, "Why don't you want *this* hat?" and holding up hats I didn't want. Finally, I got frustrated and answered, "Because my ears don't stick out like yours." My mom was horrified—she covered my mouth up and marched me out of the store.[53]

In November 1952, during her first year at Booker T. Washington High School, Colvin's life was changed by the arrest, trial, conviction, and death sentence of a sixteen-year-old friend, Jeremiah Reeves, who had been accused of raping a white woman:

> That was when I and a lot of other students really started thinking about prejudice and racism. . . . The hypocrisy of it made me so angry! Black girls were extremely vulnerable. . . . When a white man raped a black girl—something that happened all the time—it was just his word against hers, and no one would ever

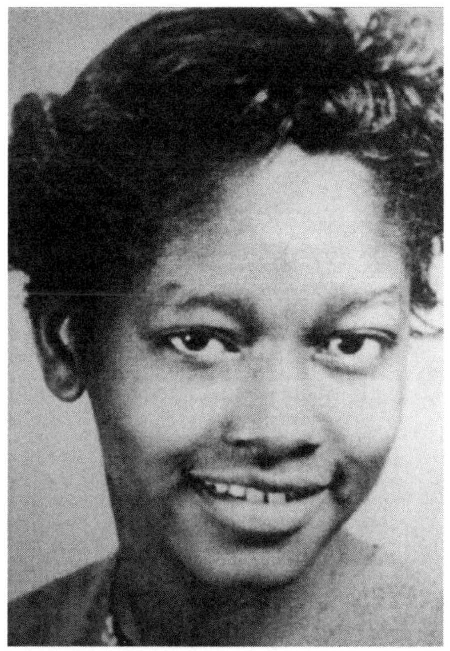

Claudette Colvin, probably in 1953. Courtesy of the Claudette Colvin Foundation.

> believe her. The white man always got off. But now they were going to hold Jeremiah for years as a minor just so they could legally execute him when he came of age. That changed me. That put a lot of anger in me. I stayed angry about Jeremiah Reeves for a long time.[54]

In 1954 the U.S. Supreme Court threw out Reeves's conviction and ordered a new trial. After a two-day trial, an all-white jury deliberated for thirty-four minutes and once again found him guilty. He was executed on March 28, 1958.[55]

Colvin was determined, however, to negotiate her world successfully and to go to college, and she became a serious, conscientious "A" student. Then on the afternoon of March 2, 1955, at age fifteen, a junior in high school, Colvin herself was arrested. She had boarded the Highland Gardens bus with twelve of her schoolmates. She and a friend took seats just in front of the rear door, well back from the ten seats reserved by law for white passengers, and two other students sat in the same row across the aisle. As it drove down Dexter Avenue, the bus quickly filled until the aisle was crowded with standing riders, mostly Black, some white.

A white woman stood in the aisle where the students were sitting. The driver then looked in the rearview mirror and said, "I need those seats." This is what drivers would typically say when they saw a white person standing and the first ten seats already filled.[56] As Colvin relates:

> The other three girls in my row got up and moved back, but I didn't. I just couldn't.
>
> Rebellion was on my mind that day. All during February we'd been talking about people who had taken stands. We had been studying the Constitution in Mrs. Nesbitt's class. I knew I had rights. . . . I knew the rule—that you didn't have to get up for a white person if there were no empty seats left on the bus—and there weren't. . . . I hadn't planned it, but my decision was built on a lifetime of nasty experiences. . . . The motorman yelled again, louder, "Why are you still sittin' there?" I didn't get up, and I didn't answer him. It got real quiet on the bus. A white rider yelled from the front, "You got to get up!" A girl named Margaret Johnson answered from the back, "She ain't got to do nothin' but stay black and die."[57]

Colvin knew her city law, at least the relevant clause. The Montgomery City Code clearly stated: "It shall be unlawful for any passenger to refuse or fail to take a seat among those assigned to the race to which he belongs, at the request of any such employee in charge, *if there is such a seat vacant*."[58] She later characterized her refusal to get up by referencing the Black history she had been studying in school just the week before: "It felt like Sojourner Truth

Sec. 10. Separation of races—Required.

Every person operating a bus line in the city shall provide equal but separate accommodations for white people and negroes on his buses, by requiring the employees in charge thereof to assign passengers seats on the vehicles under their charge in such manner as to separate the white people from the negroes, where there are both white and negroes on the same car; provided, however, that negro nurses having in charge white children or sick or infirm white persons, may be assigned seats among white people.

Nothing in this section shall be construed as prohibiting the operators of such bus lines from separating the races by means of separate vehicles if they see fit. (Code 1938, §§ 603, 606.)

Sec. 11. Same—Powers of persons in charge of vehicle; passengers to obey directions.

Any employee in charge of a bus operated in the city shall have the powers of a police officer of the city while in actual charge of any bus, for the purpose of carrying out the provisions of the preceding section, and it shall be unlawful for any passenger to refuse or fail to take a seat among those assigned to the race to which he belongs, at the request of any such employee in charge, if there is such a seat vacant. (Code 1938, § 604.)

Sec. 12. Failure to carry passengers.

It shall be unlawful for any person operating a bus line in the city to refuse, without sufficient excuse, to carry any passenger; provided, that no driver of a bus shall be required to carry any passenger who is intoxicated or disorderly, or who is afflicted with any contagious or infectious disease, or who refuses to pay in advance the fare required, or who for any other reason deemed satisfactory by the recorder should be excluded. (Code 1938, § 699.)

Sec. 13. Smoking.

It shall be unlawful for any person to smoke a cigar, pipe or cigarette upon any bus in the city; provided, however, that

A portion of the Montgomery City Code governing seating on city buses. Alabama Department of Archives and History.

was on one side pushing me down, and Harriet Tubman was on the other side of me pushing me down. I couldn't get up."[59]

The driver drove on to Court Square, the main transfer station downtown, where he called for a transit policeman to arrest Colvin. As this was happening, several people at the bus stop, not aware of the situation on board, entered the bus at the rear. A pregnant woman, Mrs. Hamilton, sat down next to Colvin. The transit policeman told both women to get up. After first refusing, Mrs. Hamilton reluctantly moved when two Black men offered her their seats in the rear and left the bus altogether. Then, for all his bluster, the transit policeman told the driver that he did not have the authority to arrest anyone.

Once again, the bus drove on. At the next block the driver saw a police car and stopped, and two policemen entered the bus. Colvin began to cry but still refused to move. The police literally dragged her off the bus as she repeatedly cried, "It's my constitutional right to sit here as much as that lady. I paid my fare, it's my constitutional right." In the squad car, Colvin, fearful of being raped, was handcuffed, cursed, ridiculed, and repeatedly insulted on the way to the police station. She was booked and fingerprinted and then driven to the city jail, where she was eventually released on bail by her pastor and her mother.[60]

As terrifying as that ordeal had been, with a court hearing only two weeks away, Colvin was proud of herself. She was especially heartened by the words of her pastor, Rev. H. H. Johnson, as he drove her home: "Claudette," he said, "I'm so proud of you. Everyone prays for freedom. We've all been praying and praying. But you're different—you want your answer the next morning. And I think you just brought the revolution to Montgomery."[61] And Reverend Johnson was right.

Word of Colvin's arrest flashed across the Black community of Montgomery. As Jo Ann Robinson wrote, "Thus a period of unrest began that permeated the thoughts of blacks." E. D. Nixon, president of the Montgomery chapter of the NAACP, asked Fred D. Gray, one of only two Black lawyers in the city, just one year out of law school, to represent Colvin. A Citizen's Coordinating Committee was formed, made up of two members from each of the more than sixty Black organizations in the city. The committee circulated a leaflet demanding that Colvin be acquitted and the driver charged. The question was raised of boycotting the buses, and some people did stop riding, but, following a meeting with the city commission in which the Black leaders were assured that "justice would be extended in this case and that Claudette would be given every fair chance to clear her name," no organized boycott was initiated.[62]

Colvin had been arrested under a city ordinance that stipulated no passenger was required to move if there was no suitable alternative vacant seat. However, she was tried according to state segregation law, which contained no such provision. State law simply stipulated that drivers had the right and authority to assign seats to passengers. Colvin was charged with breaking the segregation law, disturbing the peace, and assaulting a police officer. The charge of assault was based on the fact that one of the policemen had been scratched by Colvin, though she claimed, "I might have scratched one of them because I had long nails, but I sure didn't fight back." At her hearing in juvenile court on March 18, in the face of conflicting testimony offered by white passengers on the one hand and Black students who had been on the bus on the other, Judge Wiley Hill Jr. found Colvin guilty of all charges, placed her on indefinite probation, declared her a ward of the state, and released her to the custody of her parents.

Nixon and Gray had hopes of making the Colvin case a challenge to segregation, though some argued that Colvin was too young and perhaps too temperamental to be subjected to all that would entail. Nevertheless, Fred Gray appeared in Montgomery Circuit Court on May 6 to appeal Colvin's conviction. Judge Eugene Carter, however, cleverly brought to an end Gray's hope to make this a test case. Carter dismissed the segregation charge against Colvin, thereby eliminating the basis for appealing it. He also dismissed the charge of disorderly conduct. Given that Colvin was then no longer guilty of disorderly conduct, the fact that Carter upheld the charge of assault beggars credulity. He sentenced Colvin to a small fine, which Taylor Branch characterizes as "a sentence so much lighter than anticipated that it ruined her martyr status."[63] And it left Colvin with a criminal record that would spoil her dreams.

Colvin became pregnant during that summer, and she was expelled from school when she began to "show." Nixon and Gray knew that Colvin would not draw the sympathies of a southern court as the principal figure in a civil rights lawsuit. They had been looking for other suitable candidates, and several possible cases came up in the course of the year. However, Colvin's contribution to the cause of civil rights was not over. In February 1956 she agreed to testify as one of the plaintiffs in Fred Gray's landmark lawsuit *Browder v. Gayle*. In his memoir, Gray addresses the inclusion of Colvin's case in the suit: "Many persons had said that Claudette Colvin was not a good test case to integrate the bus lines, but they were wrong. I intentionally added Claudette Colvin as a party plaintiff because her case was a good 'test case'; ultimately her case, in fact, desegregated the buses in Montgomery." He also notes, "I believe that Claudette's act gave Mrs. Parks the moral courage to do what she later did."[64] Indeed, Gray puts Colvin's act of defiance into a far broader context, concluding,

> If Claudette Colvin had not done what she did on March 2, 1955, Mrs. Parks may never ha[ve] done what she did on December 1, 1955. If Mrs. Parks had given up her seat on December 1, 1955, she would never have been arrested; there would never have been a trial on December 5, 1955; no beginning of the Montgomery Bus Boycott; no mass meeting at Holt Street Baptist Church and Dr. Martin Luther King Jr. would not have been introduced to the nation on December 5, 1955. The whole history of the civil rights movement may have been different but for Claudette.[65]

Colvin passed her GED exam in 1957 and briefly attended Alabama State College. She took several jobs but was as often let go when her employers learned who she was. Unable to find suitable work, she spent several periods of time with her older sister Velma Colvin in New York City beginning in 1958, and she moved there permanently in 1968. She worked for thirty-six years in a Manhattan nursing home, continuing her social activism as a proud member of 1199 SEIU United Healthcare Workers East.[66] She retired in 2004, and on December 17, 2021, Claudette Colvin's criminal record was finally expunged by juvenile court judge Calvin L. Williams, in Montgomery, sixty-six years, ten months, and two weeks after she had been wrongfully arrested.[67] In 2023 Claudette Colvin and her family established the Claudette Colvin Foundation "to inspire and recognize youth and young adults for their service in significantly improving life in communities across America."[68]

Aurelia Browder, April 29, 1955

Aurelia Browder was a long-time resident of Montgomery, a graduate of Alabama State College, a member of the Women's Political Council led by Jo Ann Robinson, and the mother of six children. She supported her family by working, like Rosa Parks, as a seamstress. She is described by Robinson as a "tall, heavy-set" widow, "a good mother and citizen, well-read, highly intelligent, fearless."[69] Browder regularly rode the bus two or three times a day. On April 29, 1955, just two months after the arrest of Claudette Colvin, a driver told Browder and two other Black women to stand to vacate the entire row of seats so a white man and woman could sit.[70] Browder refused to move and was arrested and fined. In spite of this incident, with the necessity of both working and taking care of a large family, she continued to ride the bus until December 5, the first day of the bus boycott. She then became a member of the Montgomery Improvement Association and was active in the boycott. Of the four cases combined in the anti-segregation lawsuit filed in U.S. district court on February 2, 1956, by Fred Gray, Aurelia Browder's name came first alphabetically. Thus, she became the lead plaintiff in *Browder v. Gayle*.

Phillip Hoose relates an incident that illustrates both the pressures applied to frighten Black women who "stepped out of line" and the aptness of Robinson's description of Browder as "fearless." During the week following the Supreme Court ruling that ended legal segregation on the buses, there were several violent attacks against Black girls and women in Montgomery. Hoose writes, "Aurelia Browder's daughter Manervia ran to answer the phone ringing late in the night. 'Your house is gonna be blowed sky high!' a voice said. She became hysterical. Her mother grabbed the phone and told the caller, 'Blow it up. I need a new house anyway!' and slammed the phone down."[71] As a decision on *Browder v. Gayle* was pending, Browder made her car available during the boycott, and she was active in voter registration and opposition to the Alabama poll tax.

Mary Louise Smith, October 15, 1955

After graduating from the St. Jude Educational Institute in Montgomery, Alabama, in 1955, eighteen-year-old Mary Louise Smith took domestic jobs working for white families. On Friday morning, October 21, she took a bus across town to collect twelve dollars that was owed to her, but the family was not home. Disappointed and annoyed, Smith got back on a bus to return. When a white woman appeared standing over her and ordering her to give up her seat, Smith sat still. Then the bus driver told her to move, once and yet again. Each time she refused. The driver called for the police, and Smith was arrested and jailed until her father arrived a couple of hours later to pay the fine.[72]

This might have been the test case that Fred Gray was looking for to challenge the Montgomery segregated seating ordinance. Doubts were raised, however, partly, as with Claudette Colvin, on account of Smith's age, but also because her father had paid the fine without demur. E. D. Nixon discouraged Gray from taking on the case on the basis of a rumor, later denied by Smith, that her father was an alcoholic and that they lived in a house characterized by Nixon as a "low type." They actually lived in a two-story, three-bedroom house in a working-class neighborhood.[73]

Shortly after the conviction of Rosa Parks on December 5, Gray began to take a broader, more proactive approach to the bus issue. He would file a lawsuit in federal district court challenging the constitutionality of the Montgomery law, thus bypassing the inevitable long delays inherent in shepherding a case through multiple appeals in the city and state courts. Mary Louise Smith was one of four women to have her case included in *Browder v. Gayle*, which ultimately brought a legal end to bus segregation, even though the actual implementation took some time longer.

Susie McDonald, October 21, 1955

Susie McDonald, a lifelong resident of Montgomery, was a seventy-seven-year-old widow in 1955. Jo Ann Robinson writes, "Mrs. McDonald . . . was a very fair black lady. Her blue eyes, very white skin, very straight, light tan hair often misled people to believe that she was white. It angered her to be mistaken in that sense, and she spoke out on her own behalf, explaining that she was a 'member of the darker race.' When a driver cautioned her not to sit in areas on the bus reserved for blacks, she enjoyed getting him straightened out. Then she would laugh at him, while he fumed over his mistake."[74]

On October 21, just six days after the arrest of Mary Louise Smith, McDonald was arrested for refusing to give up her seat. After the conviction of Rosa Parks, Fred Gray asked if McDonald would agree to be one of the plaintiffs in *Browder v. Gayle*, and she readily agreed.

Rosa Parks and the Montgomery Bus Boycott, December 1, 1955

Rosa Louise McCauley was born in 1913 and spent most of her childhood with her mother and her grandparents on a small farm in Pine Level, Alabama. When she was eleven years old she entered the Montgomery Industrial School, popularly known as "Miss White's School," founded and run by Alice L. White, from Framingham, Massachusetts, and Margaret Beard, from Chicago. The school was staffed wholly by white women from the North who wanted to provide Black girls in Montgomery with practical skills and a better education than they would otherwise receive. Most importantly, however, they taught the girls to negotiate the complexities of life in the segregated South with dignity, self-respect, and a sense of their own self-worth.[75]

Rosa attended high school at the laboratory school of State Teachers College (now Alabama State University), for at the time there was no public high school for Black students in Montgomery. However, she had to leave school when she was sixteen to take care of her ill grandmother and then her mother. She worked occasionally cleaning white homes, and for a while she had a job in a shirt factory. When she was twenty, she married Raymond Parks, a barber. He was a member of the NAACP and worked to raise money to defend the "Scottsboro Boys," nine Black boys and young men, ages twelve to nineteen, who had been falsely charged with raping two white women on a freight train in 1931. Parks encouraged Rosa to finish her high school education, which she did in 1934. In the 1940s she too joined the NAACP and became both secretary and youth director of the Montgomery chapter, helping people in their frequently thwarted efforts to register to vote. In 1944, following the gang rape of Recy Taylor in Abbeville, Alabama, Parks, E. D. Nixon, and others formed the Committee for Equal Justice for the Rights of Mrs. Recy Taylor. The support and publicity garnered by the committee nationwide pressured the Alabama governor to convene a special grand jury. Though the rapists were never indicted, the committee continued its work on behalf of other women, and the experience its members gained was to prove valuable during the later Montgomery bus boycott.[76] In 1949 Parks organized members of the NAACP youth group to mount a protest against segregation in the Montgomery Public Library system.

December 1, 1955, was not the first time Mrs. Parks was mistreated by a Montgomery bus driver. In November 1943 she had decided go into the city to make her second attempt at registering to vote. She got on the bus and paid her fare. She started down the aisle past the empty seats reserved for white passengers to find a place to stand, because all the seats in the designated "colored" section were taken and many people were already standing in the aisle. The bus driver, James F. Blake, told her, as drivers often told African American riders, to get off the bus and get on again through the rear door. Mrs. Parks objected that to do so would be both unnecessary and difficult, because people were already crowded into the stepwell at the rear door. Blake insisted and tugged at her sleeve, telling her to "Get off my bus!" Parks dropped her purse, and as she bent over to pick it up, she sat briefly on one of the empty "white" seats. This subtly defiant act, which surely angered Blake even further, also reveals something of the determination and strength of character that sustained her in later years. Though she got off the bus that day, she did not get back on. She waited for the next bus and promised herself that never again would she ride on a bus with that driver.[77]

Twelve years later, Mrs. Parks boarded the Cleveland Avenue bus, as she did most days after work. She was a skilled seamstress and was on her way home from her job in the alterations department in the basement of the Montgomery Fair department store. As she boarded the bus that evening she may have been thinking about the Christmas shopping she had just done at the drug store or about seeing her husband after his day's work as a barber at the Maxwell Air Force Base, or she may very well have been preoccupied with the arrangements for an NAACP workshop that weekend and the upcoming NAACP election. Whatever was on her mind, she did not take notice of the driver. Had she looked up to see James Blake, she might not have stepped onto that bus at all.[78]

Montgomery City Line buses had seats for thirty-six passengers, with the ten seats at the front of the bus reserved for white people. African Americans could not sit there, even if all the rear seats were full and there were no whites on the bus at all. As a contemptuous gesture toward the pretense of equal treatment, the ten seats furthest back were unofficially "reserved" for Black riders. The seats in between were segregated, and enforcement was often according to the whim and mood of the driver. When she got on the bus and paid her fare, Mrs. Parks took a seat in the row right behind the front ten seats. It was quitting time, and the bus was quickly filling up with people on their way home. When the first ten seats were filled with white riders, Blake told the four people sitting in the next row to move back so that a white passenger boarding the bus could sit there. No Black person could be seated in the same row as a white person, not even across the aisle. There were no empty seats in the back either, but three of the passengers stood up and moved farther back. Rosa Parks, however, decided that the time had come to refuse, politely but firmly—a decision that must have become even more determined when she recognized James Blake. She may not have planned to be arrested that day, but she knew exactly what to do and how to respond.[79]

Blake asked Mrs. Parks, "Are you going to stand up?" "No," she answered. "Well," he said, "I am going to have you arrested." She replied quietly, "You may do that." Blake called his supervisor, and city police officers F. B. Day and D. W. Mixon soon arrived and arrested Mrs. Parks under Chapter 6, Section 11, of the Montgomery City Code. According to the officers' arrest report, they charged her with "refusing to obey order of bus driver."[80] She was taken to city hall, booked, and transferred to the city jail.

Throughout 1955 Black leaders in Montgomery had been preparing to challenge the bus segregation laws, and a bus boycott was one of the tactics being considered. Rosa Parks had become friends with Fred Gray, and they would often meet during their lunch hour to discuss the racial situation in Montgomery and in general. Claudette Colvin had been arrested in March, but Gray and the NAACP leaders were uncertain about putting such a young person at the center of their efforts. They wanted to make sure when they brought a test case to court that it was based on someone whose character and background were exemplary, someone whom prosecutors, courts, judges, the press, and the public could find no other cause to dislike or disparage. Rosa Parks was just right—she was married, she had a job, she was well educated, she was pleasant and respectful, and she had never been in trouble. As L. D. Reddick described her, Rosa Parks was "attractive and quiet, a churchgoer

Rosa Parks (*right*) with Septima Clark at the Highlander Folk School, summer 1955. Photo: Ida Berman. Courtesy of the Rosa and Raymond Parks Institute.

who looks like the symbol of Mother's Day." Most importantly she was determined to insist on her civil rights and those of others. During the previous summer, Mrs. Parks had accepted a scholarship to attend a two-week workshop on activism, voter registration, and school desegregation directed by Septima Clark at the interracial Highlander Folk School in Tennessee. Her experience and training there not only increased her resolve, it undoubtedly helped her to remain calm, composed, and confident when she was confronted by James Blake.[81]

Montgomery city law gave bus drivers the powers of a city police officer while in charge of a bus, and they were armed with pistols. When Mrs. Parks refused to obey Blake's order to move, tensions on the bus increased. Consistent with her character and Highlander training, Mrs. Parks remained outwardly calm, even though she knew that she was exposing herself to considerable uncertainty and danger, not only on the bus but at the hands of the police as well. She was arrested, charged, booked, and jailed. And there was no guarantee of safety for a Black woman challenging white authority. She was bailed out that evening and taken from the jail by her friends E. D. Nixon, with whom she had worked when he was president of the Montgomery NAACP, and Clifford Durr, a white lawyer, and his wife Virginia, who were friends of both Rosa and Raymond Parks.

Mrs. Parks was arrested on a Thursday evening, and her trial was set for the following Monday. Thursday night Jo Ann Robinson, who had herself been terrorized on a Montgomery bus in 1949, went into action. With the help of another Alabama State College faculty member, two students, and the college mimeograph machines, she worked through the night, using thirty-five reams of paper, at five hundred sheets per ream and three notices per sheet, to produce 52,500 copies of a notice she had written:

> Another Negro woman has been arrested and thrown in jail because she refused to get up out of her seat on the bus for a white person to sit down. It is the second time since the Claudette Colvin case that a Negro woman has been arrested for the same thing. This has to be stopped. Negroes have rights, too, for if Negroes did not ride the buses, they could not operate. Three-fourths of the riders are Negroes, yet we are arrested, or have to stand over empty seats. If we do not do something to stop these arrests, they will continue. The next time it may be you, or your daughter, or mother. This woman's case will come up on Monday. We are, therefore, asking every Negro to stay off the buses Monday in protest of the arrest and trial. Don't ride the buses to work, to town, to school, or anywhere on Monday. You can afford to stay out of school for one day if you have no other way to go except by bus. You can also afford to stay out of town for one day. If you work, take a cab, or walk. But please, children and grown-ups, don't ride the bus at all on Monday. Please stay off of all buses Monday.[82]

They began distributing the anonymous notice on Friday morning, doing so very quietly so that very few people would know where they came from. The word spread rapidly, helped by the fact that E. D. Nixon leaked the boycott plan to Joe Azbell, the city editor of the *Montgomery Advertiser*, which printed the notice on the front page. As a result, even more African Americans learned about the plan. And during Sunday church services, Black ministers told their congregations about both the arrest and the protest.[83]

When her case came up in court the following Monday, Mrs. Parks was found guilty of disorderly conduct and was fined ten dollars, plus four dollars for court costs. Her lawyers, Fred Gray and Charles D. Langford, appealed the court's decision. The daylong bus protest, however, was so successful that many people were inspired and saw the possibility that it might be a way to get the city to change the law. An impromptu mass meeting was held that evening at the Holt Street Baptist Church, presided over by the Rev. Ralph Abernathy, and between five thousand and six thousand people showed up. The participants formed the Montgomery Improvement Association (MIA) to coordinate the logistics of an ongoing boycott of the buses. A twenty-six-

Rosa Parks (*left*), E. D. Nixon (*center*), and Fred Gray, as Nixon and Gray sign the appeal bond after Parks's conviction, December 5, 1955. Courtesy of the Rosa and Raymond Parks Institute.

year-old minister who had been called to the Dexter Avenue Baptist Church just the previous year was chosen as president—Dr. Martin Luther King Jr.

That Monday, Montgomery's African American community agreed to continue the boycott. One of the first things King and the MIA leaders did was call the Rev. T. J. Jemison in Baton Rouge, Louisiana, to ask his advice about how to organize alternative transportation for people, based on his experience in the Baton Rouge boycott in June 1953, following the arrest of Martha White. The Black citizens of Montgomery pooled their small resources and combined their collective energy and determination into a powerful force for change. Those who had cars gave rides to those who did not, so they could get to work or school. Many others donated money to pay for gas for these drivers. Soon there were over three hundred cars driving people on regular routes with designated pickup and transfer stations, an impressive feat of logistics. During the hours when people would be going to and from work, many Black taxi drivers only charged ten cents per person, the same as a bus fare. When city officials learned of this, however, they ordered a fine to be imposed on any cab driver charging less than forty-five cents. People who could not find a ride walked, often for long distances, rather than get on a bus. As the boycott continued and news of it spread throughout the country, donations of money and even of shoes came pouring in. A number of churches purchased or were given station wagons, old and new, in which people could ride for free.[84]

The boycott was fiercely opposed by the city and by many in the white community. Rosa Parks lost her job at the Montgomery Fair department store. Many African Americans were threatened with violence, and some were attacked. On January 30 a bomb was set off on Dr. King's porch. His wife, his baby daughter, and a friend were in the house at the time, but fortunately they were not hurt. In spite of these attempts at intimidation, the boycott persisted. Much of the support and a great deal of the sustained enthusiasm for the protest over long months came from the Black women of Montgomery. Because three-quarters of the riders of the Montgomery city buses had been Black, the bus company was losing money every day, and it began losing sympathetic white riders as well, especially after the fare was raised from ten cents to fifteen to make up for some of the loss.

Rosa Parks's conviction for disorderly conduct was appealed, though an appeal would undoubtedly take a very long time to work its way through the Alabama court system, even if it were not perpetually delayed. Or it might be overturned without the segregation question even being addressed. In January 1956 E. D. Nixon reminded Dr. King and Ralph Abernathy how the 1944 case of Viola White had been effectively blocked.[85] Fred Gray and Charles Langford, therefore, took another tack. On February 1, 1956, they filed a civil rights lawsuit directly with the U.S. Circuit Court on behalf of Aurelia Browder, Claudette Colvin, Susie McDonald, Jeanetta Reese, and Mary Louise Smith. Rosa Parks was initially included in the suit but then withdrawn. Parks's case was still under appeal, and Gray did not want the court to think they were trying to avoid preemptively any other charges that might be brought against her.

The defendants included Mayor W. A. Gayle, members of the Montgomery Board of Commissioners, the chief of police, the Montgomery City Lines bus company, bus drivers James F. Blake and Robert Cleere, and members of the Alabama Public Service Commission. Because it was a civil rights case and not a local disorderly conduct case, *Browder v. Gayle* went directly to a U.S. district court. That evening a bomb was thrown at the house of E. D. Nixon.[86] The next day Jeanetta Reese withdrew her name from the case. She and her husband, who was ill, had both received threats. When Bayard Rustin visited her in her home and to ask why she had withdrawn, she replied, "I had to do what I did or I wouldn't be alive today."[87]

On February 21, 1956, a Montgomery grand jury, citing a 1921 Alabama statute that made boycotts illegal, indicted 115 leaders of and participants in the boycott. This move, which the editor of the *Montgomery Advertiser* called "the dumbest act that has ever been done in Montgomery," backfired spectacularly.[88] Dr. King was in Atlanta at the time, and Bayard Rustin, who had been brought in to advise and teach nonviolence as a tactic, shrewdly suggested that, rather than wait to be arrested, E. D. Nixon should simply turn himself in. So Nixon walked into the sheriff's office and said to the dumbfounded officers on duty, "Are you looking for me? Well, here I am." Soon many of the eighty-nine who were arrested that day had done the same, and the mood among the crowd of African Americans who gathered outside the courthouse that day was joyous. Dr. King returned the following day and turned himself in too. Arrest had become a public badge of honor, rather than a lifelong stigma. Ralph Abernathy described his own arrest as one of the best things that ever happened to him. Equally important, however, was the fact that this stunning reversal of expectations attracted reporters from all over the country. The ensuing wave of publicity led to much greater nationwide support and much-needed funding for continuing the boycott.[89]

Among those arrested was Rosa Parks, for the second time in less than three months. She was photographed and fingerprinted, but of the eighty-nine who were arrested that day, only Dr. King was brought to trial on March 19. He was found guilty and sentenced to pay $500 or else serve 386 days at hard labor in prison. The case was appealed, but in November 1957 the state court upheld the verdict and the fine was paid. In the meantime, the trial had raised King's stature among Montgomery's Black community even further. He was recognized unequivocally as the leading voice of the movement both locally and in the national press, and the boycott pressed on.[90]

On June 5, 1956, the three-judge U.S. district court hearing the *Browder v. Gayle* case ruled two-to-one that segregation in public transportation was unconstitutional. As expected, the defendants did not accept that ruling, and the city bus segregation rules remained in place as their appeal moved the case up to the Supreme Court. The Black citizens of Montgomery continued to walk in even greater numbers, for the city had declared the MIA car pool, with its fleet of cars and station wagons, to be an illegal public transportation business. It took six months for the Supreme Court to uphold the district court's ruling, and finally, on December 20, the Montgomery City Lines bus company was ordered to desegregate all its buses.[91]

The boycott ended joyfully, but many white citizens of Montgomery were far from happy. A shotgun was fired into Dr. King's home on December 23, and on Christmas Eve a fifteen-year-old Black girl standing at a bus stop was beaten by five white men. In the coming days, shots were fired into several integrated buses, in one case sending a pregnant woman to the hospital. On January 10, 1957, Ralph Abernathy's First Baptist Church and his home were both bombed, as were three other churches and—for the second time in four months—the home of the Rev. Robert Graetz, the white minister of Trinity Lutheran Church whose congregation was largely Black. A couple of weeks later, Dr. King, asleep at his house, was woken by something. His wife and daughter were away, but he decided to wake Bob Williams, who was also sleeping there as a guard, and they went to Williams's house. Before dawn a bomb went off near the parsonage, and when someone went there to check on King, twelve sticks of dynamite were discovered on the porch, though the fuse had fizzled out.[92] The ruling of the U.S. Supreme Court in *Browder v. Gayle* notwithstanding, the struggle for equality on the buses was not over.

Later that year, in order to escape the harassment and constant death threats that they continued to receive, Rosa Parks, her husband, and her mother moved to Detroit. She worked for some time there as a seamstress, and in 1965 she took a position as a special assistant to U.S. congressman John Conyers. Together with Coretta Scott King, she later worked to get Dr. King's birthday declared a national holiday, which was signed into federal law in 1983.

Rosa Parks died in Detroit on October 24, 2005. Her casket was flown to Montgomery, where a memorial service was held at St. Paul's African Methodist Episcopal Church, of which she had long been a member. On October 30–31, she lay in honor in the rotunda of the U.S. Capitol in Washington, D.C., the first American private citizen, the first woman, and only the second African American to be so honored.[93]

For her role in the struggle to gain equal rights and treatment for all Americans, Rosa Parks was awarded the prestigious NAACP Spingarn Award in 1977, the Presidential Medal of Freedom in 1996, and the Congressional Gold Medal in 1999. In February 2013 a life-size statue of her was unveiled in the National Statuary Hall at the U.S. Capitol. But more significant than the recognition that such high honors can bring, she is remembered now by millions as "the Mother of the American Civil Rights Movement."

CHAPTER 7

Boycotts and Freedom Rides

After *Browder v. Gayle* was filed in district court on February 1, 1956, tensions increased not only in Montgomery but also throughout the South, as the rest of the nation kept a wary watch. Would other cities integrate their buses, or would they cling to their local laws and company rules? As we saw in the case of Irene Morgan, changes in the law, even when declared by the Supreme Court, were not always readily accepted and obeyed. Just ten days before a U.S. district court issued its ruling on *Browder* in June 1956, two college students were arrested in Tallahassee, Florida, resulting in a boycott there as well. Would the Supreme Court decision in December settle the matter at last? It did not, and soon the nation was again witnessing the horrors of racist violence against a new generation of protesters—young, idealistic, dedicated, and as brave as any before them.

Wilhelmina Jakes, Carrie Patterson, and the Tallahassee Bus Boycott, May 26, 1956

In the mid-1950s Tallahassee, the capital of Florida, was only about one-seventh the size it has reached today. It was a quiet city of about thirty thousand, supported economically in large part by three institutions: the state government, Florida State University (FSU), at the time restricted to white students, and Florida Agricultural and Mechanical University (FAMU), with only African American students. Slightly more than a third of the city's population was African American, most of whom lived in two areas. White residential areas were spread out, stretching into the suburban hills. African Americans who worked in white homes as domestic servants, therefore, relied heavily on bus transportation. The bus company also depended on them: about 70 percent of the bus passengers were Black.[1]

After the 1954 Supreme Court ruling in *Brown v. Board of Education* declared segregation in public schools to be illegal, Tallahassee remained relatively calm. In their 1958 study of the Tallahassee bus boycott, local sociologists Charles U. Smith (FAMU) and Lewis M. Killian (FSU) stated, "Tallahassee has had no significant interracial conflict or 'incidents' for many years. . . . It can be said, then, that on the surface race relations in Tallahassee have been characterized by a peaceful accommodation with little evidence of racial tension. Viewed through the glass wall of segregation, Negroes in Tallahassee appeared contented and relatively well-off in the eyes of the whites."[2] But, especially as the troubled integration of the nation's schools and the bus boycott in Montgomery continued to draw attention nationwide, tension and discontent were not far below the surface among both Black and white Tallahasseeans.

On Saturday afternoon, May 26, 1956, Wilhelmina Jakes, twenty-six, from West Palm Beach, and Carrie Patterson, twenty, from Lakeland, both students at Florida A&M, got on a city bus and paid the ten-cent fare. There were only two empty seats, on the long three-person bench at the front of the bus, so they sat down there next to a white woman, who did not object. The bus driver, however, did object, and he told them to move to the back of the bus, where there was only standing room. Jakes and Patterson said they would prefer to simply get off the bus if the driver would return their money. He refused and they, in turn, decided not to move. The driver drove to a nearby filling station and called the police. The two women were taken to the police station, charged with "placing themselves in a position to cause a riot," and released on $25 bond.[3] (The charges against them were later dropped, and their case was handed over to the university.)

The following evening a cross was burned on the front lawn of the house where Jakes and Patterson lived. Out of fear they moved to a campus dormitory. At noon on Monday, May 28, FAMU students held a well-attended meeting on campus and voted to stop riding the buses for the remaining two weeks of the term. City officials were certainly watching closely and nervously, for when the first bus rode through campus at 2:00 p.m. it had a police escort. The headline of the *Tallahassee Democrat* that evening announced "FAMU Students Start Boycott of City Buses," with the subhead "Action Follows Cross Burning." The following day the police and the manager of Cities Transit, Inc., downplayed the boycott threat, as did the *Democrat*, whose front-page headline declared, "City Bus Boycott Scene Very Calm; No Disorder," with the subhead "One Sign Is Only Evidence." This was accompanied by a photograph of an abandoned, hand-painted sign reading "We'll Walk / Fight Segregation," printed undoubtedly to dismiss the event as inconsequential.

An editorial in that same edition conveys a picture of white attitudes at the time in its attempt to trivialize the event, saying that the incident "appears to have been a matter of little things and misunderstandings at the beginning." It blames Jakes and Patterson (though not by name) for a "misunderstanding of what the United States Supreme Court ruled was their right in intrastate bus seating." Most revealing, however, is the editor's facile dismissal of the cross burning: "The burning of the cross in front of the students' home naturally was something that would inflame the fears of members of their race, but it was such a crude little thing that it could have been no more than a prank or a one-man demonstration of no significance."[4]

While city authorities were warily hoping the issue would fade away, perhaps when the students left campus after their exams, the city's Black leaders were also paying close attention. About seventy-five people met at Bethel AME Church for the regular Tuesday afternoon meeting of Black pastors in the Tallahassee Interdenominational Ministerial Alliance. Some of the lay attendees invited were representatives of African American civic organizations, and some, significantly, were members of the FAMU student government. The boycott was the top agenda item. At this meeting it was decided to call a citywide gathering of Black Tallahasseeans that evening to determine whether they were interested in pursuing a boycott.

In spite of the short notice, an overflow crowd showed up at Bethel Baptist Church that evening and voted unanimously in favor of a boycott. They organized the Inter-Civic Council (ICC), led by Rev. C. K. Steele. The council "pledged itself to non-violent and legal resistance to segregation on the buses and outlined three objectives, namely: the seating of passengers on a 'first come, first served basis'; the employment of Negro bus drivers; and more courteous treatment of Negro passengers on the buses." Following the examples of the Baton Rouge and Montgomery boycotts, they also developed a car pool plan for transporting workers who lived far from their places of employment.[5]

The Tallahassee City Commission and the bus company initially responded informally by saying that they did not know what was meant by seating on a "first come, first served" basis. They met with some of the city's more conservative Black leaders, hoping to reach a compromise. On Saturday, June 2, the commission gave its response to the ICC's three-point plan. The headline above the masthead in the Sunday morning *Democrat* confidently declared, "City Commission Moves to End Bus Boycott." The commission assured people that "it would oppose permitting members of the two races to occupy the same seat, but that no member of either race should be required to relinquish a seat to a member of the other race." They also stated that they expected the bus company to require its drivers "to treat all passengers courteously" and that the company was "willing to take and consider applications from Negroes for vacancies in jobs as drivers on buses serving Negroes predominantly." Unwittingly reflecting an inability to understand the underlying causes and extent of the discontent that led to the boycott, the city commissioners concluded by expressing their hope to restore "the harmonious and cooperative spirit between white and Negro citizens which has made this a progressive, happy community."[6]

The city granted the bus company permission to discontinue the buses running through the FAMU campus (which, in any case, no one was riding), they reduced the city tax on the bus franchise from 3 percent to 0.5 percent, and they approved a rate hike to fifteen cents. By the last half of June, the city realized that in order to reach any resolution they would need to negotiate with the Inter-Civic Council. The city commission was intransigent, however, on the matter of segregated seating and insisted on reserving at least one row of seats for white passengers. The ICC, for its part, remained stalwart in demanding complete desegregation, and Black citizens stayed off the buses. The commission then broke off negotiations, complaining, "All they want is integration."[7]

Without most of its riders, Cities Transit, of course, was losing money every day, and at midnight on June 30 all bus service in the city was suspended. The Tallahassee Chamber of Commerce mounted a "Ride the Bus" campaign and promised to provide financial support to the bus company, as well as an increase in riders. Bus service resumed on August 2. The company also hired some Black drivers, especially for the route through FAMU. During July, the police began to harass car pool drivers and take them in for questioning, as the city commission considered passing an ordinance making car pools illegal. Such a law became unnecessary, however, when the state attorney general affirmed that cars in the car pool fell under the state requirement to have "hire car" license plates.

In late August, eleven drivers, including C. K. Steele and two other members of the ICC board, were charged with driving passengers without a hire car permit. A trial was postponed until October, at which time the charges against the eleven were abandoned. Instead, all twenty-one members of the ICC board were arrested on a charge of operating a transportation system without a licensed franchise. After a four-day bench trial (i.e., with no jury), they were convicted, and each was given a sixty-day suspended sentence and a $500 fine. The car pool was immediately discontinued, but Black citizens remained firm and continued the boycott, walking, riding with friends, and bicycling.[8]

On December 16, 1956, the Supreme Court ruled that segregation on buses in Montgomery, Alabama, was unconstitutional. Steele and the ICC inter-

Clergymen C. K. Steele, H. McNeal Harris, and A. C. Redd (*left to right*) ride in the front of the bus, Tallahassee, December 24, 1956. State Library and Archives of Florida.

preted this to mean that segregated seating was illegal in general. On Sunday, December 23, they announced that the boycott was officially ended, and the following morning Steele and two other ministers on the ICC board rode the bus on previously forbidden seats.[9]

Buses did not run on Christmas day, but the city commission instructed Cities Transit to enforce segregation on the buses. The company responded by saying that they would first seek a court determination as to whether the Montgomery decision applied to Florida. The day after Christmas, claiming it was in the "best interest of peace and harmony," the commission revoked the company franchise, making it illegal for buses to operate. Unsure whether that action was legal without giving prior notice, Cities Transit chose to keep its buses running while it sought advice from the court. Most of its potential Black customers, however, still chose not to ride. On the following day, nine company bus drivers were arrested on a charge of operating a transportation system without a franchise, the same charge that had been leveled against the boycott leaders two months earlier. A group of Black ministers had announced a "demonstration ride" that same day, in which they would ride a bus in a nonsegregated manner. They called off the demonstration, however, when a noisy crowd of about two hundred jeering and threatening white youths surrounded the bus as they were about to board.[10]

On January 1, the *Tallahassee Democrat* included a brief note in a longer article about desegregation efforts around the South: "The Tallahassee White Citizens Council called on Gov. Leroy Collins to seize control of the city bus line under emergency powers granted him by the recent Florida Legislature. The action came after two teams of six Negroes rode integrated on the buses as part of a campaign by Negroes to win the right to occupy seats of their own choosing."

Whatever further role the White Citizens Council might have played, acts of violence against the leaders of the ICC and against Black citizens in general had begun to proliferate. A cross was burned in front of Reverend Steele's house and rocks thrown through his windows. At 4:00 p.m. on New Year's Day, Governor Collins declared a state of emergency in Tallahassee and "ordered the buses to suspend operations to preserve peace and order. . . . Collins criticized what he called 'irresponsible Negro leadership' and 'rabid pro-segregationists' for causing the racial tension."[11]

Even though the buses were not running, the city commissioners unanimously passed a new plan to ensure the continuation of segregation. On January 7 they rescinded the bus segregation ordinance. In its place, all the seats on buses would be reserved, without mention of race, and the driver would assign a numbered seat to each entering passenger. The city also dropped the pending charges against the nine arrested bus drivers.[12] Passengers who refused to obey would be subject to arrest and a $500 fine or sixty days in jail or both. Most Black Tallahasseeans chose to continue their unofficial boycott.

On January 11 the governor lifted his ban on the buses, and service resumed. Incidents of white violence continued. On January 20 three Black and three white students decided to test the new seating system by riding nonsegregated. One FSU student and two FAMU students were arrested for refusing to sit in their assigned seats. While awaiting the final resolution to their case and the appeal to the earlier ICC convictions, Black riders slowly began to appear on the buses but not in large numbers. As enforcement of the new seating regimen gradually grew lax, the Tallahassee buses became increasingly integrated.

In a 1978 interview, C. K. Steele compared the Tallahassee boycott with that of Montgomery: "Our demands were greater than Montgomery, our results were greater than Montgomery. We had 98 percent, we put the bus company off the road, we put black drivers on before they did, and so on. And another thing, I have pictured the Montgomery effort as being the handwriting on the wall for the South, and I've considered Tallahassee as a little Daniel came along and interpreted that handwriting."[13]

Bruce Boynton, December 20, 1958

Bruce Boynton was born and raised in Selma, Alabama. His mother, Amelia Platts Boynton, and his father, Samuel Boynton, were both active in the civil rights effort and worked to help register Black Alabamians to vote. Bruce finished high school at the age of fourteen, and at eighteen he graduated from Fisk University in Nashville, after which he attended Howard University Law School in Washington, D.C.[14]

At 8:00 p.m. on December 20, 1958, Boynton boarded a Trailways bus in Washington on his way home from Howard for Christmas. At 10:40 p.m., when the bus stopped for a forty-minute layover in Richmond, Virginia, Boynton decided to get something to eat. There were two eating facilities in the Richmond bus terminal, which Boynton later described as "a clinically clean White restaurant and an absolutely filthy Black cafe."[15] Boynton took a stool at the counter of the former.

A waitress told him to go to the other restaurant, and Boynton responded that it was crowded. The waitress disappeared, and when she returned she said that she had been told not to serve him. In a 2016 interview Boynton stated, "I was hungry and just wanted a cheeseburger and a cup of hot tea on that cold night. . . . I also pointed out that, as an American citizen, I was entitled to get that burger and tea."[16] The waitress left again and came back with the assistant manager. Boynton showed his interstate ticket as evidence that he had a right to sit and eat there. The assistant manager told him to leave, and a policeman was summoned after he refused.

Boynton later said that he did think of Rosa Parks briefly at the time, but he was more intent on considering what his parents might have done in that situation.[17] The policeman tried to persuade Boynton to go to the other restaurant, and again he refused. Boynton was arrested for trespassing, jailed, convicted, and fined ten dollars. He appealed the verdict to the Virginia Supreme Court, which upheld his conviction. Boynton persisted with a further appeal to the U.S. Supreme Court.

Boynton v. Virginia was argued before the Supreme Court by Thurgood Marshall on October 12, 1960. In his oral argument, Marshall noted, "There's no question all along in this that the whole basis of asking him to move and the whole basis of refusing to serve him in this restaurant was because of his race."[18] In 1946, in the case of Irene Morgan, the Supreme Court had established that segregation was unconstitutional in interstate travel. On December 5, 1960, Justice Hugo Black began the court's opinion in *Boynton* stating, "The basic question presented in this case is whether an interstate bus passenger is denied a federal statutory or constitutional right when a restaurant in a bus terminal used by the carrier along its route discriminates in serving food to the passenger solely because of his color."[19] Citing parallels with the cases of Arthur Mitchell and Elmer Henderson regarding accommodations on trains, the court ruled 7–2 in Boynton's favor, even though the Trailways corporation did not own or operate the restaurant itself:

> Interstate passengers have to eat, and the very terms of the lease of the built-in restaurant space in this terminal constitute a recognition of the essential need of interstate passengers to be able to get food conveniently on their journey and an undertaking by the restaurant to fulfill that need. Such passengers in transit on a paid interstate Trailways journey had a right to expect that this essential transportation food service voluntarily provided for them under such circumstances would be rendered without discrimination prohibited by the Interstate Commerce Act. Under the circumstances of this case, therefore, petitioner had a federal right to remain in the white portion of the restaurant.[20]

The Supreme Court decision was delivered on February 1, 1961. As had happened after the decision in *Morgan v. Virginia*, however, enforcement of the *Boynton* ruling was minimal, to say the least. Two months later, on April 1, that failure of enforcement was brought to the attention of James Farmer, newly reelected as national director of CORE, and Farmer decided to take action with a "Freedom Ride."

On March 5, 1965, Boynton's mother and father took part in the first Selma to Montgomery March. That march was notoriously thwarted on the Edmund Pettus Bridge in Selma, when a number of marchers, including Amelia Boynton and John Lewis, were savagely beaten. Bruce Boynton went on to become a civil rights attorney, practicing in Nashville, Washington, and Selma.

Richard Burdine, Henry Nichols, and the Jackson, Tennessee, Bus Boycott, October 13–15, 1960

As the civil rights movement gained energy and strength in the late 1950s, young people, especially college students, began to take notice and take action. The Tallahassee bus boycott had been sparked by Wilhelmina Jakes and Carrie Patterson in 1956 and launched through the swift collective action of the student body at Florida A&M. The country during much of 1960 was roiled by the many sit-in protests that had begun in February in Greensboro,

North Carolina. In Jackson, Tennessee, in 1960, Richard Burdine, the student planning chairman of the Lane College chapter of the NAACP, had been organizing discussions about racial inequity among students, and as the 1960 fall semester began the chapter was considering staging protests in Jackson. Some faculty members offered training in nonviolent action. The students discovered that, while 80 percent of bus riders were Black, there was no law in Jackson requiring segregated buses: "It was just tradition," one student remarked. On October 13, 1960, four groups of five students each set out to challenge that "tradition." Three students boarded the Hayes Avenue bus, sat in the front, refused to move, and were arrested. Three students boarded the North Royal Street bus, sat in the front, refused to move, and were arrested—charged with disorderly conduct and "threatened breach of peace." Altogether, eight students were arrested that day, including Richard Burdine and Henry Nichols.

The word quickly spread, and some four hundred people, both students and townspeople, spontaneously gathered in the Lane College auditorium. A group of Black businessmen paid the bail for the arrested students. Community members and students agreed to stage a boycott. The following day people walked or carpooled to work, while a group of students picketed the Woolworth's store.[21] On October 15, the manager of Jackson City Lines, Inc., published a letter stating, "The Company's policy in the future on the seating of passengers will be not to show any discrimination between the White and Negroes. It is further agreed no charges will be filed by either party resulting from any previous incidents."[22]

Encouraged by this success, the student activists at Lane planned further protests. On October 27, five of them sat down at the whites-only lunch counter at Woolworth's. The counter was immediately closed, and the students sat quietly reading for almost three hours. A crowd of white youths gathered, insulting the protesters, attacking them with eggs and insecticide, and then dragging them out of the store. A block away, another group of students took seats at the lunch counter in McLellan's store. The manager called the police and had the protesters arrested.

Henry Nichols, president of the Student Movement Association at Lane, and some other students went to the offices of the *Jackson Sun* and paid for a half-page ad which appeared the next day in the Sunday edition. It read, in part,

> We pledge our unqualified support to those students in this nation who have recently been engaged in the significant movement to secure certain long awaited rights and privileges.

> This protest, like that in Atlanta, Georgia, and the bus boycott in Alabama, will shock many people throughout the world. Why? Because they have not quite realized the unanimity of spirit and purpose which motivates the thinking and action of the majority of the Negro People. . . .
>
> We must say, in the face of the existing situations, we intend to do everything in our power that is legal and nonviolent to secure full citizenship rights and to become as every other American, a full citizen with all the ensuing rights, obligations and privileges.[23]

The students continued to protest daily, sitting at the lunch counters and picketing on the street outside. Maintaining their commitment to nonviolence, they ignored as best they could the angry white segregationists "who kicked the students, cursed them, burned them with cigarettes and coffee, spat on them, and pelted them with eggs and tulip bulbs."[24] When the students went home for the winter break, Jackson residents took up the cause and continued the pickets. While many Woolworth stores around the country integrated their lunch counters (or shut them down completely) because of the sit-ins, the Jackson Woolworth's remained segregated until after the Civil Rights Act of 1964 was passed.

John Lewis, CORE Freedom Ride, May 4–17, 1961, and the Civil Rights Act of 1964

John Lewis, born in 1940, was the son of Eddie and Willie Mae Lewis, sharecroppers near Troy, Alabama. His parents were deeply religious, and John grew up with the intention of becoming a preacher. As a boy, he often worked alongside his parents, picking cotton, for which they received $1.40 for four hundred pounds—about two days' work. From his early youth, he was disturbed by the cruel expression and practice of segregation all around him. "When it comes down to it," he wrote in 1998, "I don't really feel I ever had a childhood. I feel childhood just passed me by."[25]

When Lewis, at the age of sixteen, first heard a sermon by Martin Luther King Jr. on the radio during the Montgomery Bus Boycott, his life changed. "From that moment on, I decided I wanted to be just like him."[26] Unable to afford a more prominent Black college such as Morehouse, Lewis went to the small American Baptist Theological Seminary in Nashville in the fall of 1957.[27] He also joined the Nashville chapter of the NAACP. Wanting to be more directly involved, and inspired by the example set by Autherine Lucy, who had integrated the University of Alabama in the midst of rioting in February 1956, Lewis wrote to King and offered to be the one to integrate Troy State

College, near his home in Alabama. He was excited when he met with Dr. King and Fred Gray, but they stressed that Lewis, still a minor, would need his parents' permission to file a lawsuit. His parents refused, in good part because his doing so would undoubtedly put the entire family in great danger.[28]

Lewis returned to his studies in Nashville, and in 1958 he began attending workshops in nonviolence theory and passive resistance held by James Lawson, a white Methodist minister, divinity student, and a field secretary for the Fellowship of Reconciliation. Lawson's practical training program was rigorous: "He showed us how to curl our bodies so that our internal organs would escape direct blows. . . . It was not enough, he would say, simply to endure a beating. It was not enough to resist the urge to strike back at an assailant. 'That urge can't *be* there,' he would tell us. 'You have to do more than just not hit back. You have to have no *desire* to hit back. You have to *love* that person who's hitting you.'"[29]

On November 28, 1959, a busy shopping day right after Thanksgiving, a group of students including Lewis, Diane Nash, and Marion Barry walked into Harvey's Department Store in downtown Nashville and sat at the lunch counter. The waitress politely refused to serve them; then the manager told them, "It is our policy not to serve colored people here." Having established that the store was indeed segregated, the group left. The next week they did the same thing at a different store, and they began planning for more direct action in the near future.[30]

Traveling home for Christmas break, Lewis and Bernard LaFayette sat right behind the driver on a bus out of Nashville, and they refused to move when asked. The driver left the bus to call the police but came back even angrier because the police refused to intervene. He shoved his seat back against them, crushing LaFayette's suitcase, but they sat still, and the driver simply drove on.[31]

Then on February 1, 1960, four students in Greensboro, North Carolina, sat down at the "white" end of the long L-shaped lunch counter at Woolworth's five and dime and asked for coffee. The next day twenty-nine students continued the protest, and the number swelled to hundreds in the following days. There had been similar "sit-ins" in the past; one of the earliest was Samuel Wilbert Tucker's 1939 library protest in Alexandria, Virginia. But the Greensboro sit-ins grabbed the nation's attention on television and in newspapers. Within two weeks, similar protests were occurring in fourteen cities. That number too grew into the hundreds as CORE threw its support behind them. Soon there were pickets in front of dime stores across the country.[32]

In solidarity with the "Greensboro Four," Lewis and other Nashville students began occupying the city's segregated lunch counters every day, sitting quietly all day at counters that had been closed down. For a while these daily sit-ins continued without incident. On Saturday morning, February 27, however, the protesters received a warning that the police were planning to stand aside to allow a group of white thugs to go into the store. When trouble started, the police would then arrest the protesters. Lewis and his companions decided to continue their protest anyway. As they entered Woolworth's, the white crowd taunted and shoved and hit them. When the protesters calmly but doggedly moved to the counter to sit, the harassment escalated. They were called names, spat on, and hit. They had lit cigarettes put down their shirts and in their hair. They were knocked to the floor and kicked, but they never struck back. After about an hour the police came and arrested *them*, not any of the rowdy mob, for disorderly conduct. The students, in response, sang out "We Shall Overcome" as they were loaded into paddy wagons. John R. Lewis had been arrested for the first time.[33]

The numerous sit-in protests around the country had inspired Ella Baker, interim director of the Southern Christian Leadership Council (SCLC), to invite 128 student sit-in leaders from twelve states to a spring conference at Shaw University in Raleigh, North Carolina. Among them were Diane Nash, Marion Barry, and John Lewis. There the assembled group created the Student Nonviolent Coordinating Committee (SNCC). They adopted a youth-oriented, nonhierarchical structure, girded by a set of nonviolent principles, to coordinate sit-ins and voter registration campaigns.[34]

Protests continued through 1960 and early 1961. White violence in response became more frequent and more threatening. At a sit-in in November 1960, Lewis and three other activists were locked inside a hamburger restaurant. The manager went out by the rear door, after turning on a fumigator that began filling the restaurant with deadly insecticide. The protesters only survived because the fire department, thinking there was a fire, arrived and got the manager to open the front door.[35] A few weeks later, in February 1961, Lewis spent his twenty-first birthday in jail for picketing a segregated movie theater.

In March, Lewis and LaFayette wrote to Rev. Fred Shuttlesworth in Birmingham, Alabama, offering to test the Supreme Court decisions in *Boynton v. Virginia* and *Morgan v. Virginia* on a bus trip to Birmingham and a visit to the bus terminal lunch counter. Shuttlesworth discouraged them, saying that Birmingham was too volatile. But new opportunities for Lewis to test his principles and his resolve against the barriers of segregation on a larger scale were soon to arise.

James Farmer, race relations secretary for the Fellowship of Reconciliation, had been one of the founders and an early director of CORE in 1942, and after a long hiatus he was reelected in 1961 as CORE's national director. On the first day at his new job, just two months after the Supreme Court had handed down its decision in *Boynton v. Virginia*, Farmer and his staff were inspired by letters asking about the failure of authorities to enforce the anti-segregation rulings stemming from the *Boynton* and *Morgan* cases. Farmer raised the question of how to address that problem at a meeting that day, and he learned that two staff members, Gordon Carey and Tom Gaither, had already come up with a solution, modeled on Bayard Rustin's Journey of Reconciliation in 1947. Thus the "Freedom Rides" were born.[36]

Just days after being turned down by Shuttlesworth, Lewis read a notice in *The Student Voice*, the SNCC newsletter, calling for volunteers to undertake "Freedom Ride 1961," sponsored by CORE. The goal of the project was nothing less than "to complete the integration of bus service and accommodations in the Deep South."[37] The Freedom Ride was to be structured much like the Journey of Reconciliation, with participants riding both Greyhound and Trailways buses for two weeks. The plan this time, however, was to follow a more dangerous, more southern route through Virginia, North Carolina, South Carolina, Georgia, Alabama, and Mississippi, ending in New Orleans, Louisiana.

Meanwhile, in February, ten students had been arrested at a lunch counter sit-in in Rock Hill, South Carolina. These ten provided a new model for future protesters—"Jail, No Bail." Rather than pay a $100 fine, they chose to endure thirty days on a road gang. By doing so, they simultaneously demonstrated their commitment to the cause and declined to provide money to fund segregationist oppression. Others soon joined them in Rock Hill, and then more in Atlanta and in Lynchburg, Virginia.[38] The stakes had been raised, and commitment to the movement continued to grow.

Participants in the first Freedom Ride were carefully chosen and vetted. Demonstrated commitment to and experience in the movement and a practical understanding of what they might be in for were high priorities. Lewis, with five arrests under his belt already, was readily accepted. He missed his graduation ceremony in order to be in Washington to take part in the journey, preceded by three days of intensive training and preparations. Central to their training were role-playing sessions in which they took turns receiving very realistic insults and blows from their compatriots to prepare them for those likely, indeed almost certain, eventualities on the road.

The night before their scheduled departure, Farmer treated everyone to a meal at a Chinese restaurant. Toward the end of the evening, he somberly told them all that it was not too late to change their minds and that if anyone chose to leave there would be no recriminations or hard feelings, and CORE would pay their transportation home. When everyone appeared at breakfast the next morning, Farmer's doubts were dispelled. As he starkly put it later, "They were prepared for anything, even death."[39]

On Thursday morning, May 4, the first Freedom Ride began. Six of the thirteen Freedom Riders boarded a bus at the Washington, D.C., Greyhound station, and seven at the Trailways station. According to the guidelines Farmer had drawn up, at least one Black rider would sit in a traditionally "white" seat, a Black and a white rider would sit together, and one rider would sit in his or her traditionally designated seat as an observer in case any or all of the others were arrested. The remaining members of the group would spread out among the passengers where they wished, to talk with them and educate them about the purpose of the Freedom Ride.

MAY 4

On the journey's first stop in **Fredericksburg**, Virginia, both groups integrated the restrooms and the lunch counters at their respective terminals without incident. The same proved true in **Richmond**, where they observed that although the "colored only" and "white only" signs had been removed, white and Black patrons were still largely acquiescing to earlier "tradition."[40]

MAY 5

On Friday, the ride continued on to **Petersburg**, where Conrad Lynn had been arrested in 1947. Both Petersburg terminals had been desegregated following sit-in protests nine months earlier, and the Freedom Riders met no opposition.[41]

MAY 6

Saturday's trip to **Farmville**, Virginia, was similar. The "white" and "colored" signs at Farmville had recently been painted over. At **Lynchburg** there were no segregating signs; however, a puzzlingly ambiguous solid partition separated the Trailways lunch counter into two sections.[42]

MAY 7

Greyhound and Trailways shared a terminal in **Danville**, Virginia. When the Greyhound load of Freedom Riders arrived, Ed Blankenheim, one of the white riders, was refused service at the "colored" lunch counter by a Black waiter. After several minutes the waiter explained that his white boss had told him he would be fired if he served anyone at the "wrong" counter. Blankenheim returned to the bus. When the Trailways bus arrived, three more white riders, Jim Peck, Genevieve Hughes, and Walter Bergman, sat down. Again the waiter refused them, but Peck, the only Freedom Rider to have been on the Journey of Reconciliation, eventually convinced the station manager to allow them to be served. They then went on to **Greensboro**, North Carolina, where they received a warm welcome from student leaders at Bennett College and took part in a mass meeting in the evening at Shiloh Baptist Church. Huge signs at the Trailways station pointed at the "colored" lunch counter, which, however, had been closed a week earlier.[43]

MAY 8

On Monday, the travelers successfully integrated the segregated facilities during stopovers in **Winston-Salem** and then in **Salisbury**, North Carolina, where they had the added pleasure of being joined at the "white" lunch counter by two Black women passengers from the bus. They all received polite, prompt service.

The city of **Charlotte**, North Carolina, was fully and determinedly segregated in 1961. The Freedom Riders experienced the first arrest of the trip there, though it came from an unexpected direction. When they arrived, Charles Person thought that his shoes needed a shine, so he went to the station shoeshine stand and sat in a seat marked "whites only." A policeman soon arrived and threatened to arrest him. Person decided to avoid arrest and left to tell the others what had happened. An impromptu meeting led to the group appointing Joe Perkins as their official shoeshine tester. Perkins went to the stand, sat down, and was arrested, with bail set at $50. He declined bail and was sentenced to two nights in jail.[44]

MAY 9

The next stop was **Rock Hill**, South Carolina, in territory never penetrated by the Journey of Reconciliation, and where students earlier in the year had chosen jail over bail. John Lewis later wrote, "I could tell we were in trouble as soon as I stepped off the bus." As Lewis and Al Bigelow approached the "white" men's room in the Greyhound terminal, they saw a large group of young white men hanging around the pinball machines in the lobby, two of them at the restroom door. One of them said, "Other way, nigger," and pointed at a door with a "colored" sign on it. Lewis later wrote,

> I didn't feel nervous at all. I really did not feel afraid. "I have a right to go in there," I said, speaking carefully and clearly, "on the grounds of the Supreme Court decision in the *Boynton* case."
>
> I don't think either of those guys had heard of the *Boynton* case. Not that it would have mattered.

> "Shit on that," one of them said.
>
> The next thing I knew, a fist smashed the right side of my head. Then another hit me square in the face. As I fell to the floor I could feel feet kicking me hard in the sides. I could taste blood in my mouth.

Al Bigelow, a large man, stepped between Lewis and the men beating him and just stood there. Momentarily nonplussed at a white man intervening, the youths paused but then began beating him. When Genevieve Hughes stepped to block the way of other youths coming to join the fight, they knocked her to the floor. At that point a policeman intervened, saying, "All right, boys. Y'all've done about enough now. Get on home."[45] Though his injuries needed medical attention, Lewis first insisted on going to the lunch counter for a cup of coffee.

The Rock Hill Trailways station had been shut down altogether. When the Trailways group arrived they were met by Rev. C. A. Ivory and other drivers, who whisked them away from a group of white men waiting in cars across the street. At a mass meeting that evening the riders met with nine members of the Rock Hill "jail-in." During the course of the evening, Lewis received a message and plane fare from the American Friends Service Committee, asking him to come to Philadelphia to interview for an overseas fellowship he had applied for. Reluctantly he left the Freedom Ride for five days.[46]

MAY 10

The riders had planned on lunch in **Chester**, South Carolina, but on arriving they discovered that, in anticipation of their coming, the bus station was locked and adorned with makeshift "Closed" signs. Both buses pressed on to **Winnsboro**, a fully segregated, conservative town with a strong Confederate tradition. As soon as Hank Thomas sat down at the whites-only lunch counter, the manager called the police. A policeman soon arrived and arrested Thomas. When Jim Peck tried to explain that Thomas had a constitutional right to eat there, the policeman arrested him as well, for "interfering with arrest." Frances Bergman, the day's designated observer, stayed behind with them, while the others took their buses on to **Sumter**, as planned.

That evening the police dropped the charges against Thomas and took him late at night to the partially closed bus station and drove away. An unusually large number of white men were hanging around the station, and the thought occurred to Thomas: "This might be my last day."[47] Nevertheless, he walked into the "white" waiting room and bought a candy bar. Fortunately, Reverend Ivory had been alerted to look after Thomas and had followed the police. He pulled his car up to the station door, yelled to Thomas to "get in the car and stay down," and then he sped away to safety. The charges against Peck were also dropped that night, but, as he was being released, the police spotted a bottle of brandy in his case. They immediately rearrested him for carrying liquor without the required South Carolina tax stamp on it, a charge very similar to one against him fourteen years earlier during the Journey of Reconciliation. He was held until dawn, when Farmer, with a lawyer, drove back from Sumter and paid the $100 bail.[48]

MAY 11

The following day, reunited with Thomas, Peck, and Bergman, the group remained in **Sumter**, though Benjamin Cox, the group's only minister, had to leave to prepare his Mother's Day sermon in High Point, North Carolina. With Lewis and Cox absent, the group's numbers were too low to continue, so Farmer accepted four new volunteers.[49]

MAY 12

Traveling into Georgia, the riders integrated the **Augusta** bus terminal without incident.

MAY 13

After a brief stop to integrate the terminal in **Athens**, they did the same on their arrival in **Atlanta**. They were heartened when Dr. King returned to the city in time to have dinner with them that evening, but they were sobered by troubling news of a plot to meet the Freedom Ride with violence in Alabama. More bad news arrived during the night, when Farmer was told that his father had died.

MAY 14

The riders, already apprehensive, woke that Mother's Day Sunday to learn that their leader would be away for two or three days just as they were about to set out on one of the most dangerous legs of the journey. CORE field secretary Joe Perkins was named "captain" of the Trailways crew, with Jim Peck temporarily taking Farmer's place in overall charge.[50] A Greyhound bus with seven Freedom Riders and seven "regular" passengers left Atlanta for Birmingham at 11:00 a.m. Among the latter, unbeknown to the CORE group, were the manager of the Birmingham Greyhound terminal and two undercover members of the Alabama highway patrol, hoping to eavesdrop on the Freedom Riders to get details of their plans. A Trailways bus with the remaining Freedom Riders left about an hour later.

John Lewis had flown to Nashville on Saturday and hoped to rejoin the

Freedom Riders by their firebombed bus near Anniston, Alabama, May 14, 1961. Photo by Joe Postiglione. Library of Congress.

Freedom Ride in Birmingham. Before he left Nashville on Sunday, however, Lewis was horrified to learn that on the way to Birmingham the Greyhound bus had been viciously attacked by a Klan-led mob at the terminal in **Anniston**, Alabama. After its rear tires had been slashed, the bus was then chased by a long line of cars and trucks. Once out of town, a car forced the bus to stop. Again it was attacked by the angry mob, and it was ultimately firebombed. Lewis did not know it at the time, but everyone managed to escape before it exploded in flames.[51]

Meanwhile, at the Trailways terminal in Atlanta, the wary Freedom Riders standing in line to buy their tickets noticed a rough-looking group of white men approaching others in the line who then disappeared. Those men—Ku Klux Klan members—boarded the bus with a few other "regular" passengers. On the way to Anniston they began to insult and threaten the Freedom Riders who were sitting toward the front of the bus. The Trailways terminal in **Anniston** was "eerily quiet," as the riders bought sandwiches at the lunch counter and went back to the bus. Soon afterward, John O. Patterson, the driver, returned, saying to the Klansmen, "We have received word that a bus has been burned to the ground and passengers are being carried to the hospital by the carloads. A mob is waiting for our bus and will do the same to us unless we get these niggers off the front seats." One of the Freedom Riders reminded him that they were interstate passengers with the right to sit anyplace. Patterson shook his head and left the bus again. One of the Klansmen threatened the Freedom Riders and then punched Charles Person in the face. Another one punched Herman Harris. The men dragged the two from their seats and began pummeling and kicking them in the aisle. Jim Peck and Walter Bergman interposed themselves and were both beaten into unconsciousness. Bergman's life was only spared when one of the Klansmen said, "Don't kill him." They dragged the four beaten men and dumped them in the laps of the people in the rear seat and then sat themselves in the middle of the bus to protect the "color line." Patterson returned and drove the bus on back roads into Birmingham.

The bus arrived in **Birmingham** two hours later only to be met by another mob of Klansmen who occupied the terminal, from which the police had let it be known they would stay away for fifteen minutes. The Klansmen on the bus rushed to the front and fled as soon as the door opened. The Freedom Riders were wary and scared, but they filed off the bus and began collecting their baggage. Peck and Person went into the waiting room and started for the lunch counter. They were set upon by several of the mob, shoved out of sight into a corridor, and beaten more. Walter Bergman had followed them and was beaten as well. He had insisted that his wife, Frances, board a city bus as soon as they arrived, so she escaped the mob. Jerry Moore and Herman Harris managed to slip away in the crowd. Ike Reynolds was badly beaten and thrown into a rubbish bin. A Black laborer, George Webb, had come to the station to meet his fiancée, Mary Spicer, one of the regular passengers on the bus. Spicer was able to escape when Gary Thomas Rowe, an undercover FBI informant, told her to run, but Webb was savagely beaten by at least a dozen men, including Rowe. Webb might have been killed, but the allotted fifteen minutes were up, the police began to move in, and the mob began to disappear. Several photographers and reporters were also beaten during the melee. Jim Peck was badly injured, requiring fifty-three stitches in his head, but even while in the hospital he was determined to get on the bus to Montgomery the next day.[52]

MAY 15

On Monday morning the group took a vote: 8–4 in favor of continuing the journey. But they knew it would not be possible to do so without protection. Much of the day was spent waiting at the bus station during negotiations among Fred Shuttlesworth, Birmingham and Alabama authorities, Greyhound officials, U.S. attorney general Robert F. Kennedy, and Kennedy's assistant, John Siegenthaler, in an effort to secure a reliable escort to Montgomery and thence to the Mississippi line. The Greyhound officials insisted that no drivers were willing to drive such a bus. The disappointed, exhausted Freedom Riders reluctantly agreed to end the ride and fly to New Orleans, where they would join a rally celebrating the seventh anniversary of the *Brown v. Board of Education* decision. They got tickets and boarded the plane, and then a bomb scare was called in. They booked a later flight, which was inexplicably canceled. By then John Siegenthaler had arrived in Birmingham. The Freedom Riders and Siegenthaler boarded a 10:38 p.m. flight to New Orleans and landed there an hour later. The first Freedom Ride, it seemed, was over.[53]

MAY 17

Back in Nashville, however, John Lewis had already been making plans on Sunday with Diane Nash, who was now working for SNCC and the SCLC and with other members of the Nashville Student Movement. Rather than let violent opposition prevail over nonviolent resistance, they were determined that the Freedom Ride should continue in spite of the palpable danger. On Wednesday morning, May 17, ten volunteers—seven men and three women, eight Black and two white, led by John Lewis—boarded a bus to Birmingham.

No one else on that bus knew they were traveling with Freedom Riders. Even though Jim Zwerg, who was white, and Paul Brooks, who was Black, insisted on sitting together near the front of the bus, no one openly objected. When they reached the city limits, however, Birmingham police boarded the bus, arrested Zwerg and Brooks, and checked everyone's ticket, thus allowing them to identify nine of the ten Freedom Riders. Salynn McCollum, who was white, had missed the bus in Nashville and only caught up with it at a later stop; thus, her ticket looked different from the others. Escorting the bus to the terminal, the police did not let anyone leave until they had checked each ticket. They kept the seven Freedom Riders they had identified in the bus and taped newspapers over the outside of the windows. McCollum slipped away and called Diane Nash, who in turn called Burke Marshall, Robert Kennedy's special deputy for civil rights, in Washington.

An increasingly troublesome white crowd had begun to gather. After four hours the Freedom Riders were let out of the bus. With police holding back the crowd, the riders went into the "white" waiting room. The lunch counter was closed, so they integrated the restrooms, which were not, and then returned to the waiting room. Theophilus "Bull" Connor, Birmingham's notorious commissioner of public safety, entered the waiting room and had all the Freedom Riders jailed under "protective custody." They spent the night singing freedom songs, as much to annoy Connor and the guards as to keep up their own spirits.

MAY 18

As the protesters mounted a hunger strike and "sing-in" on Thursday, Robert Kennedy and President Kennedy in Washington, having failed to get the Freedom Riders to agree to a "cooling off period," tried to come up with a way to get them escorted safely out of Birmingham. That evening, after CBS television broadcast to the nation a hard-hitting documentary, *Who Speaks for Birmingham*, Bull Connor himself took action, eager to get the Freedom Riders out of his jurisdiction. At 11:30 p.m. he loaded them into two unmarked cars and drove them north, letting them out around three or four o'clock Friday morning near the Tennessee border, deep in rural Klan territory.

MAY 19

They walked until they found a phone and called Diane Nash, who said she would have someone pick them up and either bring them to Nashville or take them back to Birmingham. They opted for Birmingham. Other volunteers also converged on Birmingham. That afternoon nineteen Freedom Riders found themselves at Shuttlesworth's parsonage for lunch, after which they were driven to the Greyhound terminal. A crowd of several hundred people and a dozen police were there already. The three o'clock bus to Montgomery was already idling when it was announced that the bus was canceled for lack of a driver. The riders went into the waiting room as the crowd outside grew larger.

The police allowed a few people from the crowd to come into the waiting room, some of them in Klan robes, one of whom was the "Imperial Wizard," Robert Shelton, in his black robe. For three hours Shelton tried to provoke members of the group, stepping on their toes, pouring drinks on them, and blocking the way to the restrooms. Toward dark, the police chief cleared everyone out except the Freedom Riders, disconnected the public telephones, and ordered the restaurant closed.

Still President Kennedy was trying to convince the Alabama governor, John Patterson, to provide safe passage to the Freedom Riders, but to no avail. He dispatched John Siegenthaler to Patterson's office in Montgomery to negotiate in person. Eventually the governor agreed that the Alabama Highway Patrol would escort a bus from the Birmingham city limits to the Montgomery city limits, and then from there to the Mississippi border. The Freedom Riders spent another night without food, sleeping on hard bus station benches, if indeed they slept at all.

MAY 20

At 6:00 a.m. they were ready to go. Joe Caverno, a uniformed Greyhound driver, arrived, then walked away, declaring, "I have one life to give, and I'm not going to give it to CORE or the NAACP." After further calls and back office meetings among officials, Caverno reappeared, and the Freedom Riders boarded the bus. It left, surrounded by police cars, around 8:30 a.m., and sped toward Montgomery at ninety miles per hour.

When the bus reached the **Montgomery** line, the Highway Patrol escort dropped away as planned, but only one city motorcycle cop took over. At the terminal there were no police to be seen. Nor was there a crowd. Just a dozen white men near the terminal door, some cab drivers, and a few reporters waiting to interview the Freedom Riders at the platform. But the mob *was* there, around the corners and out of sight. As the Freedom Riders got off the bus, they were approached by some reporters and cameramen. But suddenly reporters and riders alike were under attack. Lewis powerfully describes the scene in his memoir, *Walking with the Wind*:

> Out of nowhere, from every direction, came people. Men, women, and children. Dozens of them. Hundreds of them. Out of alleys, out of side streets, around corners of office buildings, they emerged from everywhere, from all directions, all at once, as if they had been let out of a gate. . . . They carried every makeshift weapon imaginable. Baseball bats, wooden boards, bricks, chains, tire irons, pipes, even garden tools—hoes and rakes. One group had women in front, their faces twisted in anger, screaming, "*Git them niggers, GIT them niggers!*"[54]

At first the Riders tried to stand together, as Lewis exhorted them, but the press of attackers was too quick and too fierce. Backed against a retaining wall, some jumped, while others were pushed over the wall and managed to escape. Several, including Lewis and Jim Zwerg, the only white male in the group, were cornered at the bus. Zwerg was kicked and hit in the head, then one Klansman held his arms while others punched him and beat him. Lucretia Collins described the horrific scene she saw as she was escaping in a taxi: "Some men held him while white women clawed his face with their nails. And they held up their little children—children who couldn't have been more than a couple years old—to claw his face. I had to turn my head because I just couldn't watch it."[55]

When Zwerg lost consciousness, he was thrown over a railing. Lewis was

John Lewis and Jim Zwerg, Montgomery, Alabama, May 21, 1961. Library of Congress.

knocked unconscious with a Coca Cola crate. "I could feel my knees collapse and then nothing. Everything turned white for an instant, then black."[56]

The violence and riot continued all around the terminal for some time. John Siegenthaler himself, trying to rescue Susan Wilbur as she was being chased, was hit over the head with a pipe, kicked, and pushed under the rear of his car, where he lay unconscious. When the police arrived about ten minutes after the riot began, they did little to quell it.

While federal and state officials in Alabama and Mississippi debated how to resolve the problem of the Freedom Riders, Diane Nash and the Nashville Student Movement were already planning their next steps. Raymond Arsenault chronicles no fewer than sixty-one Freedom Rides and related actions across the South between May 24 and December 10, 1961. He lists 436 Freedom Riders: 326 men and 110 women; 230 Black, 204 white, and 2 Asian; 111 under twenty years old, 221 in their twenties, and 104 thirty or older.[57] Many of them became well-known civil rights leaders. But all of them were the heirs of David Ruggles and Rosa Parks.[58]

In 1963 Lewis was elected chairman of SNCC. That August at the March on Washington for Jobs and Freedom, he gave a powerful speech, a speech outshone only by King's "I Have a Dream" speech. As chairman of SNCC, Lewis coordinated voter education and registration campaigns, largely student-driven, in Mississippi and Alabama during 1964 and 1965.

After a long political battle, President Lyndon Johnson signed the landmark Civil Rights Act of 1964 on July 2 that year. The law strengthened the rights of voters and banned discrimination across the board:

> SEC. 201. (a) All persons shall be entitled to the full and equal enjoyment of the goods, services, facilities, and privileges, advantages, and accommodations of any place of public accommodation, as defined in this section, without discrimination or segregation on the ground of race, color, religion, or national origin.[59]

Years of experience and numerous earlier civil rights bills had taught the legislators to define the issues more explicitly to achieve greater equality before the law. Jim Crow at last was legally dead. But although significant progress had been made, no law could eliminate the underlying prejudice. The struggle continued—and continues.

During early 1965, a voter registration campaign was under way in Selma, Alabama. On the afternoon of March 7, 1965, as they began what was to be a fifty-four-mile march for voting rights from Selma to Montgomery, Lewis and Hosea Williams, a noted SCLC leader, led a column of more than two hundred people over the Edmund Pettus Bridge. On the other side of the bridge, just across the city line, they came face to face with a blue wall of state troopers, some on foot, some on horseback, some with tear gas. After a brief standoff and an order for the marchers to disperse, the troopers attacked. Lewis was the first to be hit. He fell to the ground with a fractured skull. When he tried to get up he was hit again. "I'm going to die here," he thought.[60] Lewis and sixteen other marchers were hospitalized, including Amelia Boynton, the mother of Bruce Boynton, and Lynda Blackmon Lowery, two weeks shy of her fifteenth birthday, whose head injuries required thirty-five stitches. Fifty others were treated for lesser injuries.

John Lewis would be arrested forty-five times during his life. Five of those arrests occurred after he was elected to Congress in 1986. During his thirty-three years as a congressman, he became a moral beacon to both Congress and the nation. Lewis died in July 2020. In August 2021 the U.S. House of Representatives passed the John Lewis Voting Rights Advancement Act with the goal of preventing racially discriminatory voting laws from taking effect, but as of late 2024 it has repeatedly failed to pass in the Senate.

CHAPTER 8

Into the Twenty-First Century

The accomplishments of Rosa Parks and John Lewis, and the experiences of the people chronicled in this book, led ultimately to the Civil Rights Act of 1964 and did much to eliminate Jim Crow on buses, trains, and planes, and in bus depots, train stations, and airports, as well as other public places. The eradication of the many local and statewide Jim Crow laws, in and of itself, significantly improved the conditions long endured by people of color. A century and a half of determined effort, brave action, and incremental legal progress eventually eased, but it could not erase, the underlying prejudices that make travel difficult, demeaning, and dangerous for people of color. Racism persists, and its effects continue to plague Black and Brown travelers.

Those fortunate enough to own a car in the mid-twentieth century could avoid many of the indignities and horrors of segregation on trains and buses, but Jim Crow also lurked along the highway, making it difficult or impossible to find a hotel, restaurant, or even a service station willing to serve people of color. To address the difficulties of road travel, each April from 1936 to 1966 Victor H. Green published *The Green Book*, officially titled *The Negro Motorist Green-Book* and later *Travelers' Green Book*. This small but densely packed booklet offered information toward "vacation without aggravation." It listed hotels, motels, tourist homes, restaurants, beauty parlors and barbershops, dry cleaners, service stations, et cetera that welcomed African American customers and patrons, and it described tourist attractions and sights to see in towns and cities across the country. An important feature in later editions was a section titled "Your Rights, Briefly Speaking!"[1] Somewhat analogous to William Lloyd Garrison's Travellers' Directory in the *Liberator* in 1842–43 (see page 64), the 1963–64 edition briefly summarized "Anti-jimcro" laws in thirty-two states plus the District of Columbia and told where to go to register any violations or complaints in twenty states. *The Green Book* ceased publication shortly after the Civil Rights Act of 1964 eliminated at least the legal underpinnings of segregation.

The automobile increasingly came to dominate the movement of Americans from place to place, whether over long distances or on a daily commute between work and home. Over the decades, urban mass transit systems have continued to provide a necessary, if often inadequate, means of travel for the poorer and working classes, while the middle and upper classes have gained greater access to more exclusive modes of transportation, in private cars and taxis, or in other ride-sharing services such as Uber and Lyft, beyond the pocketbooks of many. But while racial oppression is no longer as overt on our rails or in our buses as it was, it continues to stalk Black travelers on the road.

Sandra Bland, Philando Castile, Tyre Nichols, 2015–2023

The most notorious manifestation of prejudice in modern travel is that of racial profiling by police and others in authority. Just as train conductors and bus drivers were formerly instructed—or took it upon themselves—to police public transportation, many police officers have continued the practice of discrimination by stopping Black drivers, often for minor infractions or none. Indeed, the sardonic phrase "driving while Black" gained prominence in the 1990s in reference to the trivial reasons and the frequency with which police were pulling over Black drivers more often than demographic statistics suggested was equitable.

The widespread use of racial profiling on the road was nothing new, but it gained considerable national attention with the deaths of Sandra Bland in 2015, Philando Castile in 2016, and Tyre Nichols in 2023. All three incidents were recorded on video that became important in subsequent investigations and in the widespread publicity they received. Initially, Sandra Bland had been stopped for failing to signal when she changed lanes to let the police car pass. The officer, a Texas state trooper, became increasingly agitated and forceful when Bland refused to get out of her car without an explanation as to why she should. In this she was echoing David Ruggles, Thomas Van Renselaer, Frederick Douglass, Jabez P. Campbell, J. W. C. Pennington, Miles Robinson, Adelene McBean, Bayard Rustin, and others by simply asking the question which opened this book: "Why?" After the trooper dragged Bland out of her car, she was arrested for assaulting a police officer. Three days later she was found hanged in the jail cell where she was being held. Her death was ruled a suicide.[2]

Philando Castile, driving with his girlfriend and her four-year-old child, was stopped by a patrolman in Falcon Heights, Minnesota. The pretext was that he had a broken taillight, but in actuality the officer commented to the dispatcher that he was pulling them over because "the two occupants just looked like, uh, people that were involved in a robbery."[3] In an attempt to avoid trouble, Castile told the officer that he had a gun in the car, whereupon the officer replied, "Don't reach for it then." As Castile reached for his identification, the officer shot him five times point-blank. Both Bland and Castile had been pulled over multiple times before. Neither officer was found guilty of a crime in either Bland's case or Castile's.

When Tyre Nichols was stopped, allegedly for reckless driving, on January 7, 2023, he was brutally and fatally beaten by five Memphis police officers.[4] The fact that those policemen were Black complicates the issue and brings into question the nature of police training in the use of violence. However, that training and the culture of authority that allows it grew out of the history of racism in the United States.

Anti-profiling laws have been instituted in at least thirty states, but they have proved to have insufficient effect. As part of the so-called War on Drugs in the 1970s, 1980s, and subsequently, police were trained to use minor pretexts to stop people they suspected of being drug dealers—or who looked to them like they might be drug dealers. Not surprisingly, these stops were often initiated on the basis of race. Once stopped, Black drivers were three times more likely to be searched than white drivers. To top things off, Black drivers were not only more likely to be searched, they were actually *less* likely to be found in possession of drugs than white drivers. Even if the minor infraction is actual—a broken license plate light, failure to signal a lane change, or not wearing a seat belt—Black drivers are given a ticket more often than white drivers. In some areas, the situation is getting worse rather than better. In 2017 the NAACP issued a travel advisory warning Black drivers to avoid the entire state of Missouri. In June 2023 it was estimated that Black drivers in Missouri were being stopped at rates about 60 percent higher than their share of the population would indicate.[5] Also in October 2017 the NAACP issued a travel advisory against American Airlines following reports of a number of discriminatory incidents. The company instituted an implicit bias awareness training program and the advisory was lifted the following summer.[6]

Racial profiling extends, of course, into areas other than transportation. As a result, "____ing while Black" has proliferated as an ironic, catchall meme: fill in the blank with almost any innocent activity. The March 2020 killing of Breonna Taylor as police broke into her Louisville apartment on the basis of a "no-knock warrant" was reported as "Sleeping While Black."[7] In May 2020, when Christian Cooper, an African American birdwatcher in New York's Central Park, asked a woman to keep her dog on a leash in accordance with park rules, she called the police to say that a Black man was threatening her. Joan Walsh wrote up this incident in *The Nation* under the title "Birding While Black: Just the Latest Bad Reason for White People to Call Police."[8]

A quick internet search turns up material on "Running While Black," "Walking While Black," "Banking While Black," "Aging While Black," "Eating While Black," "Living While Black" (a PBS series by that title exploring the Black experience of life in Texas), and even "Dreaming Whilst Black" (the title of a British TV series).

Yet another form of transportation has come into play in powerful and widespread public responses against racism. The Black Lives Matter movement was sparked after the 2012 murder of Trayvon Martin in Florida, and it was greatly expanded and energized following the killing of George Floyd under the knee of a Minneapolis policeman on May 25, 2020. Despite occurring as the Covid-19 pandemic was raging around the globe and keeping us all indoors, the excruciating death of George Floyd, seen by millions through a witness's cell phone video, sparked anger and outrage around the nation and throughout the world that spread quickly through the streets of cities and towns, large and small. Many protesters came on bicycles. In turn, bicycle police responded with force. They were ordered to "focus on the bicyclists." "Bike cops unleashed tear gas, shot pepper spray, tossed flash grenades, and pummeled protestors with nightsticks. The officers wielded their bikes like weapons, using them as shields and battering rams." The ferocity of such tactics so disturbed the North American distributor of Fuji Bikes that the company suspended the sale of bikes to police after seeing them being used in ways "that we did not intend or design them to be used." Throughout that summer and autumn, Black activists in New York organized Black Lives Matter actions in the form of protest rides that were joined by thousands of cyclists riding through the city.[9]

But this was not the first time that bicyclists encountered police opposition. Like Driving while Black, there is also a history of Biking while Black. Black cyclists were killed in road accidents in 2013 at a rate 30 percent higher than white cyclists, and Latino cyclists were killed at a rate 23 percent higher. A 2019 survey in Oakland found that 60 percent of cyclists pulled over by police were Black, though the city's population was only 28 percent Black. In New York, 86 percent of all cyclists ticketed for riding on the sidewalk in 2018 and 2019 were Black and Latino.[10]

Such protests as these, following the examples set by many of those chronicled in this book and carried down the years by hundreds of others, continue to show us that the human spirit cannot be cowed, cannot be diminished, cannot be extinguished as long as there are those who are willing to insist on keeping their rightful seats on the bus of life as it carries us into the future.

Transportation remains a key element in the struggle against racism on a much broader scale than we might have thought in the 1960s and earlier. In

2000 JoAnn Wypijewski wrote a damning, no-holds-barred article in *The Nation* showing how the bus system in Montgomery, Alabama, and transportation funding statewide were drastically cut or even eliminated, leaving poor, working-class, and primarily Black citizens without reliable or affordable ways to get to work, to schools, to medical care, or to social services

> Bus stops don't announce themselves in Montgomery. There are no signs, no shelters, no maps posted on the street. There are only three fixed routes, down from thirty-six in the 1980s. . . . By the fortieth anniversary of the bus boycott, service had been cut by 70 percent and fares had doubled, to $1.50. Student and old-age discounts were eliminated. In 1996 midday service stopped. Finally, in 1997, the City Council said there just weren't enough riders or revenue; the traditional system of big buses and fixed routes was finished.[11]

In the 1980s, with his study of the location of waste disposal sites near Black neighborhoods more often than white ones in Houston, Robert D. Bullard developed the concept of "environmental racism," addressing the effects of de facto segregation in urban settings.[12] As the field of environmental justice burgeoned, the centrality of transportation issues became increasingly apparent, going well beyond the matter of passengers and seating, as Martin Luther King Jr. had recognized in a speech published posthumously in 1969:

> Urban transit systems in most American cities . . . have become a genuine civil rights issue—and a valid one—because the layout of rapid-transit systems determines the accessibility of jobs to the black community. . . . A good example of this problem is my home city of Atlanta, where the rapid-transit system has been laid out for the convenience of the white upper-middle-class suburbanites who commute to their jobs downtown. The system has virtually no consideration for connecting the poor people with their jobs. There is only one possible explanation for this situation, and that is the racist blindness of city planners.[13]

It was in the context of this larger problem that in 2004 Bullard and others published *Highway Robbery: Transportation Racism and New Routes to Equity*, a collection of nine essays laying out "the anatomy of transportation racism," as Bullard's opening essay is titled.[14] Today the concerns of environmental justice, in concert with the expanded understanding of "the long civil rights movement," Black Lives Matter, and #MeToo, have generated a robust discussion of issues of equity across the board that shows promise for the future.

Eliminating the inequities in our social and civil order should not be the work of those who suffer the most under that imbalance. Active, broad support must also come from people across the social spectrum, and from public

WE, the People of the United States, in order to ſorm a more perfect Union, eſtabliſh Juſtice, inſure domeſtic Tranquility, provide for the common Defence, promote the General Welfare, and ſecure the Bleſſings of Liberty to Ourſelves and our Poſterity, do ordain and eſtabliſh this Conſtitution for the United States of America.

Preamble to the U.S. Constitution, from the original printing by Dunlap & Claypoole, 1787. Library of Congress.

and private organizations, institutions, and local, state, and federal government offices. As we have seen, the gains made through the efforts, sacrifice, and suffering of people like those outlined in this book had to be fought for repeatedly. Every concession of privilege was yielded begrudgingly. The work of white allies throughout this long period has, of course, been important, even crucial, but white resistance has been and remains strong.

With my own generation coming of age in the 1960s, there was great hope—in retrospect, a naïve hope—that we would rise above the long-standing social and racial prejudice clung to by those whose complexion, as David Ruggles might have put it, granted them great privilege. Many in today's younger generations once again show a refreshing and impressive promise, as evidenced, for example, in the widespread George Floyd protests. But the forces of privilege, prejudice, and power continue to make themselves all too visible in our streets, on our airways, and in the very halls and chambers of our local, state, and national governments.

The problem of race in this country is not a "Black problem." It is a deeply embedded condition that ultimately can only be eliminated by the refusal of white people to condone racial animosity and the personal, governmental, and cultural structures that support it. "*We shall overcome!*" The collective "we" in that iconic song of protest and hope cannot simply mean "we people of color" or "those of us singing in the street today." It has to come to mean the same "we" as in the phrase "We, the people." That is, *all* the citizens of this country. Each one of the six precepts enshrined in the oft-quoted preamble to the U.S. Constitution speaks to the need to abolish the racial prejudice that is a major impediment to achieving its goals:

> **We**, the People of the United States, in order to form a more perfect Union, establish Justice, insure domestic Tranquility, provide for the common Defence, promote the General Welfare, and secure the Blessings of Liberty to Ourselves and our Posterity, do ordain and establish this Constitution for the United States of America.

TIMELINE OF EVENTS

ACKNOWLEDGMENTS

Over the years this book has been coming together, I have received help, support, and encouragement from many colleagues and friends who have listened patiently, read and commented on excerpts, provided practical advice on matters large and small, and kept me moving forward. Among these are Stephen Darwall, Marty Dobrow, Pamela Henderson, Michael Livingston, Steven Niven, Bill Oram, and Steve Strimer. I am particularly grateful to Claudette Colvin, Victor Fleischer, Cornelia Keys Hargrave, Walter Naegle, and Amy Nathan for their kind assistance in providing photographs. Special thanks are owed to Available Potential Enterprises, Ltd., and the TOAD Fund for their support.

Nate Holly, Lea Johnson, Jon Davies, Laura Yoder, Christina Cotter, Candice Lawrence, Mary McKeon, Rebecca Norton, and the staff of the University of Georgia Press have turned this project into a book with professionalism and thoughtfulness. Erin Kirk designed an eye-catching and informative cover. Chris Dodge has been an extremely thorough, meticulous, and eagle-eyed copy editor, and Catherine B. Krusberg a keen-sighted proofreader. Classic City Composition and Sheridan Books made it all a tangible reality. Jim Gipe of Pivot Media provided technical help with various images.

Members of my family—Catrin Lloyd-Bollard, Brynley Lloyd-Bollard, Jesse Meadow, and my sister Georgiana Schmid—inspired and encouraged me as I worked, helped with research, and read and commented on various sections. No one, however, has done as much as my wife, Margaret Lloyd. In addition to countless hours of discussion, patient listening, and sound advice, she read each section as it developed and then read the entire manuscript several times, correcting my mistakes, improving the tone, and refining the argument throughout—all while simultaneously working and maintaining her own creative life as a professor, a poet, and a painter. I stand in awe!

NOTES

Preface

1. Barnes, *Journey from Jim Crow*, ix.

2. See especially Barnes, *Journey from Jim Crow*; Kelley, *Right to Ride*; and Bay, *Traveling Black*.

3. Hall, "The Long Civil Rights Movement."

4. Cha-Jua and Lang, "The 'Long Movement' as Vampire."

5. Beaupre, "Saints and the 'Long Civil Rights Movement'"; Gilmore, *Defying Dixie*; Heath W. Carter, "Emancipation Proclamation," talk at the Newberry Library, Chicago, May 18, 2020.

Introduction

1. See Gates, "Who Was the First African American?" TheRoot.com, October 22, 2012, https://www.theroot.com/who-was-the-first-african-american-1790893808. African sailors and slaves may have sailed with Christopher Columbus on his voyages. See Lyderson, "Dental Studies Give Clues"; Kingsbury, *Records of the Virginia Company*, 243.

2. Easton, "Address Delivered before the Coloured Population of Providence," 50.

3. *Liberator*, December 10, 1831.

4. Murray, *States' Laws on Race and Color*, 15.

5. *New Bedford Mercury*, July 23, 1841.

6. Child, *An Appeal*, 220.

Chapter 1. The Rise of Jim Crow

1. Child, *An Appeal*, 219–20.

2. Belton, "A Black Brazilian Immigrant and the Struggle." Details of this case and Mundrucu's career are discussed in greater detail in Belton, "A Deep Interest in Your Cause"; and Belton, "Emiliano F. B. Mundrucu."

3. *Boston Post*, October 16, 1833; *Liberator*, October 26, 1833.

4. *Liberator*, April 13, 1833.

5. *Liberator*, January 16, 1863; *Boston Daily Advertiser*, January 2, 1863.

6. *Liberator*, September 25, 1863.

7. *Emancipator*, January 28, 1834. The brackets in these passages are in Ruggles's original; a few typographical errors have been corrected silently.

8. Ruggles, *"Extinguisher" Extinguished*, 45–46n; Hodges, *Ruggles*, 57.

9. Ruggles, *"Extinguisher" Extinguished*, 14.

10. Hodges, *David Ruggles*, 11–31.

11. *Freedom's Journal*, May 9, December 12, 1828.

12. Hodges, *David Ruggles*, 46.

13. *Liberator*, June 14, 1834.

14. *Fifth Annual Report of the Board of Managers*, 9.

15. *Liberator*, July 10, 1840.

16. Appleton, "History of the Railways of Massachusetts."

17. *Liberator*, October 1, 1841.

18. Dickens, *American Notes*, 145–46.

19. *Liberator*, August 21, 1840.

20. Chace, *Anti-Slavery Reminiscences*, 10, 13, 14, 17.

21. *Frederick Douglass' Paper*, April 13, 1855; Quarles, *Black Abolitionists*, 72.

22. The Taunton Branch Railroad opened in 1836. Chace relates that "a colored man and his wife" from New Bedford entered the car in Taunton, so this incident most likely took place before the Taunton Branch was extended to New Bedford in 1840 and before the Chaces moved from Fall River to Valley Falls, Rhode Island, in 1839.

23. Chace, *Anti-Slavery Reminiscences*, 15–16.

24. Chace, *Anti-Slavery Reminiscences*, 17–18.

25. Ruggles, *Mirror of Liberty*, January 1839, 23–24; Hodges, *David Ruggles*, 131.

26. In 1780 William Lynch created a band of vigilantes and wrote up a compact stating their purpose and methods for punishing whomever they wished, without recourse to the law or legal procedures. Today "to lynch" almost always means "to put to death (as by hanging) by mob action without legal sanction," but in Ruggles's day it was used more generally in the sense of "to treat by lynch law," which the *Virginia Lancet*, as quoted by Ida B. Wells, defined as "the name given to the summary infliction of punishment by private and unauthorized citizens" (Wells, "Lynch Law," 29).

27. *Emancipator*, August 23; *Colored American*, August 25, 1838. The bracketed phrases "[viz four dollars,]" and "[or Jim Crow]" appear in the original article. The term "forties" might be an extended use of "forty" as an intensifier, or it might be from Latin *fortis*, "strong," used in the sense of "strong-arm men."

28. On the origins of "Jim Crow," see Pryor, *Colored Travelers*, 91–93; "The Origins of Jim Crow," Jim Crow Museum, https://jimcrowmuseum.ferris.edu/origins.htm.

29. *Salem (Mass.) Gazette*, October 12, 1838.

30. Luxenberg, *Separate*, 9.

31. *Liberator*, July 13, 1838.

32. *Liberator*, November 30, 1838. Van Renselaer's surname is variously spelled; I have adopted the form with which his letter is signed in the *Liberator*.

33. William C. Coffin to Debora Weston, January 1, 1841, Weston Papers, quoted in Kathryn Grover, *Fugitive's Gibraltar*, 172. Nathaniel A. Borden should not be confused with Nathaniel B. Borden, a prominent white abolitionist from Fall River, Massachusetts, whose wife Sarah was the sister of Elizabeth Buffum Chace.

34. *Liberator*, January 15, 1841. A pipe is a large barrel for holding liquids, containing about two hogsheads or 126 gallons.

35. *Liberator*, February 26, 1841.

36. Thomas Downing obituary, *New York Times*, April 12, 1866; Hewitt, "Downing and His Oyster House," 229–52.

37. *Liberator*, June 11, 1841.

38. Stimson's *Boston Directory*, 1840, 448.

39. *Liberator*, October 9, 1840.

40. *Catalogue of the Officers and Students of Harvard*, 13. An article in the *Liberator*, June 18, 1841, refers to Jinnings, not by name but as "a member of the medical class of Harvard University." See also John K. Bollard and Catrin Lloyd-Bollard, "Thomas Jinnings: The First Black Student at Harvard?," *Journal of Blacks in Higher Education*,

September 1, 2022, https://www.jbhe.com/2022/09/thomas-jinnings-the-first-black-student-at-harvard.

41. *Liberator*, June 18, 1841.

42. *Colored American*, June 19, 1841.

43. *Liberator*, July 2, 1841.

44. "Cambridge Stage and Omnibus Lines."

45. *Liberator*, August 13, 1841.

46. "Inst." is an abbreviation of Latin *instante mense*, meaning "of the present month."

47. *Liberator*, July 9, 1841.

48. *New-Bedford Register*, July 7, 1841.

49. Ruggles or the printer mistakes the judge's middle initial as *A* rather than *H*.

50. On *lynch law*, see note 26 above.

51. *Liberator*, August 6, 1841.

52. *Liberator*, July 23, 1841.

53. Hodges, *David Ruggles*, 168–85.

54. Hodges, *David Ruggles*, 187–97. In July 1848 William Lloyd Garrison underwent Ruggles's water cure with some success and described it: "The experience of the first day runs thus: —a half bath (which I should consider a whole one and a quarter) at 5 o'clock, A.M.; rubbed down with a wet sheet thrown over the body at 11 o'clock; a sitz bath at 4, P.M.; a foot-bath at half past 8, P.M.; and at 5 this morning, a shallow bath which is to be followed at 11 by a spray baptism." Higginbotham, "From the Underground Railroad to the Water-Cure." *Trumpet and Universalist Magazine*, April 15, 1848, notes in reference to a speech given by Dr. A. Means at the Medical College of Georgia in 1848: "We are pleased to see that in establishing his positions this Southern Professor, not hindered by any unworthy prejudice of complexion, takes honorable notice of the remarkable practice of our colored and blind citizen, Dr. David Ruggles, with whose great success our readers are already somewhat acquainted."

55. Reprinted in the *Liberator*, August 13, 1841.

56. Quotations here and below are from the *Liberator*, October 1, 1841.

57. See introduction, note 5.

58. Douglass, *Narrative of the Life of Frederick Douglass*, 47.

59. Douglass, *My Bondage and My Freedom*, 155.

60. Douglass, *Narrative of the Life of Frederick Douglass*, 52–53; *My Bondage and My Freedom*, 158–59; *Life and Times of Frederick Douglass*, 103–5.

61. Douglass, *Life and Times of Frederick Douglass*, 111; Douglass, *My Bondage and My Freedom*, 167.

62. Douglass, *Narrative of the Life of Frederick Douglass*, 80–81.

63. Douglass, *Narrative of the Life of Frederick Douglass*, 81.

64. Douglass, *My Bondage and My Freedom*, 334.

65. "Unspeakable joy": Douglass, *Life and Times*, 251.

66. Douglass, *Life and Times*, 253.

67. Douglass, *Life and Times*, 254.

68. Walter Scott, "The Lady of the Lake," Canto 5, verse 24. While Douglass added a second "s" to differentiate his name, early sources often printed it with only one "s".

69. Douglass, *Life and Times*, 263–64.

70. Blight, *Frederick Douglass*, 93.

71. Douglass, *My Bondage and My Freedom*, 353.

72. James, *Life of Rev. Thomas James*, 5.

73. Blight, *Frederick Douglass*, 93.

74. Blight, *Frederick Douglass*, 98–99.

75. Douglass, *Life and Times of Frederick Douglass*, 266–67; *My Bondage and My Freedom*, 357–58.

76. *Liberator*, August 20, 1841.

77. Douglass, *My Bondage and My Freedom*, 358; *Life and Times of Frederick Douglass*, 266–67.

78. *Liberator*, October 15, 1841.

79. *Liberator*, October 15, 1841.

80. *Liberator*, October 15, 1841.

81. Douglass, *Life and Times of Frederick Douglass*, 277–78; *My Bondage and My Freedom*, 399–400; *Liberator*, October 15, 1841.

82. Collins compares the conductor's fear, guilt, and shame to that of Macbeth in Shakespeare's *Tragedy of Macbeth* (act 2, scene 2). Having just killed the king, Macbeth tells his wife that when two drugged guards cried out "God bless us!" and "Amen" in their sleep, "I could not say 'Amen' / When they did say 'God bless us!'"

83. Douglass, *Life and Times of Frederick Douglass*, 278.

84. *Liberator*, October 15, 1841.

85. *Liberator*, November 5, 1841.

86. *Liberator*, November 5, 1841.

87. Reprinted in the *Liberator*, November 5, 1841. Unless otherwise noted, quotations in this account are taken from the *Liberator*.

88. Knocking off a man's hat was a potent insult and is referenced at the beginning of *Moby Dick*, when the narrator, Ishmael, comments, "Whenever I find myself growing grim . . . it requires a strong moral principle to prevent me from deliberately stepping into the street, and methodically knocking people's hats off." Melville, *Moby Dick*, 1. This trope is famously reflected in the song "Stagolee," based on an actual event in 1895 in which "Stack" Lee Shelton and Billy Lyons knocked each other's hats off before Shelton shot Lyons, saying (according to the version by Mississippi John Hurt in 1928), "You stole my Stetson hat, I'm bound to take your life." See Bollard, "Stagolee," 785.

89. The reporter mistakenly refers twice to the plaintiff, Mann, as "the defendant," but Harrington was the defendant.

90. All quotations are from the *Liberator*, November 12, 1841.

91. *Doggett's New York City Directory for 1849–1850*, 227.

92. U.S. Census, New Orleans, Louisiana, 3rd Rep. Ward, June 8, 1860, 198. The New Orleans Dental Depot was established in 1855 (*Daily Arkansas Gazette*, November 22, 1866, 4).

93. *New Orleans Daily Picayune*, May 30, 1861, quoted in Rodriguez, "We'll Hang Jeff Davis," 9.

94. *New Orleans Daily Crescent*, May 30, 1861, 1.

95. *New Orleans Daily Crescent*, May 30, 1861, 1.

96. *Pacific Appeal* (San Francisco), September 27, 1862.

97. *Liberator*, January 14, 1842.

98. *Liberator*, January 14, 1842.

99. James, *Life of Rev. Thomas James*, 3. See also Ogburn, "James, Thomas," 499–500.

100. James, *Life of Rev. Thomas James*, 3–5.

101. James, *Life of Rev. Thomas James*, 6.

102. James, *Life of Rev. Thomas James*, 8.

103. James, *Life of Rev. Thomas James*, 10–12. For an outline of the Lucy Faggins (or Louisa Fearing) case, see Grover, *Fugitive's Gibraltar*, 160–67.

104. James, *Life of Rev. Thomas James*, 12–13.

105. James, *Life of Rev. Thomas James*, 17–18.

106. James, *Life of Rev. Thomas James*, 18–19.

107. James, *Life of Rev. Thomas James*, 15 16. James's memory of the Crafts, written thirty-eight years after the fact, is not entirely accurate; see McCaskill, "Craft, William, and Ellen Craft," 195–97.

108. *New-Bedford Mercury*, February 4, 1842.

109. *New Bedford Register*, February 9, 1842; *Liberator*, February 18, 1842.

110. *Liberator*, August 6, 1841.

111. *New Bedford Register*, March 18, 1842.

112. *New Bedford Register*, March 30, 1842; *New Bedford Mercury*, April 1, 1842.

113. *Liberator*, April 22, 1842.

114. "Shadrach Howard," Black Abolitionist Archives, https://libraries.udmercy.edu/archives/special-collections/index.php?record_id=1368&collectionCode=baa.

115. Except where otherwise noted, biographical information is drawn from Sewell, "Remond, Charles Lenox"; and Hunt, "Remond, Sarah Parker," 707–10.

116. *Liberator*, February 18, 1842.

117. See *Liberator*, February 18, 1842.

118. Quotations are taken from the *Liberator*, February 25, 1842.

119. Blight, *Frederick Douglass*, 128–37.

120. Blight, *Frederick Douglass*, 218.

121. *Liberator*, September 23, 1853.

122. See especially Archer, *Jim Crow North*, 102–8.

123. Commonwealth of Massachusetts, [State Senate Report] No. 63, February 22, 1842, https://archive.org/details/insenatefeb2218400mass/page/n1/mode/2up; *Liberator*, March 4, 1842.

124. *Liberator*, April 8, 1842.

125. Alexander Pope, *Essay on Man*, Epistle IV, lines 215–16, 542.

126. *Liberator*, April 28, 1843.

127. *Liberator*, February 3, 1843.

128. Much of the debate was printed in the *Liberator*, February 17, 1843.

129. *Liberator*, March 31, 1843.

130. *Liberator*, March 31, 1843.

131. *Liberator*, April 28, 1843.

132. Pathan, "Saunders, William."

133. Quoted in Vara-Dannen, "Letters of Protest," 180.

134. *Hartford Daily Courant*, July 26, 1843.

135. *Journal of the House of Representatives of the United States* 37, no. 3: 105.

136. Purvis, "The Dorsey Brothers," 356–61.

137. The similarity of Dorsey's account to Robert Purvis's own background makes one wonder whether Dorsey was borrowing a bit of his history or the *Gazette* reporter misinterpreted Dorsey. See Purvis, "The Dorsey Brothers," 353–54.

138. Purvis, "The Dorsey Brothers," 356; *Hampshire Gazette*, April 2, 1867. The *Hampshire Gazette* may have gotten the May 14 date from Dorsey, who may have confused or conflated it with the date on which he became free according to a bill of sale dated May 14, 1851.

139. Purvis, "The Dorsey Brothers," 359–60.

140. *Hampshire Gazette*, April 2, 1867.
141. *Hampshire Gazette*, October 15, 1851.
142. Printed in the *Friends' Intelligencer* 55 (1898): 245. A copy of this bill of sale was found among the papers of the abolitionist and feminist educator Elizabeth Powell Bond, who had been the Sunday School superintendent for the Florence Congregational Society before becoming dean at Swarthmore College.
143. Douglass, *My Bondage and My Freedom*, 366–68; *Life and Times of Frederick Douglass*, 290–91.
144. Douglass, *My Bondage and My Freedom*; Elizabeth Pryor, *Colored Travelers*, 143–47.
145. Douglass, *My Bondage and My Freedom*, 390; *Life and Times of Frederick Douglass*, 318–19.
146. Douglass, *My Bondage and My Freedom*, 391; *Life and Times of Frederick Douglass*, 319.
147. Douglass, *My Bondage and My Freedom*, 391.
148. All quotations below relating to this case are drawn from the *Liberator*, June 10, 1853.
149. Porter, "The Remonds of Salem, Massachusetts," 283.
150. *Liberator*, February 17, 1860.
151. See *Dred Scott v. Sanford.*
152. Hunt, "Remond, Sarah Parker," 709. See also Pryor, *Colored Travelers*, 106–7.
153. Porter, "The Remonds of Salem, Massachusetts," 288–89; Hunt, "Remond, Sarah Parker," 709.
154. Biographical information is drawn from Thomas, "Pennington, James William Charles," 667–68.
155. *New York Times*, September 25, 1852.
156. *New York Times*, September 25, 1852.
157. *New York Times*, November 10, 1852.
158. *New York Times*, July 29, 1853.
159. *New York Times*, August 4, 1853.

Chapter 2. Streetcars and War

1. Surviving records for Elizabeth and her father, Thomas Sr., show both the spellings "Jennings" and "Jinnings"; her brother Thomas preferred the latter.
2. "Outrage upon Colored Persons," *New York Daily Tribune*, July 19, 1854; *Frederick Douglass' Paper*, July 28, 1854. Paragraphing has been added to the statement for ease of reading.
3. Hewitt, "The Search for Elizabeth Jennings," 393–96.
4. *New York Daily Tribune*, February 23, 1855; *Frederick Douglass' Paper*, March 2, 1855.
5. *New York Daily Tribune*, February 23, 1855 (italics in original).
6. *New York Daily Tribune*, February 23, 1855.
7. Hewitt, "The Search for Elizabeth Jennings," 403–8, 414.
8. For biographical information, see Eaton, "Brown, William Wells," 119–21.
9. W. Brown, *American Fugitive in Europe*, 312–14.
10. Unfortunately, the texts of these plays have not survived. Before the Civil War, "doughface" was a derogatory term for a northerner who was not opposed to slavery.
11. *New York Daily Tribune*, May 8, 1855.

12. *New York Daily Tribune*, May 8, 1855.

13. *New York Times*, May 12, 1855. The McFarland incident is also described in a letter to the *Times* from T. Bailey Myers, Secretary of the Sixth Ave. R.R. Co., *New York Times*, May 29, 1855.

14. *New York Times*, May 25, 1855.

15. *New York Times*, May 29, 1855.

16. *New York Times*, May 30, 1855.

17. *New York Times*, May 26, 1855; *Frederick Douglass' Paper*, September 7, 1855.

18. *New York Times*, December 18, 1856.

19. *New York Times*, December 20, 1856.

20. "James W. C. Pennington Award," Heidelberg Center for American Studies, https://www.hca.uni-heidelberg.de/forschung/pennington_en.html.

21. "Downing's Oyster House," Mapping the African American Past, https://maap.columbia.edu/place/1.html.

22. A rod is a formerly common measure equal to 16½ feet.

23. *Frederick Douglass' Paper*, October 5, 1855, reprinted from the *New York Evening Post*.

24. *New York Times*, April 12, 1866.

25. "Downing's Oyster House," Mapping the African American Past.

26. Blackett, "Day, William Howard," 219–20.

27. Luxenberg, *Separate*, 142.

28. See *Day v. Owen*; Luxenberg, *Separate*, 139–43.

29. *Dred Scott v. Sanford*.

30. Murray, *States' Laws on Race and Color*, 227.

31. *Harrisburg Telegraph*, April 14, 1898, quoted in Blackett, "Day, William Howard," 219.

32. *New York Daily Tribune*, December 17, 1856.

33. Kelley, *Right to Ride*, 29–31.

34. See Hepp, "Streetcars"; "Philadelphia Trolley Beginnings."

35. The classic study of streetcar segregation in Philadelphia is Philip Foner, "The Battle to End Discrimination against Negroes on Philadelphia Streetcars."

36. Still, *Brief Narrative of the Struggle*, 3.

37. Still, *Brief Narrative of the Struggle*, 4–5, 7.

38. P. Foner, "The Battle to End Discrimination (Part I)," 280, 282.

39. The letter is reprinted in Still, *Brief Narrative of the Struggle*, 8–9.

40. Still, *Brief Narrative of the Struggle*, 9.

41. Angell, "The Shadows of the Evening," 238–39.

42. McLaughlin-Stonham, *From Slavery to Civil Rights*, 56.

43. *Daily Delta* (New Orleans), October 17, 23, 1862.

44. *Clarion-Ledger* (Jackson, Miss.), March 20, 1873.

45. *George Donnell v. State of Mississippi*.

46. "Civil Rights Law of 1873."

47. *Appeal*, July 25, 1891.

48. William Still, *The Underground Rail Road*, 539.

49. *Philadelphia Press*, March 15, 1865, reprinted in the *Liberator*, March 24, 1865. Quotations below are taken from this article.

50. *Liberator*, March 24, 1865.

51. Still, *Underground Rail Road*, 540.

52. *Chicago Daily Inter-Ocean*, August 13, 1879.

53. See Truth, *Narrative of Sojourner Truth*; Painter, *Sojourner Truth*; Painter, "Truth, Sojourner," 820–22; Washington, *Sojourner Truth's America*.

54. Truth, *Narrative of Sojourner Truth*, 53.

55. "A Utopian Community in Florence, MA."

56. Douglass, "What I Found at the Northampton Association," 130.

57. New York *Independent*, April 23, 1863, reprinted in part in Truth, *Narrative of Sojourner Truth*, 131–35.

58. Truth's "I am a woman's rights" is best understood as meaning "I am (like you in the audience) a proponent of women's rights." Note: the singular "woman" in "woman's rights" was common in the nineteenth century.

59. Whether we use Gage's spelling "ar'n't," or "ain't," or the modern "aren't," this question not only became the title by which Truth's speech is now widely known. Drawing on the title of Deborah Gray White's seminal study, *Ar'n't I a Woman? Female Slaves in the Plantation South* (1985), it has become a keystone reference to the scholarly reassessment of the lives of female slaves. See also Hine, "*Ar'n't I a Woman? Female Slaves in the Plantation South*—Twenty Years After."

60. For differing perspectives on the speech, its context, and its reception and effect, see especially Painter, *Sojourner Truth*, 164–78; Washington, *Sojourner Truth's America*, 222–29; and further references cited there.

61. *Pennsylvania Freeman*, September 4, 1852, quoted in Bruno, "Rewriting Rebellion," 39–40.

62. Truth, *Narrative of Sojourner Truth*, 179.

63. On Truth's rather sophisticated relationship to and understanding of the law, see especially Accomando, "Demanding a Voice among the Pettifoggers," 61–86.

64. Truth, *Narrative of Sojourner Truth*, 184–87.

65. Painter, *Sojourner Truth*, 210.

66. Truth, *Narrative of Sojourner Truth*, 186–87. According to the description of this event in a letter Truth sent to Amy Post, Haviland's reply to the conductor was a bit more expansive: "She does not belong to me, but she belongs to Humanity, and she would have been out of the way long ago, if you had let her alone." Quoted in Painter, *Sojourner Truth*, 210.

67. Truth, *Narrative of Sojourner Truth*, 187.

68. Sojourner Truth File, Library of Congress, quoted in Accomando, "Demanding a Voice among the Pettifoggers," 78.

69. Truth, *Narrative of Sojourner Truth*, 231.

70. Truth, "Address to the American Equal Rights Association," 20.

71. P. Foner, "The Battle to End Discrimination (Part II)," 359.

72. Wallace, *Philadelphia Reports*, 30; *Philadelphia Inquirer*, April 27, 1865.

73. Wallace, *Philadelphia Reports*, 30.

74. Wallace, *Philadelphia Reports*, 30; *Inquirer*, April 27, 1865.

75. Wallace, *Philadelphia Reports*, 31.

76. Wallace, *Philadelphia Reports*, 33.

77. P. Foner, "The Battle to End Discrimination (Part II)," 361.

78. *New York Times*, May 18, 1865.

79. *Philadelphia Inquirer*, June 3, 1865, quoted in Biddle and Dubin, *Tasting Freedom*, 339–40.

80. On the possible connections between Douglass and Tubman in Maryland, see Larson, *Bound for the Promised Land*, 93–96.

81. Larson, *Bound for the Promised Land*, 42–44; Sarah H. Bradford, *Scenes in the Life of Harriet Tubman*, 74–75.

82. The site of the Ross cabin was discovered near an abandoned road in "swampy terrain" on the Eastern Shore in the spring of 2021. See Sarah Bahr, "Archaeologists Solve a Decades-Old Harriett Tubman Mystery," *New York Times*, April 20, 2021.

83. Larson gives a detailed, partially speculative account of Tubman's escape in *Bound for the Promised Land*, 80–84.

84. Larson, *Bound for the Promised Land*, 88.

85. Larson, *Bound for the Promised Land*, 143–44.

86. Larson, *Bound for the Promised Land*, 151.

87. Larson, *Bound for the Promised Land*, 173–75.

88. Larson, *Bound for the Promised Land*, 232. Bradford, *Scenes in the Life of Harriet Tubman*, 46, refers to it as a "baggage-car," which could simply have been the other half of the smoking car.

89. Martha Coffin Wright, letter to Marianna Pelham Wright, November 7, 1865, quoted in Larson, *Bound for the Promised Land*, 232.

90. Larson, *Bound for the Promised Land*, 232–33.

91. Larson, *Bound for the Promised Land*, 271–76.

92. Quoted in Larson, *Bound for the Promised Land*, 272.

93. Larson, *Bound for the Promised Land*, 230, 277–79.

94. Biographical information is drawn from Sherman, "Horton, George Moses," 414–16.

95. Still, *Underground Rail Road*, 540–41.

96. Still, *Underground Rail Road*, 540–41.

97. *National Anti-Slavery Standard*, February 23, 1867; P. Foner, "The Battle to End Discrimination (Part II)," 366.

98. Still, *Underground Rail Road*, 541.

99. Biddle and Dubin, *Tasting Freedom*. See also Scott, "Catto, Octavius Valentine."

100. Biddle and Dubin, *Tasting Freedom*, 182–83, 199.

101. Biddle and Dubin, *Tasting Freedom*, 199, 203.

102. Biddle and Dubin, *Tasting Freedom*, 290–92.

103. Biddle and Dubin, *Tasting Freedom*, 293–95.

104. Biddle and Dubin, *Tasting Freedom*, 323–25.

105. Biddle and Dubin, *Tasting Freedom*, 325–26.

106. Biddle and Dubin, *Tasting Freedom*, 25–26.

107. P. Foner, "The Battle to End Discrimination (Part II)," 363–65.

108. Biddle and Dubin, *Tasting Freedom*, 370.

109. For the text of the law, see Pauli Murray, *States' Laws on Race and Color*, 394.

110. Biddle and Dubin, *Tasting Freedom*, 415–16.

111. Biddle and Dubin, *Tasting Freedom*, 418.

112. Biddle and Dubin, *Tasting Freedom*, 429.

113. Biddle and Dubin, *Tasting Freedom*, 421–71, gives detailed accounts of the 1871 election day riot, the death of Catto, and the capture and trials of Kelly. See also Griffin, *The Trial of Frank Kelly*.

114. Downey, "Pleasant, Mary Ellen," 674–75; Hudson, *The Making of "Mammy Pleasant"*; Crowe, "Mary Ellen Pleasant," 35; E. White, "A Girl Full of Smartness"; Bennett, "Historical Detective Story," 71–86.

115. Hudson, *The Making of "Mammy Pleasant,"* 38–41.

116. *Daily Alta California*, June 30, 1863.

117. Brown: *Sacramento Bee*, June 5, 1863. Bowen: *Pacific Appeal*, June 6, 1863.

118. Both suits are cited in *Pacific Appeal*, July 11, 1863.

119. *Daily Alta California*, December 22, 1864.

120. *San Francisco Examiner* and *Daily Alta California*, January 18, 1866.

121. Quoted from *Emma J. Turner v. North Beach and Mission*, reprinted in Withrow, *American Corporation Cases*, vol. 1, 203.

122. Quoted in Hudson, *The Making of "Mammy Pleasant,"* 51.

123. *Daily Alta California*, October 18, 1866.

124. Hudson, *The Making of "Mammy Pleasant,"* 52–53.

125. *John J. Pleasants, and Mary E. v. North Beach and Mission*; *Emma J. Turner v. North Beach and Mission*.

126. *Emma J. Turner v. North Beach and Mission*, in Withrow, *The American Corporation Cases*, vol. 1, 205.

127. Hudson, *The Making of "Mammy Pleasant,"* 54.

128. See, for example, "Mammy Pleasant: Angel or Archfiend in the House of Mystery," *San Francisco Call*, May 7, 1899.

129. Hudson, *The Making of "Mammy Pleasant,"* 63–78.

130. *San Francisco Chronicle*, January 12, 1904.

131. Bennett, "Historical Detective Story," 86. In 1978 the memorial stone was surreptitiously covered with a plaque that read "Mammy Pleasant, a remarkable woman of the Gold Rush." Libby, "Mary Ellen Pleasant Grave Restoration." In June 2011 this was replaced with a stone identifying Pleasant as "MOTHER OF CIVIL RIGHTS IN CALIFORNIA" and including "SHE WAS A FRIEND OF JOHN BROWN." Find a Grave, https://www.findagrave.com/memorial/8235492/mary_ellen-pleasant/photo#view-photo=70661242.

132. Still, *Brief Narrative of the Struggle*, 23. See also P. Foner, "The Battle to End Discrimination (Part II)," 373–76; and Biddle and Dubin, *Tasting Freedom*, 352–54.

133. Still, *Brief Narrative of the Struggle*, 3–4.

134. Still, *Brief Narrative of the Struggle*, 12.

135. Still, *Brief Narrative of the Struggle*, 6.

136. Child, *An Appeal in Favor of That Class*, 120.

137. See above, pp. 4–5.

138. Still, *Brief Narrative of the Struggle*, 3–4.

139. Still, "[Letter of 1866 April 30]."

140. Evelyn Brooks Higginbotham coined the phrase "the politics of respectability" in *Righteous Discontent: The Women's Movement in the Black Baptist Church, 1880–1920*, a study of the social changes wrought especially by African American churchwomen that introduced respectability politics as an important theme in academic discourse, but respectability in general had clearly been a matter of concern and discussion before the 1880s.

141. Cooper, *Beyond Respectability*, 29, quoted in Parker, *Unceasing Militant*, 350n4.

142. Murray, *States' Laws on Race and Color*, 73.

143. *John R. Thompson Co., Inc. v. District of Columbia*, U.S. Court of Appeals, D.C. Circuit.

144. *District of Columbia v. John R. Thompson Co.*; Parker, *Unceasing Militant*, 271–81. For an examination of the role played by Black women thinkers in the late nineteenth and early twentieth centuries, see Cooper, *Beyond Respectability*; and Higginbotham, *Righteous Discontent*.

145. Parker, *Unceasing Militant*, 281.

146. Biddle and Dubin, *Tasting Freedom*, 105.

147. P. Foner, "Battle to End Discrimination (Part II)," 373.

148. P. Foner, "Battle to End Discrimination (Part II)," 373; and Biddle and Dubin, *Tasting Freedom*, 352.

149. *National Anti-Slavery Standard*, March 30, 1867; P. Foner, "Battle to End Discrimination (Part II)," 373.

150. *New Orleans Tribune*, April 21, 186, quoted in Fischer, "A Pioneer Protest," 222.

151. *New Orleans Republican*, May 1, 1867.

152. *New Orleans Tribune*, May 4, 1867, quoted in Fischer, "Pioneer Protest," 223.

153. *New Orleans Times*, May 5, 1867. In 2021 a street near where this incident occurred was renamed in honor of Joseph Guillaume; see New Orleans City Council Street Renaming Council, "Joseph Guillaume."

154. *Daily Picayune*, May 6, 1867.

155. *New Orleans Times*, May 7, 1867.

156. *Daily Picayune*, May 6, 1867.

157. *New Orleans Times*, May 7, 1867.

158. One notable exception was the Robert Charles race riot in 1900, when mobs of unruly white men invaded the cars and attacked Black passengers, killing some and injuring numerous others. See Kelley, *Right to Ride*, 96–99; and chapter 4 of this book.

159. *Constitution . . . of the State of Louisiana, 1868*, 4.

160. Act No. 38, in *Acts Passed by the General Assembly of the State of Louisiana* (1869), 37.

161. This review of the case of Madame Decuir is drawn from Beermann, *Journey to Separate but Equal*, 16–21 (on the Decuir family) and 21–22 (on Antoine Dubuclet).

162. Beermann, *Journey to Separate but Equal*, 41.

163. Beermann, *Journey to Separate but Equal*, 43.

164. Beermann, *Journey to Separate but Equal*, 43–46.

165. Beermann, *Journey to Separate but Equal*, 46–48. The quotation is drawn from the court transcript of testimony.

166. *Daily Picayune*, July 30, 1872.

167. After the judge in Decuir's case lost his seat in the 1872 election, the case was transferred to the Fifth District Court.

168. *Constitution of Louisiana* (1868), Art. 13; *Acts of Louisiana* (1869), 37.

169. Beermann, *Journey to Separate but Equal*, 63–64.

170. Beermann, *Journey to Separate but Equal*, 48–49, 69.

171. Beermann, *Journey to Separate but Equal*, 49.

172. Beermann, *Journey to Separate but Equal*, 69–70.

173. Beermann, *Journey to Separate but Equal*, 100–103.

174. Beermann, *Journey to Separate but Equal*, 108–9; E. Foner, *Reconstruction*, 237. See also *United States v. Cruikshank*.

175. Beermann, *Journey to Separate but Equal*, 114–20.

176. Beermann, *Journey to Separate but Equal*, 121–23.

177. Beermann, *Journey to Separate but Equal*, 151–52.

178. Beermann, *Journey to Separate but Equal*, 153.

179. Beermann, *Journey*, 152, 222n38. See also *Williams v. Carolina Coach Co.*, 111 F. Supp. 329 (E.D. Va. 1952).

Chapter 3. The Ladies' Car and the Law

1. See *Chicago and Northwestern v. Williams* 55 III. 185 (1870), https://cite.case.law/ill/55/185.

2. Civil Rights Act of 1875.

3. This act as passed is a greatly amended version of the Tennessee House Bill 527, originally proposed in remarkably blatantly racist language. For the text of both, see "Chapter 130, Acts of Tennessee, 1875." A note from the Tennessee House Judiciary Committee attached to the original text stated the they "fully approve[d] of the principles embodied therein" but recommended reducing it to the more anodyne but far more open-ended version adopted.

4. The present account is drawn from the handwritten report of that case and the U.S. Supreme Court's mandate of payment to Robinson, both held in the National Archives. See "Testimony from Robinson v. Memphis"; and see also François, "A Lost World," 1015–79.

5. Luxenberg, *Separate*, 349.

6. Civil Rights Cases, 109 U.S. 3 (1883).

7. *New York Times*, November 21, 1883.

8. See Luxenberg, *Separate*, 355–56.

9. Quoted in Luxenberg, *Separate*, 356.

10. *Brown v. Memphis & C. R.* (1880).

11. *Brown v. Memphis & C. R.* (1880).

12. Quoted by Hammond in denying a motion for a retrial; *Brown v. Memphis & C. R.*, Circuit Court (1881).

13. *Brown v. Memphis & C. R.* (1880).

14. *Brown v. Memphis & C. R.* (1880).

15. *Brown v. Memphis & C. R.* (1880).

16. *Brown v. Memphis & C. R.*, Circuit Court (1881).

17. *Acts of the State of Tennessee*, 1881, 211. See also Cartwright, "Black Legislators in Tennessee," 265–84.

18. For the details of Ida B. Wells-Barnett's life, see especially Paula Giddings, *Ida: A Sword Among Lions* (2008).

19. Giddings, *Ida*, 25.

20. Giddings, *Ida*, 31.

21. *The Chesapeake, Ohio and Southwestern Railroad Company v. Ida B. Wells*. This full record of the court proceedings is hereafter cited as "Transcript." Wells's testimony appears on pages 19–23. See also Giddings, *Ida*, 60–68.

22. Transcript, 23–25.

23. Transcript, 32–33.

24. Transcript, 29.

25. Transcript, 55–56.

26. Transcript, 26.

27. Transcript, 51, 47. The Tennessee Supreme Court summary written by Chief Justice Peter Turney inexplicably dates this incident as happening on May 4, 1884. Many modern accounts of Well's life, especially online, repeat this mistaken date in the court record. See *Cases Argued and Determined in the Supreme Court of Tennessee* (1887), 614.

28. Transcript, 50.

29. Transcript, 63, 64.

30. *Cases Argued . . . in Tennessee* (1887), 614–15.

31. Transcript, 51, 47.

32. Wells, *Diary*, 182–83. The diary has been edited in print by Miriam DeCosta-Willis as *The Memphis Diary of Ida B. Wells*.

33. *New York Age*, August 11, 1888, quoted in Wells, *The Memphis Diary of Ida B. Wells*, 51.

34. *New York Age*, August 8, 1891, reprinted in Wells, *Light of Truth*, 31–32.

35. Quoted in Giddings, *Ida*, 175.

36. *New York Age*, September 19, 1891, quoted in Wells, *Light of Truth*, 34.

37. All three works were reprinted in a Dover edition: Wells, *On Lynchings*.

38. Giddings, "Wells-Barnett, Ida Bell," 863–66; Giddings, *Ida*, 604–13; "Elaine Massacre of 1919," *Encyclopedia of Arkansas*, https://encyclopediaofarkansas.net/entries/elaine-massacre-of-1919-1102.

39. "Ida B. Wells," Pulitzer Prizes, 2020, https://www.pulitzer.org/winners/ida-b-wells.

40. "Stewart vs. the Sue," http://johnspinkstew.org/stewart/StewartvsSue.htm. See also *The Sue*, 22 F. 843 (D. Md. 1885).

41. *Houck v. Southern Pac. Ry. Co.*, 38 F. 226 (WD Texas, 1888). All quotations not otherwise documented are taken from this source. Curiously, the case was entered late into the 1889 *Federal Reporter* with the date November 16, 1888, and identified as from the Western District of Texas, whereas the handwritten judgment record gives the verdict date as December 12, 1888, and the court as the Eastern District of Texas. A further complication is that the judge, Aleck Boarman, served the Western District of Louisiana, not far from Galveston.

42. *Houck v. Southern Pacific Railway*, Judgment Record, http://recordsofrights.org/events/57/a-rare-victory-for-texas-woman.

43. John Smith, "Councill, William Hooper."

44. Smith, "Councill, William Hooper."

45. Luxenberg, *Separate*, 364–69.

46. Interstate Commerce Act, *Interstate Commerce Commission Reports*, vol. 1, 4. Hereafter cited as *ICC Reports*.

47. *ICC Reports*, vol. 1, 292.

48. *ICC Reports*, vol. 1, 355.

49. *ICC Reports*, vol. 1, 638; boldface as in the original.

50. John Smith, "Councill, William Hooper."

51. Heard, *From Slavery to the Bishopric*, 32.

52. See Heard, *From Slavery to the Bishopric*, 19–61.

53. *ICC Reports*, vol. 1, 720; Kelley, *Right to Ride*, 38–39.

54. *New York Times*, July 30, 1887.

55. Kelley, *Right to Ride*, 39.

56. Heard, *From Slavery to the Bishopric*, 60.

57. *New York Times*, August 9, 1937.

58. Heard obituary, *New York Times*, September 13, 1937.

Chapter 4. Jim Crow across the South

1. *Louisville, New Orleans & Texas Railway Co. v. State of Mississippi*, https://www.law.cornell.edu/supremecourt/text/133/587.

2. Louisiana Railway Accommodations Act, https://railroads.unl.edu/documents/view_document.php?id=rail.gen.0060.

3. Luxenberg, *Separate*, 393. Much of the following discussion of the Desdunes and Plessy cases draws on Luxenberg's detailed history and analysis, especially 419–87.

4. New Orleans *Times-Democrat*, May 24, 1890.

5. Luxenberg, *Separate*, 394.

6. Louisiana Railway Accommodations Act, Section 2.

7. On the arrest and court appearance of Desdunes, see Luxenberg, *Separate*, 425–30, 433–34.

8. *State ex. rel. Abbott v. Hicks*; Luxenberg, *Separate*, 429–30.

9. Luxenberg, *Separate*, 431–32.

10. Both the white-owned papers, *Times-Democrat* and *Daily Picayune*, June 9, 1892, identify him as Adolph Plessy; Martinet's *Crusader* two days later names him Homer A. Plessy.

11. *Times-Democrat*, June 9, 1892.

12. *Crusader*, probably June 11, 1892, Xavier University of Louisiana Library, Digital Archives and Collections, https://xula.contentdm.oclc.org/digital/collection/p16948coll18/id/22/rec/2. References to the lack of a successor to Judge Marr and to the Desdunes case as still pending indicate that this article was written on June 8, after Plessy appeared in court but before Judge Ferguson dismissed the Desdunes case on June 9. It would most likely have been published in the weekly *Crusader* on Saturday, June 11.

13. *Crusader*, probably June 11, 1892.

14. *Daily Picayune*, November 18, 1892.

15. *Daily Picayune*, November 18, 1892.

16. *Logwood and Wife v. Memphis & C. R. Co.*, 318.

17. *Ex parte Homer A. Plessy*, from which quotations below were taken. See also Luxenberg, *Separate*, 439.

18. An extract from Fenner's eulogy can be found on the Lee Family Digital Archive, https://leefamilyarchive.org/history-reference-misc-fenner-index. The eighty-five-foot-high monument to Lee, one of the first to be erected, was removed by order of the New Orleans City Council on May 19, 2017.

19. Lemuel Shaw, chief justice of Massachusetts, ruled in 1849 that segregated schools were constitutional in that state.

20. Luxenberg, *Separate*, 452–57.

21. *Plessy v. Ferguson*, 551.

22. *Plessy v. Ferguson*, 557–58.

23. Luxenberg, *Separate*, 489–90.

24. *Plessy v. Ferguson*, 559.

25. *New York Times*, November 12, 2021.

26. *New York Times*, January 5, 2022.

27. *Bowie v. Birmingham Railway*, 125 Ala. 397 (1899).

28. *Montgomery Advertiser*, August 8, 1900.

29. Meier and Rudwick, "The Boycott Movement against Jim Crow Streetcars," 758–59.

30. *Daily Picayune*, June 22, 1900.

31. Reprinted in Wells, *On Lynchings*, 117–63. See also Kelley, *Right to Ride*, 96–100.

32. Quoted in Wells, *Mob Rule in New Orleans*, from the New Orleans *Times-Democrat*, July 26, 1900. See also Wells, *On Lynchings*, 130.

33. *Times-Democrat*, July 26, 1900.

34. *Daily Picayune*, July 26, 1900.

35. Wells-Barnett, *Mob Rule in New Orleans*, 132–33.
36. Isaiah Scott, *Southwestern Christian Advocate*, June 5, 1902.
37. Louisiana Constitution, 1898, Article 197, Sections 3, 4.
38. "Barriers to Voting in Louisiana," 8.
39. Meier and Rudwick, "The Boycott Movement against Jim Crow Streetcars," 757.
40. Kelley, *Right to Ride*, 101–5.
41. Kelley, *Right to Ride*, 217–18n57, clarifies that the women in these organizations were not members of New Orleans's French Creole class descended from *les gens des couleur libre*, the "free people of color," but were rather members of the Black middle class.
42. Kelley, *Right to Ride*, 110.
43. *State v. Pearson et al.*, in Michie, *Railroad Reports*, 324–32. See also Kelly, *Right to Ride*, 112–15.
44. Meier and Rudwick, "The Boycott Movement against Jim Crow Streetcars," 762, 775.
45. *Georgia Edwards v. Nashville, Chattanooga & St. Louis Railway Company*, in ICC *Reports*, vol. 12, 247–48.
46. *Georgia Edwards v. Nashville, Chattanooga & St. Louis*, 248.
47. "About the *Nashville Globe*."
48. *Nashville Globe*, July 12, 1907.
49. Roosevelt, Letter from President Theodore Roosevelt to the Department of Justice.
50. Roosevelt letter.
51. Parker, *Unceasing Militant*, 13.
52. Parker, *Unceasing Militant*, 20.
53. Terrell, *A Colored Woman in a White World*, 15–16.
54. Parker, *Unceasing Militant*, 55.
55. Cooper, *Beyond Respectability*, 29, quoted in Parker, *Unceasing Militant*, 350n4.
56. Quoted in Parker, *Unceasing Militant*, 90–91.
57. Terrell, *A Colored Woman in a White World*, 417. Dyson is not named in this account.
58. Quoted in Parker, *Unceasing Militant*, 323n36.
59. Parker, *Unceasing Militant*, 92–96.
60. Parker, *Unceasing Militant*, 126–27.
61. C. Brown, "Some Incidents," 21–23. See also Lach, "Brown, Charlotte Hawkins," 105–6.
62. Brown, "Some Incidents," 4.
63. Pullman sleeping cars were an exception to segregated rail travel in the South. They were not owned by the railway companies but rather owned, staffed, and run by the Pullman Company, headquartered in Illinois, which contracted with the railways to pull them. After the passage of the 1875 Civil Rights Act, the owner, George M. Pullman, instructed his conductors to follow federal law and accept Black passengers. While it became difficult for African Americans to book Pullman tickets in much of the South, and though some states passed "sleeping car laws" to avoid any integrated travel, the Pullman cars provided the least humiliating, as well as the most comfortable, way for Black travelers who could afford it to take long journeys. See Bay, *Traveling Black*, 88–97.
64. Brown, "Some Incidents," 6–7.
65. Brown, "Some Incidents," 5–6.

66. Brown, "Some Incidents," 7–8. In 1938 Billie Holiday became the first full-time Black female vocalist with a white band, the Artie Shaw Orchestra. In a 1939 interview with *DownBeat* magazine, she commented on the reasons she quit. One of the reasons: "Artie wouldn't let me sit out front with the band. Last year, when we were at the Lincoln Hotel, the hotel management told me I had to use the back door. That was all right. But I had to ride up and down in the freight elevators, and every night Artie made me stay upstairs in a little room without a radio or anything all the time" (*DownBeat*, November 1, 1939).

67. Brown, "Some Incidents," 11.

68. Davis, *Communist Councilman from Harlem*, 33; Horne, "Davis, Benjamin Jefferson," 208–9.

69. Davis, *Communist Councilman from Harlem*, 34–35.

70. Davis, *Communist Councilman from Harlem*, 40–42.

71. Davis, *Communist Councilman from Harlem*, 44.

72. See Martin, "Herndon, Angelo," 396–98. Davis, *Communist Councilman from Harlem*, 53, gives different dates for the Georgia statute.

73. Davis, *Communist Councilman from Harlem*, 56.

74. Horne, "Davis, Benjamin Jefferson," 208–9.

75. Horne, "Davis, Benjamin Jefferson," 208.

76. Quoted, for example, in "Samuel Wilbert Tucker," Wikipedia, https://en.wikipedia.org/wiki/Samuel_Wilbert_Tucker.

77. Ackerman, "The Trials of S. W. Tucker"; For an abbreviated version, minus the trolley incident, see Ackerman, "Samuel Wilbert Tucker," 98–103.

78. J. Douglas Smith, *Managing White Supremacy*, 260–61.

79. Ackerman, "The Trials of S. W. Tucker."

80. Ackerman, "The Trials of S. W. Tucker."

81. The term "sit-down" first appeared to describe work stoppages in 1936 at tire and rubber plants in Akron, Ohio. See, for example, "'Sit-Down' Striking Affects Goodyear," *New York Times*, February 2, 1936.

82. Ackerman, "The Trials of S. W. Tucker."

83. Ackerman, "The Trials of S. W. Tucker."

84. Branch, *Parting the Waters*, 19–21.

85. *Wright v. Council of City of Emporia*, 451.

86. Ackerman, "The Trials of S. W. Tucker."

87. Baldwin, "Many Thousands Gone," 42.

88. Nordin, "Arthur Wergs Mitchell."

89. "Walter White Raps Arthur Mitchell," *Atlanta Daily World*, May 7, 1936.

90. "Walter White Raps Arthur Mitchell"; Nordin, "Arthur Wergs Mitchell."

91. *Mitchell v. United States*, 94.

92. *Mitchell v. United States*, 90–91.

93. *Mitchell v. United States*, 95.

94. *Mitchell v. United States*, 97.

95. "Pronouns, Gender, and Pauli Murray," https://www.paulimurraycenter.com/pronouns-pauli-murray. The present account uses Murray's name rather than personal pronouns.

96. For biographical information, see Murray, *Song in a Weary Throat*.

97. *Missouri ex rel. Gaines v. Canada*.

98. Murray, *Song in a Weary Throat*, 148–49, 161.

99. Murray, *Song in a Weary Throat*, 149–50.

100. Murray, *Song in a Weary Throat*, 154–55, 162.
101. Murray, *Song in a Weary Throat*, 162–63, 151–52.
102. Murray, *Song in a Weary Throat*, 178.
103. *Carolina Times*, April 6, 1940.
104. Murray, *Song in a Weary Throat*, 179.
105. *Carolina Times*, April 6, 1940.
106. Murray, *Song in a Weary Throat*, 181.
107. *Carolina Times*, April 6, 1940.
108. Murray, *Song in a Weary Throat*, 183.
109. Murray, *Song in a Weary Throat*, 183–89.
110. Murray, *Song in a Weary Throat*, 189.
111. Murray, *Song in a Weary Throat*, 190.
112. Murray, *Song in a Weary Throat*, 191–93.
113. Murray, *Song in a Weary Throat*, 141.
114. Murray, *Song in a Weary Throat*, 194–228.
115. Murray, *Song in a Weary Throat*, 338–39.
116. Murray, *Song in a Weary Throat*, 452–61.
117. Murray and Eastwood, "Jane Crow and the Law," 232–56.
118. Murray, *Song in a Weary Throat*, 473, 480.
119. "Who Is the Rev. Dr. Pauli Murray?"
120. Murray, *Song in a Weary Throat*, 569.
121. All quotations are taken from the U.S. Supreme Court decision in *Henderson v. United States*. See also Bay, *Traveling Black*, 261.
122. Rustin obituary, *New York Times*, August 25, 1987. See also Niven, "Rustin, Bayard Taylor," 741–42.
123. Rustin obituary, *New York Times*.
124. The *Christian Century* is a nondenominational Protestant magazine published since the late nineteenth century. During World War II it helped bring to public attention the plight of interned Japanese Americans.
125. Reprinted by permission of the Fellowship of Reconciliation, www.forusa.org. All rights reserved.
126. Full text of the letter: "I Must Resist: Bayard Rustin's Letter to the Draft Board," American Friends Service Committee, February 19, 2015, https://www.afsc.org/blogs/acting-in-faith/i-must-resist-bayard-rustin%E2%80%99s-letter-to-draft-board.
127. "Bayard Rustin," *Making Gay History*, https://makinggayhistory.com/podcast/bayard-rustin.
128. Anderson, *Bayard Rustin*, 111.
129. Swingler, "Thrown from Train," 20.
130. Swingler, "Thrown from Train," 20.
131. Swingler, "Thrown from Train," 20–21.
132. Swingler, "Thrown from Train," 20–21.
133. Swingler, "Thrown from Train," 22.
134. S. Brown, "Out of Their Mouths," 23–36.
135. Biographical information is drawn from DeGregory, "Gloster, Hugh Morris"; and Hugh Gloster obituary, *New York Times*, March 7, 2002.

Chapter 5. World War II and the Black Soldier

1. Lee, *The Employment of Negro Troops*, 349.
2. Wynn, *The African American Experience during World War II*, 118.

3. *People's Voice*, July 29, 1944.

4. *Lubbock Avalanche-Journal*, January 17, 1943. See also Burran, *The Beaumont Race Riot*, 43–49.

5. "Killing of Henry Williams in Alabama in 1942."

6. *Crisis*, November 1942, 361.

7. Moye, *Freedom Flyers*, 89.

8. Roundtree and McCabe, *Mighty Justice*, 9–10.

9. Wynn, *The African American Experience during World War II*, 106.

10. Roundtree and McCabe, *Mighty Justice*, 43.

11. Roundtree and McCabe, *Mighty Justice*, 65–66.

12. Roundtree and McCabe, *Mighty Justice*, 67–71.

13. Roundtree and McCabe, *Mighty Justice*, 119.

14. Roundtree and McCabe, *Mighty Justice*, 126.

15. Phillips, *War! What Is It Good For?*, 87.

16. Much of the information in this account is drawn from Rampersad, *Jackie Robinson*, especially 102–9.

17. Rampersad, *Jackie Robinson*, 91.

18. Images of this letter and other relevant documents are included in Vernon, "Jim Crow, Meet Lieutenant Robinson."

19. Quoted in Rampersad, *Jackie Robinson*, 103.

20. Gibson and Huntley, *Knocking Down Barriers*, 238. See also Jabbar and Walton, *Brothers in Arms*, 55.

21. "Summary of Telephone Conversation," in Vernon, "Jim Crow, Meet Lieutenant Robinson." See also Rampersad, *Jackie Robinson*, 104.

22. Rampersad, *Jackie Robinson*, 105–9.

23. Quotations are from the trial transcript. See Rampersad, Jackie Robinson, 106–7.

24. Rampersad, *Jackie Robinson*, 107.

25. Quoted in Rampersad, *Jackie Robinson*, 108.

26. Rampersad, *Jackie Robinson*, 109.

27. Rampersad, *Jackie Robinson*, 136–39.

28. Some accounts suggest that they sat in the front seat right behind the driver. See, for example, "Spicely, Booker T.," Open Durham, http://www.opendurham.org/people/spicely-booker-t.

29. "Killing of Booker T. Spicely."

30. *Massachusetts Register of Marriages*, 347; *Greater Hartford Directory*, 923; U.S. Census Bureau, Hartford, Conn., SU 1, ED 1–44, Sheet 61A, April 13, 1940; Pinder, "Morgan, Irene."

31. This account is drawn largely from Arsenault, *Freedom Riders*, 11–19.

32. *Morgan v. Virginia*, 328 U.S. 375, footnote 6; emphasis added.

33. Arsenault, *Freedom Riders*, 13.

34. Arsenault, *Freedom Riders*, 14.

35. See above, pp. 150–51; and Beermann, *The Journey to Separate but Equal.*

36. Arsenault, *Freedom Riders*, 17; *Morgan v. Commonwealth.*

37. Arsenault, *Freedom Riders*, 17–18.

38. *Morgan v. Virginia*, 328 U.S. 386.

39. Arsenault, *Freedom Riders*, 18–20.

40. Arsenault, *Freedom Riders*, 592n1.

41. "Kirkaldy, Irene Morgan," *New York Times*, August 13, 2007.

42. Theoharis, *The Rebellious Life of Mrs. Rosa Parks*, 48.

43. Nixon, E. D., interview.
44. Nixon, E. D., interview.
45. Hughes, "Adventures in Dining."
46. Murray, *States' Laws on Race and Color*, 227.
47. *Bob-Lo Excursion Co. v. Michigan*, 30n5.
48. "Zoot Suit Riots," Wikipedia, https://en.wikipedia.org/wiki/Zoot_Suit_Riots; Arellano, "The Untold Story of the Zoot Suit Riots."
49. *Bob-Lo Excursion Co. v. Michigan*, 31.
50. Murray, *States' Laws on Race and Color*, 228.
51. *Bob-Lo Excursion Co. v. Michigan*, 33n11.
52. *Bob-Lo Excursion Co. v. Michigan*, 40.
53. "Sarah Elizabeth Ray."
54. Unless otherwise noted, the present account is drawn from Gergel, *Unexampled Courage*. The incident itself is described on pages 12–23.
55. McMillan, "Race Justice in Aiken," *Nation*, November 23, 1946, in *Reporting Civil Rights*, pt. 1, 83.
56. Gergel, *Unexampled Courage*, 14–15.
57. Gergel, *Unexampled Courage*, 15.
58. Gergel, *Unexampled Courage*, 17.
59. Gergel, *Unexampled Courage*, 15.
60. Gergel, *Unexampled Courage*, 33.
61. Gergel, *Unexampled Courage*, 39–44.
62. Guthrie, *Born to Win*, 73, 231.
63. Gergel, *Unexampled Courage*, 73.
64. Gergel, *Unexampled Courage*, 84–91.
65. Gergel, *Unexampled Courage*, 118–26.
66. Gergel, *Unexampled Courage*, 127–28.
67. Gergel, *Unexampled Courage*, 128.
68. Harry S. Truman, "Address before the National Association for the Advancement of Colored People," June 29, 1947, Voices of Democracy, https://voicesofdemocracy.umd.edu/harry-s-truman-naacp-speech-text.
69. Gergel, *Unexampled Courage*, 145–50.
70. Truman, "Executive Order 9981."
71. Gergel, *Unexampled Courage*, 156.
72. Gergel, *Unexampled Courage*, 158–59.
73. Gergel, *Unexampled Courage*, 200–205.
74. Gergel, *Unexampled Courage*, 238–39.
75. *Brown v. Board of Education of Topeka*, https://tile.loc.gov/storage-services/service/ll/usrep/usrep347/usrep347483/usrep347483.pdf.
76. Gergel, *Unexampled Courage*, 259–61.
77. Gergel, *Unexampled Courage*, 269.

Chapter 6. "You Don't Have to Ride Jim Crow"

1. The dates and parameters of the civil rights movement remain a matter of debate. See preface.
2. Catsam, *Freedom's Main Line*, 20–21, 320nn30–31; Arsenault, *Freedom Riders*, 35, 596n38.
3. Rustin and Houser, *You Don't Have to Ride Jim Crow*. © Fellowship of Reconciliation, www.forusa.org, Reprinted by permission. All rights reserved.

4. Houser and Rustin, *We Challenged Jim Crow!*
5. Houser and Rustin, *We Challenged Jim Crow*, 3–9.
6. Houser and Rustin, *We Challenged Jim Crow*, 3–4.
7. Houser and Rustin, *We Challenged Jim Crow*, 10–11.
8. Houser and Rustin, *We Challenged Jim Crow*, 3.
9. Houser and Rustin, *We Challenged Jim Crow*, 5.
10. Peck, "Not So Deep Are the Roots," 95.
11. Peck, *Freedom Ride*, 25.
12. Houser and Rustin, *We Challenged Jim Crow*, 7.
13. Houser and Rustin, *We Challenged Jim Crow*, 8.
14. Houser and Rustin, *We Challenged Jim Crow*, 8.
15. The accompanying map is based on Houser and Rustin, *We Challenged Jim Crow*, as is that in Arsenault, *Freedom Riders*, on page 42.
16. Peck, "Not So Deep Are the Roots," 96.
17. Arsenault, *Freedom Riders*, 53.
18. Arsenault, *Freedom Riders*, 53; Catsam, *Freedom's Main Line*, 36–37.
19. Houser and Rustin, *We Challenged Jim Crow*, 13.
20. Nair, "Bayard Rustin," March 28, 2012.
21. Foreman, "Freedom Riders' Convictions Vacated."
22. Thornton, "Robinson, Jo Ann," 723–24.
23. Robinson, *Montgomery Bus Boycott*, 15–16.
24. Robinson, *Montgomery Bus Boycott*, 23, 24–25.
25. Robinson, *Montgomery Bus Boycott*, 26–27.
26. Williams and Greenhaw, *Thunder of Angels*, 5–14. Various versions of the incident give Brooks's name as Hilliard Brooks, including the Department of Justice File No. 144-2-1426, "Hilliard Brooks—Notice to Close File," https://www.justice.gov/crt/case-document/officer-marvin-e-mills-deceased-montgomery-police-dept-montgomery-alabama-subject. The names of the driver and the police officer are given in Thornton, *Dividing Lines*, 35.
27. Thornton, *Dividing Lines*, 35, 591. See also Graetz, *A White Preacher's Message*, 51.
28. The account of this incident and the subsequent ICC case is based on Roundtree, *Mighty Justice*, 125–55, and on personal communications with Amy Nathan, Keys's biographer, March 19, 2024. See also Nathan, *Sarah Keys v. Carolina Coach Company*.
29. Sarah Keys Evans, interview for the Military Women's Memorial Oral History Collection, January 30, 2006, courtesy of Amy Nathan.
30. Roundtree and McCabe, *Mighty Justice*, 127.
31. Roundtree and McCabe, *Mighty Justice*, 126.
32. Roundtree and McCabe, *Mighty Justice*, 128.
33. Roundtree and McCabe, *Mighty Justice*, 138.
34. Roundtree and McCabe, *Mighty Justice*, 143.
35. Roundtree and McCabe, *Mighty Justice*, 143–44.
36. *Brown v. Board of Education* at 493.
37. Roundtree and McCabe, *Mighty Justice*, 147.
38. *Sarah Keys v. Carolina Coach Company*, 152–53.
39. NAACP *v. St. Louis-San Francisco Railway Company*. In addition to the St. Louis-San Francisco line, twelve other railway companies and the Richmond Terminal Company were defendants in this case. See *New York Times*, November 26, 1955.
40. Huston, "ICC Orders End of Segregation."

41. *New York Post*, November 27, 1955, quoted in Roundtree and McCabe, *Mighty Justice*, 154.

42. "We Walk Together," *New York Post*, November 28, 1955, quoted in Roundtree and McCabe, *Mighty Justice*, 154.

43. Both the old seating system and the new are outlined in an Associated Press report printed in the *Crowley (La.) Daily Signal*, June 15, 1953. For an analysis of the boycott, see Catsam, "The Onward March of a People." See also "The Baton Rouge Bus Boycott"; and Melton, "Baton Rouge Bus Boycott."

44. *Crowley (La.) Daily Signal*, June 15, 1953.

45. Seelye, "Martha White, 99."

46. *Crowley (La.) Daily Signal*, June 15, 1953.

47. Branch, *Parting the Waters*, 146.

48. *Crowley Daily Signal*, June 20, 1953.

49. *Crowley Daily Signal*, June 26, 1953.

50. *Monroe Morning World*, June 28, 1953.

51. Branch, *Parting the Waters*, 145–46.

52. Vitello, "Rev. T. J. Jemison."

53. Hoose, *Claudette Colvin*, 17. Quotations here and below from Colvin herself are taken from Hoose's record of fourteen interviews that he did with her in 2007. See also Robinson, *The Montgomery Bus Boycott and the Women*, 37–43; and Branch, *Parting the Waters*, 120–23.

54. Hoose, *Claudette Colvin*, 24–26.

55. Hoose, *Claudette Colvin*, 26; J. Gray, "The Execution of Jeremiah Reeves."

56. F. Gray, *Bus Ride to Justice*, 48.

57. Hoose, *Claudette Colvin*, 32.

58. *Code of the City of Montgomery*, C.6, Section 11; emphasis added.

59. Adler, "Before Rosa Parks, There Was Claudette Colvin."

60. Hoose, *Claudette Colvin*, 33–36

61. Hoose, *Claudette Colvin*, 37.

62. Robinson, *The Montgomery Bus Boycott and the Women*, 40–41.

63. Branch, *Parting the Waters*, 123.

64. F. Gray, *Bus Ride to Justice*, 72, 47.

65. F. Gray, *Bus Ride to Justice*, 96.

66. "Before Rosa Parks."

67. Reeves, "Judge Clears 1955 Court Record." See also Medina, "A Civil Rights Pioneer Seeks to Have Her Record Cleared."

68. Claudette Colvin Foundation, https://www.claudettecolvinfoundation.com/.

69. Robinson, *The Montgomery Bus Boycott and the Women*, 136–37.

70. Williams and Greenhaw, *Thunder of Angels*, 213–14. Some sources give the date as April 19.

71. Hoose, *Claudette Colvin*, 110.

72. Hoose, *Claudette Colvin*, 58–60; Williams and Greenhaw, *Thunder of Angels*, 215.

73. Hoose, *Claudette Colvin*, 60; Theoharis, *Rebellious Life of Mrs. Rosa Parks*, 59.

74. Robinson, *The Montgomery Bus Boycott and the Women*, 137.

75. Parks and Haskins, *My Story*, 42–50; Morice, "Alice White."

76. See Theoharis, *Rebellious Life of Mrs. Rosa Parks*, 23–24; McGuire, "They'd Kill Me If I Told," chap. 1 in *Dark End of the Street*.

77. Brinkley, *Rosa Parks*, 57–60; Parks and Haskins, *My Story*, 72–79. Parks's 1992 autobiography, *My Story*, is a small volume aimed at a teenage audience; however,

because it is based on Jim Haskins's tapes of numerous interviews with her, it has a powerful first-person voice that conveys her personality quite vividly. Theoharis and Brinkley provide the historian's perspective.

78. Parks and Haskins, *My Story*, 113; Theoharis, *The Rebellious Life of Mrs. Rosa Parks*, 61; Brinkley, *Rosa Parks*, 104; Woo, "She Set Wheels of Justice."

79. For more detailed narratives of this confrontation and the arrest, see Theoharis, *The Rebellious Life of Mrs. Rosa Parks*, 61–71; Brinkley, *Rosa Parks*, 104–14; Parks and Haskins, *My Story*, 113–24.

80. Police Report, December 1, 1955, 2. See also Bredhoff, Schamel, and Potter, "An Act of Courage," 207–11.

81. On Parks's friendship with Gray, see F. Gray, "The Making of a Lawyer," chap. 2 in *Bus Ride to Justice*. For the quotation from Reddick, see Reddick, "The Bus Boycott in Montgomery," 253. On Septima Clark and the Highlander Folk School, see Theoharis, *The Rebellious Life of Mrs. Rosa Parks*, 39–42; Brinkley, *Rosa Parks*, 90–97; Parks and Haskins, *My Story*, 101–7; and Rouse, "Clark, Septima Poinsette."

82. Robinson, *The Montgomery Bus Boycott and the Women*, 45–46.

83. Theoharis, *The Rebellious Life of Mrs. Rosa Parks*, 82; Brinkley, *Rosa Parks*, 125.

84. Robinson, *The Montgomery Bus Boycott and the Women*, 91–95.

85. E. D. Nixon interview.

86. Brinkley, *Rosa Parks*, 152–53; Robinson, *The Montgomery Bus Boycott and the Women*, 135–38.

87. Theoharis, *The Rebellious Life of Mrs. Rosa Parks*, 231.

88. Branch, *Parting the Waters*, 183.

89. Branch, *Parting the Waters*, 176–79.

90. Brinkley, *Rosa Parks*, 155–60; Robinson, *The Montgomery Bus Boycott and the Women*, 149–61.

91. On July 7, 2022, Fred Gray was awarded the Medal of Freedom for his role in defending civil rights for African Americans in numerous cases.

92. Branch, *Parting the Waters*, 199, 201.

93. Janofsky, "Thousands Gather at the Capitol."

Chapter 7. Boycotts and Freedom Rides

1. C. Smith and Killian, *Tallahassee Bus Protest*, 1958.

2. C. Smith and Killian, *Tallahassee Bus Protest*, 5 and erratum to 5.

3. *Tallahassee Democrat*, May 28 and 29, 1956.

4. *Tallahassee Democrat*, May 29, 1956.

5. C. Smith and Killian, *Tallahassee Bus Protest*, 8.

6. *Tallahassee Democrat*, June 3, 1956.

7. C. Smith and Killian, *Tallahassee Bus Protest*, 9.

8. C. Smith and Killian, *Tallahassee Bus Protest*, 9–12; *Tallahassee Democrat*, October 21, 1956.

9. *Tallahassee Democrat*, December 24, 1956.

10. Smith and Killian, *Tallahassee Bus Boycott*, 13.

11. *Tallahassee Democrat*, January 2, 1957.

12. *Tallahassee Democrat*, January 8, 1957.

13. Killian, "Organization, Rationality and Spontaneity," 775.

14. See obituaries for Boynton from the Associated Press, November 25, 2020; *Washington Post*, November 26, 2020; and *New York Times*, November 27, 2020.

15. *Washington Post*, November 26, 2020.

16. *New York Times*, November 27, 2020, quoted from a 2016 article in the *Montgomery Advertiser.*

17. *Washington Post*, November 26, 2020.

18. *Boynton v. Virginia.*

19. *Boynton v. Virginia.*

20. *Boynton v. Virginia.*

21. Ross, "Jackson, Tennessee Students Campaign."

22. The letter is reproduced in Carson, *Student Voice*, 22.

23. Carson, *Student Voice*, 23.

24. Lovett, *The Civil Rights Movement in Tennessee*, 152. No explanation is given for the tulip bulbs, which are also mentioned in other sources.

25. Meacham, *His Truth Is Marching On*, 33, quoted in Lewis, *Walking with the Wind*, 63.

26. Meacham, *His Truth Is Marching On*, 35, quoted in Lewis, *Across That Bridge*, 80.

27. Meacham, *His Truth Is Marching On*, 33–43.

28. Meacham, *His Truth Is Marching On*, 50–52.

29. Meacham, *His Truth Is Marching On*, 66, quoted in Lewis, *Walking with the Wind*, 85.

30. Meacham, *His Truth Is Marching On*, 67–68.

31. Arsenault, *Freedom Riders*, 105–6. See also Meacham, *His Truth Is Marching On*, 85.

32. Arsenault, *Freedom Riders*, 84–86.

33. Meacham, *His Truth Is Marching On*, 68–71.

34. SNCC Digital Gateway, https://snccdigital.org/; Meacham, *His Truth Is Marching On*, 60–62; Arsenault, *Freedom Riders*, 86–90.

35. Meacham, *His Truth Is Marching On*, 76–78.

36. Arsenault, *Freedom Riders*, 93–94.

37. *Student Voice*, March 1961, 7, quoted in Meacham, *His Truth Is Marching On*, 85.

38. Arsenault, *Freedom Riders*, 94–95.

39. Arsenault, *Freedom Riders*, 109.

40. Arsenault, *Freedom Riders*, 112–14.

41. Arsenault, *Freedom Riders*, 115–16.

42. Arsenault, *Freedom Riders*, 116–17.

43. Arsenault, *Freedom Riders*, 118–19.

44. Arsenault, *Freedom Riders*, 120–21. The stop at Winston-Salem is not mentioned by Arsenault but is included in Catsam, *Freedom's Main Line*, 113.

45. Quotations in Arsenault, *Freedom Riders*, 121–22, quoted in Lewis, *Walking with the Wind*, 141–42.

46. Arsenault, *Freedom Riders*, 121–24.

47. Catsam, *Freedom's Main Line*, 132. See also Arsenault, *Freedom Riders*, 125–26.

48. Arsenault, *Freedom Riders*, 125–27.

49. Arsenault, *Freedom Riders*, 128.

50. Arsenault, *Freedom Riders*, 132–35.

51. Arsenault, *Freedom Riders*, 135, 141–61; Catsam, *Freedom's Main Line*, 149–68.

52. Arsenault, *Freedom Riders*, 148–61; Catsam, *Freedom's Main Line*, 149–77.

53. Arsenault, *Freedom Riders*, 162–76; Catsam, *Freedom's Main Line*, 177–84.

54. Lewis, *Walking with the Wind*, 157–58, quoted in Arsenault, *Freedom Riders*, 212.

55. Arsenault, *Freedom Riders*, 214.

56. Arsenault, *Freedom Riders*, 214.

57. Arsenault, *Freedom Riders*, 587.

58. On July 7, 2022, Diane Nash was awarded the Medal of Freedom for her role in organizing numerous Freedom Rides and her continuing work to establish equality in civil rights.

59. The portion of the act (Title VII) dealing with Equal Employment Opportunity adds "sex" to the list of categories under which discrimination is banned. In 2020 the Supreme Court further clarified that discrimination on the basis of sexual orientation or gender identity falls under the category of discrimination on the basis of sex. See *Bostock v. Clayton County*, 590 U.S. __ (2020).

60. Meacham, *His Truth Is Marching On*, 197.

Chapter 8. Into the Twenty-First Century

1. *Travelers' Green Book*, 1963–64, 2–4.

2. Montgomery, "Death of Sandra Bland."

3. Jacobo, "Cops May Have Thought Philando Castile Was a Robbery Suspect." See also LaFraniere and Smith, "Philando Castile Was Pulled Over."

4. Cardia et al., "Timeline of Tyre Nichols's Lethal Police Encounter."

5. "NAACP: Missouri Travel Advisory." See also Bay, *Traveling Black*, 313–20.

6. Lee, "NAACP Lifts Its Warning," July 18, 2018.

7. Mystal, "Breonna Taylor," May 15, 2020. On August 4, 2022, the US Dept. of Justice charged four current and former Louisville police officers with violating Taylor's civil rights, providing false information to obtain the warrant, and lying afterward to investigators.

8. Walsh, "Birding While Black."

9. Rosen, *Two Wheels Good*, 315–18.

10. Rosen, *Two Wheels Good*, 317–18.

11. Wypijewski, "Back to the Back of the Bus," 18–23.

12. Robert Bullard, "Solid Waste Sites," 273–88; see also his *Confronting Environmental Racism*, 1983.

13. Quoted in Bullard, *Transportation Racism*, 17, from King, *Testament of Hope*, 325–26.

14. See also Robert Bullard, "All Transit," 9–13; Sanchez and Brenman, *The Right to Transportation*. Numerous additional sources are referenced in Cantilina, Daly, and Hamphire, "Approaches and Barriers," 972–85, and in Adli and Chowdhury, "Review of Social Justice Theories," https://doi.org/10.3390/su13084289.

BIBLIOGRAPHY

Newspapers

AFRICAN AMERICAN AND ABOLITIONIST NEWSPAPERS

The Appeal (St. Paul, Minn., 1885–1923)
Atlanta Daily World (1928–present)
Carolina Times (Durham, N.C., 1919–2020)
Chicago Daily Inter-Ocean (1865–1914)
Chicago Defender (1905–present)
Clarion-Ledger (Jackson, Miss.)
The Colored American (New York, 1837–1841)
Daily Alta California (San Francisco, 1849–1891)
Emancipator (New York, 1833–41)
Frederick Douglass' Paper (Rochester, N.Y., 1851–1860)
Freedom's Journal (New York, 1827–1829)
Independent (New York)
Liberator (Boston, 1831–1865)
Nashville Globe (1906–1937)
National Anti-Slavery Standard (New York, 1840–1870)
New National Era (Washington, D.C., 1870–1874)
New Orleans Crusader (1889–1898)
New Orleans Tribune (1864–187?)
New York Age (1887–1960)
Pacific Appeal (San Francisco, 1862–1880)
Pennsylvania Freeman (Philadelphia, 1838–1854)
People's Voice (New York, 1941–1948)
St. Louis American (1928–present)
Southwestern Christian Advocate (1877–1929)

OTHER NEWSPAPERS

Boston Daily Advertiser
Boston Post
Crowley (La.) Daily Signal
Daily Arkansas Gazette
Daily Delta (New Orleans)
Daily Picayune (New Orleans)
Harrisburg (Pa.) Telegraph
Lubbock Avalanche-Journal
Monroe (La.) Morning World
Montgomery Advertiser
New-Bedford (Mass.) Mercury
New Bedford (Mass.) Register
New Orleans Daily Crescent
New Orleans Republican
New Orleans Times(-Democrat)
New York Daily Tribune
New York Evening Post
New York Times
Philadelphia Inquirer
Philadelphia Press
Sacramento Bee
Salem (Mass.) Gazette
San Francisco Call
San Francisco Chronicle
San Francisco Examiner
Tallahassee Democrat
Trumpet and Universalist Magazine
Washington Post

Court Decisions

Bob-Lo Excursion Co. v. Michigan, 333 U.S. 28 (1948)
Bostock v. Clayton County, 590 U.S. __ (2020)
Bowie v. Birmingham Railway & Electric Co., 125 Ala. 397 (1899)
Boynton v. Virginia, 364 U.S. 454 (1960)
Brown v. Board of Education of Topeka, 347 U.S. 483 (1954)
Brown v. Memphis & C. R. Co., 5 F. 499 (1880)
Brown v. Memphis & C. R. Co., Circuit Court, WD Tennessee (1881)

Chesapeake, Ohio & S. W. Railroad v. Ida Wells, Tennessee Sup. Ct. (1885)
Chicago and Northwestern Railway Co. v. Williams, 55 III. 185 (1870)
Civil Rights Cases, 109 U.S. 3 (1883)
Day v. Owen, 5 Mich. 520 (1858)
District of Columbia v. John R. Thompson Co., Inc., 346 U.S. 100 (1953)
Dred Scott v. Sanford, U.S, 60 U.S. (19 How.) 393
Emma J. Turner v. The North Beach and Mission Railroad Company, 34 Cal. 594 (1868)
Ex parte Homer A. Plessy, 45 La. Ann. 80 (1892)
George Donnell v. State of Mississippi, 48 Miss. 661, 12 Am. Rep. 375
Georgia Edwards v. Nashville, Chattanooga & St. Louis Railway Company, ICC (1908)
Henderson v. United States, 339 U.S. 816 (1950)
Houck v. Southern Pacific Railway Co., 38 F. 226 (WD Texas, 1888)
John J. Pleasants, and Mary E., his wife, v. The North Beach and Mission Railroad Company, 34 Cal. 586 (1868)
John R. Thompson Co., Inc. v. District of Columbia, 203 F.2d 579 (1953)
Logwood and Wife v. Memphis & C. R. Co. (1885), 318–19
Louisville, New Orleans & Texas Railway Co. v. State of Mississippi, 133 U.S. 587
Missouri ex rel. Gaines v. Canada, 305 U.S. 337 (1938)
Mitchell v. United States, 313 U.S. 80 (1941)
Morgan v. Commonwealth, 184 Va. 24 (Va. 1945)
Morgan v. Virginia, 328 U.S. 373 (1946)
NAACP *v. St. Louis-San Francisco Railway Company*, 298 ICC 355 (1955)
Plessy v. Ferguson, 163 U.S. 537 (1896)
Sarah Keys v. Carolina Coach Company, 64 MCC 769 (1955)
State ex. rel. Abbott v. Hicks, 44 La. Ann. 770 (1892)
State v. Pearson et al., 110 La. 387, 34 So. 575 (1903)
The Sue, 22 F. 843 (D. Md. 1885)
United States v. Cruikshank, 92 U.S. 542 (1875)
Williams v. Carolina Coach Co., 111 F. Supp. 329 (E.D. Va. 1952)
Wright v. Council of City of Emporia, 407 U.S. 451 (1972)

Works Cited

"About the *Nashville Globe*." *Chronicling America*, Library of Congress, https://chroniclingamerica.loc.gov/lccn/sn86064259.
Accomando, Christina. "Demanding a Voice among the Pettifoggers: Sojourner Truth as Legal Actor." *MELUS* 28 (2003): 61–86.
Ackerman, S. J. "Samuel Wilbert Tucker: The Unsung Hero of the School Desegregation Movement." *Journal of Blacks in Higher Education* 28 (Summer 2000): 98–103.
Ackerman, S. J. "The Trials of S. W. Tucker." *Washington Post*, June 11, 2000.
Acts of the State of Tennessee, 1881. Nashville: Tavel and Howell, 1881.
Acts Passed by the General Assembly of the State of Louisiana at the Second Session of the First Legislature. New Orleans: A. L. Lee, 1869.
Adler, Margot. "Before Rosa Parks, There Was Claudette Colvin." *Weekend Edition*, National Public Radio, March 15, 2009. https://www.npr.org/2009/03/15/101719889/before-rosa-parks-there-was-claudette-colvin.
Adli, Saeid Nazari, and Subeh Chowdhury. "A Critical Review of Social Justice Theories in Public Transit Planning." *Sustainability* 13 (2021): 4289.
Anderson, Jarvis. *Bayard Rustin: Troubles I've Seen*. New York: Harper Collins, 1997.
Angell, Stephen W. "'The Shadows of the Evening Stretched Out': Richard Robinson and the Shaping of African Methodist Identity." *Journal of Africana Religions* 3, no. 3 (2015): 238–39.
Appleton, Edward. "History of the Railways of Massachusetts. *Catskill*

Archive, http://www.catskillarchive.com/rrextra/abnere1.Html. "Written for publication in . . . 1871."

Archer, Richard. *Jim Crow North*. Oxford: Oxford University Press, 2017.

Arellano, Gustavo. "The Untold Story of the Zoot Suit Riots: How Black L.A. Defended Mexican Americans." *Los Angeles Times*, June 2, 2023.

Arsenault, Raymond. *Freedom Riders: 1961 and the Struggle for Racial Justice*. Oxford: Oxford University Press, 2006.

Bahr, Sarah. "Archaeologists Solve a Decades-Old Harriett Tubman Mystery." *New York Times*, April 20, 2021.

Baldwin, James. "Many Thousands Gone." In *Notes of a Native Son*, 24–45. Boston: Beacon, 1955.

Barnes, Catherine A. *Journey from Jim Crow: The Desegregation of Southern Transit*. New York: Columbia University Press, 1983.

"Barriers to Voting in Louisiana." Louisiana Advisory Committee for the United States Commission on Civil Rights, June 2018. https://www.usccr.gov/files/pubs/2018/08-20-LA-Voting-Barriers.pdf.

"Basil Dorsey." *Hampshire Gazette*, April 2, 1867.

"The Baton Rouge Bus Boycott of 1953." https://www.lib.lsu.edu/sites/all/files/sc/exhibits/e-exhibits/boycott/index.html.

Bay, Mia. *Traveling Black*. Cambridge: Harvard University Press, 2021.

"Bayard Rustin." *Making Gay History: The Podcast*. https://makinggayhistory.com/podcast/bayard-rustin.

Beaupre, Lauren Elizabeth. "Saints and the 'Long Civil Rights Movement': Claiming Space in Memphis." *Journal of Urban History* 38, no. 6 (2013): 971–1002.

Beermann, Jack M. *The Journey to Separate but Equal: Madame Decuir's Quest for Racial Justice in the Reconstruction Era*. Lawrence: University of Kansas Press, 2021.

"Before Rosa Parks." *Our Life and Times: A Journal of 1199 SEIU*, March/April 2015, 10.

Belton, Lloyd. "A Black Brazilian Immigrant and the Struggle [for] Civil Rights in the U.S." *Black Perspectives*, January 26, 2021, https://www.aaihs.org/a-black-brazilian-immigrant-and-the-struggle-civil-rights-in-the-u-s.

———. "'A Deep Interest in Your Cause': The Inter-American Sphere of Black Abolitionism and Civil Rights." *Slavery and Abolition* 42 (2021): 589–609.

———. "Emiliano F. B. Mundrucu: Inter-American Revolutionary and Abolitionist (1791–1863)." *Atlantic Studies* 15, no. 1 (2018): 62–82.

Bennett, Lerone, Jr. "A Historical Detective Story: Part II, Mystery of Mary Ellen Pleasant." *Ebony*, May 1979, 71–86.

Berry, Dana Ramey. "Teaching *Ar'n't I a Woman*." *Journal of Women's History* 19 (2007): 139–145.

Biddle, Daniel R., and Murray Dubin. *Tasting Freedom: Octavius Catto and the Battle for Equality in Civil War America*. Philadelphia: Temple University Press, 2010.

Black Abolitionist Archives, Doc. No. 27197. Special Collections, University of Detroit Mercy.

Blackett, R. J. M. "Day, William Howard." In Gates and Higginbotham, *African American Lives*, 219–20.

Blight, David W. *Frederick Douglass: Prophet of Freedom*. New York: Simon and Schuster, 2018.

Bollard, John K. "Stagolee." In Gates and Higginbotham, *African American Lives*, 784–85.

Bollard, John K., and Catrin Lloyd-Bollard. "Thomas Jinnings: The First Black Student at Harvard?" *Journal of Blacks in Higher Education*, September 1, 2022. https://jbhe.com/2022/09/thomas-jinnings-the-first-black-student-at-harvard.

Bradford, Sarah H. *Scenes in the Life of*

Harriet Tubman. Auburn, N.Y.: W. J. Moses, 1869.

Branch, Taylor. *Parting the Waters: America in the King Years, 1954–63*. New York: Simon & Schuster, 1988.

Bredhoff, Stacey, Wynell Schamel, and Lee Ann Potter. "An Act of Courage: The Arrest Records of Rosa Parks." *Social Education* 63, no. 4 (May/June 1999): 207–11. https://www.archives.gov/education/lessons/rosa-parks.

Brinkley, Douglas. *Rosa Parks: A Life*. New York: Viking Penguin, 2005.

Brown, Charlotte Hawkins. "Some Incidents in the Life and Career of Charlotte Hawkins Brown Growing out of Racial Situations, at the Request of Dr. Ralph Bunche." Unpublished paper, no date. Papers of Charlotte Hawkins Brown, 1900–1961, box 1, folder 2, Schlesinger Library, Radcliffe Institute for Advanced Study, Cambridge, Massachusetts. https://iiif.lib.harvard.edu/manifests/view/drs:51234610$1i.

Brown, Sterling A. "Out of Their Mouths." *Survey Graphic*, November 1942; in *Reporting Civil Rights*, pt. 1, 23–36.

Brown, William Wells. *The American Fugitive in Europe: Sketches of Places and People Abroad*. Boston: John P. Jewett, 1855.

Bruno, Tim. "Rewriting Rebellion: The Douglass-Truth Debate." *ESQ: A Journal of Nineteenth-Century American Literature and Culture* 65 (2019): 39–40.

Bullard, Robert. "All Transit Is Not Created Equal." *Race, Poverty, and the Environment*, Winter 2005/2006, 9–12.

———. *Confronting Environmental Racism: Voices from the Grassroots*. Boston: South End Press, 1983.

———. "Solid Waste Sites and the Black Houston Community." *Sociological Inquiry* 53 (1983): 273–88.

Bullard, Robert, Glenn S. Johnson, and Angel O. Torres, eds. *Highway Robbery: Transportation Racism and New Routes to Equity*. Cambridge, Mass.: South End Press, 2004.

Burran, James Albert, III. *The Beaumont Race Riot, 1943*. Master's thesis, Texas Tech University, 1973.

"Cambridge Stage and Omnibus Lines." Celebrate Boston. http://www.celebrateboston.com/mbta/omnibus-cambridge.htm.

Cantilina, Kaylla, Shanna R. Daly, and Robert C. Hampshire. "Approaches and Barriers to Addressing Equity in Transportation: Experiences of Transportation Practitioners." *Journal of the Transportation Research Board* 2675, no. 10 (October 2021): 972–85.

Cardia, Alexander, Jason Kao, Christoph Koettl, Eleanor Lutz, Anjali Singhvi, and Robin Stein. "A Timeline of Tyre Nichols's Lethal Police Encounter." *New York Times*, January 27, 2023.

Carson, Clayborne, ed. *The Student Voice, 1960–1965: Periodical of the Student Nonviolent Coordinating Committee*. Westport, Conn: Meckler, 1990.

Cartwright, Joseph H. "Black Legislators in Tennessee in the 1800's: A Case Study in Black Political Leadership." *Tennessee Historical Quarterly* 32, no. 3 (1973): 265–84.

Cases Argued and Determined in the Supreme Court of Tennessee (1887), 614–15. https://www.lib.uchicago.edu/ead/pdf/ibwells-0008-011-02.pdf.

Catalogue of the Officers and Students of Harvard University for the Academical Year 1841–42. Cambridge, Mass.: Harvard University, 1841.

Catsam, Derek Charles. *Freedom's Main Line: The Journey of Reconciliation and the Freedom Rides*. Lexington: University Press of Kentucky, 2009.

———. "'The Onward March of a People Who Desire to Be Totally Free': The 1953 Baton Rouge Bus Boycott." In *Boycotts Past and Present: From the American Revolution to the Campaign to Boycott Israel*, edited by David

Feldman, 139–56. New York: Palgrave Macmillan, 2019.

Chace, Elizabeth Buffum. *Anti-Slavery Reminiscences*. Central Falls, R.I.: Freeman & Sons, 1891.

Cha-Jua, Sundiata Keita, and Clarence Lang. "The 'Long Movement' as Vampire: Temporal and Spatial Fallacies in Recent Black Freedom Studies." *Journal of African American History* 92, no. 2 (March 2007): 265–88.

"Chapter 130, Acts of Tennessee, 1875." https://sharetngov.tnsosfiles.com/tsla/exhibits/aale/pdfs/chapter130.pdf.

The Chesapeake, Ohio & S. W. Railroad vs. Ida B. Wells. Tennessee Virtual Archive. https://teva.contentdm.oclc.org/digital/collection/p15138coll18/id/176.

Child, Lydia Maria. *An Appeal in Favor of That Class of Americans Called Africans*. Boston: Allen & Ticknor, 1833.

Civil Rights Act of 1875. https://www.senate.gov/artandhistory/history/resources/pdf/Civil_Rights_Act_1875.pdf.

"Civil Rights Law of 1873." Mississippi Encyclopedia Online. https://mississippiencyclopedia.org/entries/civil-rights-law-of-1873.

Code of the City of Montgomery, Alabama. Charlottesville, Va.: Michie City Publications, 1952.

Constitution Adopted by the State Constitutional Convention of the State of Louisiana, March 7, 1868. New Orleans, 1868.

Cooper, Brittney C. *Beyond Respectability: The Intellectual Thought of Race Women*. Urbana: University of Illinois Press, 2017.

Crowe, Steve. "Mary Ellen Pleasant: Unsung Heroine." *Crisis*, January/February 1999, 35.

Davis, Benjamin J. *Communist Councilman from Harlem: Autobiographical Notes Written in a Federal Prison*. New York: International Publishers, 1969.

DeGregory, Crystal A. "Gloster, Hugh Morris." In Gates and Higginbotham, *African American National Biography*, vol. 3, 520–21.

Dexter, Dave, Jr. "Billie Holiday for the First Time Tells Why She Left Shaw and Basie: 'Too Many Bad Kicks.'" *DownBeat*, November 1, 1939. https://downbeat.com/archives/detail/billie-holiday-for-the-first-time-tells-why-she-left-shaw-basie-too-many.

Dickens, Charles. *American Notes for General Circulation*. London: Chapman and Hall, 1842.

Doggett's New York City Directory for 1849–1850. New York: John Doggett, 1849.

Douglass, Frederick. *Life and Times of Frederick Douglass*. Boston: De Wolfe & Fiske, 1892. First published 1881.

———. *My Bondage and My Freedom*. New York: Dover, 1969. First published 1855.

———. *Narrative of the Life of Frederick Douglass*. New York: Signet, 1997.

———. "What I Found at the Northampton Association." In *The History of Florence, Massachusetts*, edited by Charles A. Sheffeld, 129–32. Florence, Mass.: C. Sheffeld, 1895.

Downey, Lynn. "Pleasant, Mary Ellen." In Gates and Higginbotham, *African American Lives*, 674–75.

"Downing's Oyster House." Mapping the African American Past. https://maap.columbia.edu/place/1.html.

Easton, Hosea. "An Address Delivered before the Coloured Population of Providence, Rhode Island, on Thanksgiving Day, November 27, 1828." In *Preaching with Sacred Fire: An Anthology of African American Sermons, 1750 to the Present*, edited by Martha Simmons and Frank A. Thomas, 47–55. New York: Norton, 2010.

Eaton, Alice Knox. "Brown, William Wells." In Gates and Higginbotham, *African American Lives*, 119–21.

Federal Reporter, vol. 22, *Cases Argued and Determined in the Circuit and District Courts of the United States*,

December, 1884–March, 1885. St. Paul: West Publishing, 1885.
Federal Reporter, vol. 38, *Cases Argued and Determined in the Circuit and District Courts of the United States, May–July 1889*. St. Paul: West Publishing, 1889.
Fifth Annual Report of the Board of Managers of the Massachusetts Anti-Slavery Society. Boston, 1837.
Fischer, Roy A. "A Pioneer Protest: The New Orleans Streetcar Controversy of 1867." *Journal of Negro History* 53 (1968): 219–33.
Foner, Eric. *Reconstruction: America's Unfinished Revolution 1863–1877*. New York: HarperCollins, 1988.
Foner, Philip S. "The Battle to End Discrimination against Negroes on Philadelphia Streetcars: (Part I) Background and Beginning of the Battle." *Pennsylvania History* 40, no. 3 (July 1973): 261–90.
———. "The Battle to End Discrimination against Negroes on Philadelphia Streetcars: (Part II) The Victory." *Pennsylvania History* 40, no. 4 (October 1973): 355–79.
Foreman, Tom, Jr. "Freedom Riders' 1947 Convictions Vacated in North Carolina." Associated Press, June 17, 2022. https://apnews.com/article/north-carolina-race-and-ethnicity-racial-injustice-government-politics-eb1a6308edb82eb271ed92c32dbe432d.
François, Aderson Bellegarde. "A Lost World: Sallie Robinson, the Civil Rights Cases, and Missing Narratives of Slavery in the Supreme Court's Reconstruction Jurisprudence." *Georgetown Law Journal* 109, no. 5 (2021): 1015–79.
Gates, Henry Louis, Jr. "Who Was the First African American?" *The Root*, October 22, 2012. https://www.theroot.com/who-was-the-first-african-american-1790893808.
Gates, Henry Louis, Jr., and Evelyn Brooks Higginbotham, eds. *African American Lives*. New York: Oxford University Press, 2004.
———. *African American National Biography*. 8 volumes. New York: Oxford University Press, 2008.
Georgia Edwards v. Nashville, Chattanooga & St. Louis. In Interstate Commerce Commission, *Interstate Commerce Commission Reports*, vol. 12 (1908): 247–50.
Gergel, Richard. *Unexampled Courage: The Blinding of Sgt. Isaac Woodard and the Awakening of America*. New York: Picador, 2019.
Gibson, Truman K., Jr., and Steve Huntley. *Knocking Down Barriers: My Fight for Black America*. Chicago University Press, 2005.
Giddings, Paula. *Ida: A Sword among Lions*. New York: Amistad, 2008.
———. "Wells-Barnett, Ida Bell." In Gates and Higginbotham, *African American Lives*, 863–66.
Gilmore, Glenda Elizabeth. *Defying Dixie: The Radical Roots of Civil Rights, 1919–1950*. New York: Norton, 2007.
Gorsuch, P. "The Bill of Sale for Basil Dorsey." *Friends' Intelligencer* 55 (April 2, 1898): 245.
Gray, Fred D. *Bus Ride to Justice*. Montgomery, Ala.: NewSouth Books, 1995.
Gray, Jeremy. "The Execution of Jeremiah Reeves: Alabama Teen's Death Sentence Helped Drive Civil Rights Movement." AL.com, February 4, 2015. https://www.al.com/news/2015/02/the_execution_of_jeremiah_reev.html.
Graetz, Robert S. *A White Preacher's Message on Race and Reconciliation*. Athens: University of Georgia Press, 2006.
Greater Hartford Directory, 1940.
Griffin, Henry H. *The Trial of Frank Kelly, for the Assassination and Murder of Octavius V. Catto, on October 10, 1871*. Philadelphia: Daily Tribune, 1977.
Grover, Kathryn. *Fugitive's Gibraltar: Escaping Slaves and Abolitionism in New*

Bedford, Massachusetts. Amherst: University of Massachusetts Press, 2001.

Guthrie, Woody. *Born to Win*. New York: Collier, 1965.

Hall, Jacquelyn Dowd. "The Long Civil Rights Movement and the Political Uses of the Past." *Journal of American History* 91, no. 4 (March 2005): 1233–63.

Heard, William H. *From Slavery to the Bishopric in the A.M.E. Church: An Autobiography*. Philadelphia: AME Book Concern, 1928. https://docsouth.unc.edu/neh/heard/menu.html.

Hepp, John. "Streetcars." *The Encyclopedia of Greater Philadelphia*. https://philadelphiaencyclopedia.org/essays/streetcars.

Hewitt, John H. "Mr. Downing and His Oyster House." *New York History* 74, no. 3 (July 1, 1993): 229–52.

———. "The Search for Elizabeth Jennings, Heroine of a Sunday Afternoon in New York City." *New York History* 71, no. 4 (October 1990): 393–96.

Higginbotham, Evelyn Brooks. *Righteous Discontent: The Women's Movement in the Black Baptist Church, 1880–1920*. Cambridge, Mass.: Harvard University Press, 1994.

Higginbotham, Susan. "From the Underground Railroad to the Water-Cure: David Ruggles." *Susan Higginbotham: History Refreshed: New Perspectives on Old Times*. https://www.susanhigginbotham.com/posts/from-the-underground-railroad-to-the-water-cure-david-ruggles.

Hine, Darlene Clark. "*Ar'n't I a Woman? Female Slaves in the Plantation South*—Twenty Years After." *Journal of African American History* 92 (2007): 13–21.

———. "Rosa Parks." In Gates and Higginbotham, *African American Lives*, 655–57. New York: Oxford University Press, 2004.

Hodges, Graham. *David Ruggles: A Radical Black Abolitionist and the Underground Railroad in New York City*. Chapel Hill: University of North Carolina Press, 2010.

Hoose, Phillip. *Claudette Colvin: Twice toward Justice*. New York: Farrar Straus Giroux, 2000.

Horne, Gerald. "Davis, Benjamin Jefferson." In Gates and Higginbotham, *African American Lives*, 208–9.

Houck v. Southern Pacific Railway Co., Judgment Record. "Records of Rights exhibition," National Archives Museum, Washington, D.C.

Houser, George, and Bayard Rustin. *We Challenged Jim Crow! A Report on the Journey of Reconciliation, April 9–23, 1947*. New York: FOR and CORE, 1947. https://gateway.uncg.edu/islandora/object/ghm:22289!.

Hudson, Lynn M. *The Making of "Mammy Pleasant": A Black Entrepreneur in Nineteenth-century San Francisco*. Urbana: University of Illinois Press, 2008.

Hughes, Langston. "Adventures in Dining." *Chicago Defender*, June 2, 1945, in *Reporting Civil Rights*, pt. 1, 68–70.

Hunt, Karen Jean. "Remond, Sarah Parker." In Gates and Higginbotham, *African American Lives*, 708–10.

Huston, Luther A. "ICC Orders End of Segregation on Trains, Buses." *New York Times*, November 26, 1955.

Interstate Commerce Act. *Interstate Commerce Commission Reports*, vol. 1, 1887. https://www.archives.gov/milestone-documents/interstate-commerce-act.

Interstate Commerce Commission. *Interstate Commerce Commission Reports*, vol. 12, 1908. https:// babel.hathitrust.org/cgi/pt?id=uc1.b2910867&seq=9.

Jabbar, Kareem Abdul, and Anthony Walton. *Brothers in Arms: The Epic Story of the 751st Tank Battalion, World War II's Forgotten Heroes*. New York: Broadway Books, 2004.

Jacobo, Julia. "Cops May Have Thought Philando Castile Was a Robbery Suspect, Noting 'Wide-Set Nose,' Dispatch Audio Indicates." ABC News, July 11,

2016. https://abc7.com/news/cops-may-have-thought-philando-castile-was-a-robbery-suspect/1422991.

James, Thomas. *Life of Rev. Thomas James by Himself*. Rochester, N.Y.: Post Express, 1886.

Janofsky, Michael. "Thousands Gather at the Capitol to Remember a Hero." *New York Times*, October 31, 2005.

Journal of the House of Representatives of the United States, vol. 37, no. 3 (1863).

Kelley, Blair L. M. *Right to Ride: Streetcar Boycotts and African American Citizenship in the Era of "Plessy v. Ferguson."* Chapel Hill: University of North Carolina Press, 2010.

Killian, Lewis M. "Organization, Rationality and Spontaneity in the Civil Rights Movement." *American Sociological Review* 49, no. 6 (December 1984): 770–83.

"Killing of Booker T. Spicely." CRRJ Archive, https://crrjarchive.org/incidents/894.

"Killing of Henry Williams in Alabama in 1942." CRRJ Archive, https://crrjarchive.org/incidents/329.

King, Martin Luther, Jr. *A Testament of Hope: The Essential Writings and Speeches of Martin Luther King, Jr.* Edited by James M. Washington. San Francisco: Harper and Row, 1986.

Kingsbury, Susan Myra, ed. *Records of the Virginia Company of London*, vol. 3. Washington, D.C.: U.S. Government Printing Office, 1953. https://www.loc.gov/item/06035006.

"Kirkaldy, Irene Morgan, 90, Rights Pioneer, Dies." *New York Times*, August 13, 2007.

Lach, Edward L., Jr. "Brown, Charlotte Hawkins." In Gates and Higginbotham, *African American Lives*, 105–6.

LaFraniere, Sharon, and Mitch Smith. "Philando Castile Was Pulled Over 49 Times in 13 Years, Often for Minor Infractions." *New York Times*, July 16, 2016.

Larson, Kate Clifford. *Bound for the Promised Land: Harriet Tubman, Portrait of an American Hero*. New York: Ballantine Books, 2004.

Lee, Davis. "NAACP Lifts Its Warning against American Airlines." *Courthouse News Service*, July 18, 2018. https://www.courthousenews.com/naacp-lifts-its-warning-against-american-airlines.

Lee Family Digital Archive. https://leefamilyarchive.org/.

Lee, Ulysses. *The Employment of Negro Troops*. Washington, D.C.: Center for Military History, 2000.

Lerner, Max. "We Walk Together." *New York Post*, November 28, 1955.

Lewis, John, with Brenda Jones. *Across That Bridge*. New York: Hyperion, 2012.

Lewis, John, with Michael D'Orso. *Walking with the Wind: A Memoir of the Movement*. New York: Simon & Schuster, 1998.

Libby, Jean. "Mary Ellen Pleasant Grave Restoration in California: 'She was a friend of John Brown.'" *John Brown Today: A Biographer's Blog*, December 30, 2010. https://abolitionist-john-brown.blogspot.com/2010/12/mary-ellen-pleasant-grave-restoration.html.

Louisiana Constitution, 1898. https://lasc.libguides.com/c.php?g=967774&p=6992545.

Louisiana Railway Accommodations Act. In *Railroads and the Making of Modern America*, https://railroads.unl.edu/documents/view_document.php?id=rail.gen.0060 (citing Louisiana Laws, 1890).

Lovett, Bobby L. *The Civil Rights Movement in Tennessee: A Narrative History*. Knoxville: University of Tennessee, 2005.

Luxenberg, Steve. *Separate: The Story of* Plessy v. Ferguson *and America's Journey from Slavery to Segregation*. New York: Norton, 2019.

Lydersen, Kari. "Dental Studies Give Clues about Christopher Columbus's Crew." *Washington Post*, May 18, 2009.

"Mammy Pleasant: Angel or Archfiend in the House of Mystery." *The Call*, May 7, 1899.

Martin, Charles H. "Herndon, Angelo." In Gates and Higginbotham, *African American Lives*, 397–98.

Massachusetts Register of Marriages, 1939, vol. 86.

Massachusetts State Senate Report No. 63 on the Rights of Colored Persons, February 22, 1842.

McCaskill, Barbara. "Craft, William and Ellen Craft." In Gates and Higginbotham, *African American Lives*, 195–97.

McLaughlin-Stonham, Hilary. *From Slavery to Civil Rights on the Streetcars of New Orleans*. Liverpool: Liverpool University Press, 2020.

McGuire, Danielle L. *At the Dark End of the Street: Black Women, Rape, and Resistance*. New York: Vintage, 2011.

McMillan, George. "Race Justice in Aiken." *The Nation*, November 23, 1946, in *Reporting Civil Rights*, pt. 1, 82–84.

Meacham, John. *His Truth Is Marching On: John Lewis and the Power of Hope*. New York: Random House, 2020.

Medina, Eduardo. "A Civil Rights Pioneer Seeks to Have Her Record Cleared." *New York Times*, October 26, 2021.

Meier, August, and Elliott Rudwick. "The Boycott Movement against Jim Crow Streetcars in the South." *Journal of American History* 55, no. 4 (March 1969): 758–59.

Melton, Christina. "Baton Rouge Bus Boycott." *64 Parishes*, February 12, 2016, https://64parishes.org/entry/baton-rouge-bus-boycott.

Melville, Herman. *Moby Dick; or, The Whale*. New York: Harper and Brothers, 1851.

Michie, Thomas J., ed. *Railroad Reports: A Collection of All Cases Affecting Railroads of Every Kind, Decided by the Courts of Last Resort in the United States*, vol. 8. Charlottesville, Va.: Michie, 1904.

Montgomery, David. "The Death of Sandra Bland: Is There Anything Left to Investigate?" *New York Times*, May 8, 2019.

Morice, Linda. "Alice White: The Principal Who Influenced Rosa Parks." *Vitae Scholasticae* 23 (2006). https://link.gale.com/apps/doc/A173922134/AONE?u=mlin_oweb&sid=googleScholar&xid=9bf60636.

Moye, J. Todd. *Freedom Flyers: The Tuskegee Airmen of World War II*. New York: Oxford University Press, 2010.

Murray, Pauli. *Song in a Weary Throat: Memoir of an American Pilgrimage*. New York: Liveright, 2018.

———, ed. *States' Laws on Race and Color*. Athens: University of Georgia Press, 2016. First published 1951.

Murray, Pauli, and Mary O. Eastwood. "Jane Crow and the Law: Sex Discrimination and Title VII." *George Washington Law Review* 34, no. 2 (December 1965): 232–56.

Mystal, Elie. "Breonna Taylor Was Murdered for Sleeping While Black." *The Nation*, May 15, 2020. https://www.thenation.com/article/society/breonna-taylor-was-murdered-for-sleeping-while-black.

"NAACP: Missouri Travel Advisory Is Still in Effect." *St. Louis American*, June 8, 2023.

Nair, Yasmin. "Bayard Rustin: A Complex Legacy." *Windy City Times*, March 28, 2012.

Nathan, Amy, with Sarah Keys Evans. *Sarah Keys v. Carolina Coach Company: One Black Woman's Journey to Desegregate Interstate Travel before the Montgomery Bus Boycott*. Durham, NC: Duke University Press, forthcoming.

New Orleans City Council Street Renaming Council. "Joseph Guillaume." https://nolaccsrc.org/guillaume.

Niven, Steven J. "Rustin, Bayard Taylor."

In Gates and Higginbotham, *African American Lives*, 741–42.

Nixon, E. D., interview conducted by Blackside, Inc., 1979. Washington University Libraries. http://repository.wustl.edu/concern/videos/v405sc21t.

Nordin, Dennis S. "Arthur Wergs Mitchell." *Encyclopedia of Alabama*, September 18, 2007. https://encyclopediaofalabama.org/article/arthur-wergs-mitchell.

Ogburn, Floyd, Jr. "James, Thomas." In Gates and Higginbotham, *African American National Biography*, 499–500.

Painter, Nell Irvin. *Sojourner Truth: A Life, a Symbol*. New York: Norton, 1996.

———. "Truth, Sojourner." In Gates and Higginbotham, *African American Lives*, 820–22.

Parker, Alison M. *Unceasing Militant: The Life of Mary Church Terrell*. Chapel Hill: University of North Carolina Press, 2020.

Parks, Rosa, with Jim Haskins. *My Story*. New York: Puffin Books, 1992.

Pathan, Vajid. "Saunders, William." Oxford African American Studies Center. https://oxfordaasc.com/.

Peck, James. *Freedom Ride*. New York: Simon and Schuster, 1962.

———. "Not So Deep Are the Roots." *Crisis*, September 1947, in *Reporting Civil Rights*, pt. 1, 92–97.

"Philadelphia Trolley Beginnings." Philadelphia Trolley Tracks. http://www.phillytrolley.org/Phila_trolley_history_1924/Phila_trolley_history_1924.html.

Phillips, Kimberley L. *War! What Is It Good For?* Chapel Hill: University of North Carolina Press, 2012.

Pinder, Sherrow O. "Morgan, Irene." Oxford African American Studies Center. https://oxfordaasc.com/.

Pope, Alexander. "An Essay on Man." In *The Poems of Alexander Pope*, edited by John Butt, 501–47. New Haven: Yale University Press, 1963.

Porter, Dorothy Burnett. "The Remonds of Salem, Massachusetts: A Nineteenth-Century Family Revisited." *Proceedings of the American Antiquarian Society* 95, no. 2 (1985), 259–95.

"Pronouns, Gender, and Pauli Murray." Pauli Murray Center for History and Social Justice. November 2, 2020. https://www.paulimurraycenter.com/pronouns-pauli-murray.

Pryor, Elizabeth. *Colored Travelers*. Chapel Hill: University of North Carolina Press, 2016.

Purvis, Robert. "The Dorsey Brothers." In *History of the Underground Railroad in Chester and the Neighboring Counties of Pennsylvania*, by R. C. Smedley, 356–61. Lancaster, Pa.: Office of the Journal, 1883.

Quarles, Benjamin. *Black Abolitionists*. New York: Oxford University Press, 1969.

Rampersad, Arnold J. *Jackie Robinson: A Biography*. New York: Ballantine Books, 1997.

Reddick, L. D. "The Bus Boycott in Montgomery." *Dissent*, Winter 1956, in *Reporting Civil Rights*, pt. 1, 252–65.

Reeves, Jay. "Judge Clears 1955 Court Record of Civil Rights Pioneer." Associated Press, December 17, 2021.

Reporting Civil Rights, pt. 1, *American Journalism 1941–1963*. New York: Library of America, 2003.

Robinson, Jo Ann. *The Montgomery Bus Boycott and the Women Who Started It*. Knoxville: University of Tennessee Press, 1987.

Robinson, Richard J. and Sallie J. Jury Report 2611, US Circuit Court, Western District of Tennessee, October Term 1883.

Rodriguez, Junius P. "'We'll Hang Jeff Davis on the Sour Apple Tree': Civil War Era Slave Resistance in Louisiana." *Gulf Coast Historical Review* 10, no. 2 (Spring 1995): 7–23.

Roosevelt, Theodore. Letter from President Theodore Roosevelt to the

Department of Justice Regarding Train Segregation, April 2, 1908. National Archives Catalog, https://catalog.archives.gov/id/7455571.

Ross, Alexa. "Jackson, Tennessee Students Campaign for U.S. Civil Rights, 1960–1961." Global Nonviolent Action Database. https://nvdatabase.swarthmore.edu/content/jackson-tennessee-students-campaign-us-civil-rights-1960-1961.

Rosen, Jody. *Two Wheels Good: The History and Mystery of the Bicycle*. New York: Crown, 2022.

Roundtree, Dovey Johnson, and Kate McCabe. *Mighty Justice: My Life in Civil Rights*. Chapel Hill: Algonquin Books of Chapel Hill, 2019.

Rouse, Jacqueline A. "Clark, Septima Poinsette." In Gates and Higginbotham, *African American Lives*, 172–73.

Ruchames, Louis. "Jim Crow Railroads in Massachusetts." *American Quarterly* 8, no. 1 (Spring 1956): 61–65.

Ruggles, David. Advertisement in *Freedom's Journal*, May 9, December 12, 1828.

———. *The "Extinguisher" Extinguished, or David M. Reese, M. D., "Used Up," by David Ruggles, a Man of Color, Together With Some Remarks upon a Late Production Entitled "An Address on Slavery and against Immediate Emancipation with a Plan of Their Being Gradually Emancipated and Colonized in Thirty-Two Years" by Herman Howlett*. New York: D. Ruggles, 1834.

———. Letter to *The Emancipator*, January 28, 1834.

———. *The Mirror of Liberty* 1, no. 2 (January 1839).

Rustin, Bayard. "Non-Violence vs. Jim Crow." *Fellowship: The Journal of the Fellowship of Reconciliation*, July 1942, in *Reporting Civil Rights*, pt. 1, 15–18.

Rustin, Bayard, and George Houser. *You Don't Have to Ride Jim Crow*. Washington, D.C.: Interracial Workshop, 1947.

Sanchez, Thomas W., and Marc Brenman. *The Right to Transportation: Moving to Equity*. New York: Routledge, 2017.

"Sarah Elizabeth Ray, Detroit's Other Rosa Parks." BLAC Detroit, March 8, 2017. https://www.blac.media/people-places/sarah-elizabeth-ray-detroits-other-rosa-parks.

Scott, Donald, Sr. "Catto, Octavius Valentine." In Gates and Higginbotham, *African American National Biography*, vol. 2, 217–18.

Seelye, Katharine Q. "Martha White, 99, Dies; Before Rosa Parks She Sparked a Bus Boycott." *New York Times*, June 11, 2021.

Sewell, Stacy Kinlock. "Remond, Charles Lenox." In Gates and Higginbotham, *African American Lives*, 707–8.

Sherman, Joan R. "Horton, George Moses." In Gates and Higginbotham, *African American Lives*, 414–16.

Smith, Charles U., and Lewis M. Killian. *The Tallahassee Bus Protest*. New York: Anti-Defamation League of B'nai B'rith, 1958.

Smith, J. Douglas. *Managing White Supremacy: Race, Politics, and Citizenship in Jim Crow Virginia*. Chapel Hill: University of North Carolina Press, 2002.

Smith, John David. "Councill, William Hooper." In Gates and Higginbotham, *African American National Biography*, vol. 2, 448–49.

SNCC Digital Gateway. https://snccdigital.org/.

Still, William. *A Brief Narrative of the Struggle for the Rights of the Colored People of Philadelphia in the City Railway Cars*. Philadelphia, 1867.

———. "[Letter of 1866 April 30]." William Still: An African American Abolitionist. Temple University Libraries. https://web.archive.org/web/20171004184844/http://stillfamily.library.temple.edu/items/show/188.

———. *The Underground Rail Road*. Philadelphia: Porter & Coates, 1872.

Stimson's Boston Directory, 1840.

Swingler, L. O. "Thrown from Train, Attacked." *Atlanta Daily World,* August 27, 1942, in *Reporting Civil Rights,* pt. 1, 19–22.

Terrell, Mary Church. *A Colored Woman in a White World.* Washington, D.C.: Ransdell, 1940.

"Testimony from Robinson v. Memphis and Charleston Railroad Co." DocsTeach, National Archives. https://www.docsteach.org/documents/document/testimony-robinson.

Theoharis, Jeanne. *The Rebellious Life of Mrs. Rosa Parks.* Boston: Beacon, 2013.

Thomas, Herman E. "Pennington, James William Charles." In Gates and Higginbotham, *African American Lives,* 667–68.

Thornton, J. Mills. *Dividing Lines: Municipal Politics and the Struggle for Civil Rights in Montgomery, Birmingham, and Selma.* Tuscaloosa: University of Alabama Press, 2002.

———. "Robinson, Jo Ann." In Gates and Higginbotham, *African American Lives,* 723–24.

Travelers' Green Book, 1963–64. International ed. New York: Victor H. Green, 1963.

Truman, Harry S. "Executive Order 9981: Desegregation of the Armed Forces (1948)." National Archives. https://www.archives.gov/milestone-documents/executive-order-9981.

Truth, Sojourner. "Address to the First Annual Meeting of the American Equal Rights Association." In *Proceedings of the First Anniversary of the American Equal Rights Association Held at the Church of the Puritans, New York, May 9 and 10, 1867.* New York: Robert J. Johnston, 1867, 20–21.

———. *Narrative of Sojourner Truth: A Bondswoman of Olden Time.* Boston, 1875.

"A Utopian Community in Florence, MA (1842–1846)." David Ruggles Center for History and Education. https://davidrugglescenter.org/northampton-association-education-industry.

Vara-Dannen, Theresa. "Letters of Protest: Responding to Racial Prejudice against Frederick Douglass and Others in Connecticut." *Connecticut History Review* 51, no. 2 (Fall 2012): 172–202.

Vernon, John. "Jim Crow, Meet Lieutenant Robinson: A 1944 Court-Martial." *Prologue Magazine,* Spring 2008. https://www.archives.gov/publications/prologue/2008/spring/robinson.html

Vitello, Paul. "Rev. T. J. Jemison, Civil Rights Leader Who Organized Early Boycott, Dies at 95." *New York Times,* November 22, 2013.

Wallace, Henry E. *The Philadelphia Reports, Containing the Decisions Published in the "Legal Intelligencer" from 1865 to 1868,* vol. 6. Philadelphia: J. B. Hunter, 1870.

Walsh, Joan. "Birding While Black: Just the Latest Bad Reason for White People to Call Police." *The Nation,* May 26, 2020. https://www.thenation.com/article/society/amy-cooper-birding-police.

Washington, Margaret. *Sojourner Truth's America.* Urbana: University of Illinois Press, 2009.

Weaver, Harold D., et al., eds. *Black Fire: American Quakers on Spirituality and Human Rights.* Philadelphia: Quaker Press, 2011.

Wells, Ida B. *Diary.* 1885. Ida B. Wells Papers. University of Chicago Library. https://www.lib.uchicago.edu/ead/pdf/ibwells-0009-008.pdf.

———. *The Light of Truth: Writings of an Anti-Lynching Crusader.* Edited by Mia Bay. New York: Penguin, 2014.

———. "Lynch Law." In *The Reason Why the Colored American Is Not in the Columbian Exposition,* edited by Robert W. Rydell, 29–43. Urbana: University of Illinois Press, 1999.

———. *The Memphis Diary of Ida B.*

Wells. Edited by Miriam DeCosta-Willis. New York: Beacon Press, 1995.

———. *Mob Rule in New Orleans: Robert Charles and His Fight to the Death*. Chicago, 1900. Reprinted in *On Lynchings*.

———. *On Lynchings*. New York: Dover, 2014.

White, Deborah Gray. *Ar'n't I a Woman? Female Slaves in the Plantation South*. New York: Norton, 1985.

White, Edward. "A Girl Full of Smartness." *The Lives of Others* (*Paris Review* blog), June 2, 2017. https://www.theparisreview.org/blog/2017/06/02/a-girl-full-of-smartness.

"Who Is the Rev. Dr. Pauli Murray?" Pauli Murray Center for History and Social Justice. https://www.paulimurraycenter.com/who-is-pauli.

Williams, Donnie, and Wayne Greenhaw. *The Thunder of Angels: The Montgomery Bus Boycott and the People Who Broke the Back of Jim Crow*. Chicago: Lawrence Hill, 2006.

Withrow, Thomas F., ed. *The American Corporation Cases*, vol. 1. Chicago: Myers, 1872.

Woo, Elaine. "She Set Wheels of Justice in Motion." *Los Angeles Times*, October 25, 2005.

Wynn, Neil A. *The African American Experience during World War II*. New York: Rowman & Littlefield, 2010.

Wypijewski, JoAnn. "Back to the Back of the Bus." *The Nation*, December 2000, 18–23.

INDEX

Boldface numbers indicate a section in which the person or item indexed is a primary subject. Numbers in *italics* indicate a page with an illustration of the subject.